PLEASE PRAY
FOR THE DONOR

LIFE

OF

GEORGE WASHINGTON.

Original in Possession of G.W.P. Custis Esq.

C.W. Peale

J.H. Forrest

G Washington

1772. Æt. 40.

NEW YORK, G.P. PUTNAM & CO

LIFE

OF

GEORGE WASHINGTON.

BY

WASHINGTON IRVING.

IN FIVE VOLS.

VOL. II.

NEW YORK:
G. P. PUTNAM, 441 BROADWAY.
1863.

Entered according to Act of Congress, in the year 1855,

BY G. P. PUTNAM & CO.,

In the Clerk's Office of the District Court of the United States for the Southern
District of New York.

JOHN F. TROW,
Printer, Stereotyper, and Electrotyper,
46, 48 & 50 Greene Street,
Between Grand & Broome, New York.

CONTENTS OF VOL. II.

CHAPTER XV.

CHAPTER XVI.

CHAPTER XVII.

CHAPTER XVIII.

CHAPTER XIX.

CHAPTER XX.

CHAPTER XLI.

CHAPTER XLII.

CHAPTER XLIII.

CHAPTER XLIV.

CHAPTER XLV.

CHAPTER XLVI.

LIFE OF WASHINGTON.

CHAPTER I.

WASHINGTON TAKES COMMAND OF THE ARMIES—SKETCH OF GENERAL LEE—
CHARACTERS OF THE BRITISH COMMANDERS, HOWE, CLINTON, AND BUR-
GOYNE—SURVEY OF THE CAMPS FROM PROSPECT HILL—THE CAMPS CON-
TRASTED—DESCRIPTION OF THE REVOLUTIONARY ARMY—RHODE ISLAND
TROOPS—CHARACTER OF GENERAL GREENE—WASHINGTON REPRESENTS THE
DEFICIENCIES OF THE ARMY—HIS APOLOGY FOR THE MASSACHUSETTS
TROOPS — GOVERNOR TRUMBULL — CRAGIE HOUSE, WASHINGTON'S HEAD-
QUARTERS.

On the 3d of July, the morning after his arrival at Cambridge,
Washington took formal command of the army. It was drawn
up on the Common about half a mile from head-quarters. A
multitude had assembled there, for as yet military spectacles
were novelties, and the camp was full of visitors, men, women,
and children, from all parts of the country, who had relatives
among the yeoman soldiery.

An ancient elm is still pointed out, under which Washington,
as he arrived from head-quarters accompanied by General Lee and

a numerous suite, wheeled his horse, and drew his sword as commander-in-chief of the armies. We have cited the poetical description of him furnished by the pen of Mrs. Adams; we give her sketch of his military compeer—less poetical, but no less graphic.

"General Lee looks like a careless, hardy veteran; and by his appearance brought to my mind his namesake, Charles XII. of Sweden. The elegance of his pen far exceeds that of his person." *

Accompanied by this veteran campaigner, on whose military judgment he had great reliance, Washington visited the different American posts, and rode to the heights, commanding views over Boston and its environs, being anxious to make himself acquainted with the strength and relative position of both armies: and here we will give a few particulars concerning the distinguished commanders with whom he was brought immediately in competition.

Congress, speaking of them reproachfully, observed, "Three of England's most experienced generals are sent to wage war with their fellow-subjects." The first here alluded to was the Honorable William Howe, next in command to Gage. He was a man of a fine presence, six feet high, well proportioned, and of graceful deportment. He is said to have been not unlike Washington in appearance, though wanting his energy and activity. He lacked also his air of authority; but affability of manners, and a generous disposition, made him popular with both officers and soldiers.

There was a sentiment in his favor even among Americans at the time when he arrived at Boston. It was remembered that

---

* Mrs. Adams to John Adams, 1775.

he was brother to the gallant and generous youth, Lord Howe, who fell in the flower of his days, on the banks of Lake George, and whose untimely death had been lamented throughout the colonies. It was remembered that the general himself had won reputation in the same campaign, commanding the light infantry under Wolfe, on the famous plains of Abraham. A mournful feeling had therefore gone through the country, when General Howe was cited as one of the British commanders who had most distinguished themselves in the bloody battle of Bunker's Hill. Congress spoke of it with generous sensibility, in their address to the people of Ireland already quoted. "America is amazed," said they, "to find the name of Howe on the catalogue of her enemies—*she loved his brother!*"

General Henry Clinton, the next in command, was grandson of the Earl of Lincoln, and son of George Clinton, who had been Governor of the province of New York for ten years, from 1743. The general had seen service on the continent in the Seven Years' War. He was of short stature, and inclined to corpulency; with a full face and prominent nose. His manners were reserved, and altogether he was in strong contrast with Howe, and by no means so popular.

Burgoyne, the other British general of note, was natural son of Lord Bingley, and had entered the army at an early age. While yet a subaltern, he had made a runaway match with a daughter of the Earl of Derby, who threatened never to admit the offenders to his presence. In 1758, Burgoyne was a lieutenant-colonel of light dragoons. In 1761, he was sent with a force to aid the Portuguese against the Spaniards, joined the army commanded by the Count de la Lippe, and signalized himself by surprising and capturing the town of Alcantara. He had since been elected to Parliament for the borough of Middlesex, and displayed considerable parliamentary talents. In 1772, he was made a major-general. His taste, wit, and intelligence, and his aptness at devising and promoting elegant amusements, made him for a time a leader in the gay world; though Junius accuses him of unfair practices at the gaming table. His reputation for talents and services had gradually mollified the heart of his father-in-law, the Earl of Derby. In 1774, he gave celebrity to the marriage of a son of the Earl with Lady Betty Hamilton, by producing an elegant dramatic trifle, entitled, " The Maid of the Oaks," afterwards performed at Drury Lane, and honored with a biting sarcasm by Horace Walpole. "There is a new puppet-show at Drury Lane," writes the wit, " as fine as the scenes can make it, and as dull as the author could not help making it." *

It is but justice to Burgoyne's memory to add, that in after years he produced a dramatic work, "The Heiress," which extorted even Walpole's approbation, who pronounced it the genteelest comedy in the English language.

Such were the three British commanders at Boston, who were considered especially formidable; and they had with them eleven thousand veteran troops, well appointed and well disciplined.

In visiting the different posts, Washington halted for a time at Prospect Hill, which, as its name denotes, commanded a wide view over Boston and the surrounding country. Here Putnam had taken his position after the battle of Bunker's Hill, fortifying himself with works which he deemed impregnable; and here the veteran was enabled to point out to the commander-in-chief,

---

* Walpole to the Hon. W. S. Conway.

and to Lee, the main features of the belligerent region, which lay spread out like a map before them.

Bunker's Hill was but a mile distant to the east; the British standard floating as if in triumph on its summit. The main force under General Howe was intrenching itself strongly about half a mile beyond the place of the recent battle. Scarlet uniforms gleamed about the hill; tents and marquees whitened its sides. All up there was bright, brilliant, and triumphant. At the base of the hill lay Charlestown in ashes, "nothing to be seen of that fine town but chimneys and rubbish."

Howe's sentries extended a hundred and fifty yards beyond the neck or isthmus, over which the Americans retreated after the battle. Three floating batteries in Mystic River commanded this isthmus, and a twenty-gun ship was anchored between the peninsula and Boston.

General Gage, the commander-in-chief, still had his head-quarters in the town, but there were few troops there besides Burgoyne's light-horse. A large force, however, was intrenched south of the town on the neck leading to Roxbury,—the only entrance to Boston by land.

The American troops were irregularly distributed in a kind of semicircle eight or nine miles in extent; the left resting on Winter Hill, the most northern post; the right extending on the south to Roxbury and Dorchester Neck.

Washington reconnoitred the British posts from various points of view. Every thing about them was in admirable order. The works appeared to be constructed with military science, the troops to be in a high state of discipline. The American camp, on the contrary, disappointed him. He had expected to find eighteen or twenty thousand men under arms; there were not much more than fourteen thousand. He had expected to find some degree of system and discipline; whereas all were raw militia. He had expected to find works scientifically constructed, and proofs of knowledge and skill in engineering; whereas, what he saw of the latter was very imperfect, and confined to the mere manual exercise of cannon. There was abundant evidence of aptness at trenching and throwing up rough defences; and in that way General Thomas had fortified Roxbury Neck, and Putnam had strengthened Prospect Hill. But the semicircular line which linked the extreme posts, was formed of rudely-constructed works, far too extensive for the troops which were at hand to man them.

Within this attenuated semicircle, the British forces lay concentrated and compact; and having command of the water, might suddenly bring their main strength to bear upon some weak point, force it, and sever the American camp.

In fact, when we consider the scanty, ill-conditioned and irregular force which had thus stretched itself out to beleaguer a town and harbor defended by ships and floating batteries, and garrisoned by eleven thousand strongly posted veterans, we are at a loss whether to attribute its hazardous position to ignorance, or to that daring self-confidence, which at times, in our military history, has snatched success in defiance of scientific rules. It was revenge for the slaughter at Lexington which, we are told, first prompted the investment of Boston. "The universal voice," says a contemporary, "is, starve them out. Drive them from the town, and let His Majesty's ships be their only place of refuge."

In riding throughout the camp, Washington observed that nine thousand of the troops belonged to Massachusetts; the rest were from other provinces. They were encamped in separate bodies, each with its own regulations, and officers of its own appointment. Some had tents, others were in barracks, and others sheltered themselves as best they might. Many were sadly in want of clothing, and all, said Washington, were strongly imbued with the spirit of insubordination, which they mistook for independence.

A chaplain of one of the regiments * has left on record a graphic sketch of this primitive army of the Revolution. "It is very diverting," writes he, "to walk among the camps. They are as different in their forms, as the owners are in their dress; and every tent is a portraiture of the temper and taste of the persons who encamp in it. Some are made of boards, and some are made of sail-cloth; some are partly of one, and partly of the other. Again others are made of stone and turf, brick and brush. Some are thrown up in a hurry, others curiously wrought with wreaths and withes."

One of the encampments, however, was in striking contrast with the rest, and might vie with those of the British for order and exactness. Here were tents and marquees pitched in the English style; soldiers well drilled and well equipped; every thing had an air of discipline and subordination. It was a body of Rhode Island troops, which had been raised, drilled, and brought to the camp by Brigadier-general Greene, of that province, whose subsequent renown entitles him to an introduction to the reader.

Nathaniel Greene was born in Rhode Island, on the 26th of May, 1742. His father was a miller, an anchor-smith, and a Quaker preacher. The waters of the Potowhammet turned the

* The Rev. William Emerson.

wheels of the mill, and raised the ponderous sledge-hammer of the forge. Greene, in his boyhood, followed the plough, and occasionally worked at the forge of his father. His education was of an ordinary kind; but having an early thirst for knowledge, he applied himself sedulously to various studies, while subsisting by the labor of his hands. Nature had endowed him with quick parts, and a sound judgment, and his assiduity was crowned with success. He became fluent and instructive in conversation, and his letters, still extant, show that he held an able pen.

In the late turn of public affairs, he had caught the belligerent spirit prevalent throughout the country. Plutarch and Cæsar's Commentaries became his delight. He applied himself to military studies, for which he was prepared by some knowledge of mathematics. His ambition was to organize and discipline a corps of militia to which he belonged. For this purpose, during a visit to Boston, he had taken note of every thing about the discipline of the British troops. In the month of May, he had been elected commander of the Rhode Island contingent of the army of observation, and in June had conducted to the lines before Boston, three regiments, whose encampment we have just described, and who were pronounced the best disciplined and appointed troops in the army.

Greene made a soldier-like address to Washington, welcoming him to the camp. His appearance and manner were calculated to make a favorable impression. He was about thirty-nine years of age, nearly six feet high, well built and vigorous, with an open, animated, intelligent countenance, and a frank, manly demeanor. He may be said to have stepped at once into the confidence of the commander-in-chief, which he never forfeited, but became one of his most attached, faithful, and efficient coadjutors throughout the war.

Having taken his survey of the army, Washington wrote to the President of Congress, representing its various deficiencies, and, among other things, urging the appointment of a commissary-general, a quartermaster-general, a commissary of musters, and a commissary of artillery. Above all things, he requested a supply of money as soon as possible. "I find myself already much embarrassed for want of a military chest."

In one of his recommendations we have an instance of frontier expediency, learnt in his early campaigns. Speaking of the ragged condition of the army, and the difficulty of procuring the requisite kind of clothing, he advises that a number of hunting-shirts, not less than ten thousand, should be provided; as being the cheapest and quickest mode of supplying this necessity. "I know nothing in a speculative view more trivial," observes he, "yet which, if put in practice, would have a happier tendency to unite the men, and abolish those provincial distinctions that lead to jealousy and dissatisfaction."

Among the troops most destitute, were those belonging to Massachusetts, which formed the larger part of the army. Washington made a noble apology for them. "This unhappy and devoted province," said he, "has been so long in a state of anarchy, and the yoke has been laid so heavily on it, that great allowances are to be made for troops raised under such circumstances. The deficiency of numbers, discipline, and stores, can only lead to this conclusion, *that their spirit has exceeded their strength.*"

This apology was the more generous, coming from a Southerner; for there was a disposition among the Southern officers to regard the Eastern troops disparagingly.   But Washington already felt as commander-in-chief, who looked with an equal eye on all ; or rather as a true patriot, who was above all sectional prejudices.

One of the most efficient co-operators of Washington at this time, and throughout the war, was Jonathan Trumbull, the Governor of Connecticut.   He was a well educated man, experienced in public business, who had sat for many years in the legislative councils of his native province.   Misfortune had cast him down from affluence, at an advanced period of life, but had not subdued his native energy.   He had been one of the leading spirits of the Revolution, and the only colonial governor who, at its commencement, proved true to the popular cause.   He was now sixty-five years of age, active, zealous, devout, a patriot of the primitive New England stamp, whose religion sanctified his patriotism.   A letter addressed by him to Washington, just after the latter had entered upon the command, is worthy of the purest days of the Covenanters.   " Congress," writes he, " have, with one united voice, appointed you to the high station you possess.   The Supreme Director of all events hath caused a wonderful union of hearts and counsels to subsist among us.

" Now, therefore, be strong, and very courageous.   May the God of the armies of Israel shower down the blessings of his Divine providence on you; give you wisdom and fortitude, cover your head in the day of battle and danger, add success, convince our enemies of their mistaken measures, and that all their attempts to deprive these colonies of their inestimable constitutional rights and liberties, are injurious and vain."

NOTE.

We are obliged to Professor Felton, of Cambridge, for correcting an error in our first volume in regard to Washington's head-quarters, and for some particulars concerning a house, associated with the history and literature of our country.

The house assigned to Washington for head-quarters, was that of the president of the Provincial Congress, not of the University. It had been one of those tory mansions noticed by the Baroness Reidesel, in her mention of Cambridge. "Seven families, who were connected by relationship, or lived in great intimacy, had here farms, gardens, and splendid mansions, and not far off, orchards; and the buildings were at a quarter of a mile distant from each other. The owners had been in the habit of assembling every afternoon in one or other of these houses, and of diverting themselves with music or dancing; and lived in affluence, in good humor, and without care, until this unfortunate war dispersed them, and transformed all these houses into solitary abodes.

The house in question was confiscated by Government. It stood on the Watertown road, about half a mile west of the college, and has long been known as the Cragie house, from the name of Andrew Cragie, a wealthy gentleman, who purchased it after the war, and revived its former hospitality. He is said to have acquired great influence among the leading members of the "great and general court," by dint of jovial dinners. He died long ago, but his widow survived until within fifteen years. She was a woman of much talent and singularity. She refused to have the canker worms destroyed, when they were making sad ravages among the beautiful trees on the lawn before the house. "We are all worms," said she, "and they have as good a right here as I have." The consequence was that more than half of the trees perished.

The Cragie House is associated with American literature through some of its subsequent occupants. Mr. Edward Everett resided in it the first year or two after his marriage. Later, Mr. Jared Sparks, during part of the time that he was preparing his collection of Washington's writings; editing a volume or two of his letters in the very room from which they were written. Next came Mr. Worcester, author of the pugnacious dictionary, and of many excellent books, and lastly Longfellow, the poet, who, having married the heroine of Hyperion, purchased the house of the heirs of Mr. Cragie and refitted it.

CHAPTER II.

THE justice and impartiality of Washington were called into exercise as soon as he entered upon his command, in allaying discontents among his general officers, caused by the recent appointments and promotions made by the Continental Congress. General Spencer was so offended that Putnam should be promoted over his head, that he left the army, without visiting the commander-in-chief; but was subsequently induced to return. General Thomas felt aggrieved by being outranked by the veteran Pomeroy; the latter, however, declining to serve, he found himself senior brigadier, and was appeased.

The sterling merits of Putnam soon made every one acquiesce in his promotion. There was a generosity and buoyancy about the brave old man that made him a favorite throughout the army; especially with the younger officers, who spoke of him familiarly and fondly as "Old Put;" a sobriquet by which he is called even in one of the private letters of the commander-in-chief.

The Congress of Massachusetts manifested considerate liberality with respect to head-quarters. According to their minutes, a committee was charged to procure a steward, a housekeeper, and two or three women cooks; Washington, no doubt, having brought with him none but the black servants who had accompanied him to Philadelphia, and who were but little fitted for New England housekeeping. His wishes were to be consulted in regard to the supply of his table. This his station, as commander-in-chief, required should be kept up in ample and hospitable style. Every day a number of his officers dined with him. As he was in the neighborhood of the seat of the Provincial Government, he would occasionally have members of Congress and other functionaries at his board. Though social, however, he was not convivial in his habits. He received his guests with courtesy; but his mind and time were too much occupied by grave and anxious concerns, to permit him the genial indulgence of the table. His own diet was extremely simple. Sometimes nothing but baked apples or berries, with cream and milk. He would retire early from the board, leaving an aide-de-camp or one of his officers to take his place. Colonel Mifflin was the first person who officiated as aide-de-camp. He was a Philadelphia gentleman of high respectability, who had accompanied him from that city, and received his appointment shortly after their arrival at Cambridge. The second aide-de-camp was John Trumbull,* son of the Governor of Connecticut. He had accompanied General Spencer to

* In after years distinguished as a historical painter.

the camp, and had caught the favorable notice of Washington by some drawings which he had made of the enemy's works. "I now suddenly found myself," writes Trumbull, "in the family of one of the most distinguished and dignified men of the age; surrounded at his table by the principal officers of the army, and in constant intercourse with them—it was further my duty to receive company, and do the honors of the house to many of the first people of the country of both sexes." Trumbull was young, and unaccustomed to society, and soon found himself, he says, unequal to the elegant duties of his situation; he gladly exchanged it, therefore, for that of major of brigade.

The member of Washington's family most deserving of mention at present, was his secretary, Mr. Joseph Reed. With this gentleman he had formed an intimacy in the course of his visits to Philadelphia, to attend the sessions of the Continental Congress. Mr. Reed was an accomplished man, had studied law in America, and at the Temple in London, and had gained a high reputation at the Philadelphia bar. In the dawning of the Revolution he had embraced the popular cause, and carried on a correspondence with the Earl of Dartmouth, endeavoring to enlighten that minister on the subject of colonial affairs. He had since been highly instrumental in rousing the Philadelphians to co-operate with the patriots of Boston. A sympathy of views and feelings had attached him to Washington, and induced him to accompany him to the camp. He had no definite purpose when he left home, and his friends in Philadelphia were surprised, on receiving a letter from him written from Cambridge, to find that he had accepted the post of secretary to the commander-in-chief.

They expostulated with him by letter. That a man in the thirty-fifth year of his age, with a lucrative profession, a young wife and growing family, and a happy home, should suddenly abandon all to join the hazardous fortunes of a revolutionary camp, appeared to them the height of infatuation. They remonstrated on the peril of the step. " I have no inclination," replied Reed, "to be hanged for half treason. When a subject draws his sword against his prince, he must cut his way through, if he means to sit down in safety. I have taken too active a part in what may be called the civil part of opposition, to renounce, without disgrace, the public cause when it seems to lead to danger; and have a most sovereign contempt for the man who can plan measures he has not the spirit to execute."

Washington has occasionally been represented as cold and reserved; yet his intercourse with Mr. Reed is a proof to the contrary. His friendship towards him was frank and cordial, and the confidence he reposed in him full and implicit. Reed, in fact, became, in a little time, the intimate companion of his thoughts, his bosom counsellor. He felt the need of such a friend in the present exigency, placed as he was in a new and untried situation, and having to act with persons hitherto unknown to him.

In military matters, it is true he had a shrewd counsellor in General Lee; but Lee was a wayward character; a cosmopolite, without attachment to country, somewhat splenetic, and prone to follow the bent of his whims and humors, which often clashed with propriety and sound policy. Reed on the contrary, though less informed on military matters, had a strong common sense, unclouded by passion or prejudice, and a pure patriotism, which regarded every thing as it bore upon the welfare of his country.

Washington's confidence in Lee had always to be measured and guarded in matters of civil policy.

The arrival of Gates in camp, was heartily welcomed by the

commander-in-chief, who had received a letter from that officer, gratefully acknowledging his friendly influence in procuring him the appointment of adjutant-general. Washington may have promised himself much cordial co-operation from him, recollecting the warm friendship professed by him when he visited at Mount Vernon, and they talked together over their early companionship in arms; but of that kind of friendship there was no further manifestation. Gates was certainly of great service, from his practial knowledge and military experience at this juncture, when the whole army had in a manner to be organized; but from the familiar intimacy of Washington he gradually estranged himself. A contemporary has accounted for this, by alleging that he was secretly chagrined at not having received the appointment of major-general, to which he considered himself well fitted by his military knowledge and experience, and which he thought Washington might have obtained for him had he used his influence with Congress. We shall have to advert to this estrangement of Gates on subsequent occasions.

The hazardous position of the army from the great extent and weakness of its lines, was what most pressed on the immediate attention of Washington; and he summoned a council of war, to take the matter into consideration. In this it was urged that, to abandon the line of works, after the great labor and expense of their construction, would be dispiriting to the troops and encouraging to the enemy, while it would expose a wide extent of the surrounding country to maraud and ravage. Beside, no safer position presented itself, on which to fall back. This being generally admitted, it was determined to hold on to the works, and defend them as long as possible; and, in the mean time, to augment the army to at least twenty thousand men.

Washington now hastened to improve the defences of the camp, strengthen the weak parts of the line, and throw up additional works round the main forts. No one seconded him more effectually in this matter than General Putnam. No works were thrown up with equal rapidity to those under his superintendence. " You seem, general," said Washington, " to have the faculty of infusing your own spirit into all the workmen you employ ;"—and it was the fact.

The observing chaplain already cited, gazed with wonder at the rapid effects soon produced by the labors of an army. " It is surprising," writes he, " how much work has been done. The lines are extended almost from Cambridge to Mystic River; very soon it will be morally impossible for the enemy to get between the works, except in one place, which is supposed to be left purposely unfortified, to entice the enemy out of their fortresses. Who would have thought, twelve months past, that all Cambridge and Charlestown would be covered over with American camps, and cut up into forts and intrenchments, and all the lands, fields, orchards, laid common,—horses and cattle feeding on the choicest mowing land, whole fields of corn eaten down to the ground, and large parks of well-regulated forest trees cut down for fire-wood and other public uses."

Beside the main dispositions above mentioned, about seven hundred men were distributed in the small towns and villages along the coast, to prevent depredations by water; and horses were kept ready saddled at various points of the widely extended lines, to convey to head-quarters intelligence of any special movement of the enemy.

The army was distributed by Washington into three grand divisions. One, forming the right wing, was stationed on the heights of Roxbury. It was commanded by Major-general Ward, who had under him Brigadier-generals Spencer and Thomas. Another, forming the left wing under Major-general Lee, having with him Brigadier-generals Sullivan and Greene, was stationed on Winter and Prospect Hills; while the centre, under Major-general Putnam and Brigadier-general Heath, was stationed at Cambridge. With Putnam was encamped his favorite officer Knowlton, who had been promoted by Congress to the rank of major for his gallantry at Bunker's Hill.

At Washington's recommendation, Joseph Trumbull, the eldest son of the governor, received on the 24th of July the appointment of commissary-general of the continental army. He had already officiated with talent in that capacity in the Connecticut militia. "There is a great overturning in the camp as to order and regularity," writes the military chaplain; "new lords, new laws. The generals Washington and Lee are upon the lines every day. New orders from his excellency are read to the respective regiments every morning after prayers. The strictest government is taking place, and great distinction is made between officers and soldiers. Every one is made to know his place and keep it, or be tied up and receive thirty or forty lashes according to his crime. Thousands are at work every day from four till eleven o'clock in the morning."

Lee was supposed to have been at the bottom of this rigid discipline; the result of his experience in European campaigning. His notions of military authority were acquired in the armies of the North. Quite a sensation was, on one occasion, produced in camp by his threatening to cane an officer for unsoldierly conduct. His laxity in other matters occasioned almost equal scandal. He scoffed, we are told, "with his usual profaneness," at a resolution of Congress appointing a day of fasting and prayer, to obtain the favor of Heaven upon their cause. "Heaven," he observed, "was ever found favorable to strong battalions."*

Washington differed from him in this respect. By his orders the resolution of Congress was scrupulously enforced. All labor, excepting that absolutely necessary, was suspended on the appointed day, and officers and soldiers were required to attend divine service, armed and equipped and ready for immediate action.

Nothing excited more gaze and wonder among the rustic visitors to the camp, than the arrival of several rifle companies, fourteen hundred men in all, from Pennsylvania, Maryland and Virginia; such stalwart fellows as Washington had known in his early campaigns. Stark hunters and bush fighters; many of them upwards of six feet high, and of vigorous frame; dressed in fringed frocks, or rifle shirts, and round hats. Their displays of sharp shooting were soon among the marvels of the camp. We are told that while advancing at quick step, they could hit a mark of seven inches diameter, at the distance of two hundred and fifty yards.†

One of these companies was commanded by Captain Daniel Morgan, a native of New Jersey, whose first experience in war had been to accompany Braddock's army as a waggoner. He had since carried arms on the frontier and obtained a command. He and his riflemen in coming to the camp had marched six hundred miles in three weeks. They will be found of signal efficiency in the sharpest conflicts of the revolutionary war.

While all his forces were required for the investment of Boston, Washington was importuned by the Legislature of Massachusetts and the Governor of Connecticut, to detach troops for

<hr>

* Graydon's Memoirs, p. 138.   † Thacher's Military Journal, p. 37.

the protection of different points of the sea-coast, where depredations by armed vessels were apprehended. The case of New London was specified by Governor Trumbull, where Captain Wallace of the Rose frigate, with two other ships of war, had entered the harbor, landed men, spiked the cannon, and gone off threatening future visits.

Washington referred to his instructions, and consulted with his general officers and such members of the Continental Congress as happened to be in camp, before he replied to these requests; he then respectfully declined compliance.

In his reply to the General Assembly of Massachusetts, he stated frankly and explicitly the policy and system on which the war was to be conducted, and according to which he was to act as commander-in-chief. "It has been debated in Congress and settled," writes he, "that the militia, or other internal strength of each province, is to be applied for defence against those small and particular depredations, which were to be expected, and to which they were supposed to be competent. This will appear the more proper, when it is considered that every town, and indeed every part of our sea-coast, which is exposed to these depredations, would have an equal claim upon this army.

"It is the misfortune of our situation which exposes us to these ravages, and against which, in my judgment, no such temporary relief could possibly secure us. The great advantage the enemy have of transporting troops, by being masters of the sea, will enable them to harass us by diversions of this kind; and should we be tempted to pursue them, upon every alarm, the army must either be so weakened as to expose it to destruction, or a great part of the coast be still left unprotected. Nor, indeed, does it appear to me that such a pursuit would be attended with the least effect.   The first notice of such an excursion would be its actual execution, and long before any troops could reach the scene of action, the enemy would have an opportunity to accomplish their purpose and retire.   It would give me great pleasure to have it in my power to extend protection and safety to every individual; but the wisdom of the General Court will anticipate me on the necessity of conducting our operations on a general and impartial scale, so as to exclude any just cause of complaint and jealousy."

His reply to the Governor of Connecticut was to the same effect.   " I am by no means insensible to the situation of the people on the coast.   I wish I could extend protection to all, but the numerous detachments necessary to remedy the evil would amount to a dissolution of the army, or make the most important operations of the campaign depend upon the piratical expeditions of two or three men-of-war and transports."

His refusal to grant the required detachments gave much dissatisfaction in some quarters, until sanctioned and enforced by the Continental Congress.   All at length saw and acquiesced in the justice and wisdom of his decision.   It was in fact a vital question, involving the whole character and fortune of the war; and it was acknowledged that he met it with a forecast and determination befitting a commander-in-chief.

CHAPTER III.

THE great object of Washington at present, was to force the enemy to come out of Boston and try a decisive action. His lines
had for some time cut off all communication of the town with
the country, and he had caused the live stock within a considerable distance of the place to be driven back from the coast, out of
reach of the men-of-war's boats. Fresh provisions and vegetables
were consequently growing more and more scarce and extrava-
gantly dear, and sickness began to prevail. " I have done and
shall do every thing in my power to distress them," writes he to
his brother John Augustine. " The transports have all arrived,
and their whole reinforcement is landed, so that I see no reason
why they should not, if they ever attempt it, come boldly out and
put the matter to issue at once."

" We are in the strangest state in the world," writes a lady
from Boston, " surrounded on all sides. The whole country is
in arms and intrenched. We are deprived of fresh provisions,

subject to continual alarms and cannonadings, the Provincials being very audacious and advancing to our lines, since the arrival of Generals Washington and Lee to command them."

At this critical juncture, when Washington was pressing the siege, and endeavoring to provoke a general action, a startling fact came to light; the whole amount of powder in the camp would not furnish more than nine cartridges to a man! *

A gross error had been made by the committee of supplies when Washington, on taking command, had required a return of the ammunition. They had returned the whole amount of powder collected by the province, upwards of three hundred barrels; without stating what had been expended. The blunder was detected on an order being issued for a new supply of cartridges. It was found that there were but thirty-two barrels of powder in store.

This was an astounding discovery. Washington instantly despatched letters and expresses to Rhode Island, the Jerseys, Ticonderoga and elsewhere, urging immediate supplies of powder and lead; no quantity, however small, to be considered beneath notice. In a letter to Governor Cooke of Rhode Isand, he suggested that an armed vessel of that province might be sent to seize upon a magazine of gunpowder, said to be in a remote part of the Island of Bermuda. "I am very sensible," writes he, "that at first view the project may appear hazardous, and its success must depend on the concurrence of many circumstances; but we are in a situation which requires us to run all risks. * * * Enterprises which appear chimerical, often prove successful from that very circumstance. Common sense and prudence will suggest vigilance and care, where the danger is plain and obvious;

* Letter to the President of Congress, Aug. 4.

but where little danger is apprehended, the more the enemy will be unprepared, and, consequently, there is the fairest prospect of success."

Day after day elapsed without the arrival of any supplies; for in these irregular times, the munitions of war were not readily procured. It seemed hardly possible that the matter could be kept concealed from the enemy. Their works on Bunker's Hill commanded a full view of those of the Americans on Winter and Prospect Hills. Each camp could see what was passing in the other. The sentries were almost near enough to converse. There was furtive intercourse occasionally between the men. In this critical state, the American camp remained for a fortnight; the anxious commander incessantly apprehending an attack. At length a partial supply from the Jerseys put an end to this imminent risk. Washington's secretary, Reed, who had been the confidant of his troubles and anxieties, gives a vivid expression of his feelings on the arrival of this relief. "I can hardly look back, without shuddering, at our situation before this increase of our stock. *Stock* did I say? it was next to nothing. Almost the whole powder of the army was in the cartridge-boxes."*

It is thought that, considering the clandestine intercourse carried on between the two camps, intelligence of this deficiency of ammunition on the part of the besiegers must have been conveyed to the British commander; but that the bold face with which the Americans continued to maintain their position, made him discredit it.

Notwithstanding the supply from the Jerseys, there was not more powder in camp than would serve the artillery for one

* Reed to Thomas Bradford. Life and Correspondence, vol. i. p. 118.

day of general action. None, therefore, was allowed to be wasted; the troops were even obliged to bear in silence an occasional cannonading. "Our poverty in ammunition," writes Washington, "prevents our making a suitable return."

One of the painful circumstances attending the outbreak of a revolutionary war is, that gallant men, who have held allegiance to the same government, and fought side by side under the same flag, suddenly find themselves in deadly conflict with each other. Such was the case at present in the hostile camps. General Lee, it will be recollected, had once served under General Burgoyne, in Portugal, and had won his brightest laurels when detached by that commander to surprise the Spanish camp, near the Moorish castle of Villa Velha. A soldier's friendship had ever since existed between them, and when Lee had heard at Philadelphia, before he had engaged in the American service, that his old comrade and commander was arrived at Boston, he wrote a letter to him giving his own views on the points in dispute between the colonies and the mother country, and inveighing with his usual vehemence and sarcastic point, against the conduct of the court and ministry. Before sending the letter, he submitted it to the Boston delegates and other members of Congress, and received their sanction.

Since his arrival in camp he had received a reply from Burgoyne, couched in moderate and courteous language, and proposing an interview at a designated house on Boston Neck, within the British sentries; mutual pledges to be given for each other's safety.

Lee submitted this letter to the Provincial Congress of Massachusetts, and requested their commands with respect to the proposed interview. They expressed, in reply, the highest confidence in his wisdom, discretion and integrity, but questioned whether the interview might not be regarded by the public with distrust; "a people contending for their liberties being naturally disposed to jealousy." They suggested, therefore, as a means of preventing popular misconception, that Lee on seeking the interview, should be accompanied by Mr. Elbridge Gerry; or that the advice of a council of war should be taken in a matter of such apparent delicacy.

Lee became aware of the surmises that might be awakened by the proposed interview, and wrote a friendly note to Burgoyne declining it.

A correspondence of a more important character took place between Washington and General Gage. It was one intended to put the hostile services on a proper footing. A strong disposition had been manifested among the British officers to regard those engaged in the patriot cause as malefactors, outlawed from the courtesies of chivalric warfare. Washington was determined to have a full understanding on this point. He was peculiarly sensitive with regard to Gage. They had been companions in arms in their early days; but Gage might now affect to look down upon him as the chief of a rebel army. Washington took an early opportunity to let him know, that he claimed to be the commander of a legitimate force, engaged in a legitimate cause, and that both himself and his army were to be treated on a footing of perfect equality. The correspondence arose from the treatment of several American officers.

"I understand," writes Washington to Gage, "that the officers engaged in the cause of liberty and their country, who by the fortune of war have fallen into your hands, have been thrown indiscriminately into a common jail, appropriated to felons; that no consideration has been had for those of the most respectable rank, when languishing with wounds and sickness, and that some have been amputated in this unworthy situation.   Let your opinion, sir, of the principles which actuate them, be what it may, they suppose that they act from the noblest of all principles, love of freedom and their country.   But political principles, I conceive, are foreign to this point.   The obligations arising from the rights of humanity and claims of rank are universally binding and extensive, except in case of retaliation.   These, I should have hoped, would have dictated a more tender treatment of those individuals whom chance or war had put in your power. Nor can I forbear suggesting its fatal tendency to widen that unhappy breach which you, and those ministers under whom you act, have repeatedly declared your wish to see for ever closed. My duty now makes it necessary to apprise you that, for the future, I shall regulate all my conduct towards those gentlemen who are, or may be, in our possession, exactly by the rule you shall observe towards those of ours, now in your custody.

"If severity and hardships mark the line of your conduct, painful as it may be to me, your prisoners will feel its effects. But if kindness and humanity are shown to us, I shall with pleasure consider those in our hands only as unfortunate, and they shall receive from me that treatment to which the unfortunate are ever entitled."

The following are the essential parts of a letter from General Gage in reply.

"SIR,—To the glory of civilized nations, humanity and war have been compatible, and humanity to the subdued has become almost a general system.   Britons, ever pre-eminent in mercy, have outgone common examples, and overlooked the criminal in the captive. Upon these principles your prisoners, whose lives by the law of the land are destined to the cord, have hitherto been treated with care and kindness, and more comfortably lodged than the King's troops in the hospitals; indiscriminately it is true, for I acknowledge no rank that is not derived from the King.

"My intelligence from your army would justify severe recriminations. I understand there are of the King's faithful subjects, taken some time since by the rebels, laboring, like negro slaves to gain their daily subsistence, or reduced to the wretched alternative to perish by famine or take arms against their King and country. Those who have made the treatment of the prisoners in my hands, or of your other friends in Boston, a pretence for such measures, found barbarity upon falsehood.

"I would willingly hope, sir, that the sentiments of liberality which I have always believed you to possess, will be exerted to correct these misdoings. Be temperate in political disquisition; give free operation to truth, and punish those who deceive and misrepresent; and not only the effects, but the cause, of this unhappy conflict will be removed. Should those, under whose usurped authority you act, control such a disposition, and dare to call severity retaliation; to God, who knows all hearts, be the appeal of the dreadful consequences," &c.

There were expressions in the foregoing letter well calculated to rouse indignant feelings in the most temperate bosom. Had Washington been as readily moved to transports of passion as some are pleased to represent him, the *rebel* and the *cord* might readily have stung him to fury; but with him, anger was checked in its impulses by higher energies, and reined in to give a grander effect to the dictates of his judgment. The following was his noble and dignified reply to General Gage:

'I addressed you, sir, on the 11th instant, in terms which gave the fairest scope for that humanity and politeness which were supposed to form a part of your character. I remonstrated with you on the unworthy treatment shown to the officers and citizens of America, whom the fortune of war, chance, or a mistaken confidence had thrown into your hands. Whether British or American mercy, fortitude and patience, are most pre-eminent; whether our virtuous citizens, whom the hand of tyranny has forced into arms to defend their wives, their children and their property, or the merciless instruments of lawless domination, avarice, and revenge, best deserve the appellation of rebels, and the punishment of that cord, which your affected clemency has forborne to inflict; whether the authority under which I act is usurped, or founded upon the genuine principles of liberty, were altogether foreign to the subject. I purposely avoided all political disquisition; nor shall I now avail myself of those advantages which the sacred cause of my country, of liberty, and of human nature give me over you; much less shall I stoop to retort and invective; but the intelligence you say you have received from our army requires a reply. I have taken time, sir, to make a strict inquiry, and find it has not the least foundation in truth. Not only your officers and soldiers have been treated with the tenderness due to fellow-citizens and brethren, but even those execrable parricides, whose counsels and aid have deluged their country with blood, have been protected from the fury of a justly enraged people. Far from compelling or permitting their assistance, I am embarrassed with the numbers who crowd to our camp, animated with the purest principles of virtue and love to their country. *　　*　　*　　*　　*　　*　　*　　*

" You affect, sir, to despise all rank not derived from the same source with your own. I cannot conceive one more honorable, than that which flows from the uncorrupted choice of a brave and free people, the purest source and original fountain of all power. Far from making it a plea for cruelty, a mind of true magnanimity and enlarged ideas would comprehend and respect it.

"What may have been the ministerial views which have precipitated the present crisis, Lexington, Concord, and Charlestown can best declare. May that God, to whom you, too, appeal, judge between America and you. Under his providence, those who influence the councils of America, and all the other inhabitants of the united colonies, at the hazard of their lives, are determined to hand down to posterity those just and invaluable privileges which they received from their ancestors.

"I shall now, sir, close my correspondence with you, perhaps for ever. If your officers, our prisoners, receive a treatment from me different from that which I wished to show them, they and you will remember the occasion of it."

We have given these letters of Washington almost entire, for they contain his manifesto as commander-in-chief of the armies of the Revolution; setting forth the opinions and motives by which he was governed, and the principles on which hostilities on his part would be conducted. It was planting with the pen, that standard which was to be maintained by the sword.

In conformity with the threat conveyed in the latter part of his letter, Washington issued orders that British officers at Watertown and Cape Ann, who were at large on parole, should be confined in Northampton jail; explaining to them that this conduct, which might appear to them harsh and cruel, was contrary to his disposition, but according to the rule of treatment observed by General Gage toward the American prisoners in his hands;

making no distinction of rank. Circumstances, of which we have no explanation, induced subsequently a revocation of this order; the officers were permitted to remain as before, at large upon parole, experiencing every indulgence and civility consistent with their security.

CHAPTER IV.

DANGERS IN THE INTERIOR—MACHINATIONS OF THE JOHNSON FAMILY—RIVAL-
RY OF ETHAN ALLEN AND BENEDICT ARNOLD—GOVERNMENT PERPLEXITIES
ABOUT THE TICONDEROGA CAPTURE—MEASURES TO SECURE THE PRIZE—
ALLEN AND ARNOLD AMBITIOUS OF FURTHER LAURELS—PROJECTS FOR THE
INVASION OF CANADA—ETHAN ALLEN AND SETH WARNER HONORED BY
CONGRESS—ARNOLD DISPLACED BY A COMMITTEE OF INQUIRY—HIS INDIG-
NATION—NEWS FROM CANADA—THE REVOLUTION TO BE EXTENDED INTO
THAT PROVINCE—ENLISTMENT OF GREEN MOUNTAIN BOYS—SCHUYLER AT
TICONDEROGA—STATE OF AFFAIRS THERE—ELECTION FOR OFFICERS OF
THE GREEN MOUNTAIN BOYS—ETHAN ALLEN DISMOUNTED—JOINS THE ARMY
AS A VOLUNTEER—PREPARATIONS FOR THE INVASION OF CANADA—GENE-
RAL MONTGOMERY—INDIAN CHIEFS AT CAMBRIDGE—COUNCIL FIRE—PLAN
FOR AN EXPEDITION AGAINST QUEBEC—DEPARTURE OF TROOPS FROM TI-
CONDEROGA—ARRIVAL AT ISLE AUX NOIX.

WE must interrupt our narrative of the siege of Boston to give
an account of events in other quarters, requiring the superintending care of Washington as commander-in-chief.   Letters from
General Schuyler, received in the course of July, had awakened
apprehensions of danger from the interior.   The Johnsons were
said to be stirring up the Indians in the western parts of New
York to hostility, and preparing to join the British forces in
Canada; so that, while the patriots were battling for their rights
along the seaboard, they were menaced by a powerful combination
in rear.   To place this matter in a proper light, we will give a

brief statement of occurrences in the upper part of New York, and on the frontiers of Canada, since the exploits of Ethan Allen and Benedict Arnold, at Ticonderoga and on Lake Champlain.

Great rivalry, as has already been noted, had arisen between these doughty leaders. Both had sent off expresses to the provincial authorities, giving an account of their recent triumphs. Allen claimed command at Ticonderoga, on the authority of the committee from the Connecticut Assembly, which had originated the enterprise. Arnold claimed it on the strength of his instructions from the Massachusetts committee of safety. He bore a commission, too, given him by that committee; whereas Allen had no other commission than that given him before the war by the committees in the Hampshire Grants, to command their Green Mountain Boys against the encroachments of New York.

"Colonel Allen," said Arnold, "is a proper man to head his own wild people, but entirely unacquainted with military service, and as I am the only person who has been legally authorized to take possession of this place, I am determined to insist on my right; * * * and shall keep it [the fort] at every hazard, until I have further orders." *

The public bodies themselves seemed perplexed what to do with the prize, so bravely seized upon by these bold men. Allen had written to the Albany committee, for men and provisions, to enable him to maintain his conquest. The committee feared this daring enterprise might involve the northern part of the province in the horrors of war and desolation, and asked advice of the New York committee. The New York committee did not think themselves authorized to give an opinion upon a matter of such importance, and referred it to the Continental Congress.

* Arnold to Mass. Comm. of Safety. Am. Arch. ii. 557.

The Massachusetts committee of safety, to whom Arnold had written, referred the affair to the Massachusetts Provincial Congress. That body, as the enterprise had begun in Connecticut, wrote to its General Assembly to take the whole matter under their care and direction, until the advice of the Continental Congress could be had.

The Continental Congress at length legitimated the exploit, and, as it were, accepted the captured fortress. As it was situated within New York, the custody of it was committed to that province, aided if necessary by the New England colonies, on whom it was authorized to call for military assistance.

The Provincial Congress of New York forthwith invited the "Governor and Company of the English colony of Connecticut" to place part of their forces in these captured posts, until relieved by New York troops; and Trumbull, the Governor of Connecticut, soon gave notice that one thousand men under Colonel Hinman, were on the point of marching, for the reinforcement of Ticonderoga and Crown Point.

It had been the idea of the Continental Congress to have those posts dismantled, and the cannon and stores removed to the south end of Lake George, where a strong post was to be established. But both Allen and Arnold exclaimed against such a measure; vaunting, and with reason, the importance of those forts.

Both Allen and Arnold were ambitious of further laurels. Both were anxious to lead an expedition into Canada; and Ticonderoga and Crown Point would open the way to it. "The Key is ours," writes Allen to the New York Congress. "If the colonies would suddenly push an army of two or three thousand men into Canada, they might make an easy conquest of all that would oppose them, in the extensive province of Quebec, except a reinforcement from England should prevent it. Such a diversion would weaken Gage, and insure us Canada. I wish to God America would, at this critical juncture, exert herself agreeably to the indignity offered her by a tyrannical ministry. She might rise on eagles' wings, and mount up to glory, freedom, and immortal honor, if she did but know and exert her strength. Fame is now hovering over her head. A vast continent must now sink to slavery, poverty, horror and bondage, or rise to unconquerable freedom, immense wealth, inexpressible felicity, and immortal fame.

"I will lay my life on it, that with fifteen hundred men, and a proper train of artillery, I will take Montreal. Provided I could be thus furnished, and if an army could command the field, it would be no insuperable difficulty to take Quebec."

A letter to the same purport, and with the same rhetorical flourish, on which he appeared to value himself, was written by Allen to Trumbull, the Governor of Connecticut. Arnold urged the same project, but in less magniloquent language, upon the attention of the Continental Congress. His letter was dated from Crown Point; where he had a little squadron, composed of the sloop captured at St. Johns, a schooner, and a flotilla of bateaux. All these he had equipped, armed, manned, and officered; and his crews were devoted to him. In his letter to the Continental Congress he gave information concerning Canada, collected through spies and agents. Carleton, he said, had not six hundred effective men under him. The Canadians and Indians were disaffected to the British Government, and Montreal was ready to throw open its gates to a patriot force. Two thousand men, he was certain, would be sufficient to get possession of the province.

"I beg leave to add," says he, "that if no person appears who will undertake to carry the plan into execution, I will undertake, and, with the smiles of Heaven, answer for the success, provided I am supplied with men, &c., to carry it into execution without loss of time."

In a postcript of his letter, he specifies the forces requisite for his suggested invasion. "In order to give satisfaction to the different colonies, I propose that Colonel Hinman's regiment, now on their march from Connecticut to Ticonderoga, should form part of the army; say one thousand men; five hundred men to be sent from New York, five hundred of General Arnold's regiment, including the seamen and marines on board the vessels (no *Green Mountain* Boys)."

Within a few days after the date of this letter, Colonel Hinman with the Connecticut troops arrived. The greater part of the Green Mountain Boys now returned home, their term of enlistment having expired. Ethan Allen and his brother in arms, Seth Warner, repaired to Congress to get pay for their men, and authority to raise a new regiment. They were received with distinguished honor by that body. The same pay was awarded to the men who had served under them as that allowed to the continental troops; and it was recommended to the New York Convention that, should it meet the approbation of General Schuyler, a fresh corps of Green Mountain Boys about to be raised, should be employed in the army under such officers as they (the Green Mountain Boys) should choose.

To the New York Convention, Allen and Warner now repaired. There was a difficulty about admitting them to the hall of Assembly, for their attainder of outlawry had not been repealed. Patriotism, however, pleaded in their behalf. They obtained an audience. A regiment of Green Mountain Boys, five hundred strong, was decreed, and General Schuyler notified the people of the New Hampshire Grants of the resolve, and requested them to raise the regiment.

Thus prosperously went the affairs of Ethan Allen and Seth Warner. As to Arnold, difficulties instantly took place between him and Colonel Hinman. Arnold refused to give up to him the command of either post, claiming on the strength of his instructions from the committee of safety of Massachusetts, a right to the command of all the posts and fortresses at the south end of Lake Champlain and Lake George. This threw every thing into confusion. Colonel Hinman was himself perplexed in this conflict of various authorities; being, as it were, but a *locum tenens* for the province of New York.

Arnold was at Crown Point, acting as commander of the fort and admiral of the fleet; and having about a hundred and fifty resolute men under him, was expecting with confidence to be authorized to lead an expedition into Canada.

At this juncture arrived a committee of three members of the Congress of Massachusetts, sent by that body to inquire into the manner in which he had executed his instructions; complaints having been made of his arrogant and undue assumption of command.

Arnold was thunderstruck at being subjected to inquiry, when he had expected an ovation. He requested a sight of the committee's instructions. The sight of them only increased his indignation. They were to acquaint themselves with the manner in which he had executed his commission; with his spirit, capacity, and conduct. Should they think proper, they might order him to return to Massachusetts, to render account of the moneys, ammunition and stores he had received, and the debts he had contracted on behalf of the colony. While at Ticonderoga, he and his men were to be under command of the principal officer from Connecticut.

Arnold was furious. He swore he would be second in command to no one, disbanded his men, and threw up his commission. Quite a scene ensued. His men became turbulent; some refused to serve under any other leader; others clamored for their pay, which was in arrears. Part joined Arnold on board of the vessels which were drawn out into the lake; and among other ebullitions of passion, there was a threat of sailing for St. Johns.

At length the storm was allayed by the interference of several of the officers, and the assurances of the committee that every man should be paid. A part of them enlisted under Colonel Easton, and Arnold set off for Cambridge to settle his accounts with the committee of safety.

The project of an invasion of Canada, urged by Allen and Arnold, had at first met with no favor, the Continental Congress having formally resolved to make no hostile attempts upon that province. Intelligence subsequently received, induced it to change its plans. Carleton was said to be strengthening the fortifications and garrison at St. Johns, and preparing to launch vessels on the lake wherewith to regain command of it, and retake the captured posts. Powerful reinforcements were coming from England and elsewhere. Guy Johnson was holding councils with the fierce Cayugas and Senecas, and stirring up the Six Nations to hostility. On the other hand, Canada was full of religious and political dissensions. The late exploits of the Americans on Lake Champlain, had produced a favorable effect on the Canadians, who would flock to the patriot standard if unfurled among them by an imposing force. Now was the time to strike a blow to paralyze all hostility from this quarter; now, while Carleton's regular force was weak, and before the arrival of additional troops. Influenced by these considerations, Congress now determined to extend the revolution into Canada, but it was an enterprise too important to be entrusted to any but discreet hands. General Schuyler, then in New York, was accordingly ordered, on the 27th June, to proceed to Ticonderoga, and "should he find it practicable, and not disagreeable to the Canadians, immediately to take possession of St Johns and Montreal, and pursue such other measures in Canada as might have a tendency to promote the peace and security of these provinces."

It behooved General Schuyler to be on the alert, lest the enterprise should be snatched from his hands. Ethan Allen and Seth Warner were at Bennington, among the Green Mountains. Enlistments were going on, but too slow for Allen's impatience, who had his old hankering for a partisan foray. In a letter to Governor Trumbull (July 12th), he writes, "Were it not that the grand Continental Congress had totally incorporated the Green Mountain Boys into a battalion under certain regulations and command, I would forthwith advance them into Canada and invest Montreal, *exclusive of any help from the colonies;* though under present circumstances I would not, for my right arm, act without or contrary to order. *If my fond zeal for reducing the King's fortresses and destroying or imprisoning his troops in Canada be the result of enthusiasm,* I hope and expect the wisdom of the Continent will treat it as such; and on the other hand, if it proceed from sound policy, that the plan will be adopted." *

Schuyler arrived at Ticonderoga on the 18th of July. A

* Force's Am. Archives, ii. 1649.

letter to Washington, to whom, as commander-in-chief, he made constant reports, gives a striking picture of a frontier post in those crude days of the Revolution.

" You will expect that I should say something about this place and the troops here. Not one earthly thing for offence or defence has been done; *the commanding officer has no orders; he only came to reinforce the garrison, and he expected the general.* About ten last night I arrived at the landing-place, at the north end of Lake George; a post occupied by a captain and one hundred men. A sentinel, on being informed that I was in the boat, quitted his post to go and awaken the guard, consisting of three men, in which he had no success. I walked up and came to another, a sergeant's guard. Here the sentinel challenged, but suffered me to come up to him; the whole guard, like the first, in the soundest sleep. With a penknife only I could have cut off both guards, and then have set fire to the block house, destroyed the stores, and starved the people here. At this post I had pointedly recommended vigilance and care, as all the stores from Lake George must necessarily be landed here. But I hope to get the better of this inattention. The officers and men are all good-looking people, and decent in their deportment, and I really believe will make good soldiers as soon as I can get the better of this *nonchalance* of theirs. Bravery, I believe, they are far from wanting."

Colonel Hinman, it will be recollected, was in temporary command at Ticonderoga, if that could be called a command where none seemed to obey. The garrison was about twelve hundred strong: the greater part Connecticut men brought by himself; some were New York troops, and some few Green Mountain Boys. Schuyler, on taking command, despatched a confidential agent into Canada, Major John Brown, an American, who resided on the Sorel River, and was popular among the Canadians. He was to collect information as to the British forces and fortifications, and to ascertain how an invasion and an attack on St. Johns would be considered by the people of the province : in the mean time, Schuyler set diligently to work to build boats and prepare for the enterprise, should it ultimately be ordered by Congress.

Schuyler was an authoritative man, and inherited from his Dutch ancestry a great love of order ; he was excessively annoyed, therefore, by the confusion and negligence prevalent around him, and the difficulties and delays thereby occasioned. He chafed in spirit at the disregard of discipline among his yeoman soldiery, and their opposition to all system and regularity. This was especially the case with the troops from Connecticut, officered generally by their own neighbors and familiar companions, and unwilling to acknowledge the authority of a commander from a different province. He poured out his complaints in a friendly letter to Washington ; the latter consoled him by stating his own troubles and grievances in the camp at Cambridge, and the spirit with which he coped with them. "From my own experience," writes he (July 28), "I can easily judge of your difficulties in introducing order and discipline into troops, who have, from their infancy, imbibed ideas of the most contrary kind. It would be far beyond the compass of a letter, for me to describe the situation of things here [at Cambridge], on my arrival. Perhaps you will only be able to judge of it, from my assuring you, that mine must be a portrait at full length of what you have had in miniature. Confusion and discord reigned in every department, which, in a little time, must have ended either in the separation of the army, or fatal contests with one another. The better genius of America has prevailed, and most happily, the ministerial troops have not availed themselves of these advantages, till, I trust, the opportunity is in a great measure passed over. * * * We mend every day, and, I flatter myself, that in a little time we shall work up these raw materials into a good manufacture. I must recommend to you, what I endeavor to practise myself, patience and perseverance."

Schuyler took the friendly admonition in the spirit in which it was given. "I can easily conceive," writes he (Aug. 6th), that my difficulties are only a faint semblance of yours. Yes, my general, I will strive to copy your bright example, and patiently and steadily persevere in that line which only can promise the wished-for reformation."

He had calculated on being joined by this time by the regiment of Green Mountain Boys which Ethan Allen and Seth Warner had undertaken to raise in the New Hampshire Grants. Unfortunately, a quarrel had arisen between those brothers in arms, which filled the Green Mountains with discord and party feuds. The election of officers took place on the 27th of July. It was made by committees from the different townships. Ethan Allen was entirely passed by, and Seth Warner nominated as Lieutenant-colonel of the regiment. Allen was thunderstruck at finding himself thus suddenly dismounted. His patriotism and love of adventure, however, were not quelled : and he forthwith repaired to the army at Ticonderoga to offer himself as a volunteer.

Schuyler, at first, hesitated to accept his services. He was aware of his aspiring notions, and feared there would be a difficulty in keeping him within due bounds, but was at length persuaded by his officers to retain him, to act as a pioneer on the Canadian frontier.

In a letter from camp, Allen gave Governor Trumbull an account of the downfall of his towering hopes. "Notwithstanding my zeal and success in my country's cause, the old farmers on the New Hampshire Grants, who do not incline to go to war, have met in a committee meeting, and in their nomination of officers for the regiment of Green Mountain Boys, have wholly omitted me."

His letter has a consolatory postscript. "I find myself in the favor of the officers of the army and the young Green Mountain Boys. How the old men came to reject me I cannot conceive, inasmuch as I saved them from the encroachments of New York."*—The old men probably doubted his discretion.

Schuyler was on the alert with respect to the expedition against Canada. From his agent Major Brown, and from other sources, he had learnt that there were but about seven hundred king's troops in that province; three hundred of them at St. Johns, about fifty at Quebec, the remainder at Montreal, Chamblee, and the upper posts. Colonel Guy Johnson was at Montreal with three hundred men, mostly his tenants, and with a number of Indians. Two batteries had been finished at St. Johns, mounting nine guns each : other works were intrenched and picketed. Two large row galleys were on the stocks, and would soon be finished. Now was the time, according to his informants, to carry Canada. It might be done with great ease and little cost. The Canadians were disaffected to British rule, and would join the Americans, and so would many of the Indians.

" I am prepared," writes he to Washington, " to move against

* Am. Archives, 4th Series, iii. 17.

the enemy, unless your Excellency and Congress should direct otherwise. In the course of a few days I expect to receive the ultimate determination. Whatever it may be, I shall try to execute it in such a manner as will promote the just cause in which we are engaged."

While awaiting orders on this head, he repaired to Albany, to hold a conference and negotiate a treaty with the Caughnawagas, and the warriors of the Six Nations, whom, as one of the commissioners of Indian affairs, he had invited to meet him at that place. General Richard Montgomery was to remain in command at Ticonderoga, during his absence, and to urge forward the military preparations. As the subsequent fortunes of this gallant officer are inseparably connected with the Canadian campaign, and have endeared his name to Americans, we pause to give a few particulars concerning him.

General Richard Montgomery was of a good family in the north of Ireland, where he was born in 1736. He entered the army when about eighteen years of age; served in America in the French war; won a lieutenancy by gallant conduct at Louisburg; followed General Amherst to Lake Champlain, and, after the conquest of Canada, was promoted to a captaincy for his services in the West Indies.

After the peace of Versailles he resided in England; but, about three years before the breaking out of the Revolution, he sold out his commission in the army and emigrated to New York. Here he married the eldest daughter of Judge Robert R. Livingston, of the Clermont branch of that family; and took up his residence on an estate which he had purchased in Dutchess County on the banks of the Hudson.

Being known to be in favor of the popular cause, he was

drawn reluctantly from his rural abode, to represent his county in the first convention of the province; and on the recent organization of the army, his military reputation gained him the unsought commission of Brigadier-general. "It is an event," writes he to a friend, "which must put an end for a while, perhaps for ever, to the quiet scheme of life I had prescribed for myself; for, though entirely unexpected and undesired by me, the will of an oppressed people, compelled to choose between liberty and slavery, must be obeyed."

At the time of receiving his commission, Montgomery was about thirty-nine years of age, and the *beau ideal* of a soldier. His form was well proportioned and vigorous; his countenance expressive and prepossessing; he was cool and discriminating in council, energetic and fearless in action. His principles commanded the respect of friends and foes, and he was noted for winning the affections of the soldiery.

While these things were occurring at Ticonderoga, several Indian chiefs made their appearance in the camp at Cambridge. They came in savage state and costume, as ambassadors from their respective tribes, to have a talk about the impending invasion of Canada. One was chief of the Caughnawaga tribe, whose residence was on the banks of the St. Lawrence, six miles above Montreal. Others were from St. Francis, about forty-five leagues above Quebec, and were of a warlike tribe, from which hostilities had been especially apprehended.

Washington, accustomed to deal with the red warriors of the wilderness, received them with great ceremonial. They dined at head-quarters among his officers, and it is observed that to some of the latter they might have served as models; such was their grave dignity and decorum.

A council fire was held. The sachems all offered, on behalf of their tribes, to take up the hatchet for the Americans, should the latter invade Canada. The offer was embarrassing. Congress had publicly resolved to seek nothing but neutrality from the Indian nations, unless the ministerial agents should make an offensive alliance with them. The chief of the St. Francis tribe declared that Governor Carleton had endeavored to persuade him to take up the hatchet against the Americans, but in vain. "As our ancestors gave this country to you," added he grandly, "we would not have you destroyed by England; but are ready to afford you our assistance."

Washington wished to be certain of the conduct of the enemy, before he gave a reply to these Indian overtures. He wrote by express, therefore, to General Schuyler, requesting him to ascertain the intentions of the British governor with respect to the native tribes.

By the same express, he communicated a plan which had occupied his thoughts for several days. As the contemplated movement of Schuyler would probably cause all the British force in Canada to be concentrated in the neighborhood of Montreal and St. Johns, he proposed to send off an expedition of ten or twelve hundred men, to penetrate to Quebec by the way of the Kennebec River. "If you are resolved to proceed," writes he to Schuyler, "which I gather from your last letter is your intention, it would make a diversion that would distract Carleton. He must either break up, and follow this party to Quebec, by which he would leave you a free passage, or he must suffer that important place to fall into other hands; an event that would have a decisive effect and influence on the public interest. * * * * The few whom I have consulted on the project approve it much, but the final determination is deferred until I hear from you. Not a moment's time is to be lost in the preparations for this enterprise, if the advices from you favor it. With the utmost expedition the season will be considerably advanced, so that you will dismiss the express as soon as possible."

The express found Schuyler in Albany, where he had been attending the conference with the Six Nations. He had just received intelligence which convinced him of the propriety of an expedition into Canada; had sent word to General Montgomery to get every thing ready for it, and was on the point of departing for Ticonderoga to carry it into effect. In reply to Washington, he declared his conviction, from various accounts which he had received, that Carleton and his agents were exciting the Indian tribes to hostility. "I should, therefore, not hesitate one moment," adds he, "to employ any savages that might be willing to join us."

He expressed himself delighted with Washington's project of sending off an expedition to Quebec, regretting only that it had not been thought of earlier. "Should the detachment from your body penetrate into Canada," added he, "and we meet with success, Canada must inevitably fall into our hands."

Having sent off these despatches, Schuyler, hastened back to Ticonderoga. Before he reached there, Montgomery had received intelligence that Carleton had completed his armed vessels at St. Johns, and was about to send them into Lake Champlain by the Sorel River. No time, therefore, was to be lost in getting possession of the Isle aux Noix, which commanded the entrance to that river. Montgomery hastened, therefore, to embark with about a thousand men, which were as many as the boats now ready could hold, taking with him two pieces of artillery; with this force he set off down the lake. A letter to General Schuyler explained the cause of his sudden departure, and entreated him to follow on in a whale-boat, leaving the residue of the artillery to come on as soon as conveyances could be procured.

Schuyler arrived at Ticonderoga on the night of the 30th of August, but too ill of a bilious fever to push on in a whale-boat. He caused, however, a bed to be prepared for him in a covered bateau, and, ill as he was, continued forward on the following day. On the 4th of September he overtook Montgomery at the Isle la Motte, where he had been detained by contrary weather, and, assuming command of the little army, kept on the same day to the Isle aux Noix, about twelve miles south of St. Johns—where for the present we shall leave him, and return to the head-quarters of the commander-in-chief.

CHAPTER V.

A CHALLENGE DECLINED—A BLOW MEDITATED—A CAUTIOUS COUNCIL OF WAR—PREPARATION FOR THE QUEBEC EXPEDITION—BENEDICT ARNOLD THE LEADER—ADVICE AND INSTRUCTIONS—DEPARTURE—GENERAL SCHUYLER ON THE SOREL—RECONNOITRES ST. JOHNS—CAMP AT ISLE AUX NOIX—ILLNESS OF SCHUYLER—RETURNS TO TICONDEROGA—EXPEDITION OF MONTGOMERY AGAINST ST. JOHNS—LETTER OF ETHAN ALLEN—HIS DASH AGAINST MONTREAL—ITS CATASTROPHE—A HERO IN IRONS—CORRESPONDENCE OF WASHINGTON WITH SCHUYLER AND ARNOLD—HIS ANXIETY ABOUT THEM.

THE siege of Boston had been kept up for several weeks without any remarkable occurrence. The British remained within their lines, diligently strengthening them; the besiegers having received further supplies of ammunition, were growing impatient of a state of inactivity. Towards the latter part of August there were rumors from Boston, that the enemy were preparing for a sortie. Washington was resolved to provoke it by a kind of challenge. He accordingly detached fourteen hundred men to seize at night upon a height within musket shot of the enemy's line on Charlestown Neck, presuming that the latter would sally forth on the following day to dispute possession of it, and thus be drawn into a general battle. The task was executed with silence and celerity, and by daybreak the hill presented to the astonished foe, the aspect of a fortified post.

The challenge was not accepted. The British opened a heavy cannonade from Bunker's Hill, but kept within their works. The Americans, scant of ammunition, could only reply with a single nine-pounder; this, however, sank one of the floating batteries which guarded the neck. They went on to complete and strengthen this advanced post, exposed to daily cannonade and bombardment, which, however, did but little injury. They continued to answer from time to time with a single gun; reserving their ammunition for a general action. "We are just in the situation of a man with little money in his pocket," writes Secretary Reed; "he will do twenty mean things to prevent his breaking in upon his little stock. We are obliged to bear with the rascals on Bunker's Hill, when a few shot now and then in return, would keep our men attentive to their business and give the enemy alarms." *

The evident unwillingness of the latter to come forth was perplexing. "Unless the ministerial troops in Boston are waiting for reinforcements," writes Washington, "I cannot devise what they are staying there for, nor why, as they affect to despise the Americans, they do not come forth and put an end to the contest at once."

Perhaps they persuaded themselves that his army, composed of crude, half-disciplined levies from different and distant quarters, would gradually fall asunder and disperse, or that its means of subsistence would be exhausted. He had his own fears on the subject, and looked forward with doubt and anxiety to a winter's campaign; the heavy expense that would be incurred in providing barracks, fuel and warm clothing; the difficulty there would be of keeping together, through the rigorous season, troops unaccus-

* Life of Reed, vol. i. 119.

tomed to military hardships, and none of whose terms of enlistment extended beyond the 1st of January : the supplies of ammunition, too, that would be required for protracted operations; the
stock of powder on hand, notwithstanding the most careful hus-
bandry, being fearfully small.   Revolving these circumstances in
his mind, he rode thoughtfully about the commanding points in
the vicinity of Boston, considering how he might strike a decisive
blow that would put an end to the murmuring inactivity of the
army, and relieve the country from the consuming expense of
maintaining it.   The result was, a letter to the major and brigadier-generals, summoning them to a council of war to be held at
the distance of three days, and giving them previous intimation
of its purpose.   It was to know whether, in their judgment, a
successful attack might not be made upon the troops at Boston
by means of boats, in co-operation with an attempt upon their
lines at Roxbury.   " The success of such an enterprise," adds he,
" depends, I well know, upon the Allwise Disposer of events, and
it is not within the reach of human wisdom to foretell the issue ;
but if the prospect is fair, the undertaking is justifiable."

He proceeded to state the considerations already cited, which
appeared to justify it.   The council having thus had time for
previous deliberation, met on the 11th of September.   It was
composed of Major-generals Ward, Lee, and Putnam, and Brigadier-generals Thomas, Heath, Sullivan, Spencer, and Greene.
They unanimously pronounced the suggested attempt inexpedi-
ent, at least for the present.

It certainly was bold and hazardous, yet it seems to have
taken strong hold on the mind of the commander-in-chief, usually
so cautious.   " I cannot say," writes he to the President of Congress, " that I have wholly laid it aside ; but new events may oc-

casion new measures. Of this I hope the honorable Congress can need no assurance, that there is not a man in America who more earnestly wishes such a termination of the campaign, as to make the army no longer necessary."

In the mean time, as it was evident the enemy did not intend to come out, but were only strengthening their defences and preparing for winter, Washington was enabled to turn his attention to the expedition to be sent into Canada by the way of the Kennebec River.

A detachment of about eleven hundred men, chosen for the purpose, was soon encamped on Cambridge Common. There were ten companies of New England infantry, some of them from General Greene's Rhode Island regiments; three rifle companies from Pennsylvania and Virginia, one of them Captain Daniel Morgan's famous company; and a number of volunteers; among whom was Aaron Burr, then but twenty years of age, and just commencing his varied, brilliant, but ultimately unfortunate career.

The proposed expedition was wild and perilous, and required a hardy, skilful and intrepid leader. Such a one was at hand. Benedict Arnold was at Cambridge, occupied in settling his accounts with the Massachusetts committee of safety. These were nearly adjusted. Whatever faults may have been found with his conduct in some particulars, his exploits on Lake Champlain had atoned for them; for valor in time of war, covers a multitude of sins. It was thought too, by some, that he had been treated harshly, and there was a disposition to soothe his irritated pride. Washington had given him an honorable reception at head-quarters, and now considered him the very man for the present enterprise. He had shown aptness for military service, whether on land or water. He was acquainted, too, with Canada, and especially with Quebec, having, in the course of his checkered life, traded in horses between that place and the West Indies. With these considerations he intrusted him with the command of the expedition, giving him the commission of lieutenant-colonel in the continental army.

As he would be intrusted with dangerous powers, Washington, beside a general letter of instructions, addressed a special one to him individually, full of cautious and considerate advice. "Upon your conduct and courage, and that of the officers and soldiers detailed on this expedition, not only the success of the present enterprise, and your own honor, but the safety and welfare of the whole continent, may depend. I charge you, therefore, and the officers and soldiers under your command, as you value your own safety and honor, and the favor and esteem of your country, that you consider yourselves as marching, not through the country of an enemy, but of our friends and brethren; for such the inhabitants of Canada and the Indian nations have approved themselves, in this unhappy contest between Great Britain and America; and that you check by every motive of duty and fear of punishment every attempt to plunder or insult the inhabitants of Canada. Should any American soldier be so base and infamous as to injure any Canadian or Indian in his person or property, I do most earnestly enjoin you to bring him to such severe and exemplary punishment as the enormity of the crime may require. Should it extend to death itself, it will not be disproportioned to its guilt at such a time and in such a cause. * * * * I also give in charge to you, to avoid all disrespect to the religion of the country and its ceremonies. * * While we are contending for our own liberty, we should be very cautious not to violate the rights of conscience in others, ever considering that God alone is the judge of the hearts of men, and to him only, in this case, are they answerable."

In the general letter of instructions, Washington inserted the following clause. "If Lord Chatham's son should be in Canada, and in any way fall into your power, you are enjoined to treat him with all possible deference and respect. You cannot err in paying too much honor to the son of so illustrious a character and so true a friend to America."

Arnold was, moreover, furnished with handbills for distribution in Canada, setting forth the friendly objects of the present expedition, as well as of that under General Schuyler; and calling on the Canadians to furnish necessaries and accommodations of every kind; for which they were assured ample compensation.

On the 13th of September, Arnold struck his tents, and set out in high spirits. More fortunate than his rival, Ethan Allen, he had attained the object of his ambition, the command of an expedition into Canada; and trusted in the capture of Quebec, to eclipse even the surprise of Ticonderoga.

Washington enjoined upon him to push forward, as rapidly as possible, success depending upon celerity; and counted the days as they elapsed after his departure, impatient to receive tidings of his progress up the Kennebec, and expecting that the expedition would reach Quebec about the middle of October. In the interim came letters from General Schuyler, giving particulars of the main expedition.

In a preceding chapter we left the general and his little army at the Isle aux Noix, near the Sorel River, the outlet of the lake. Thence, on the 5th of September, he sent Colonel Ethan Allen and Major Brown to reconnoitre the country between that river and the St. Lawrence, to distribute friendly addresses among the people and ascertain their feelings. This done, and having landed his baggage and provisions, the general proceeded along the Sorel River the next day with his boats, until within two miles of St. Johns, when a cannonade was opened from the fort. Keeping on for half a mile further, he landed his troops in a deep, close swamp, where they had a sharp skirmish with an ambuscade of tories and Indians, whom they beat off with some loss on both sides. Night coming on, they cast up a small intrenchment, and encamped, disturbed occasionally by shells from the fort, which, however, did no other mischief than slightly wounding a lieutenant.

In the night the camp was visited secretly by a person, who informed General Schuyler of the state of the fort. The works were completed, and furnished with cannon. A vessel pierced for sixteen guns was launched, and would be ready to sail in three or four days. It was not probable that any Canadians would join the army, being disposed to remain neutral. This intelligence being discussed in a council of war in the morning, it was determined that they had neither men nor artillery sufficient to undertake a siege. They returned, therefore, to the Isle aux Noix, cast up fortifications, and threw a boom across the channel of the river to prevent the passage of the enemy's vessels into the lake, and awaited the arrival of artillery and reinforcements from Ticonderoga.

In the course of a few days the expected reinforcements arrived, and with them a small train of artillery. Ethan Allen also returned from his reconnoitring expedition, of which he made a most encouraging report. The Canadian captains of militia were ready, he said, to join the Americans, whenever they should appear with sufficient force. He had held talks, too, with the Indians, and found them well disposed. In a word, he was convinced that an attack on St. Johns, and an inroad into the province, would meet with hearty co-operation.

Preparations were now made for the investment of St. Johns by land and water. Major Brown, who had already acted as a scout, was sent with one hundred Americans, and about thirty Canadians towards Chamblee, to make friends in that quarter, and to join the army as soon as it should arrive at St. Johns.

To quiet the restless activity of Ethan Allen, who had no command in the army, he was sent with an escort of thirty men to retrace his steps, penetrate to La Prairie, and beat up for recruits among the people whom he had recently visited.

For some time past, General Schuyler had been struggling with a complication of maladies, but exerting himself to the utmost in the harassing business of the camp, still hoping to be able to move with the army. When every thing was nearly ready, he was attacked in the night by a severe access of his disorder, which confined him to his bed, and compelled him to surrender the conduct of the expedition to General Montgomery. Since he could be of no further use, therefore, in this quarter, he caused his bed, as before, to be placed on board a covered bateau, and set off for Ticonderoga, to hasten forward reinforcements and supplies. An hour after his departure, he met Colonel Seth Warner, with one hundred and seventy Green Mountain Boys, steering for the camp, "being the first," adds he, "that have appeared of that boasted corps." Some had mutinied and deserted the colonel, and the remainder were at Crown Point; whence they were about to embark.

Such was the purport of different letters received from

Schuyler; the last bearing date September 20th. Washington was deeply concerned when informed that he had quitted the army, supposing that General Wooster, as the eldest brigadier, would take rank and command of Montgomery, and considering him deficient in the activity and energy required by the difficult service in which he was engaged. "I am, therefore," writes he to Schuyler, "much alarmed for Arnold, whose expedition was built upon yours, and who will infallibly perish, if the invasion and entry into Canada are abandoned by your successor. I hope by this time the penetration into Canada by your army is effected; but if it is not, and there are any intentions to lay it aside, I beg it may be done in such a manner that Arnold may be saved, by giving him notice; and in the mean time, your army may keep such apearances as to fix Carleton, and to prevent the force of Canada being turned wholly upon Arnold.

"Should this find you at Albany, and General Wooster about taking the command, I entreat you to impress him strongly with the importance and necessity of proceeding, or so to conduct, that Arnold may have time to retreat."

What caused this immediate solicitude about Arnold, was a letter received from him, dated ten days previously from Fort Western, on the Kennebec River. He had sent reconnoitring parties ahead in light canoes, to gain intelligence from the Indians, and take the courses and distances to Dead River, a branch of the Kennebec, and he was now forwarding his troops in bateaux in five divisions, one day's march apart; Morgan with his riflemen in the first division, Lieutenant-colonel Roger Enos commanding the last. As soon as the last division should be under way, Arnold was to set off in a light skiff to overtake the advance. Chaudiere Pond on the Chaudiere River, was the appointed rendezvous, whence they were to march in a body towards Quebec.

Judging from the date of the letter, Arnold must at this time be making his way, by land and water, through an uninhabited and unexplored wilderness; and beyond the reach of recall; his situation, therefore, would be desperate should General Wooster fail to follow up the campaign against St. Johns. The solicitude of Washington on his account was heightened by the consciousness, that the hazardous enterprise in which he was engaged had chiefly been set on foot by himself, and he felt in some degree responsible for the safety of the resolute partisan and his companions.

Fortunately, Wooster was not the successor to Schuyler in the command of the expedition. Washington was mistaken as to the rank of his commission, which was one degree lower than that of Montgomery. The veteran himself, who was a gallant soldier, and had seen service in two wars, expressed himself nobly in the matter, in reply to some inquiry made by Schuyler. " I have the cause of my country too much at heart," said he, "to attempt to make any difficulty or uneasiness in the army, upon whom the success of an enterprise of almost infinite importance to the country is now depending. I shall consider my rank in the army what my commission from the Continental Congress makes it, and shall not attempt to dispute the command with General Montgomery at St. Johns." We shall give some further particulars concerning this expedition against St. Johns, towards which Washington was turning so anxious an eye.

On the 16th of September, the day after Schuyler's departure for Ticonderoga, Montgomery proceeded to carry out the plans which had been concerted between them. Landing on the

17th at the place where they had formerly encamped, within a mile and a half of the fort, he detached a force of five hundred men, among whom were three hundred Green Mountain Boys under Colonel Seth Warner, to take a position at the junction of two roads leading to Montreal and Chamblee, so as to intercept relief from those points. He now proceeded to invest St. Johns. A battery was erected on a point of land commanding the fort, the ship yards and the armed schooner. Another was thrown up in the woods on the east side of the fort, at six hundred yards distance, and furnished with two small mortars. All this was done under an incessant fire from the enemy, which, as yet, was but feebly returned.

St. Johns had a garrison of five or six hundred regulars and two hundred Canadian militia. Its commander, Major Preston, made a brave resistance. Montgomery had not proper battering cannon; his mortars were defective; his artillerists unpractised, and the engineer ignorant of the first principles of his art. The siege went on slowly, until the arrival of an artillery company under Captain Lamb, expedited from Saratoga by General Schuyler. Lamb, who was an able officer, immediately bedded a thirteen-inch mortar, and commenced a fire of shot and shells upon the fort. The distance, however, was too great, and the positions of the batteries were ill chosen.

A flourishing letter was received by the general from Colonel Ethan Allen, giving hope of further reinforcement. "I am now," writes he, "at the Parish of St. Ours, four leagues from Sorel to the south. I have two hundred and fifty Canadians under arms. As I march, they gather fast. You may rely on it, that I shall join you in about three days, with five hundred or more Canadian volunteers. I could raise one or two thousand in a week's time; but I will first visit the army with a less number, and, if necessary, go again recruiting. Those that used to be enemies to our cause, come cap in hand to me; and I swear by the Lord, I can raise three times the number of our army in Canada, provided you continue the siege. * * * The eyes of all America, nay, of Europe, are or will be on the economy of this army and the consequences attending it." *

Allen was actually on his way toward St. Johns, when, between Longueil and La Prairie, he met Colonel Brown with his party of Americans and Canadians. A conversation took place between them. Brown assured him that the garrison at Montreal did not exceed thirty men, and might easily be surprised. Allen's partisan spirit was instantly excited. Here was a chance for another bold stroke equal to that at Ticonderoga. A plan was forthwith agreed upon. Allen was to return to Longueil, which is nearly opposite Montreal, and cross the St. Lawrence in canoes in the night, so as to land a little below the town. Brown, with two hundred men, was to cross above, and Montreal was to be attacked simultaneously at opposite points.

All this was arranged and put in action without the consent or knowledge of General Montgomery; Allen was again the partisan leader, acting from individual impulse. His late letter also to General Montgomery, would seem to have partaken of fanfaronade; for the whole force with which he undertook his part of this inconsiderate enterprise, was thirty Americans, and eighty Canadians. With these he crossed the river on the night of the 24th of September, the few canoes found at Longueil having to pass to and fro repeatedly, before his petty force could be landed. Guards were stationed on the roads to prevent any one

---

* Am. Archives, 4th Series, iii. 754.

passing and giving the alarm in Montreal. Day dawned, but there was no signal of Major Brown having performed his part of the scheme. The enterprise seems to have been as ill concerted, as it was ill advised. The day advanced, but still no signal; it was evident Major Brown had not crossed. Allen would gladly have recrossed the river, but it was too late. An alarm had been given to the town, and he soon found himself encountered by about forty regular soldiers, and a hasty levy of Canadians and Indians. A smart action ensued; most of Allen's Canadian recruits gave way and fled, a number of Americans were slain, and he at length surrendered to the British officer, Major Campbell, being promised honorable terms for himself and thirty-eight of his men, who remained with him, seven of whom were wounded. The prisoners were marched into the town and delivered over to General Prescott, the commandant. Their rough appearance, and rude equipments, were not likely to gain them favor in the eyes of the military tactician, who doubtless considered them as little better than a band of freebooters on a maraud. Their leader, albeit a colonel, must have seemed worthy of the band; for Allen was arrayed in rough frontier style; a deer-skin jacket, a vest and breeches of coarse serge, worsted stockings, stout shoes, and a red woollen cap.

We give Allen's own account of his reception by the British officer. "He asked me my name, which I told him. He then asked me whether I was that Colonel Allen who took Ticonderoga. I told him I was the very man. Then he shook his cane over my head, calling me many hard names, among which, he frequently used the word rebel, and put himself in a great rage." *

* Am. Archives, III. 800.

Ethan Allen, according to his own account, answered with becoming spirit. Indeed he gives somewhat of a melodramatic scene, which ended by his being sent on board of the Gaspee schooner of war, heavily ironed, to be transported to England for trial; Prescott giving him the parting assurance, sealed with an emphatic oath, that he would grace a halter at Tyburn.

Neither Allen's courage nor his rhetorical vein deserted him on this trying occasion. From his place of confinement, he indited the following epistle to the general:—

"HONORABLE SIR,—In the wheel of transitory events I find myself prisoner, and in irons. Probably your honor has certain reasons to me inconceivable, though I challenge an instance of this sort of economy of the Americans during the late war to any officers of the crown. On my part, I have to assure your honor, that when I had the command and took Captain Delaplace and Lieutenant Fulton, with the garrison of Ticonderoga, I treated them with every mark of friendship and generosity, the evidence of which is notorious, even in Canada. I have only to add, that I expect an honorable and humane treatment, as an officer of my rank and merit should have, and subscribe myself your honor's most obedient servant,

"ETHAN ALLEN."

In the British publication from which we cite the above, the following note is appended to the letter, probably on the authority of General Prescott: "N. B.—The author of the above letter is an outlaw, and a reward is offered by the New York Assembly for apprehending him." *

* Remembrancer, ii. 51.

The reckless dash at Montreal, was viewed with concern by the American commander. "I am apprehensive of disagreeable consequences arising from Mr. Allen's imprudence," writes General Schuyler. "I always dreaded his impatience of subordination, and it was not until after a solemn promise made me in the presence of several officers, that he would demean himself with propriety, that I would permit him to attend the army; nor would I have consented then, had not his solicitations been backed by several officers."

The conduct of Allen was also severely censured by Washington. "His misfortune," said he, "will, I hope, teach a lesson of prudence and subordination to others who may be ambitious to outshine their general officers, and, regardless of order and duty, rush into enterprises which have unfavorable effects on the public, and are destructive to themselves."

Partisan exploit had, in fact, inflated the vanity and bewildered the imagination of Allen, and unfitted him for regular warfare. Still his name will ever be a favorite one with his countrymen. Even his occasional rhodomontade will be tolerated with a good-humored smile, backed as it was by deeds of daring courage; and among the hardy pioneers of our Revolution whose untutored valor gave the first earnests of its triumphs, will be remembered, with honor, the rough Green Mountain partisan, who seized upon the "Keys of Champlain."

In the letters of Schuyler, which gave Washington accounts, from time to time, of the preceding events, were sad repinings at his own illness, and the multiplied annoyances which beset him. "The vexation of spirit under which I labor," writes he, "that a barbarous complication of disorders should prevent me from reaping those laurels for which I have unweariedly wrought since

I was honored with this command; the anxiety I have suffered since my arrival here (at Ticonderoga), lest the army should starve, occasioned by a scandalous want of subordination and inattention to my orders, in some of the officers that I left to command at the different posts; the vast variety of disagreeable and vexatious incidents that almost every hour arise in some department or other,—not only retard my cure, but have put me considerably back for some days past. If Job had been a general in my situation, his memory had not been so famous for patience. But the glorious end we have in view, and which I have confident hope will be attained, will atone for all." Washington replied in that spirit of friendship which existed between them. "You do me justice in believing that I feel the utmost anxiety for your situation, that I sympathize with you in all your distresses, and shall most heartily share in the joy of your success. My anxiety extends itself to poor Arnold, whose fate depends upon the issue of your campaign. * * * * * The more I reflect upon the importance of your expedition, the greater is my concern, lest it should sink under insuperable difficulties. I look upon the interests and salvation of our bleeding country in a great degree as depending upon your success."

Shortly after writing the above, and while he was still full of solicitude about the fate of Arnold, he received a despatch from the latter, dated October 13th, from the great portage or carrying-place between the Kennebec and Dead River.

"Your Excellency," writes Arnold, "may possibly think we have been tardy in our march, as we have gained so little; but when you consider the badness and weight of the bateaux, and large quantities of provisions, &c., we have been obliged to force up against a very rapid stream, where you would have taken the men for amphibious animals, as they were a great part of the time under water : add to this the great fatigue in the portage, you will think I have pushed the men as fast as they could possibly bear."

The toils of the expedition up the Kennebec River had indeed been excessive. Part of the men of each division managed the boats—part marched along the banks. Those on board had to labor against swift currents; to unload at rapids; transport the cargoes, and sometimes the boats themselves, for some distance on their shoulders, and then to reload. They were days in making their way round stupendous cataracts; several times their boats were upset and filled with water, to the loss or damage of arms, ammunition, and provisions.

Those on land had to scramble over rocks and precipices, to struggle through swamps and fenny streams; or cut their way through tangled thickets, which reduced their clothes to rags. With all their efforts, their progress was but from four to ten miles a day. At night the men of each division encamped together.

By the time they arrived at the place whence the letter was written, fatigue, swamp fevers and desertion had reduced their numbers to about nine hundred and fifty effective men. Arnold, however, wrote in good heart. "The last division," said he, "is just arrived; three divisions are over the first carrying-place, and as the men are in high spirits, I make no doubt of reaching the river Chaudiere in eight or ten days, the greatest difficulty being, I hope, already past."

He had some days previously despatched an Indian, whom he considered trusty, with a letter for General Schuyler, apprising him of his whereabouts, but as yet had received no intelligence either of, or from the general, nor did he expect to receive any until he should reach Chaudiere Pond. There he calculated to meet the return of his express, and then to determine his plan of operations.

CHAPTER VI.

BRITISH IN BOSTON SEND OUT CRUISERS—DEPREDATIONS OF CAPTAIN WALLACE ALONG THE COAST—TREASON IN THE CAMP—ARREST OF DR. CHURCH—HIS TRIAL AND FATE—CONFLAGRATION OF FALMOUTH—IRRITATION THROUGHOUT THE COUNTRY—FITTING OUT OF VESSELS OF WAR—EMBARKATION OF GENERAL GAGE FOR ENGLAND—COMMITTEE FROM CONGRESS—CONFERENCES WITH WASHINGTON—RESOLUTIONS OF CONGRESS TO CARRY ON THE WAR—RETURN OF SECRETARY REED TO PHILADELPHIA.

WHILE the two expeditions were threatening Canada from different quarters, the war was going on along the seaboard. The British in Boston, cut off from supplies by land, fitted out small armed vessels to seek them along the coast of New England. The inhabitants drove their cattle into the interior, or boldly resisted the aggressors. Parties landing to forage were often repulsed by hasty levies of the yeomanry. Scenes of ravage and violence occurred. Stonington was cannonaded, and further measures of vengeance were threatened by Captain Wallace of the Rose man-of-war, a naval officer, who had acquired an almost piratical reputation along the coast, and had his rendezvous in the harbor of Newport: domineering over the waters of Rhode Island.[*]

About this time there was an occurrence, which caused great

* Gov. Trumbull to Washington. Sparks' Corresp. of the Rev., i. 27.

excitement in the armies. A woman, coming from the camp at Cambridge, applied to a Mr. Wainwood of Newport, Rhode Island, to aid her in gaining access to Captain Wallace, or Mr. Dudley, the collector. Wainwood, who was a patriot, drew from her the object of her errand. She was the bearer of a letter from some one in camp, directed to Major Kane in Boston; but which she was to deliver either to the captain or the collector. Suspecting something wrong, he prevailed upon her to leave it with him for delivery. After her departure he opened the letter. It was written in cipher, which he could not read. He took it to Mr. Henry Ward, secretary of the colony. The latter, apprehending it might contain treasonable information to the enemy, transmitted it to General Greene, who laid it before Washington.

A letter in cipher, to a person in Boston hostile to the cause, and to be delivered into the hands of Captain Wallace the nautical marauder!—there evidently was treason in the camp; but how was the traitor to be detected? The first step was to secure the woman, the bearer of the letter, who had returned to Cambridge. Tradition gives us a graphic scene connected with her arrest. Washington was in his chamber at head-quarters, when he beheld from his window, General Putnam approaching on horseback, with a stout woman *en croupe* behind him. He had pounced upon the culprit. The group presented by the old general and his prize, overpowered even Washington's gravity. It was the only occasion throughout the whole campaign, on which he was known to laugh heartily. He had recovered his gravity by the time the delinquent was brought to the foot of the broad staircase in head-quarters, and assured her in a severe tone from the head of it, that, unless she confessed every thing before the next morning, a halter would be in readiness for her.

So far the tradition;—his own letter to the President of Congress states that, for a long time, the woman was proof against every threat and persuasion to discover the author, but at length named Dr. Benjamin Church. It seemed incredible. He had borne the character of a distinguished patriot; he was the author of various patriotic writings; a member of the Massachusetts House of Representatives; one of the committee deputed to conduct Washington to the army, and at present he discharged the functions of surgeon-general and director of the hospitals. That such a man should be in traitorous correspondence with the enemy, was a thunderstroke. Orders were given to secure him and his papers. On his arrest he was extremely agitated, but acknowledged the letter, and said it would be found, when deciphered, to contain nothing criminal. His papers were searched, but nothing of a treasonable nature discovered. "It appeared, however, on inquiry," says Washington, "that a confidant had been among the papers before my messenger arrived."

The letter was deciphered. It gave a description of the army. The doctor made an awkward defence, protesting that he had given an exaggerated account of the American force, for the purpose of deterring the enemy from attacking the American lines in their present defenceless condition from the want of powder. His explanations were not satisfactory. The army and country were exceedingly irritated. In a council of war he was convicted of criminal correspondence; he was expelled from the Massachusetts House of Representatives, and the Continental Congress ultimately resolved that he should be confined in some secure jail in Connecticut, without the use of pen, ink, or paper; "and that no person be allowed to converse with him, except in the presence and hearing of a magistrate or the sheriff of the county."

His sentence was afterwards mitigated on account of his health, and he was permitted to leave the country. He embarked for the West Indies, and is supposed to have perished at sea.

What had caused especial irritation in the case of Dr. Church, was the kind of warfare already mentioned, carried on along the coast by British cruisers, and notoriously by Captain Wallace. To check these maraudings, and to capture the enemy's transports laden with supplies, the provinces of Massachusetts, Rhode Island and Connecticut, fitted out two armed vessels each, at their own expense, without seeking the sanction or aid of Congress. Washington, also, on his own responsibility, ordered several to be equipped for like purpose, which were to be manned by hardy mariners, and commanded by able sea captains, actually serving in the army. One of these vessels was despatched as soon as ready, to cruise between Cape Ann and Cape Cod. Two others were fitted out with all haste, and sent to cruise in the waters of the St. Lawrence, to intercept two unarmed brigantines which Congress had been informed had sailed from England for Quebec, with ammunition and military stores. Among the sturdy little New England seaports, which had become obnoxious to punishment by resistance to nautical exactions, was Falmouth (now Portland), in Maine.

On the evening of the 11th of October, Lieutenant Mowat, of the royal navy, appeared before it with several armed vessels, and sent a letter on shore, apprising the inhabitants that he was come to execute a just punishment on them for their "premeditated attacks on the legal prerogatives of the best of sovereigns." Two hours were given them, " to remove the human species out of the town," at the period of which, a red pendant hoisted at the main-topgallant masthead, and a gun, would be the signal for destruction.

The letter brought a deputation of three persons on board. The lieutenant informed them verbally, that he had orders from Admiral Graves to set fire to all the seaport towns between Boston and Halifax; and he expected New York, at the present moment, was in ashes.

With much difficulty, and on the surrendering of some arms, the committee obtained a respite until nine o'clock the next morning, and the inhabitants employed the interval in removing their families and effects. The next morning the committee returned on board before nine o'clock. The lieutenant now offered to spare the town on certain conditions, which were refused. About half past nine o'clock the red pendant was run up to the masthead, and the signal gun fired. Within five minutes several houses were in flames, from a discharge of carcasses and bombshells, which continued throughout the day. The inhabitants, "standing on the heights, were spectators of the conflagration, which reduced many of them to penury and despair." One hundred and thirty-nine dwelling houses, and two hundred and twenty-eight stores, are said to have been burnt.* All the vessels in the harbor, likewise, were destroyed or carried away as prizes.

Having satisfied his sense of justice with respect to Falmouth, the gallant lieutenant left it a smoking ruin, and made sail, as was said, for Boston, to supply himself with more ammunition, having the intention to destroy Portsmouth also.†

The conflagration of Falmouth was as a bale fire throughout

* Holmes's Annals, ii. 220.   † Letter of P. Jones.

the country. Lieutenant Mowat was said to have informed the committee at that place, that orders had come from England to burn all the seaport towns that would not lay down and deliver up their arms, and give hostages for their good behavior.*

Washington himself supposed such to be the case. " The desolation and misery," writes he, " which ministerial vengeance had planned, in contempt of every principle of humanity, and so lately brought on the town of Falmouth, I know not how sufficiently to commiserate, nor can my compassion for the general suffering be conceived beyond the true measure of my feelings."

General Greene, too, in a letter to a friend, expresses himself with equal warmth. " O, could the Congress behold the distresses and wretched condition of the poor inhabitants driven from the seaport towns, it must, it would, kindle a blaze of indignation against the commissioned pirates and licensed robbers * * * People begin heartily to wish a declaration of independence." †

General Sullivan was sent to Portsmouth, where there was a fortification of some strength, to give the inhabitants his advice and assistance in warding off the menaced blow. Newport, also, was put on the alert, and recommended to fortify itself. " I expect every hour," writes Washington, " to hear that Newport has shared the same fate of unhappy Falmouth." ‡ Under the feeling roused by these reports, the General Court of Massachusetts, exercising a sovereign power, passed an act for encouraging the fitting out of armed vessels to defend the sea coast of America, and for erecting a court to try and condemn all vessels that should be found infesting the same. This act, granting letters

* Letter from Gen. Greene to Gov. Cooke.   ‡ Am. Archives, iii. 1145.
† Letter to the President of Congress.

of marque and reprisal, anticipated any measure of the kind on the part of the General Government, and was pronounced by John Adams, "one of the most important documents in history."*

The British ministry have, in later days, been exculpated from the charge of issuing such a desolating order as that said to have been reported by Lieutenant Mowat. The orders under which that officer acted, we are told, emanated from General Gage and Admiral Graves. The former intended merely the annoyance and destruction of rebel shipping, whether on the coast or in the harbors to the eastward of Boston; the burning of the town is surmised to have been an additional thought of Admiral Graves. Naval officers have a passion for bombardments.

Whatever part General Gage may have had in this most ill-advised and discreditable measure, it was the last of his military government, and he did not remain long enough in the country to see it carried into effect. He sailed for England on the 10th of October. The tidings of the battle of Bunker's Hill had withered his laurels as a commander. Still he was not absolutely superseded, but called home, "in order," as it was considerately said, "to give his majesty exact information of every thing, and suggest such matters as his knowledge and experience of the service might enable him to furnish." During his absence, Major-general Howe would act as commander-in-chief of the colonies on the Atlantic Ocean, and Major-general Carleton of the British forces in Canada and on the frontiers. Gage fully expected to return and resume the command. In a letter written to the minister, Lord Dartmouth, the day before sailing, he

---

* See Life of Gerry, 109.

urged the arrival, early in the spring, of reinforcements which had been ordered, anticipating great hazard at the opening of the campaign. In the mean time he trusted that two thousand troops, shortly expected from Ireland, would enable him " to distress the rebels by incursions along the coast,"—and—" he hoped Portsmouth in New Hampshire would feel the weight of his majesty's arms." "Poor Gage," writes Horace Walpole, "is to be the scape-goat for what was a reason against employing him— incapacity." He never returned to America.

On the 15th of October a committee from Congress arrived in camp, sent to hold a conference with Washington, and with delegates from the governments of Connecticut, Rhode Island, Massachusetts and New Hampshire, on the subject of a new organization of the army. The committee consisted of Benjamin Franklin, Thomas Lynch of Carolina, and Colonel Harrison of Virginia. It was just twenty years since Washington had met Franklin in Braddock's camp, aiding that unwary general by his sagacious counsels and prompt expedients. Franklin was regarded with especial deference in the camp at Cambridge. Greene, who had never met with him before, listened to him as to an oracle.

Washington was president of the board of conference, and Mr. Joseph Reed secretary. The committee brought an intimation from Congress that an attack upon Boston was much desired, if practicable.

Washington called a council of war of his generals on the subject ; they were unanimously of the opinion that an attack would not be prudent at present.

Another question now arose. An attack upon the British forces in Boston, whenever it should take place, might require a bombardment ; Washington inquired of the delegates how far it might be pushed to the destruction of houses and property, They considered it a question of too much importance to be decided by them, and said it must be referred to Congress. But though they declined taking upon themselves the responsibility, the majority of them were strongly in favor of it; and expressed themselves so, when the matter was discussed informally in camp. Two of the committee, Lynch and Harrison, as well as Judge Wales, delegate from Connecticut, when the possible effects of a bombardment were suggested at a dinner table, declared that they would be willing to see Boston in flames. Lee, who was present, observed that it was impossible to burn it unless they sent in men with bundles of straw to do it. "It could not be done with carcasses and red-hot shot. Isle Royal," he added, "in the river St. Lawrence, had been fired at for a long time in 1760, with a fine train of artillery, hot-shot and carcasses, without effect." *

The board of conference was repeatedly in session, for three or four days. The report of its deliberations rendered by the committee, produced a resolution of Congress, that a new army of twenty-two thousand two hundred and seventy-two men and officers, should be formed, to be recruited as much as possible from the troops actually in service. Unfortunately the term for which they were to be enlisted was to be *but for one year*. It formed a precedent which became a recurring cause of embarrassment throughout the war.

Washington's secretary, Mr. Reed, had, after the close of the conference, signified to him his intention to return to Philadelphia, where his private concerns required his presence. His de-

* Life of Dr. Belknap, p. 96. The doctor was present at the above-cited conversation.

parture was deeply regretted. His fluent pen had been of great
assistance to Washington in the despatch of his multifarious correspondence, and his judicious counsels and cordial sympathies had
been still more appreciated by the commander-in-chief, amid the
multiplied difficulties of his situation. On the departure of Mr.
Reed, his place as secretary was temporarily supplied by Mr.
Robert Harrison of Maryland, and subsequently by Colonel
Mifflin; neither, however, attained to the affectionate confidence
reposed in their predecessor.

We shall have occasion to quote the correspondence kept up
between Washington and Reed, during the absence of the latter.
The letters of the former are peculiarly interesting, as giving
views of what was passing, not merely around him, but in the recesses of his own heart. No greater proof need be given of the
rectitude of that heart, than the clearness and fulness with
which, in these truthful documents, every thought and feeling is
laid open.

CHAPTER VII.

MEASURES OF GENERAL HOWE—DESECRATION OF CHURCHES—THREE PROCLA-
MATIONS—SEIZURE OF TORIES—WANT OF ARTILLERY—HENRY KNOX, THE
ARTILLERIST—HIS MISSION TO TICONDEROGA—RE-ENLISTMENT OF TROOPS
—LACK OF PUBLIC SPIRIT—COMMENTS OF GENERAL GREENE.

THE measures which General Howe had adopted after taking
command in Boston, rejoiced the royalists, seeming to justify
their anticipations. He proceeded to strengthen the works on
Bunker's Hill and Boston Neck, and to clear away houses and
throw up redoubts on eminences within the town. The patriot
inhabitants were shocked by the desecration of the Old South
Church, which for more than a hundred years had been a favorite
place of worship, where some of the most eminent divines had
officiated. The pulpit and pews were now removed, the floor was
covered with earth, and the sacred edifice was converted into a
riding-school for Burgoyne's light dragoons. To excuse its desecration, it was spoken of scoffingly as a "meeting-house, where
sedition had often been preached."

The North Church, another "meeting-house," was entirely
demolished and used for fuel. "Thus," says a chronicler of the
day, "thus are our houses devoted to religious worship, profaned
and destroyed by the subjects of his royal majesty." *

* Thacher's Military Journal, p. 50.

About the last of October, Howe issued three proclamations. The first forbade all persons to leave Boston without his permission under pain of military execution; the second forbade any one, so permitted, to take with him more than five pounds sterling, under pain of forfeiting all the money found upon his person and being subject to fine and imprisonment; the third called upon the inhabitants to arm themselves for the preservation of order within the town; they to be commanded by officers of his appointment.

Washington had recently been incensed by the conflagration of Falmouth; the conduct of Governor Dunmore who had proclaimed martial law in Virginia, and threatened ruin to the patriots, had added to his provocation; the measures of General Howe seemed of the same harsh character, and he determined to retaliate.

"Would it not be prudent," writes he to Governor Trumbull of Connecticut, "to seize those tories who have been, are, and we know will be active against us? Why should persons who are preying upon the vitals of their country, be suffered to stalk at large, whilst we know they will do us every mischief in their power?"

In this spirit he ordered General Sullivan, who was fortifying Portsmouth, "to seize upon such persons as held commissions under the crown, and were acting as open and avowed enemies to their country, and hold them as hostages for the security of the town." Still he was moderate in his retaliation, and stopped short of private individuals. "For the present," said he, "I shall avoid giving the like order with regard to the *tories* of Portsmouth; but the day is not far off when they will meet with this, or a worse fate, if there is not a considerable reformation in their conduct." *

The season was fast approaching when the bay between the camp and Boston would be frozen over, and military operations might be conducted upon the ice. General Howe, if reinforced, would then very probably " endeavor to relieve himself from the disgraceful confinement in which the ministerial troops had been all summer." Washington felt the necessity, therefore, of guarding the camps wherever they were most assailable; and of throwing up batteries for the purpose. He had been embarrassed throughout the siege by the want of artillery and ordnance stores; but never more so than at the present moment. In this juncture, Mr. Henry Knox stepped forward, and offered to proceed to the frontier forts on Champlain in quest of a supply.

Knox was one of those providential characters which spring up in emergencies, as if they were formed by and for the occasion. A thriving bookseller in Boston, he had thrown up business to take up arms for the liberties of his country. He was one of the patriots who had fought on Bunker's Hill, since when he had aided in planning the defences of the camp before Boston. The aptness and talent here displayed by him as an artillerist, had recently induced Washington to recommend him to Congress for the command of the regiment of artillery in place of the veteran Gridley, who was considered by all the officers of the camp, too old for active employment. Congress had not yet acted on that recommendation; in the mean time Washington availed himself of the offered services of Knox in the present instance. He was, accordingly, instructed to examine into the state of the artillery

* Letter to William Palfrey. Sparks, iii. **158.**

in camp, and take an account of the cannon, mortars, shells, lead and ammunition that were wanting. He was then to hasten to New York, procure and forward all that could be had there; and thence proceed to the head-quarters of General Schuyler, who was requested by letter to aid him in obtaining what further supplies of the kind were wanting from the forts at Ticonderoga, Crown Point, St. Johns, and even Quebec, should it be in the hands of the Americans. Knox set off on his errand with promptness and alacrity, and shortly afterwards the commission of colonel of the regiment of artillery which Washington had advised, was forwarded to him by Congress.

The re-enlistment of troops actually in service was now attempted, and proved a fruitful source of perplexity. In a letter to the President of Congress, Washington observes that half of the officers of the rank of captain were inclined to retire; and it was probable their example would influence their men. Of those who were disposed to remain, the officers of one colony were unwilling to mix in the same regiment with those of another. Many sent in their names, to serve in expectation of promotion; others stood aloof, to see what advantages they could make for themselves; while those who had declined sent in their names again to serve.* The difficulties were greater, if possible, with the soldiers than with the officers. They would not enlist unless they knew their colonel, lieutenant-colonel and captain; Connecticut men being unwilling to serve under officers from Massachusetts, and Massachusetts men under officers from Rhode Island; so that it was necessary to appoint the officers first.

Twenty days later he again writes to the President of Con-

* Washington to the President of Congress, Nov. 8.

gress: "I am sorry to be necessitated to mention to you the egregious want of public spirit which prevails here. Instead of pressing to be engaged in the cause of their country, which I vainly flattered myself would be the case, I find we are likely to be deserted in a most critical time. * * * Our situation is truly alarming, and of this General Howe is well apprised. No doubt when he is reinforced he will avail himself of the information."

In a letter to Reed he disburdened his heart more completely. "Such dearth of public spirit, and such want of virtue; such stock-jobbing, and fertility in all the low arts to obtain advantage of one kind or another in this great change of military arrangement, I never saw before, and I pray God's mercy that I may never be witness to again. What will be the end of these manœuvres is beyond my scan. I tremble at the prospect. We have been till this time (Nov. 28) enlisting about three thousand five hundred men. To engage these, I have been obliged to allow furloughs as far as fifty men to a regiment, and the officers I am persuaded indulge many more. The Connecticut troops will not be prevailed upon to stay longer than their term, saving those who have enlisted for the next campaign, and are mostly on furlough; and such a mercenary spirit pervades the whole, that I should not be surprised at any disaster that may happen. * * * Could I have foreseen what I have experienced and am likely to experience, no consideration upon earth should have induced me to accept this command."

No one drew closer to Washington in this time of his troubles and perplexities than General Greene. He had a real veneration for his character, and thought himself "happy in an opportunity to serve under so good a general." He grieved at

Washington's annoyances, but attributed them in part to his being somewhat of a stranger in New England. "He has not had time," writes he, "to make himself acquainted with the genius of this people; they are naturally as brave and spirited as the peasantry of any other country, but you cannot expect veterans of a raw militia from only a few months' service. The common people are exceedingly avaricious; the genius of the people is commercial, from their long intercourse with trade. The sentiment of honor, the true characteristic of a soldier, has not yet got the better of interest. His Excellency has been taught to believe the people here a superior race of mortals; and finding them of the same temper and dispositions, passions and prejudices, virtues and vices of the common people of other governments, they sank in his esteem." *

* Greene to Dep. Gov. Ward.   Am. Arch. 4th Series, iii. 1145.

CHAPTER VIII.

AFFAIRS IN CANADA—CAPTURE OF FORT CHAMBLEE—SIEGE OF ST. JOHNS—
MACLEAN AND HIS HIGHLANDERS—MONTGOMERY ON THE TREATMENT OF
ETHAN ALLEN—REPULSE OF CARLETON—CAPITULATION OF THE GARRISON
OF ST. JOHNS—GENEROUS CONDUCT OF MONTGOMERY—MACLEAN RE-
EMBARKS FOR QUEBEC—WEARY STRUGGLE OF ARNOLD THROUGH THE
WILDERNESS—DEFECTION OF COLONEL ENOS—ARNOLD IN THE VALLEY OF
THE CHAUDIERE—HIS ARRIVAL OPPOSITE QUEBEC—SURRENDER OF MON-
TREAL—ESCAPE OF CARLETON—HOME SICKNESS OF THE AMERICAN TROOPS.

DESPATCHES from Schuyler dated October 26th, gave Washington another chapter of the Canada expedition. Chamblee, an
inferior fort, within five miles of St. Johns, had been taken by
Majors Brown and Livingston at the head of fifty Americans and
three hundred Canadians. A large quantity of gunpowder and
other military stores found there, was a seasonable supply to the
army before St. Johns, and consoled General Montgomery for his
disappointment in regard to the aid promised by Colonel Ethan
Allen. He now pressed the siege of St. Johns with vigor. The
garrison, cut off from supplies, were suffering from want of provisions; but the brave commander, Major Preston, still held out
manfully, hoping speedy relief from General Carleton, who was
assembling troops for that purpose at Montreal.

Carleton, it is true, had but about one hundred regulars

several hundred Canadians, and a number of Indians with him; but he calculated greatly on the co-operation of Colonel Maclean, a veteran Scot, brave and bitterly loyal, who had enlisted three hundred of his countrymen at Quebec, and formed them into a regiment called "The Royal Highland Emigrants." This doughty Highlander was to land at the mouth of the Sorel, where it empties into the St. Lawrence, and proceed along the former river to St. Johns, to join Carleton, who would repair thither by the way of Longueil.

In the mean time Montgomery received accounts from various quarters that Colonel Ethan Allen and his men, captured in the ill-advised attack upon Montreal, were treated with cruel and unnecessary severity, being loaded with irons; and that even the colonel himself was subjected to this "shocking indignity." Montgomery addressed a letter to Carleton on the subject, strong and decided in its purport, but written in the spirit of a courteous and high-minded gentleman, and ending with an expression of that sad feeling which gallant officers must often have experienced in this revolutionary conflict, on being brought into collision with former brothers in arms.

" Your character, sir," writes he, "induces me to hope I am ill informed. Nevertheless, the duty I owe the troops committed to my charge, lays me under the necessity of acquainting your Excellency, that, if you allow this conduct and persist in it, I shall, though with the most painful regret, execute with rigor the just and necessary law of retaliation upon the garrison of Chamblee, now in my possession, and upon all others who may hereafter fall into my hands. * * * * I shall expect your Excellency's answer in six days. Should the bearer not return in that time, I must interpret your silence into a declaration of a barbarous war. I cannot pass this opportunity without lamenting the melancholy and fatal necessity, which obliges the firmest friends of the constitution to oppose one of the most respectable officers of the crown."

While waiting for a reply, Montgomery pressed the siege of St. Johns, though thwarted continually by the want of subordination and discipline among his troops; hasty levies from various colonies, who, said he, "carry the spirt of freedom into the field, and think for themselves." Accustomed as he had been, in his former military experience, to the implicit obedience of European troops, the insubordination of these yeoman soldiery was intolerable to him. "Were I not afraid," writes he, "the example would be too generally followed, and that the public service might suffer, I would not stay an hour at the head of troops whose operations I cannot direct. I must say I have no hopes of success, unless from the garrison's wanting provisions."

He had advanced his lines and played from his batteries on two sides of the fort for some hours, when tidings brought by four prisoners, caused him to cease his fire.

General Carleton, on the 31st of September, had embarked his motley force at Montreal in thirty-four boats, to cross the St. Lawrence, land at Longueil, and push on for St. Johns, where, as concerted, he was to be joined by Maclean and his Highlanders. As the boats approached the right bank of the river at Longueil, a terrible fire of artillery and musketry was unexpectedly opened upon them, and threw them into confusion. It was from Colonel Seth Warner's detachment of Green Mountain Boys and New Yorkers. Some of the boats were disabled, some were driven on shore on an island; Carleton retreated with the rest to Montreal, with some loss in killed and wounded. The Americans captured two Canadians and two Indians; and it was these prisoners who brought tidings to the camp of Carleton's signal repulse.

Aware that the garrison held out merely in expectation of the relief thus intercepted, Montgomery ceased his fire, and sent a flag by one of the Canadian prisoners with a letter informing Major Preston of the event, and inviting a surrender to spare the effusion of blood.

Preston in reply expressed a doubt of the truth of the report brought by the prisoners, but offered to surrender if not relieved in four days. The condition was refused and the gallant major was obliged to capitulate. His garrison consisted of five hundred regulars and one hundred Canadians; among the latter were several of the provincial noblesse.

Montgomery treated Preston and his garrison with the courtesy inspired by their gallant resistance. He had been a British officer himself, and his old associations with the service, made him sympathize with the brave men whom the fortune of war had thrown into his hands. Perhaps, their high-bred and aristocratic tone contrasted favorably in his eyes, with the rough demeanor of the crude swordsmen with whom he had recently associated, and brought back the feelings of early days, when war with him was a gay profession, not a melancholy duty. According to capitulation, the baggage of both officers and men was secured to them, and each of the latter received a new suit of clothing from the captured stores. This caused a murmur among the American soldiery, many of whom were nearly naked, and the best but scantily provided. Even some of the officers were indignant that all the articles of clothing had not been treated as lawful spoil. "I would not have sullied my own reputation, nor disgraced the Continental arms by such a breach of capitulation for the universe," said Montgomery. Having sent his prisoners up Lake Champlain to Ticonderoga, he prepared to proceed immediately to Montreal; requesting General Schuyler to forward all the men he could possibly spare.

The royal Highland Emigrants who were to have co-operated with General Carleton, met with no better fortune than that commander. Maclean landed at the mouth of the Sorel, and added to his force by recruiting a number of Canadians in the neighborhood, at the point of the bayonet. He was in full march for St. Johns when he was encountered by Majors Brown and Livingston with their party, fresh from the capture of Chamblee, and reinforced by a number of Green Mountain Boys. These pressed him back to the mouth of the Sorel, where, hearing of the repulse of Carleton, and being deserted by his Canadian recruits, he embarked the residue of his troops, and set off down the St. Lawrence to Quebec. The Americans now took post at the mouth of the Sorel, where they erected batteries so as to command the St. Lawrence, and prevent the descent of any armed vessels from Montreal.

Thus closed another chapter of the invasion of Canada. "Not a word of Arnold yet," said Montgomery, in his last despatch. "I have sent two expresses to him lately, one by an Indian who promised to return with expedition. The instant I have any news of him, I will acquaint you by express."

We will anticipate his express, by giving the reader the purport of letters received by Washington direct from Arnold himself, bringing forward the collateral branch of this eventful enterprise.

The transportation of troops and effects across the carrying-place between the Kennebec and Dead Rivers, had been a work of severe toil and difficulty to Arnold and his men, but performed with admirable spirit. There were ponds and streams full of trout and salmon, which furnished them with fresh provisions. Launching their boats on the sluggish waters of the Dead River, they navigated it in divisions, as before, to the foot of snow-crowned mountains; a part of the great granite chain which extends from south-west to north-east throughout our continent. Here, while Arnold and the first division were encamped to repose themselves, heavy rains set in, and they came near being swept away by sudden torrents from the mountains. Several of their boats were overturned, much of their provisions was lost, the sick list increased, and the good spirits which had hitherto sustained them began to give way. They were on scanty allowance, with a prospect of harder times, for there were still twelve or fifteen days of wilderness before them, where no supplies were to be had. A council of war was now held, in which it was determined to send back the sick and disabled, who were mere incumbrances. Arnold, accordingly, wrote to the commanders of the other divisions, to press on with as many of their men as they could furnish with provisions for fifteen days, and to send the rest back to a place on the route called Norridgewock. This order was misunderstood, or misinterpreted by Colonel Enos, who commanded the rear division; he gave all the provisions he could spare to Colonel Greene of the third division, retaining merely enough to supply his own corps of three hundred men on their way back to Norridgewock, whither he immediately returned.

Letters from Arnold and Enos apprised Washington of this grievous flaw in the enterprise. He regarded it, however, as usual, with a hopeful eye. "Notwithstanding this great defection," said he, "I do not despair of Colonel Arnold's success. He will have, in all probability, many more difficulties to encounter, than if he had been a fortnight sooner; as it is likely that Governor Carleton will, with what forces he can collect after the surrender of the rest of Canada, throw himself into Quebec, and there make his last effort." *

Washington was not mistaken in the confidence he had placed in the energy of Arnold. Though the latter found his petty force greatly reduced by the retrograde move of Enos and his party, and although snow and ice rendered his march still more bleak among the mountains, he kept on with unflinching spirit until he arrived at the ridge which divides the streams of New England and Canada. Here, at Lake Megantic, the source of the Chaudiere, he met an emissary whom he had sent in advance to ascertain the feelings of the *habitans*, or French yeomanry, in the fertile valley of that stream. His report being favorable, Arnold shared out among the different companies the scanty provisions which remained, directing them to make the best of their way for the Chaudiere settlements; while he, with a light foraging party, would push rapidly ahead, to procure and send back supplies.

He accordingly embarked with his little party in five bateaux and a birch canoe, and launched forth without a guide on the swift current of the Chaudiere. It was little better than a mountain torrent, full of rocks and rapids. Three of their boats were dashed to pieces, the cargoes lost, and the crews saved with difficulty. At one time, the whole party came near being precipitated over a cataract, where all might have perished; at

* Washington to the President of Congress, Nov. 19th.

length they reached Sertigan, the first French settlement, where they were cordially received. Here Arnold bought provisions, which he sent back by the Canadians and Indians to his troops. The latter were in a state of starvation. Some had not tasted food for eight and forty hours; others had cooked two dogs, followers of the camp; and others had boiled their moccasins, cartouch boxes, and other articles of leather, in the hope of rendering them eatable.

Arnold halted for a short time in the hospitable valley of the Chaudiere, to give his troops repose, and distributed among the inhabitants the printed manifesto with which he had been furnished by Washington. Here he was joined by about forty Norridgewock Indians. On the 9th of November, the little army emerged from the woods at Point Levi, on the St. Lawrence, opposite to Quebec. A letter written by an inhabitant of that place, speaks of their sudden apparition.

"There are about 500 Provincials arrived at Point Levi, opposite to the town, by the way of Chaudiere across the woods. Surely a miracle must have been wrought in their favor. It is an undertaking above the common race of men in this debauched age. They have travelled through woods and bogs, and over precipices, for the space of one hundred and twenty miles, attended with every inconvenience and difficulty, to be surmounted only by men of indefatigable zeal and industry."

Leaving Arnold in full sight of Quebec, which, after his long struggle through the wilderness, must have appeared like a land of promise; we turn to narrate the events of the upper expedition into Canada, of which the letters of Schuyler kept Washington faithfully informed.

Montgomery appeared before Montreal on the 12th of November. General Carleton had embarked with his little garrison, and several of the civil officers of the place, on board of a flotilla of ten or eleven small vessels, and made sail in the night, with a favorable breeze, carrying away with him the powder and other important stores. The town capitulated, of course; and Montgomery took quiet possession. His urbanity and kindness soon won the good will of the inhabitants, both English and French, and made the Canadians sensible that he really came to secure their rights, not to molest them. Intercepted letters acquainted him with Arnold's arrival in the neighborhood of Quebec, and the great alarm of "the king's friends," who expected to be besieged: "which, with the blessing of God, they shall be," said Montgomery, "if the severe season holds off, and I can prevail on the troops to accompany me."

His great immediate object was the capture of Carleton; which would form a triumphal close to the enterprise, and might decide the fate of Canada. The flotilla in which the general was embarked, had made repeated attempts to escape down the St. Lawrence; but had as often been driven back by the batteries thrown up by the Americans at the mouth of the Sorel. It now lay anchored about fifteen miles above that river; and Montgomery prepared to attack it with bateaux and light artillery, so as to force it down upon the batteries.

Carleton saw his imminent peril. Disguising himself as a Canadian voyager, he set off on a dark night accompanied by six peasants, in a boat with muffled oars, which he assisted to pull; slipped quietly and silently past all the batteries and guard-boats, and effected his escape to Three Rivers, where he embarked in a vessel for Quebec. After his departure the flotilla surrendered, and all those who had taken refuge on board were made prisoners of war. Among them was General Prescott, late commander of Montreal.

Montgomery now placed garrisons in Montreal, St. Johns and Chamblee, and made final preparations for descending the St. Lawrence, and co-operating with Arnold against Quebec. To his disappointment and deep chagrin, he found but a handful of his troops disposed to accompany him. Some pleaded ill health; the term of enlistment of many had expired, and they were bent on returning home; and others, who had no such excuses to make, became exceedingly turbulent, and indeed mutinous. Nothing but a sense of public duty, and gratitude to Congress for an unsought commission, had induced Montgomery to engage in the service; wearied by the continual vexations which beset it, he avowed, in a letter to Schuyler, his determination to retire as soon as the intended expedition against Quebec was finished. "Will not your health permit you to reside at Montreal this winter?" writes he to Schuyler; "I must go home, if I walk by the side of the lake. I am weary of power, and totally want that patience and temper so requisite for such a command." Much of the insubordination of the troops he attributed to the want of tact and cultivation in their officers; who had been suddenly advanced from inferior stations and coarse employments. "An affair happened yesterday," writes he to Schuyler on the 24th of November, "which had very near sent me home. A number of officers presumed to remonstrate against the indulgence I had given some of the king's troops. Such an insult I could not bear, and immediately resigned. To-day they qualified it by such an apology, as put it in my power to resume the command." In the same spirit he writes: "I wish some method could be fallen upon for engaging *gentlemen* to serve. A point of honor and more knowledge of the world, to be found in that class of men, would greatly reform discipline, and render the troops much more tractable."

The troops which had given Montgomery so much annoyance and refused to continue with him in Canada, soon began to arrive at Ticonderoga.   Schuyler, in a letter to Congress, gives a half querulous, half humorous account of their conduct. "About three hundred of the troops raised in Connecticut, passed here within a few days.   An unhappy home-sickness prevails.   These all came down as invalids, not one willing to re-engage for the winter's service ; and, unable to get any work done by them, I discharged them *en groupe.*   Of all the specifics ever invented for *any,* there is none so efficacious as a discharge for *this* prevailing disorder.   No sooner was it administered but it perfected the cure of nine out of ten; who, refusing to wait for boats to go by the way of Lake George, slung their heavy packs, crossed the lake at this place, and undertook a march of two hundred miles with the greatest good-will and alacrity."

This home-sickness in rustic soldiers after a rough campaign, was natural enough, and seems only to have provoked the testy and subacid humor of Schuyler; but other instances of conduct roused his indignation.

A schooner and tow galley arrived at Crown Point, with upwards of a hundred persons.   They were destitute of provisions; none were to be had at the Point, and the ice prevented them from penetrating to Ticonderoga.   In starving condition they sent an express to General Schuyler, imploring relief.   He immediately ordered three captains of General Wooster's regiment, with a considerable body of men in bateaux, to "attempt a relief for the unhappy sufferers."   To his surprise and disgust, they manifested the utmost unwillingness to comply, and made a variety of excuses, which he spurned at as frivolous, and as evincing the greatest want of humanity. He expressed himself to that effect the next day, in a general order, adding the following stinging words: "The general, therefore, not daring to trust a matter of so much importance to men of so little feeling, has ordered Lieutenant Riker, of Col. Holmes's regiment, to make the attempt. He received the order with the alacrity becoming a gentleman, an officer, and a Christian."

This high-minded rebuke, given in so public a manner, rankled in the breasts of those whose conduct had merited it, and insured to Schuyler that persevering hostility with which mean minds revenge the exposure of their meanness.

CHAPTER IX.

WASHINGTON'S ANTICIPATIONS OF SUCCESS AT QUEBEC—HIS EULOGIUM OF
ARNOLD—SCHUYLER AND MONTGOMERY TALK OF RESIGNING—EXPOSTULA-
TIONS OF WASHINGTON—THEIR EFFECT—SCHUYLER'S CONDUCT TO A CAPTIVE
FOE.

WE have endeavored to compress into a succinct account various
events of the invasion of Canada, furnished to Washington by
letters from Schuyler and Arnold. The tidings of the capture
of Montreal had given him the liveliest satisfaction. He now
looked forward to equal success in the expedition against Quebec.
In a letter to Schuyler, he passed a high eulogium on Arnold.
"The merit of this gentleman is certainly great," writes he,
"and I heartily wish that fortune may distinguish him as one of
her favorites. I am convinced that he will do every thing that
prudence and valor shall suggest to add to the success of our
arms, and for reducing Quebec to our possession. Should he not
be able to accomplish so desirable a work with the forces he has,
I flatter myself that it will be effected when General Montgomery joins him, and our conquest of Canada will be complete."

Certain passages of Schuyler's letters, however, gave him deep
concern, wherein that general complained of the embarrassments
and annoyances he had experienced from the insubordination of

the army. "Habituated to order," said he, "I cannot without pain see that disregard of discipline, confusion and inattention, which reign so generally in this quarter, and I am determined to retire. Of this resolution I have advised Congress."

He had indeed done so. In communicating to the President of Congress the complaints of General Montgomery, and his intention to retire, "my sentiments," said he, "exactly coincide with his. I shall, with him, do every thing in my power to put a finishing stroke to the campaign, and make the best arrangement in my power, in order to insure success to the next. This done, I must beg leave to retire."

Congress, however, was too well aware of his value, readily to dispense with his services. His letter produced a prompt resolution expressive of their high sense of his attention and perseverance, "which merited the thanks of the United Colonies." He had alleged his impaired health,—they regretted the injuries it had sustained in the service, but begged he would not insist on a measure "which would deprive America of the benefits of his zeal and abilities, and rob him of the honor of completing the work he had so happily begun."

What, however, produced a greater effect upon Schuyler than any encomium or entreaty on the part of Congress, were the expostulations of Washington, inspired by strong friendship and kindred sympathies. "I am exceedingly sorry," writes the latter, "to find you so much embarrassed by the disregard of discipline, confusion, and want of order among the troops, as to have occasioned you to mention to Congress an inclination to retire. I know that your complaints are too well founded, but would willingly hope that nothing will induce you to quit the service. * * * * I have met with difficulties of the same sort, and such as I never expected; but they must be borne with. The cause we are engaged in is so just and righteous, that we must try to rise superior to every obstacle in its support; and, therefore, I beg that you will not think of resigning, unless you have carried your application to Congress too far to recede."

And in another letter he makes a still stronger appeal to his patriotism. "I am sorry that you, and General Montgomery, incline to quit the service. Let me ask you, sir, when is the time for brave men to exert themselves in the cause of liberty and their country, if this is not? Should any difficulties that they may have to encounter at this important crisis deter them? God knows there is not a difficulty that you both very justly complain of, that I have not in an eminent degree experienced, that I am not every day experiencing; but we must bear up against them, and make the best of mankind, as they are, since we cannot have them as we wish. Let me, therefore, conjure you, and Mr. Montgomery, to lay aside such thoughts—as thoughts injurious to yourselves, and extremely so to your country, which calls aloud for gentlemen of your ability."

This noble appeal went straight to the heart of Schuyler, and brought out a magnanimous reply. "I do not hesitate," writes he, "to answer my dear general's question in the affirmative, by declaring that now or never is the time for every virtuous American to exert himself in the cause of liberty and his country; and that it is become a duty cheerfully to sacrifice the sweets of domestic felicity to attain the honest and glorious end America has in view."

In the same letter he reveals in confidence the true cause of his wish to retire from an official station; it was the annoyance he had suffered throughout the campaign from sectional prejudice and jealousy. " I could point out particular persons of rank in the army," writes he, "who have frequently declared that the general commanding in this quarter, ought to be of the colony from whence the majority of the troops came. But it is not from opinions or principles of individuals that I have drawn the following conclusion : that troops from the colony of Connecticut will not bear with a general from another colony ; it is from the daily and common conversation of all ranks of people from that colony, both in and out of the army ; and I assure you that I sincerely lament that people of so much public virtue should be actuated by such an unbecoming jealousy, founded on such a narrow principle." Having made this declaration, he adds, "although I frankly own that I feel a resentment, yet I shall continue to sacrifice it to a nobler object, the weal of that country in which I have drawn the breath of life, resolved ever to seek, with unwearied assiduity, for opportunities to fulfil my duty to it."

It is with pride we have quoted so frequently the corespondence of these two champions of our Revolution, as it lays open their hearts, and shows the lofty patriotism by which they were animated.

A letter from John Adams to General Thomas, alleges as one cause of Schuyler's unpopularity with the eastern troops, the "politeness" shown by him to Canadian and British prisoners; which "enabled them and their ministerial friends to impose upon him." *

The "politeness" in fact, was that noble courtesy which a high-minded soldier extends towards a captive foe. If his cour-

* Letter Book of Gen. Thomas. MS.

tesy was imposed upon, it only proved that, incapable of double-dealing himself, he suspected it not in others. All generous natures are liable to imposition; their warm impulses being too quick for selfish caution. It is the cold, the calculating and the mean, whose distrustful wariness is never taken in.

CHAPTER X.

DIFFICULTIES IN FILLING UP THE ARMY—THE CONNECTICUT TROOPS PERSIST IN GOING HOME—THEIR RECEPTION THERE—TIMELY ARRIVAL OF SPOILS IN THE CAMP—PUTNAM AND THE PRIZE MORTAR—A MARAUD BY AMERICANS—REBUKED BY WASHINGTON—CORRESPONDENCE OF WASHINGTON WITH GEN. HOWE ABOUT THE TREATMENT OF ETHAN ALLEN—FRATERNAL ZEAL OF LEVI ALLEN—TREATMENT OF GEN. PRESCOTT—PREPARATIONS TO BOMBARD BOSTON—BATTERY AT LECHMERE'S POINT—PRAYER OF PUTNAM FOR POWDER.

THE forming even of the skeleton of an army under the new regulations, had been a work of infinite difficulty; to fill it up was still more difficult.. The first burst of revolutionary zeal had passed away; enthusiasm had been chilled by the inaction and monotony of a long encampment; an encampment, moreover, destitute of those comforts which, in experienced warfare, are provided by a well-regulated commissariat. The troops had suffered privations of every kind, want of fuel, clothing, provisions. They looked forward with dismay to the rigors of winter, and longed for their rustic homes and their family firesides.

Apprehending that some of them would incline to go home when the time of their enlistment expired, Washington summoned the general officers at head-quarters, and invited a delegation of the General Court to be present, to adopt measures for the

defence and support of the lines. The result of their deliberations was an order that three thousand of the minute men and
militia of Massachusetts, and two thousand from New Hampshire,
should be at Cambridge by the 10th of December, to relieve the
Connecticut regiments, and supply the deficiency that would be
caused by their departure, and by the absence of others on
furlough.

With this arrangement the Connecticut troops were made acquainted, and, as the time of most of them would not be out
before the 10th, they were ordered to remain in camp until relieved. Their officers assured Washington that he need apprehend no defection on the part of their men; they would not leave
the lines. The officers themselves were probably mistaken in
their opinion of their men, for on the 1st of December, many of
the latter, some of whom belonged to Putnam's regiment, resolved to go home immediately. Efforts were made to prevent
them, but in vain; several carried off with them their arms and
ammunition. Washington sent a list of their names to Governor
Trumbull. "I submit it to your judgment," writes he, "whether
an example should not be made of these men who have deserted
the cause of their country at this critical juncture, when the
enemy are receiving reinforcements?"

We anticipate the reply of Governor Trumbull, received
several days subsequently. "The late extraordinary and repre-
hensible conduct of some of the troops of this colony," writes he,
"impresses me, and the minds of many of our people, with great
surprise and indignation, since the treatment they met with, and the
order and request made to them, were so reasonable, and apparently necessary for the defence of our common cause, and safety
of our rights and privileges, for which they freely engaged."

We will here add, that the homeward-bound warriors seem to have run the gauntlet along the road; for their conduct on quitting the army drew upon them such indignation, that they could hardly get any thing to eat on their journey, and when they arrived at home they met with such a reception (to the credit of the Connecticut women be it recorded), that many were soon disposed to return again to the camp. *

On the very day after the departure homeward of these troops, and while it was feared their example would be contagious, a long, lumbering train of waggons, laden with ordnance and military stores, and decorated with flags, came wheeling into the camp escorted by continental troops and country militia. They were part of the cargo of a large brigantine laden with munitions of war, captured and sent in to Cape Ann by the schooner Lee, Captain Manly, one of the cruisers sent out by Washington. "Such universal joy ran through the whole camp," writes an officer, "as if each one grasped a victory in his own hands."

Beside the ordnance captured, there were two thousand stand of arms, one hundred thousand flints, thirty thousand round shot, and thirty-two tons of musket balls.

"Surely nothing," writes Washington, "ever came more *apropos.*"

It was indeed a cheering incident, and was eagerly turned to account. Among the ordnance was a huge brass mortar of a new construction, weighing near three thousand pounds. It was considered a glorious trophy, and there was a resolve to christen it. Mifflin, Washington's secretary, suggested the name. The mortar was fixed in a bed; old Putnam mounted it, dashed

* See Letter of Gen. Greene to Samuel Ward. Am. Arch. 4th Series, vol. iv.

on it a bottle of rum, and gave it the name of Congress. The shouts which rent the air were heard in Boston. When the meaning of them was explained to the British, they observed, that "should their expected reinforcements arrive in time, the rebels would pay dear in the spring for all their petty triumphs."

With Washington, this transient gleam of nautical success was soon overshadowed by the conduct of the cruisers he had sent to the St. Lawrence. Failing to intercept the brigantines, the objects of their cruise, they landed on the island of St. Johns, plundered the house of the governor and several private dwellings, and brought off three of the principal inhabitants prisoners; one of whom, Mr. Callbeck, was president of the council, and acted as governor.

These gentlemen made a memorial to Washington of this scandalous maraud. He instantly ordered the restoration of the effects which had been pillaged;—of his conduct towards the gentlemen personally, we may judge by the following note addressed to him by Mr. Callbeck.

"I should ill deserve the generous treatment which your Excellency has been pleased to show me, had I not the gratitude to acknowledge so great a favor. I cannot ascribe any part of it to my own merit, but must impute the whole to the philanthropy and humane disposition that so truly characterize General Washington. Be so obliging, therefore, as to accept the only return in my power, that of my most grateful thanks." *

Shortly after the foregoing occurrence, information was received of the indignities which had been heaped upon Colonel Ethan Allen, when captured at Montreal by General Prescott,

---

* Sparks. Washington's Writings, vol. iii. p. 194.

who, himself, was now a prisoner in the hands of the Americans. It touched Washington on a point on which he was most sensitive and tenacious, the treatment of American officers when captured; and produced the following letter from him to General Howe:

" SIR,—We have just been informed of a circumstance which, were it not so well authenticated, I should scarcely think credible. It is that Colonel Allen, who, with his small party, was defeated and made prisoner near Montreal, has been treated without regard to decency, humanity, or the rules of war; that he has been thrown into irons, and suffers all the hardships inflicted upon common felons.

" I think it my duty, sir, to demand, and do expect from you, an eclaircissement on this subject. At the same time, I flatter myself, from the character which Mr. Howe bears as a man of honor, gentleman and soldier, that my demand will meet with his approbation. I must take the liberty, also, of informing you that I shall consider your silence as a confirmation of the report, and further assuring you, that whatever treatment Colonel Allen receives, whatever fate he undergoes, such exactly shall be the treatment and fate of Brigadier Prescott, now in our hands. The law of retaliation is not only justifiable in the eyes of God and man, but absolutely a duty, which, in our present circumstances, we owe to our relations, friends and fellow-citizens.

" Permit me to add, sir, that we have all here the highest regard and reverence for your great personal qualities and attainments, and the Americans in general esteem it as not the least of their misfortunes, that the name of Howe, a name so dear to them, should appear at the head of the catalogue of the instruments employed by a wicked ministry for their destruction.",

General Howe felt acutely the sorrowful reproach in the latter part of the letter. It was a reiteration of what had already been expressed by Congress; in the present instance it produced irritation, if we may judge from the reply.

"Sir,—In answer to your letter, I am to acquaint you that my command does not extend to Canada. Not having any accounts wherein the name of Allen is mentioned, I cannot give you the smallest satisfaction upon the subject of your letter. But trusting Major-general Carleton's conduct will never incur censure upon any occasion, I am to conclude in the instance of your inquiry, that he has not forfeited his past pretensions to decency and humanity.

"It is with regret, considering the character you have always maintained among your friends, as a gentleman of the strictest honor and delicacy, that I find cause to resent a sentence in the conclusion of your letter, big with invective against my superiors, and insulting to myself, which should obstruct any further intercourse between us. I am, sir, &c."

In transmitting a copy of his letter to the President of Congress, Washington observed: "My reason for pointing out Brigadier-general Prescott as the object, who is to suffer for Mr. Allen's fate, is, that by letters from General Schuyler and copies of letters from General Montgomery to Schuyler, I am given to understand that Prescott is the cause of Allen's sufferings. I thought it best to be decisive on the occasion, as did the generals whom I consulted thereon."

For the sake of continuity we will anticipate a few facts connected with the story of Ethan Allen. Within a few weeks after the preceding correspondence, Washington received a letter from Levi Allen, a brother to the colonel, and of like enterprising and enthusiastic character. It was dated from Salisbury in Connecticut; and enclosed affidavits of the harsh treatment his brother had experienced, and of his being confined on board of the Gaspee, " with a bar of iron fixed to one of his legs and iron to his hands." Levi was bent upon effecting his deliverance, and the mode proposed was in unison with the bold, but wild schemes of the colonel. We quote his crude, but characteristic letter.

"Have some thoughts of going to England *incognito*, after my brother; but am not positively certain he is sent there, though believe he is. Beg your excellency will favor me with a line, and acquaint me if any intelligence concerning him, and if your excellency please, your opinion of the expediency of going after him, and whether your excellency would think proper to advance any money for that purpose, as my brother was a man blessed with more fortitude than fortune. Your excellency may think, at first thought, I can do nothing by going to England; I feel as if I could do a great deal, by raising a mob in London, bribing the jailer, or by getting into some servile employment with the jailer, and over-faithfulness make myself master of the key, or at least be able to lay my hand on it some night. I beg your excellency will countenance my going; can muster more than one hundred pounds, my own property; shall regard spending that no more than one copper. Your excellency must know Allen was not only a brother, but a real friend that sticketh closer than a brother."

In a postscript he adds, " cannot live without going to England, if my brother is sent there."

In reply, Washington intimated a belief that the colonel had been sent to England, but discountenanced Levi's wild project of following him thither; as there was no probability of its success, and he would be running himself into danger without a prospect of rendering service to his brother.

The measure of retaliation mentioned in Washington's letter to Howe, was actually meted out by Congress on the arrival of General Prescott in Philadelphia. He was ordered into close confinement in the jail; though not put in irons. He was subsequently released from confinement, on account of ill health, and was treated by some Philadelphia families with unmerited hospitality.*

At the time of the foregoing correspondence with Howe, Washington was earnestly occupied preparing works for the bombardment of Boston, should that measure be resolved upon by Congress. General Putnam, in the preceding month, had taken possession in the night of Cobble Hill without molestation from the enemy, though a commanding eminence; and in two days had constructed a work, which, from its strength, was named Putnam's impregnable fortress.

He was now engaged on another work on Lechmere Point, to be connected with the works at Cobble Hill by a bridge thrown across Willis's Creek, and a covered way. Lechmere Point is im-

---

* Thomas Walker, a merchant of Montreal, who, accused of traitorous dealings with the Americans, had been thrown into prison during Prescott's sway, and his country-house burnt down, undertook a journey to Philadelphia in the depth of winter, when he understood the general was a captive there, trusting to obtain satisfaction for his ill-treatment. To his great surprise, he found Mr. Prescott lodged in the best tavern of the place, walking or riding at large through Philadelphia and Bucks counties, feasting with gentlemen of the first rank in the province, and keeping a levée for the reception of the grandees. In consequence of which unaccountable phenomena, and the little prospect of his obtaining any adequate redress in the present unsettled state of public affairs, Mr. Walker has returned to Montreal.—*Am. Archives, 4th Series,* vol. iv. 1178.

mediately opposite the west part of Boston; and the Scarborough ship-of-war was anchored near it. Putnam availed himself of a dark and foggy day (Dec. 17), to commence operations, and broke ground with four hundred men, at ten o'clock in the morning, on a hill at the Point. "The mist," says a contemporary account, "was so great as to prevent the enemy from discovering what he was about until near twelve o'clock, when it cleared up, and opened to their view our whole party at the Point, and another at the causeway throwing a bridge over the creek. The Scarborough, anchored off the Point, poured in a broadside. The enemy from Boston threw shells. The garrison at Cobble Hill returned fire. Our men were obliged to decamp from the Point, but the work was resumed by the brave old general at night."

On the next morning, a cannonade from Cobble Hill obliged the Scarborough to weigh anchor, and drop down below the ferry; and General Heath was detached with a party of men to carry on the work which Putnam had commenced. The enemy resumed their fire. Sentinels were placed to give notice of a shot or shell; the men would crouch down or dodge it, and continue on with their work. The fire ceased in the afternoon, and Washington visited the hill accompanied by several officers, and inspected the progress of the work. It was to consist of two redoubts, on one of which was to be a mortar battery. There was, as yet, a deficiency of ordnance; but the prize mortar was to be mounted which Putnam had recently christened, "The Congress." From the spirit with which the work was carried on, Washington trusted that it would soon be completed, "and then," said he, "if we have powder to sport with, and Congress gives the word, Boston can be bombarded from this point."

For several days the labor at the works was continued; the redoubts were thrown up, and a covered way was constructed leading down to the bridge. All this was done notwithstanding the continual fire of the enemy. The letter of a British officer gives his idea of the efficiency of the work.

"The rebels for some days past have been erecting a battery on Phipps' Farm. The new constructed mortar taken on board the ordnance brig, we are told, will be mounted upon it, and we expect a warm salute from the shells, another part of that vessel's cargo; so that, in spite of her capture, we are likely to be complimented with the contents of her lading."

"If the rebels can complete their battery, this town will be on fire about our ears a few hours after; all our buildings being of wood, or a mixture of brick and wood-work. Had the rebels erected their battery on the other side of the town, at Dorchester, the admiral and all his booms would have made the first blaze, and the burning of the town would have followed. If we cannot destroy the rebel battery by our guns, we must march out and take it sword in hand."

Putnam anticipated great effects from this work, and especially from his grand mortar, "The Congress." Shells there were in abundance for a bombardment; the only thing wanting was a supply of powder. One of the officers, writing of the unusual mildness of the winter, observes: "Every thing thaws here except old Put. He is still as hard as ever, crying out for powder—powder—powder. Ye gods, give us powder!"

CHAPTER XI.

AMID the various concerns of the war, and the multiplied per-plexities of the camp, the thoughts of Washington continually reverted to his home on the banks of the Potomac. A constant correspondence was kept up between him and his agent, Mr. Lund Washington, who had charge of his various estates. The general gave clear and minute directions as to their management, and the agent rendered as clear and minute returns of every thing that had been done in consequence.

According to recent accounts, Mount Vernon had been con-sidered in danger. Lord Dunmore was exercising martial law in the Ancient Dominion, and it was feared that the favorite abode of the "rebel commander-in-chief" would be marked out for hos-tility, and that the enemy might land from their ships in the Potomac, and lay it waste. Washington's brother, John Augus-tine, had entreated Mrs. Washington to leave it. The people of

Loudoun had advised her to seek refuge beyond the Blue Ridge, and had offered to send a guard to escort her. She had declined the offer, not considering herself in danger. Lund Washington was equally free from apprehensions on the subject. "Lord Dunmore," writes he, "will hardly himself venture up this river, nor do I believe he will send on that errand. You may depend I will be watchful, and upon the least alarm persuade her to move."

Though alive to every thing concerning Mount Vernon, Washington agreed with them in deeming it in no present danger of molestation by the enemy. Still he felt for the loneliness of Mrs. Washington's situation, heightened as it must be by anxiety on his own account. On taking command of the army, he had held out a prospect to her, that he would rejoin her at home in the autumn; there was now a probability of his being detained before Boston all winter. He wrote to her, therefore, by express, in November, inviting her to join him at the camp. He at the same time wrote to Lund Washington, engaging his continued services as an agent. This person, though bearing the same name, and probably of the same stock, does not appear to have been in any near degree of relationship. Washington's letter to him gives a picture of his domestic policy.

"I will engage for the year coming, and the year following, if these troubles and my absence continue, that your wages shall be standing and certain at the highest amount that any one year's crop has produced you yet. I do not offer this as any temptation to induce you to go on more cheerfully in prosecuting those schemes of mine. I should do injustice to you were I not to acknowledge, that your conduct has ever appeared to me above every thing sordid; but I offer it in consideration of the great charge you have upon your hands, and my entire dependence upon your fidelity and industry.

"It is the greatest, indeed it is the only comfortable reflection I enjoy on this score, that my business is in the hands of a person concerning whose integrity I have not a doubt, and on whose care I can rely. Were it not for this, I should feel very unhappy on account of the situation of my affairs. But I am persuaded you will do for me as you would for yourself."

The following were his noble directions concerning Mount Vernon.

"Let the hospitality of the house with respect to the poor be kept up. Let no one go hungry away. If any of this kind of people should be in want of corn, supply their necessaries, provided it does not encourage them to idleness; and I have no objection to your giving my money in charity to the amount of forty or fifty pounds a year, when you think it well bestowed. What I mean by having no objection is, that it is my desire it should be done. You are to consider that neither myself nor wife, is now in the way to do those good offices."

Mrs. Washington came on with her own carriage and horses, accompanied by her son, Mr. Custis, and his wife. She travelled by very easy stages, partly on account of the badness of the roads, partly out of regard to the horses, of which Washington was always very careful, and which were generally remarkable for beauty and excellence. Escorts and guards of honor attended her from place to place, and she was detained some time at Philadelphia, by the devoted attention of the inhabitants.

Her arrival at Cambridge was a glad event in the army. Incidental mention is made of the equipage in which she appeared there. A chariot and four, with black postilions in scarlet and white liveries. It has been suggested that this was an English style of equipage, derived from the Fairfaxes; but in truth it was a style still prevalent at that day in Virginia.

It would appear that dinner invitations to head-quarters, were becoming matters of pride and solicitude. " I am much obliged to you," writes Washington to Reed, "for the hints respecting the jealousies which you say are gone abroad. I cannot charge myself with incivility, or what in my opinion is tantamount, ceremonious civility to gentlemen of this colony; but if such my conduct appears, I will endeavor at a reformation; as I can assure you, my dear Reed, that I wish to walk in such a line as will give most general satisfaction. You know that it was my wish at first to invite a certain number to dinner, but unintentionally we somehow or other missed of it. If this has given rise to the jealousy, I can only say that I am very sorry for it; at the same time I add, that it was rather owing to inattention, or more properly, too much attention to other matters, which caused me to neglect it."

And in another letter :

" My constant attention to the great and perplexing objects which continually arise to my view, absorbs all lesser considerations; and, indeed, scarcely allows me to reflect that there is such a body as the General Court of this colony, but when I am reminded of it by a committee; nor can I, upon recollection, discover in what instance I have been inattentive to, or slighted them. They could not surely conceive that there was a propriety in unbosoming the secrets of the army to them; that it was necessary to ask their opinion in throwing up an intrenchment or forming a battalion. It must be, therefore, what I before hinted to you; and how to remedy it I hardly know, as I am acquainted with few of the members, never go out of my own lines, nor see any of them in them."

The presence of Mrs. Washington soon relieved the general from this kind of perplexity. She presided at head-quarters with mingled dignity and affability. We have an anecdote or two of the internal affairs of head-quarters, furnished by the descendant of one who was an occasional inmate there.

Washington had prayers morning and evening, and was regular in his attendance at the church in which he was a communicant. On one occasion, for want of a clergyman, the Episcopal service was read by Colonel William Palfrey, one of Washington's aides-de-camp; who substituted a prayer of his own composition in place of the one formerly offered up for the king.

Not long after her arrival in camp, Mrs. Washington claimed to keep twelfth-night in due style, as the anniversary of her wedding. "The general," says the same informant, "was somewhat thoughtful, and said he was afraid he must refuse it." His objections were overcome, and twelfth-night and the wedding anniversary were duly celebrated.

There seems to have been more conviviality at the quarters of some of the other generals; their time and minds were less intensely engrossed by anxious cares, having only their individual departments to attend to. Adjutant-general Mifflin's house appears to have been a gay one. "He was a man of education, ready apprehension and brilliancy," says Graydon; "had spent some time in Europe, particularly in France, and was very easy of access, with the manners of genteel life, though occasionally evolving those of the Quaker." *

* Graydon's Memoirs, p. 154.

Mrs. Adams gives an account of an evening party at his house. "I was very politely entertained and noticed by the generals," writes she, "more especially General Lee, who was very urgent for me to tarry in town, and dine with him and the ladies present at Hobgoblin Hall; but I excused myself. The general was determined that I should not only be acquainted with him, but with his companions too; and therefore placed a chair before me, into which he ordered Mr. Spada (his dog) to mount, and present his paw to me for a better acquaintance. I could not do otherwise than accept it." *

John Adams, likewise, gives us a picture of festivities at head-quarters, where he was a visitant on the recess of Congress.

"I dined at Col. Mifflin's with the general (Washington) and lady, and a vast collection of other company, among whom were six or seven sachems and warriors of the French Caughnawaga Indians, with their wives and children. A savage feast they made of it; yet were very polite in the Indian style. I was introduced to them by the general as one of the grand council at Philadelphia, which made them prick up their ears. They came and shook hands with me." †

While giving these familiar scenes and occurrences at the camp, we are tempted to subjoin one furnished from the manuscript memoir of an eye witness. A large party of Virginia riflemen, who had recently arrived in camp, were strolling about Cambridge, and viewing the collegiate buildings, now turned into barracks. Their half-Indian equipments, and fringed and ruffled hunting garbs, provoked the merriment of some troops from

* Letters of Mr. Adams, vol. i. p. 85.

† Adams's Letters, vol. ii. p. 80. Adams adds, that they made him "low bows and scrapes"—a kind of homage never paid by an Indian warrior.

Marblehead, chiefly fishermen and sailors, who thought nothing equal to the round jacket and trowsers. A bantering ensued between them. There was snow upon the ground, and snowballs began to fly when jokes were wanting. The parties waxed warm with the contest. They closed, and came to blows; both sides were reinforced, and in a little while at least a thousand were at fisticuffs, and there was a tumult in the camp worthy of the days of Homer. "At this juncture," writes our informant, "Washington made his appearance, whether by accident or design, I never knew. I saw none of his aides with him; his black servant just behind him mounted. He threw the bridle of his own horse into his servant's hands, sprang from his seat, rushed into the thickest of the melée, seized two tall brawny riflemen by the throat, keeping them at arm's-length, talking to and shaking them."

As they were from his own province, he may have felt peculiarly responsible for their good conduct; they were engaged, too, in one of those sectional brawls which were his especial abhorrence; his reprimand must, therefore, have been a vehement one. He was commanding in his serenest moments, but irresistible in his bursts of indignation. On the present occasion, we are told, his appearance and strong-handed rebuke put an instant end to the tumult. The combatants dispersed in all directions, and in less than three minutes none remained on the ground but the two he had collared.

The veteran who records this exercise of military authority, seems at a loss which most to admire, the simplicity of the process or the vigor with which it was administered. "Here," writes he, "bloodshed, imprisonments, trials by court-martial, revengeful feelings between the different corps of the army, were happily prevented by the physical and mental energies of a single person, and the only damage resulting from the fierce encounter was, a few torn hunting frocks and round jackets." *

* From memoranda written at an advanced age, by the late Hon. Israel Trask; who, when but ten years old, was in the camp at Cambridge with his father, who was a lieutenant.

CHAPTER XII.

WE again turn from the siege of Boston, to the invasion of Canada, which at that time shared the anxious thoughts of Washington. His last accounts of the movements of Arnold, left him at
Point Levi, opposite to Quebec. Something brilliant from that
daring officer was anticipated. It was his intention to cross the
river immediately. Had he done so, he might have carried the
town by a *coup de main;* for terror as well as disaffection prevailed among the inhabitants. At Point Levi, however, he was
brought to a stand; not a boat was to be found there. Letters
which he had despatched some days previously, by two Indians,
to Generals Schuyler and Montgomery, had been carried by his
faithless messengers, to Caramhe, the lieutenant-governor, who,
thus apprised of the impending danger, had caused all the boats
of Point Levi to be either removed or destroyed.

Arnold was not a man to be disheartened by difficulties.
With great exertions he procured about forty birch canoes from

the Canadians and Indians, with forty of the latter to navigate them; but stormy winds arose, and for some days the river was too boisterous for such frail craft. In the mean time the garrison at Quebec was gaining strength. Recruits arrived from Nova Scotia. The veteran Maclean, too, who had been driven from the mouth of the Sorel by the detachment under Brown and Livingston, arrived down the river with his corps of Royal Highland Emigrants, and threw himself into the place. The Lizard frigate, the Hornet sloop-of-war, and two armed schooners were stationed in the river, and guard-boats patrolled at night. The prospect of a successful attack upon the place was growing desperate.

On the 13th of November, Arnold received intelligence that Montgomery had captured St. Johns. He was instantly roused to emulation. His men, too, were inspirited by the news. The wind had abated: he determined to cross the river that very night. At a late hour in the evening he embarked with the first division, principally riflemen. The river was wide; the current rapid; the birch canoes, easy to be upset, required skilful management. By four o'clock in the morning, a large part of his force had crossed without being perceived, and landed about a mile and a half above Cape Diamond, at Wolfe's Cove, so called from being the landing-place of that gallant commander.

Just then a guard-boat, belonging to the Lizard, came slowly along shore and discovered them. They hailed it, and ordered it to land. Not complying, it was fired into, and three men were killed. The boat instantly pulled for the frigate, giving vociferous alarm.

Without waiting the arrival of the residue of his men, for whom the canoes had been despatched, Arnold led those who had landed to the foot of the cragged defile, once scaled by the intrepid Wolfe, and scrambled up it in all haste. By daylight he had planted his daring flag on the far-famed Heights of Abraham.

Here the main difficulty stared him in the face. A strong line of walls and bastions traversed the promontory from one of its precipitous sides to the other; enclosing the upper and lower towns. On the right, the great bastion of Cape Diamond crowned the rocky height of that name. On the left was the bastion of La Potasse, close by the gate of St. Johns opening upon the barracks; the gate where Wolfe's antagonist, the gallant Montcalm, received his death wound.

A council of war was now held. Arnold, who had some knowledge of the place, was for dashing forward at once and storming the gate of St. Johns. Had they done so, they might have been successful. The gate was open and unguarded. Through some blunder and delay, a message from the commander of the Lizard to the lieutenant-governor had not yet been delivered, and no alarm had reached the fortress.

The formidable aspect of the place, however, awed Arnold's associates in council. They considered that their whole force was but between seven and eight hundred men; that nearly one third of their fire-arms had been rendered useless, and much of their ammunition damaged in their march through the wilderness; they had no artillery, and the fortress looked too strong to be carried by a *coup de main*. Cautious counsel is often fatal to a daring enterprise. While the council of war deliberated, the favorable moment passed away. The lieutenant-governor received the tardy message. He hastily assembled the merchants, officers of militia, and captains of merchant vessels. All promised to stand by him; he had strong distrust, however, of the French part of the population and the Canadian militia; his main reliance was on Colonel Maclean and his Royal Highland Emigrants.

The din of arms now resounded through the streets. The cry was up—"The enemy are on the Heights of Abraham! The gate of St. Johns is open!" There was an attempt to shut it. The keys were not to be found. It was hastily secured by ropes and handspikes, and the walls looking upon the heights were soon manned by the military, and thronged by the populace.

Arnold paraded his men within a hundred yards of the walls, and caused them to give three hearty cheers; hoping to excite a revolt in the place, or to provoke the scanty garrison to a sally. There were a few scatterd cheerings in return; but the taunting bravado failed to produce a sortie; the governor dared not venture beyond the walls with part of his garrison, having too little confidence in the loyalty of those who would remain behind. There was some firing on the part of the Americans, but merely as an additional taunt; they were too far off for their musketry to have effect. A large cannon on the ramparts was brought to bear on them, and matches were procured from the Lizard, with which to fire it off. A few shots obliged the Americans to retire and encamp.

In the evening Arnold sent a flag, demanding in the name of the United Colonies the surrender of the place. Some of the disaffected and the faint-hearted were inclined to open the gates, but were held in check by the mastiff loyalty of Maclean. The veteran guarded the gate with his Highlanders; forbade all communication with the besiegers, and fired upon their flag as an ensign of rebellion.

Several days elapsed. Arnold's flags of truce were repeatedly insulted, but he saw the futility of resenting it, and attacking

VOL. II.—6

the place with his present means. The inhabitants gradually recovered from their alarm, and armed themselves to defend their property. The sailors and marines proved a valuable addition to the garrison, which now really meditated a sortie.

Arnold received information of all this from friends within the walls; he heard about the same time of the capture of Montreal, and that General Carleton, having escaped from that place, was on his way down to Quebec. He thought at present, therefore, to draw off on the 19th to *Point aux Trembles* (Aspen-tree Point), twenty miles above Quebec, there to await the arrival of General Montgomery with troops and artillery. As his little army wended its way along the high bank of the river towards its destined encampment, a vessel passed below, which had just touched at Point aux Trembles. On board of it was General Carleton, hurrying on to Quebec.

It was not long before the distant booming of artillery told of his arrival at his post, where he resumed a stern command. He was unpopular among the inhabitants; even the British merchants and other men of business, were offended by the coldness of his manners, and his confining his intimacy to the military and the Canadian noblesse. He was aware of his unpopularity, and looked round him with distrust; his first measure was to turn out of the place all suspected persons, and all who refused to aid in its defence. This caused a great "trooping out of town," but what was lost in numbers was gained in strength. With the loyally disposed who remained, he busied himself in improving the defences.

Of the constant anxiety, yet enduring hope, with which Washington watched this hazardous enterprise, we have evidence in his various letters. To Arnold, when at Point Levi, baffled in the expectation of finding the means of making a dash upon Quebec, he writes: "It is not in the power of any man to command success, but you have done more, you have deserved it; and before this time (Dec. 5th), I hope you have met with the laurels which are due to your toils, in the possession of Quebec.

"I have no doubt but a junction of your detachment with the army under General Montgomery, is effected before this. If so, you will put yourself under his command, and will, I am persuaded, give him all the assistance in your power, to finish the glorious work you have begun."

CHAPTER XIII.

In the month of December a vessel had been captured, bearing
supplies from Lord Dunmore, to the army at Boston. A letter
on board, from his lordship to General Howe, invited him to
transfer the war to the southern colonies; or, at all events, to
send reinforcements thither; intimating at the same time his plan
of proclaiming liberty to indentured servants, negroes, and others
appertaining to rebels, and inviting them to join his majesty's
troops. In a word,—to inflict upon Virginia the horrors of a
servile war.

"If this man is not crushed before spring," writes Washington, "he will become the most formidable enemy America has.
His strength will increase as a snowball. * * * Motives of
resentment actuate his conduct to a degree equal to the destruction of the colony."

General Lee took the occasion to set forth his own system of policy, which was particularly rigid wherever men in authority and tories were concerned. It was the old grudge against ministers and their adherents set on edge.

"Had my opinion been thought worthy of attention," would he say, "Lord Dunmore would have been disarmed of his teeth and claws." He would have seized Tryon too, "and all his tories at New York," and, having struck the stroke, would have applied to Congress for approbation.

"I propose the following measures," would he add: "To seize every governor, government man, placeman, tory and enemy to liberty on the continent, to confiscate their estates; or at least lay them under heavy contributions for the public. Their persons should be secured, in some of the interior towns, as hostages for the treatment of those of our party, whom the fortune of war shall throw into their hands; they should be allowed a reasonable pension out of their fortunes for their maintenance." *

Such was the policy advocated by Lee in his letters and conversation, and he soon had an opportunity of carrying it partly into operation. Rhode Island had for some time past been domineered over by Captain Wallace of the royal navy; who had stationed himself at Newport with an armed vessel, and obliged the place to furnish him with supplies. Latterly he had landed in Conanicut Island, opposite to Newport, with a number of sailors and marines, plundered and burnt houses, and driven off cattle for the supply of the army. In his exactions and maraudings, he was said to have received countenance from the tory part of the inhabitants. It was now reported that a naval armament was

* Lee to Rich. Henry Lee. Am. Archives, 4th Series, iv. 248.

coming from Boston against the island. In this emergency, the governor (Cooke) wrote to Washington, requesting military aid, and an efficient officer to put the island in a state of defence, suggesting the name of General Lee for the purpose.

Lee undertook the task with alacrity. " I sincerely wish," said Washington, " he may be able to do it with effect ; as that place, in its present state, is an asylum for such as are disaffected to American liberty."

Lee set out for Rhode Island with his guard and a party of riflemen, and at Providence was joined by the cadet company of that place, and a number of minute men. Preceded by these, he entered the town of Newport on Christmas day, in military style. While there, he summoned before him a number of persons who had supplied the enemy ; some according to a convention originally made between Wallace and the authorities, others, as it was suspected, through tory feelings. All were obliged by Lee to take a test oath of his own devising, by which they "religiously swore that they would neither directly, nor indirectly, assist the wicked instruments of ministerial tyranny and villainy commonly called the king's troops and navy, by furnishing them with provisions and refreshments." They swore, moreover, to " denounce all traitors before the public authority, and to take arms in defence of American liberty, whenever required by Congress or the provincial authority." Two custom-house officers, and another person, who refused to take the oath, were put under guard and sent to Providence. Having laid out works, and given directions for fortifications, Lee returned to camp after an absence of ten days. Some of his proceedings were considered too high-handed, and were disapproved by Congress. Lee made light of legislative censures. "One must not be trammelled by laws in war time," said he; "in a revolution, all means are legal."

Washington approved of his measures. "I have seen General Lee since his expedition," writes he, "and hope Rhode Island will derive some advantage from it. I am told that Captain Wallace's ships have been supplied for some time by the town of Newport, on certain conditions stipulated between him and the committee. * * * I know not what pernicious consequences may result from a precedent of this sort. Other places, circumstanced as Newport is, may follow the example, and by that means their whole fleet and army will be furnished with what it highly concerns us to keep from them. * * * Vigorous regulations, and such as at another time would appear extraordinary, are now become absolutely necessary for preserving our country against the strides of tyranny, making against it." *

December had been throughout a month of severe trial to Washington; during which he saw his army dropping away piecemeal before his eyes. Homeward every face was turned as soon as the term of enlistment was at an end. Scarce could the disbanding troops be kept a few days in camp until militia could be procured to supply their place. Washington made repeated and animated appeals to their patriotism; they were almost unheeded. He caused popular and patriotic songs to be sung about the camp. They passed by like the idle wind. Home! home! home! throbbed in every heart. "The desire of retiring into a chimney-corner," says Washington reproachfully, "seized the troops as soon as their terms expired."

Can we wonder at it? They were for the most part yeoman-

---

* Washington to Gov. Cooke. Sparks, iii. 227.

ry, unused to military restraint, and suffering all the hardships of a starveling camp, almost within sight of the smoke of their own firesides.

Greene, throughout this trying month, was continually by Washington's side. His letters expressing the same cares and apprehensions, and occasionally in the same language with those of the commander-in-chief, show how completely he was in his councils. He could well sympathize with him in his solicitudes. Some of his own Rhode Island troops were with Arnold in his Canada expedition. Others encamped on Prospect Hill, and whose order and discipline had been his pride, were evincing the prevalent disposition to disband. "They seem to be so sick of this way of life, and so homesick," writes he, "that I fear the greater part of the best troops from our colony will soon go home." To provide against such a contingency, he strengthened his encampment, so that, "if the soldiery should not engage as cheerfully as he expected, he might defend it with a less number." *

Still he was buoyant and cheerful; frequently on his white horse about Prospect Hill, haranguing his men, and endeavoring to keep them in good humor. "This is no time for disgusting the soldiery," would he say, "when their aid is so essential to the preservation of the rights of human nature and the liberties of America."

He wore the same cheery aspect to the commander-in-chief; or rather he partook of his own hopeful spirit. "I expect," would he say, "the army, notwithstanding all the difficulties we meet with, will be full in about six weeks."

* Greene to Henry Ward.

It was this loyalty in time of trouble; this buoyancy under depression, this thorough patriotism, which won for him the entire confidence of Washington.

The thirty-first of December arrived, the crisis of the army; for with that month expired the last of the old terms of enlistment. "We never have been so weak," writes Greene, "as we shall be to-morrow, when we dismiss the old troops." On this day Washington received cheering intelligence from Canada. A junction had taken place, a month previously, between Arnold and Montgomery at Point aux Trembles. They were about two thousand strong, and were making every preparation for attacking Quebec. Carleton was said to have with him but about twelve hundred men, the majority of whom were sailors. It was thought that the French would give up Quebec, if they could get the same conditions that were granted to the inhabitants of Montreal. *

Thus the year closed upon Washington with a ray of light from Canada, while all was doubt around him.

On the following morning (January 1st, 1776), his army did not amount to ten thousand men, and was composed of but half-filled regiments. Even in raising this inadequate force, it had been necessary to indulge many of the men with furloughs, that they might visit their families and friends. The expedients resorted to in equipping the army, show the prevailing lack of arms. Those soldiers who retired from service, were obliged to leave their weapons for their successors; receiving their appraised value. Those who enlisted, were required to bring a gun, or were charged a dollar for the use of one during the campaign.

* Letter of Washington to the President of Congress, Dec. 31.

He who brought a blanket was allowed two dollars. It was impossible to furnish uniforms; the troops, therefore, presented a motley appearance, in garments of divers cuts and colors; the price of each man's garb being deducted from his pay.

The detachments of militia from the neighboring provinces which replaced the disbanding troops, remained but for brief periods; so that, in despite of every effort, the lines were often but feebly manned, and might easily have been forced.

The anxiety of Washington, in this critical state of the army, may be judged from his correspondence with Reed. "It is easier to conceive than to describe the situation of my mind for some time past, and my feelings under our present circumstances," writes he on the 4th of January. "Search the volumes of history through, and I much question whether a case similar to ours is to be found; namely, to maintain a post against the power of the British troops for six months together, without powder, and then to have one army disbanded and another raised within the same distance (musket shot) of a reinforced enemy. What may be the issue of the last manœuvre, time only can unfold. I wish this month were well over our head. * * * We are now left with a good deal less than half-raised regiments, and about five thousand militia, who only stand engaged to the middle of this month; when, according to custom, they will depart, let the necessity of their stay be ever so urgent. Thus, for more than two months past, I have scarcely emerged from one difficulty before I have been plunged in another. How it will end, God, in his great goodness, will direct. I am thankful for his protection to this time. We are told that we shall soon get the army completed, but I have been told so many things which have never come to pass, that I distrust every thing."

In a subsequent letter to Mr. Reed, he reverts to the subject, and pours forth his feelings with confiding frankness. What can be more touching than the picture he draws of himself and his lonely vigils about his sleeping camp? "The reflection on my situation and that of this army, produces many an unhappy hour, when all around me are wrapped in sleep. Few people know the predicament we are in on a thousand accounts; fewer still will believe, if any disaster happens to these lines, from what cause it flows. I have often thought how much happier I should have been, if, instead of accepting the command, under such circumstances, I had taken my musket on my shoulder and entered the ranks; or, if I could have justified the measure to posterity and my own conscience, had retired to the back country and lived in a wigwam. If I shall be able to rise superior to these and many other difficulties, which might be enumerated, I shall most religiously believe that the finger of Providence is in it, to blind the eyes of our enemies; for surely if we get well through this month, it must be for want of their knowing the disadvantages which we labor under."

Recurring to the project of an attack upon Boston, which he had reluctantly abandoned in deference to the adverse opinions of a council of war—"Could I have foreseen the difficulties which have come upon us; could I have known that such a backwardness would have been discovered among the old soldiers to the service, all the generals upon earth should not have convinced me of the propriety of delaying an attack upon Boston till this time. When it can now be attempted, I will not undertake to say; but thus much I will answer for, that no opportunity can present itself earlier than my wishes."

In the midst of his discouragements, Washington received letters from Knox, showing the spirit and energy with which he was executing his mission, in quest of cannon and ordnance stores. He had struggled manfully and successfully with all kinds of difficulties from the advanced season, and head winds, in getting them from Ticonderoga to the head of Lake George. "Three days ago," writes he, on the 17th of December, "it was very uncertain whether we could get them over until next spring; but now, please God, they shall go. I have made forty-two exceedingly strong sleds, and have provided eighty yoke of oxen to drag them as far as Springfield, where I shall get fresh cattle to take them to camp."

It was thus that hardships and emergencies were bringing out the merits of the self-made soldiers of the Revolution; and showing their commander-in-chief on whom he might rely.

CHAPTER XIV.

EARLY in the month of January, there was a great stir of preparation in Boston harbor. A fleet of transports were taking in
supplies, and making arrangements for the embarkation of troops.
Bomb-ketches and flat-bottomed boats were getting ready for sea,
as were two sloops-of-war, which were to convey the armament.
Its destination was kept secret; but was confidently surmised by
Washington.

In the preceding month of October, a letter had been laid
before Congress, written by some person in London of high cred-
ibility, and revealing a secret plan of operations said to have been
sent out by ministers to the commanders in Boston. The following is the purport: Possession was to be gained of New York
and Albany, through the assistance of Governor Tryon, on whose
influence with the tory part of the poplulation, much reliance was
placed. These cities were to be very strongly garrisoned. All

who did not join the king's forces were to be declared rebels. The Hudson River, and the East River or Sound, were to be commanded by a number of small men-of-war and cutters, stationed in different parts, so as wholly to cut off all communication by water between New York and the provinces to the northward of it; and between New York and Albany, except for the king's service; and to prevent, also, all communication between the city of New York and the provinces of New Jersey, Pennsylvania, and those to the southward of them. "By these means," said the letter, "the administration and their friends fancy they shall soon either starve out or retake the garrisons of Crown Point and Ticonderoga, and open and maintain a safe intercourse and correspondence between Quebec, Albany and New York; and thereby offer the fairest opportunity to their soldiery and the Canadians, in conjunction with the Indians to be procured by Guy Johnson, to make continual irruptions into New Hampshire, Massachusetts and Connecticut, and so distract and divide the Provincial forces, as to render it easy for the British army at Boston to defeat them, break the spirits of the Massachusetts people, depopulate their country, and compel an absolute subjection to Great Britain." *

It was added that a lord, high in the American department, had been very particular in his inquiries about the Hudson River; what sized vessels could get to Albany; and whether, if batteries were erected in the Highlands, they would not control the navigation of the river, and prevent vessels from going up and down.

This information had already excited solicitude respecting th

* Am. Archives, 4th Series, iii. 1281.

Hudson, and led to measures for its protection. It was now surmised that the expedition preparing to sail from Boston, and which was to be conducted by Sir Henry Clinton, might be destined to seize upon New York. How was the apprehended blow to be parried? General Lee, who was just returned from his energetic visit to Rhode Island, offered his advice and services in the matter. In a letter to Washington, he urged him to act at once, and on his own responsibility, without awaiting the tardy and doubtful sanction of Congress, for which, in military matters, Lee had but small regard.

"New York must be secured," writes he, "but it will never, I am afraid, be secured by due order of the Congress, for obvious reasons. They find themselves awkwardly situated on this head. You must step in to their relief. I am sensible no man can be spared from the lines under present circumstances; but I would propose that you should detach me into Connecticut, and lend your name for collecting a body of volunteers. I am assured that I shall find no difficulty in assembling a sufficient number for the purposes wanted. This body, in conjunction (if there should appear occasion to summon them) with the Jersey regiment under the command of Lord Stirling, now at Elizabethtown, will effect the security of New York, and the expulsion or suppression of that dangerous banditti of tories, who have appeared on Long Island, with the professed intention of acting against the authority of Congress. Not to crush these serpents before their rattles are grown would be ruinous.

"This manœuvre, I not only think prudent and right, but absolutely necessary to our salvation; and if it meets, as I ardently hope it will, with your approbation, the sooner it is entered upon the better; the delay of a single day may be fatal."

Washington, while he approved of Lee's military suggestions, was cautious in exercising the extraordinary powers so recently vested in him, and fearful of transcending them. John Adams was at that time in the vicinity of the camp, and he asked his opinion as to the practicability and expediency of the plan, and whether it " might not be regarded as beyond his line."

Adams, resolute of spirit, thought the enterprise might easily be accomplished by the friends of liberty in New York, in connection with the Connecticut people, " who are very ready," said he, " upon such occasions."

As to the expediency, he urged the vast importance, in the progress of this war, of the city and province of New York, and the Hudson River, being the *nexus* of the northern and southern colonies, a kind of key to the whole continent, as it is a passage to Canada, to the Great Lakes, and to all the Indian nations. No effort to secure it ought to be omitted.

That it was within the limits of Washington's command, he considered perfectly clear, he being " vested with full power and authority, to act as he should think for the good and welfare of the service."

If there was a body of people on Long Island, armed to oppose the American system of defence, and furnishing supplies to the British army and navy, they were invading American liberty as much as those besieged in Boston.

If, in the city of New York, a body of tories were waiting only for a force to protect them, to declare themselves on the side of the enemy, it was high time that city was secured.*

* Adams to Washington, Corr. of Rev., i. 113.

Thus fortified, as it were, by congressional sanction, through one of its most important members, who pronounced New York as much within his command as Massachusetts; he gave Lee authority to carry out his plans. He was to raise volunteers in Connecticut; march at their head to New York; call in military aid from New Jersey; put the city and the posts on the Hudson, in a posture of security against surprise; disarm all persons on Long Island and elsewhere, inimical to the views of Congress, or secure them in some other manner if necessary; and seize upon all medicines, shirts and blankets, and send them on for the use of the American army.

Lee departed on his mission on the 8th of January. On the 16th, he was at New Haven, railing at the indecision of Congress. They had ordered the enlistment of troops for the security of New York. A Connecticut regiment under Colonel Waterbury had been raised, equipped, and on the point of embarking for Oyster Bay, on Long Island, to attack the tories, who were to be attacked on the other side by Lord Stirling, " when suddenly," says Lee, " Colonel Waterbury received an order to disband his regiment; and the tories are to remain unmolested till they are joined by the king's assassins."

Trumbull, the governor of Connecticut, however, " like a man of sense and spirit," had ordered the regiment to be re-assembled, and Lee trusted it would soon be ready to march with him. " I shall send immediately," said he, " an express to the Congress, informing them of my situation, and at the same time, conjuring them not to suffer the accursed Provincial Congress of New York to defeat measures so absolutely necessary to salvation."

Lee's letter to the President of Congress, showed that the instructions dictated by the moderate and considerate spirit of Washington, were not strong enough on some points, to suit his stern military notions. The scheme, simply of disarming the tories, seemed to him totally ineffectual; it would only embitter their minds, and add virus to their venom. They could and would always be supplied with fresh arms by the enemy. That of seizing the most dangerous, would, from its vagueness, be attended with some bad consequences, and could answer no good one. "The plan of explaining to these deluded people the justice of the American cause, is certainly generous and humane," observed he; "but I am afraid will be fruitless. They are so riveted in their opinions, that I am persuaded, should an angel descend from heaven with his golden trumpet, and ring in their ears that their conduct was criminal, he would be disregarded."

Lee's notion of the policy proper in the present case was, to disarm the disaffected of all classes, supplying our own troops with the arms thus seized; to appraise their estates, and oblige them to deposit at least one half the value with the Continental Congress, as a security for good behavior; to administer the strongest oath that could be devised, that they would act offensively and defensively in support of the common rights; and finally, to transfer all such as should prove refractory, to some place in the interior, where they would not be dangerous.

The people of New York, at all times very excitable, were thrown into a panic on hearing that Lee was in Connecticut, on his way to take military possession of the city. They apprehended his appearance there would provoke an attack from the ships in the harbor. Some, who thought the war about to be brought to their own doors, packed up their effects, and made off

into the country with their wives and children. Others beleaguered the committee of safety with entreaties against the depre-
cated protection of General Lee. The committee, through Pierre
Van Cortlandt, their chairman, addressed a letter to Lee, inquiring into the motives of his coming with an army to New York,
and stating the incapacity of the city to act hostilely against the
ships of war in port, from deficiency of powder, and a want of
military works. For these, and other reasons, they urged the
impropriety of provoking hostilities for the present, and the necessity of "saving appearances," with the ships of war, till at
least the month of March, when they hoped to be able to face
their enemies with some countenance.

"We, therefore," continued the letter, "ardently wish to remain in peace for a little time, and doubt not we have assigned
sufficient reasons for avoiding at present, a dilemma, in which the
entrance of a large body of troops into the city, will almost certainly involve us. Should you have such an entrance in design,
we beg at least the troops may halt on the western confines of
Connecticut, till we have been honored by you with such an explanation on this important subject, as you may conceive your
duty may permit you to enter upon with us, the grounds of
which, you may easily see, ought to be kept an entire secret."

Lee, in reply, dated Stamford, Jan. 23d, disclaimed all intention of commencing actual hostilities against the men-of-war in
the harbor ; his instructions from the commander-in-chief being
solely to prevent the enemy from taking post in the city, or lodg-
ing themselves on Long Island. Some subordinate purposes
were likewise to be executed, which were much more proper to be
communicated by word of mouth than by writing. In compliance with the wishes of the committee, he promised to carry with

him into the town just troops enough to secure it against any present designs of the enemy, leaving his main force on the western border of Connecticut. "I give you my word," added he, "that no active service is proposed, as you seem to apprehend. If the ships of war are quiet, I shall be quiet; but I declare solemnly, that if they make a pretext of my presence to fire on the town, the first house set on flames by their guns shall be the funeral pile of some of their best friends."

In a letter to Washington, written on the following day, he says of his recruiting success in Connecticut: "I find the people throughout this province, more alive and zealous than my most sanguine expectations. I believe I might have collected two thousand volunteers. I take only four companies with me, and Waterbury's regiment. * * * These Connecticutians are, if possible, more eager to go out of their country, than they are to return home, when they have been absent for any considerable time."

Speaking of the people of New York, and the letter from their Provincial Congress, which he encloses: "The whigs," says he, "I mean the stout ones, are, it is said, very desirous that a body of troops should march and be stationed in the city—the timid ones are averse, merely from the spirit of procrastination, which is the characteristic of timidity. The letter from the Provincial Congress, you will observe, breathes the very essence of this spirit; it is wofully hysterical."

By the by, the threat contained in Lee's reply about a "funeral pile," coming from a soldier of his mettle, was not calculated to soothe the hysterical feelings of the committee of safety. How he conducted himself on his arrival in the city, we shall relate in a future chapter.

CHAPTER XV.

FROM amid surrounding perplexities, Washington still turned a hopeful eye to Canada. He expected daily to receive tidings that Montgomery and Arnold were within the walls of Quebec, and he had even written to the former to forward as much as could be spared of the large quantities of arms, blankets, clothing and other military stores, said to be deposited there; the army before Boston being in great need of such supplies.

On the 18th of January came despatches to him from General Schuyler, containing withering tidings. The following is the purport. Montgomery, on the 2d of December, the day after his arrival at Point aux Trembles, set off in face of a driving snow-storm for Quebec, and arrived before it on the 5th. The works, from their great extent, appeared to him incapable of being defended by the actual garrison; made up, as he said, of "Maclean's banditti," the sailors from the frigates and other vessels, together with the citizens obliged to take up arms; most of whom were impatient of the fatigues of a siege, and wished to see matters accommodated amicably. " I propose," added he, " amusing Mr. Carleton with a formal attack, erecting batteries, &c., but mean to assault the works, I believe towards the lower town, which is the weakest part."

According to his own account, his whole force did not exceed nine hundred effective men, three hundred of whom he had brought with him; the rest he found with Colonel Arnold. The latter he pronounced an exceeding fine corps, inured to fatigue, and well accustomed to a cannon shot, having served at Cambridge. "There is a style of discipline among them," adds he, " much superior to what I have been used to see in this campaign. He, himself (Arnold), is active, intelligent and enterprising. Fortune often baffles the sanguine expectations of poor mortals. I am not intoxicated with her favors, but I do think there is a fair prospect of success." *

On the day of his arrival, he sent a flag with a summons to surrender. It was fired upon, and obliged to retire. Exasperated at this outrage, which, it is thought, was committed by the veteran Maclean, Montgomery wrote an indignant, reproachful, and even menacing letter to Carleton, reiterating the demand, magnifying the number of his troops, and warning him against the consequences of an assault. Finding it was rejected from the walls, it was conveyed in by a woman, together with letters addressed to the principal merchants, promising great indulgence in case of immediate submission. By Carleton's orders, the messenger was sent to prison for a few days, and then drummed out of town.

* Montgomery to Schuyler, Dec. 5.

Montgomery now prepared for an attack. The ground was frozen to a great depth, and covered with snow; he was scantily provided with intrenching tools, and had only a field train of artillery, and a few mortars. By dint of excesssive labor a breastwork was thrown up, four hundred yards distant from the walls and opposite to the gate of St. Louis, which is nearly in the centre. It was formed of gabions, ranged side by side, and filled with snow, over which water was thrown until thoroughly frozen. Here Captain Lamb mounted five light pieces and a howitzer. Several mortars were placed in the suburbs of St. Roque, which extends on the left of the promontory, below the heights, and nearly on a level with the river.

From the "Ice Battery" Captain Lamb opened a well-sustained and well-directed fire upon the walls, but his field-pieces were too light to be effective. With his howitzer he threw shells into the town and set it on fire in several places. For five days and nights the garrison was kept on the alert by the teasing fire of this battery. The object of Montgomery was to harass the town, and increase the dissatisfaction of the inhabitants. His flag of truce being still fired upon, he caused the Indians in his camp to shoot arrows into the town, having letters attached to them, addressed to the inhabitants, representing Carleton's refusal to treat, and advising them to rise in a body, and compel him. It was all in vain; whatever might have been the disposition of the inhabitants, they were completely under the control of the military.

On the evening of the fifth day, Montgomery paid a visit to the ice battery. The heavy artillery from the wall had repaid its ineffectual fire with ample usury. The brittle ramparts had been shivered like glass; several of the guns had been rendered useless. Just as they arrived at the battery, a shot from the fortress dismounted one of the guns, and disabled many of the men. A second shot immediately following, was almost as destructive. "This is warm work, sir," said Montgomery to Captain Lamb. "It is indeed, and certainly no place for you, sir." "Why so, captain?" "Because there are enough of us here to be killed, without the loss of you, which would be irreparable."

The general saw the insufficiency of the battery, and, on retiring, gave Captain Lamb permission to leave it whenever he thought proper. The veteran waited until after dark, when, securing all the guns, he abandoned the ruined redoubt. The general in this visit was attended by Aaron Burr, whom he had appointed his aide-de-camp. Lamb wondered that he should encumber himself with such a boy. The perfect coolness and self-possession with which the youth mingled in this dangerous scene, and the fire which sparkled in his eye, soon convinced Lamb, according to his own account, that "the young volunteer was no ordinary man." *

Nearly three weeks had been consumed in these futile operations. The army, ill-clothed, and ill-provided, was becoming impatient of the rigors of a Canadian winter; the term for which part of the troops had enlisted would expire with the year, and they already talked of returning home. Montgomery was sadly conscious of the insufficiency of his means; still he could not endure the thoughts of retiring from before the place without striking a blow. He knew that much was expected from him, in consequence of his late achievements, and that the eyes of the public were fixed upon this Canadian enterprise. He deter-

* Life of John Lamb, p. 125.

mined, therefore, to attempt to carry the place by *escalade*. One third of his men were to set fire to the houses and stockades of the suburb of St. Roque, and force the barriers of the lower town; while the main body should scale the bastion of Cape Diamond.

It was a hazardous, almost a desperate project, yet it has met with the approbation of military men. He calculated upon the devotion and daring spirit of his men; upon the discontent which prevailed among the Canadians, and upon the incompetency of the garrison for the defence of such extensive works.

In regard to the devotion of his men, he was threatened with disappointment. When the plan of assault was submitted to a council of war, three of the captains in Arnold's division, the terms of whose companies were near expiring, declined to serve, unless they and their men could be transferred to another command. This almost mutinous movement, it is supposed, was fomented by Arnold's old adversary, Major Brown, and it was with infinite difficulty Montgomery succeeded in overcoming it.

The ladders were now provided for the *escalade*, and Montgomery waited with impatience for a favorable night to put it into execution. Smallpox and desertion had reduced his little army to seven hundred and fifty men. From certain movements of the enemy, it was surmised that the deserters had revealed his plan. He changed, therefore, the arrangement. Colonel Livingston was to make a false attack on the gate of St. Johns and set fire to it; Major Brown, with another detachment, was to menace the bastion of Cape Diamond. Arnold, with three hundred and fifty of the hardy fellows who had followed him through the wilderness, strengthened by Captain Lamb and forty of his company, was to assault the suburbs and batteries of St. Roque;

VOL. II.—7

while Montgomery, with the residue of his forces, was to pass below the bastion at Cape Diamond, defile along the river, carry the defences at Drummond's Wharf, and thus enter the lower town on one side, while Arnold forced his way into it on the other. These movements were all to be made at the same time, on the discharge of signal rockets, thus distracting the enemy, and calling their attention to four several points.

On the 31st of December, at two o'clock in the morning, the troops repaired to their several destinations, under cover of a violent snow-storm. By some accident or mistake, such as is apt to occur in complicated plans of attack, the signal rockets were let off before the lower divisions had time to get to their fighting ground. They were descried by one of Maclean's Highland officers, who gave the alarm. Livingston, also, failed to make the false attack on the gate of St. Johns, which was to have caused a diversion favorable to Arnold's attack on the suburb below.

The feint by Major Brown, on the bastion of Cape Diamond, was successful, and concealed the march of General Montgomery. That gallant commander descended from the heights to Wolfe's Cove, and led his division along the shore of the St. Lawrence, round the beetling promontory of Cape Diamond. The narrow approach to the lower town in that direction was traversed by a picket or stockade, defended by Canadian militia; beyond which was a second defence, a kind of block-house, forming a battery of small pieces, manned by Canadian militia, and a few seamen, and commanded by the captain of a transport. The aim of Montgomery was to come upon these barriers by surprise. The pass which they defended is formidable at all times, having a swift river on one side, and overhanging precipices on the other; but at this time was rendered peculiarly difficult by drifting snow, and by great masses of ice piled on each other at the foot of the cliffs.

The troops made their way painfully, in extended and straggling files, along the narrow footway, and over the slippery piles of ice. Among the foremost, were some of the first New York regiment, led on by Captain Cheeseman. Montgomery, who was familiar with them, urged them on. "Forward, men of New York!" cried he. "You are not the men to flinch when your general leads you on!" In his eagerness, he threw himself far in the advance, with his pioneers and a few officers, and made a dash at the first barrier. The Canadians stationed there, taken by surprise, made a few random shots, then threw down their muskets and fled. Montgomery sprang forward, aided with his own hand to pluck down the pickets, which the pioneers were sawing, and having made a breach sufficiently wide to admit three or four men abreast, entered sword in hand, followed by his staff, Captain Cheeseman, and some of his men. The Canadians had fled from the picket to the battery or block-house, but seemed to have carried the panic with them, for the battery remained silent. Montgomery felt for a moment as if the surprise had been complete. He paused in the breach to rally on the troops, who were stumbling along the difficult pass. "Push on, my brave boys," cried he, " Quebec is ours !"

He again dashed forward, but, when within forty paces of the battery, a discharge of grape-shot from a single cannon, made deadly havoc. Mongtomery, and McPherson, one of his aides, were killed on the spot. Captain Cheeseman, who was leading on his New Yorkers, received a canister shot through the body; made an effort to rise and push forward, but fell back a corpse; with him fell his orderly sergeant and several of his men. This fearful slaughter, and the death of their general, threw every thing in confusion. The officer next in lineal rank to the general, was far in the rear; in this emergency, Colonel Campbell, quarter-master-general, took the command, but, instead of rallying the men, and endeavoring to effect the junction with Arnold, ordered a retreat, and abandoned the half-won field, leaving behind him the bodies of the slain.

While all this was occurring on the side of Cape Diamond, Arnold led his division against the opposite side of the lower town along the suburb and street of St. Roque. Like Montgomery, he took the advance at the head of a forlorn hope of twenty-five men, accompanied by his secretary Oswald, formerly one of his captains at Ticonderoga. Captain Lamb and his artillery company came next, with a field-piece mounted on a sledge. Then came a company with ladders and scaling implements, followed by Morgan and his riflemen. In the rear of all these came the main body. A battery on a wharf commanded the narrow pass by which they had to advance. This was to be attacked with the field-piece, and then scaled with ladders by the forlorn hope; while Captain Morgan with his riflemen, was to pass round the wharf on the ice.

The false attack which was to have been made by Livingston on the gate of St. Johns, by way of diversion, had not taken place; there was nothing, therefore, to call off the attention of the enemy in this quarter from the detachment. The troops, as they straggled along in lengthened file through the drifting snow, were sadly galled by a flanking fire on the right, from walls and pickets. The field-piece at length became so deeply embedded in a snow-drift, that it could not be moved. Lamb sent word to Arnold of the impediment; in the mean time, he and his artillery company were brought to a halt. The company with the scaling ladders would have halted also, having been told to keep in the rear of the artillery; but they were urged on by Morgan with a thundering oath, who pushed on after them with his riflemen, the artillery company opening to the right and left to let them pass.

They arrived in the advance, just as Arnold was leading on his forlorn hope to attack the barrier. Before he reached it, a severe wound in the right leg with a musket ball completely disabled him, and he had to be borne from the field. Morgan instantly took the command. Just then Lamb came up with his company, armed with muskets and bayonets, having received orders to abandon the field-piece, and support the advance. Oswald joined him with the forlorn hope. The battery which commanded the defile mounted two pieces of cannon. There was a discharge of grape-shot when the assailants were close under the muzzles of the guns, yet but one man was killed. Before there could be a second discharge, the battery was carried by assault, some firing into the embrasures; others scaling the walls. The captain and thirty of his men were taken prisoners.

The day was just dawning as Morgan led on to attack the second barrier, and his men had to advance under a fire from the town walls on their right, which incessantly thinned their ranks. The second barrier was reached; they applied their scaling ladders to storm it. The defence was brave and obstinate, but the defenders were at length driven from their guns, and the battery was gained. At the last moment one of the gunners ran back, linstock in hand, to give one more shot. Captain Lamb snapped a fusee at him. It missed fire. The cannon was discharged, and a grape-shot wounded Lamb in the head, carrying away part of the cheek-bone. He was borne off senseless, to a neighboring shed.

The two barriers being now taken, the way on this side into the lower town seemed open. Morgan prepared to enter it with the victorious vanguard; first stationing Captain Dearborn and some provincials at Palace Gate, which opened down into the defile from the upper town. By this time, however, the death of Montgomery and retreat of Campbell, had enabled the enemy to turn all their attention in this direction. A large detachment sent by General Carleton, sallied out of Palace Gate after Morgan had passed it, surprised and captured Dearborn and the guard, and completely cut off the advanced party. The main body, informed of the death of Montgomery, and giving up the game as lost, retreated to the camp, leaving behind the field-piece which Lamb's company had abandoned, and the mortars in the battery of St. Roque.

Morgan and his men were now hemmed in on all sides, and obliged to take refuge in a stone house, from the inveterate fire which assailed them. From the windows of this house they kept up a desperate defence, until cannon were brought to bear upon it. Then, hearing of the death of Montgomery, and seeing that there was no prospect of relief, Morgan and his gallant handful of followers were compelled to surrender themselves prisoners of war.

Thus foiled at every point, the wrecks of the little army abandoned their camp, and retreated about three miles from the town; where they hastily fortified themselves, apprehending a pursuit by the garrison. General Carleton, however, contented himself with having secured the safety of the place, and remained cautiously passive until he should be properly reinforced; distrusting the good faith of the motley inhabitants. He is said to have treated the prisoners with a humanity the more honorable, considering the "habitual military severity of his temper;" their heroic daring, displayed in the assault upon the lower town, having excited his admiration.

The remains of the gallant Montgomery received a soldier's grave, within the fortifications of Quebec, by the care of Cramahé, the lieutenant-governor, who had formerly known him.

Arnold, wounded and disabled, had been assisted back to the camp, dragging one foot after the other for nearly a mile in great agony, and exposed continually to the musketry from the walls at fifty yards' distance, which shot down several at his side.

He took temporary command of the shattered army, until General Wooster should arrive from Montreal, to whom he sent an express, urging him to bring on succor. "On this occasion," says a contemporary writer, "he discovered the utmost vigor of a determined mind, and a genius full of resources. Defeated and wounded, as he was, he put his troops into such a situation as to keep them still formidable. *

With a mere handful of men, at one time not exceeding five hundred, he maintained a blockade of the strong fortress from which he had just been repulsed. "I have no thoughts," writes he, "of leaving this proud town until I enter it in triumph. *I am in the way of my duty, and I know no fear!*" †

Happy for him had he fallen at this moment.—Happy for him had he found a soldier's and a patriot's grave, beneath the rock-built walls of Quebec. Those walls would have remained

* Civil War in America, vol. i. p. 112.
† See Arnold's Letter. Remembrancer, ii. 368.

enduring monuments of his renown. His name, like that of
Montgomery, would have been treasured up among the dearest
though most mournful recollections of his country, and that
country would have been spared the single traitorous blot that
dims the bright page of its revolutionary history.

CHAPTER XVI.

CORRESPONDENCE OF WASHINGTON AND SCHUYLER ON THE DISASTERS IN CANADA—REINFORCEMENTS REQUIRED FROM NEW ENGLAND—DANGERS IN THE INTERIOR OF NEW YORK—JOHNSON HALL BELEAGUERED—SIR JOHN CAPITULATES—GENEROUS CONDUCT OF SCHUYLER—GOVERNOR TRYON AND THE TORIES—TORY MACHINATIONS—LEE AT NEW YORK—SIR HENRY CLINTON IN THE HARBOR—MENACES OF LEE—THE CITY AND RIVER FORTIFIED—LEE'S TREATMENT OF THE TORIES—HIS PLANS OF FORTIFICATION—ORDERED TO THE COMMAND IN CANADA—HIS SPECULATIONS ON TITLES OF DIGNITY.

SCHUYLER'S letter to Washington, announcing the recent events, was written with manly feeling. "I wish," said he, "I had no occasion to send my dear general this melancholy account. My amiable friend, the gallant Montgomery, is no more; the brave Arnold is wounded; and we have met with a severe check in an unsuccessful attempt on Quebec. May Heaven be graciously pleased that the misfortune may terminate here! I tremble for our people in Canada."

Alluding to his recent request to retire from the army, he writes: "Our affairs are much worse than when I made the request. This is motive sufficient for me to continue to serve my country in any way I can be thought most serviceable; but my utmost can be but little, weak and indisposed as I am."

Washington was deeply moved by the disastrous intelligence. "I most sincerely condole with you," writes he, in reply to Schuyler, "upon the fall of the brave and worthy Montgomery. In the death of this gentleman, America has sustained a heavy loss. I am much concerned for the intrepid and enterprising Arnold, and greatly fear that consequences of the most alarming nature will result from this well-intended, but unfortunate attempt."

General Schuyler, who was now in Albany, urged the necessity of an immediate reinforcement of three thousand men for the army in Canada. Washington had not a man to spare from the army before Boston. He applied, therefore, on his own responsibility, to Massachusetts, New Hampshire and Connecticut, for three regiments, which were granted. His prompt measure received the approbation of Congress, and further reinforcements were ordered from the same quarters.

Solicitude was awakened about the interior of the province of New York. Arms and ammunition were said to be concealed in Tryon County, and numbers of the tories in that neighborhood preparing for hostilities. Sir John Johnson had fortified Johnson Hall, gathered about him his Scotch Highland tenants and Indian allies, and it was rumored he intended to carry fire and sword along the valley of the Mohawk.

Schuyler, in consequence, received orders from Congress to take measures for securing the military stores, disarming the disaffected, and apprehending their chiefs. He forthwith hastened from Albany, at the head of a body of soldiers; was joined by Colonel Herkimer, with the militia of Tryon County marshalled forth on the frozen bosom of the Mohawk River, and appeared

before Sir John's stronghold, near Johnstown, on the 19th of
January.

Thus beleaguered, Sir John, after much negotiation, capitulated. He was to surrender all weapons of war and military
stores in his possession, and to give his parole not to take arms
against America. On these conditions he was to be at liberty
to go as far westward in Tryon County as the German Flats and
Kingsland districts, and to every part of the colony to the southward and eastward of these districts; provided he did not go
into any seaport town.

Sir John intimated a trust, that he, and the gentlemen with
him, would be permitted to retain such arms as were their own
property. The reply was characteristic: "General Schuyler's
feelings as a gentleman, induce him to consent that Sir John
Johnson may retain the few favorite family arms, he making a
list of them. General Schuyler never refused a gentleman his
side-arms."

The capitulation being adjusted, Schuyler ordered his troops
to be drawn up in line at noon (Jan. 20th), between his quarters
and the Court House, to receive the surrender of the Highlanders, enjoining profound silence on his officers and men, when the
surrender should be made. Every thing was conducted with
great regard to the feelings of Sir John's Scottish adherents;
they marched to the front, grounded their arms, and were dismissed with exhortations to good behavior.

The conduct of Schuyler, throughout this affair, drew forth a
resolution of Congress, applauding him for his fidelity, prudence
and expedition, and the proper temper he had maintained toward
the "deluded people" in question. Washington, too, congratu-
lated him on his success. "I hope," writes he, "General Lee

will execute a work of the same kind on Long Island. It is high time to begin with our internal foes, when we are threatened with such severity of chastisement from our kind parent without."

The recent reverses in Canada had, in fact, heightened the solicitude of Washington about the province of New York. That province was the central and all-important link in the confederacy; but he feared it might prove a brittle one. We have already mentioned the adverse influences in operation there. A large number of friends to the crown, among the official and commercial classes; rank tories, (as they were called,) in the city and about the neighboring country; particularly on Long and Staten Islands; king's ships at anchor in the bay and harbor, keeping up a suspicious intercourse with the citizens; while Governor Tryon, castled, as it were, on board one of these ships, carried on intrigues with those disaffected to the popular cause, in all parts of the neighborhood. County committees had been empowered by the New York Congress and convention, to apprehend all persons notoriously disaffected, to examine into their conduct, and ascertain whether they were guilty of any hostile act or machination. Imprisonment or banishment was the penalty. The committees could call upon the militia to aid in the discharge of their functions. Still, disaffection to the cause was said to be rife in the province, and Washington looked to General Lee for effective measures to suppress it.

Lee arrived at New York on the 4th of February, his caustic humors sharpened by a severe attack of the gout, which had rendered it necessary, while on the march, to carry him for a considerable part of the way in a litter. His correspondence is a complete mental barometer. " I consider it as a piece of the greatest good fortune," writes he to Washington (Feb. 5th), " that the

Congress have detached a committee to this place, otherwise I should have made a most ridiculous figure, besides bringing upon myself the enmity of the whole province. My hands were effectually tied up from taking any step necessary for the public service by the late resolve of Congress, putting every detachment of the continental forces under the command of the Provincial Congress where such detachment is."

By a singular coincidence, on the very day of his arrival Sir Henry Clinton, with the squadron which had sailed so mysteriously from Boston, looked into the harbor. " Though it was Sabbath," says a letter-writer of the day, " it threw the whole city into such a convulsion as it never knew before. Many of the inhabitants hastened to move their effects into the country, expecting an immediate conflict. All that day and all night, were there carts going and boats loading, and women and children crying, and distressed voices heard in the roads in the dead of the night." *

Clinton sent for the mayor, and expressed much surprise and concern at the distress caused by his arrival; which was merely, he said, on a short visit to his friend Tryon, and to see how matters stood. He professed a juvenile love for the place, and desired that the inhabitants might be informed of the purport of his visit, and that he would go away as soon as possible.

" He brought no troops with him," writes Lee, " and pledges his honor that none are coming. He says it is merely a visit to his friend Tryon. If it is really so, it is the most whimsical piece of civility I ever heard of."

A gentleman in New York, writing to a friend in Philadelphia, reports one of the general's characteristic menaces, which kept the town in a fever.

* Remembrancer, vol. iii.

"Lee says, he will send word on board of the men-of-war, that, if they set a house on fire, he will chain a hundred of their friends by the neck, and make the house their funeral pile." *

For this time, the inhabitants of New York were let off for their fears. Clinton, after a brief visit, continued his mysterious cruise, openly avowing his destination to be North Carolina— which nobody believed, simply because he avowed it.

The Duke of Manchester, speaking in the House of Lords of the conduct of Clinton, contrasts it with that of Lôrd Dunmore, who wrapped Norfolk in flames. "I will pass no censure on that noble lord," said he, "but I could wish that he had acted with that generous spirit that forbade Clinton uselessly to destroy the town of New York. My lords, Clinton visited New York; the inhabitants expected its destruction. Lee appeared before it with an army too powerful to be attacked, and Clinton passed by without doing any wanton damage."

The necessity of conferring with committees at every step, was a hard restraint upon a man of Lee's ardent and impatient temper, who had a soldierlike contempt for the men of peace around him; yet at the outset he bore it better than might have been expected.

"The Congress committees, a certain number of the committees of safety, and your humble servant," writes he to Washington, "have had two conferences. The result is such as will agreeably surprise you. It is in the first place agreed, and justly, that to fortify the town against shipping is impracticable; but we are to fortify lodgments on some commanding part of the city for two thousand men. We are to erect enclosed batteries on

* Am. Archives, 5th Series, iv. 941.

both sides of the water, near Hell Gate, which will answer the double purpose of securing the town against piracies through the Sound, and secure our communication with Long Island, now become a more important point than ever; as it is determined to form a strong fortified camp of three thousand men, on the Island, immediately opposite to New York. The pass in the Highlands is to be made as respectable as possible, and guarded by a battalion. In short, I think the plan judicious and complete."

The pass in the Highlands above alluded to, is that grand defile of the Hudson, where, for upwards of fifteen miles, it wends its deep channel between stern, forest-clad mountains and rocky promontories. Two forts, about six miles distant from each other, and commanding narrow parts of the river at its bends through these Highlands, had been commenced in the preceding autumn, by order of the Continental Congress; but they were said to be insufficient for the security of that important pass, and were to be extended and strengthened.

Washington had charged Lee, in his instructions, to keep a stern eye upon the tories, who were active in New York. "You can seize upon the persons of the principals," said he; "they must be so notoriously known, that there will be little danger of committing mistakes." Lee acted up to the letter of these instructions, and weeded out with a vigorous hand, some of the rankest of the growth. This gave great offence to the peace-loving citizens, who insisted that he was arrogating a power vested solely in the civil authority. One of them, well-affected to the cause, writes: "To see the vast number of houses shut up, one would think the city almost evacuated. Women and children are scarcely to be seen in the streets. Troops are daily coming in;

they break open and quarter themselves in any house they find shut." *

The enemy, too, regarded his measures with apprehension. "That arch rebel Lee," writes a British officer, "has driven all the well-affected people from the town of New York. If something is not speedily done, his Britannic majesty's American dominions will be confined within a very narrow compass." †

In the exercise of his military functions, Lee set Governor Tryon and the captain of the Asia at defiance. "They had threatened perdition to the town," writes he to Washington, "if the cannon were removed from the batteries and wharves, but I ever considered their threats as a *brutum fulmen*, and even persuaded the town to be of the same way of thinking. We accordingly conveyed them to a place of safety in the middle of the day, and no cannonade ensued. Captain Parker publishes a pleasant reason for his passive conduct. He says that it was manifestly my intention, and that of the New England men under my command, to bring destruction on this town, so hated for their loyal principles, but that he was determined not to indulge us; so remained quiet out of spite. The people here laugh at his nonsense, and begin to despise the menaces which formerly used to throw them into convulsions."

Washington appears to have shared the merriment. In his reply to Lee, he writes, "I could not avoid laughing at Captain Parker's reasons for not putting his repeated threats into execution,"—a proof, by the way, under his own hand, that he could laugh occasionally; and even when surrounded by perplexities.

According to Lee's account, the New Yorkers showed a won-

* Fred. Rhinelander to Peter Van Schaack, Feb. 23.
† Am. Archives, v. 425.

derful alacrity in removing the cannon. "Men and boys of all ages," writes he, "worked with the greatest zeal and pleasure. I really believe the generality are as well affected as any on the continent." Some of the well-affected, however, thought he was rather too self-willed and high-handed. "Though General Lee has many things to recommend him as a general," writes one of them, "yet I think he was out of luck when he ordered the removal of the guns from the battery; as it was without the approbation or knowledge of our Congress." *—Lee seldom waited for the approbation of Congress in moments of exigency.

He now proceeded with his plan of defences. A strong redoubt, capable of holding three hundred men, was commenced at Horen's Hook, commanding the pass at Hell Gate, so as to block up from the enemy's ships, the passage between the mainland and Long Island. A regiment was stationed on the island, making fascines, and preparing other materials for constructing the works for an intrenched camp, which Lee hoped would render it impossible for the enemy to get a footing there. "What to do with this city," writes he, "I own, puzzles me. It is so encircled with deep navigable water, that whoever commands the sea must command the town. To-morrow I shall begin to dismantle that part of the fort next to the town, to prevent its being converted into a citadel. I shall barrier the principal streets, and, at least, if I cannot make it a continental garrison, it shall be a disputable field of battle." Batteries were to be erected on an eminence behind Trinity Church, to keep the enemy's ships at so great a distance as not to injure the town.

King's Bridge, at the upper end of Manhattan or New York

* Fred. Rhinelander to Peter Van Schaack.

Island, linking it with the mainland, was pronounced by Lee "a most important pass, without which the city could have no communication with Connecticut." It was, therefore, to be made as strong as possible.

Heavy cannon were to be sent up to the forts in the Highlands; which were to be enlarged and strengthened.

In the midst of his schemes, Lee received orders from Congress to the command in Canada, vacant by the death of Montgomery. He bewailed the defenceless condition of the city; the Continental Congress, as he said, not having, as yet, taken the least step for its security. "The instant I leave it," said he, "I conclude the Provincial Congress, and inhabitants in general, will relapse into their former hysterics. The men-of-war and Mr. Tryon will return to their old station at the wharves, and the first regiments who arrive from England, will take quiet possession of the town and Long Island."

It must be observed that, in consequence of his military demonstrations in the city, the enemy's ships had drawn off and dropped down the bay; and he had taken vigorous measures, without consulting the committees, to put an end to the practice of supplying them with provisions.

"Governor Tryon and the Asia," writes he to Washington, "continue between Nutten and Bedlow's Islands. It has pleased his excellency, in violation of the compact he has made, to seize several vessels from Jersey laden with flour. It has, in return, pleased my excellency to stop all provisions from the city, and cut off all intercourse with him,—a measure which has thrown the mayor, council, and tories into agonies. The propensity, or rather rage, for paying court to this great man, is inconceivable. They cannot be weaned from him. We must put wormwood on his paps, or they will cry to suck, as they are in their second childhood."

We would observe, in explanation of a sarcasm in the above quoted letter, that Lee professed a great contempt for the titles of respect which it was the custom to prefix to the names of men in office or command. He scoffed at them, as unworthy of "a great, free, manly, equal commonwealth." "For my own part," said he, "I would as lief they would put ratsbane in my mouth, as the excellency with which I am daily crammed. How much more true dignity was there in the simplicity of address among the Romans! Marcus Tullius Cicero, Decius Bruto Imperatori, or Caio Marcello Consuli, than to 'His Excellency Major-general Noodle,' or to the 'Honorable John Doodle.'"

CHAPTER XVII.

MONOTONOUS STATE OE AFFAIRS BEFORE BOSTON—WASHINGTON ANXIOUS FOR ACTION—EXPLOIT OF PUTNAM—ITS DRAMATIC CONSEQUENCES—THE FARCE OF THE BLOCKADE OF BOSTON—AN ALARMING INTERRUPTION—DISTRESSES OF THE BESIEGED—WASHINGTON'S IRKSOME PREDICAMENT—HIS BOLD PROPOSITION—DEMUR OF THE COUNCIL OF WAR—ARRIVAL OF KNOX WITH ARTILLERY—DORCHESTER HEIGHTS TO BE SEIZED AND FORTIFIED—PREPARATIONS FOR THE ATTEMPT.

THE siege of Boston continued through the winter, without any striking incident to enliven its monotony. The British remained within their works, leaving the beleaguering army slowly to augment its forces. The country was dissatisfied with the inaction of the latter. Even Congress was anxious for some successful blow that might revive popular enthusiasm. Washington shared this anxiety, and had repeatedly, in councils of war, suggested an attack upon the town, but had found a majority of his general officers opposed to it. He had hoped some favorable opportunity would present, when, the harbor being frozen, the troops might approach the town upon the ice. The winter, however, though severe at first, proved a mild one, and the bay continued open. General Putnam, in the mean time, having completed the new works at Lechmere Point, and being desirous of keeping up the spirit of his men, resolved to treat them to an exploit. Accordingly, from his "impregnable fortress" of Cobble Hill, he detached a party of about two hundred, under his favorite officer, Major Knowlton, to surprise and capture a British guard stationed at Charlestown. It was a daring enterprise, and executed with spirit. As Charlestown Neck was completely protected, Knowlton led his men across the mill-dam, round the base of the hill, and immediately below the fort; set fire to the guard-house and some buildings in its vicinity; made several prisoners, and retired without loss; although thundered upon by the cannon of the fort. The exploit was attended by a dramatic effect on which Putnam had not calculated. The British officers, early in the winter, had fitted up a theatre, which was well attended by the troops and tories. On the evening in question, an afterpiece was to be performed, entitled "The Blockade of Boston," intended as a burlesque on the patriot army which was beleaguering it. Washington is said to have been represented in it as an awkward lout, equipped with a huge wig, and a long rusty sword, attended by a country booby as orderly sergeant, in rustic garb, with an old firelock seven or eight feet long.

The theatre was crowded, especially by the military. The first piece was over, and the curtain was rising for the farce, when a sergeant made his appearance, and announced that "the alarm guns were firing at Charlestown, and the Yankees attacking Bunker's Hill." At first this was supposed to be a part of the entertainment, until General Howe gave the word, "Officers, to your alarm posts."

Great confusion ensued; every one scrambled out of the theatre as fast as possible. There was, as usual, some shrieking and fainting of ladies; and the farce of "The Blockade of Boston" had a more serious than comic termination.

The London Chronicle, in a sneering comment on Boston affairs, gave Burgoyne as the author of this burlesque afterpiece, though perhaps unjustly. "General Burgoyne has opened a theatrical campaign, of which himself is sole manager, being determined to act with the Provincials on the defensive only. Tom Thumb has been already represented; while, on the other hand, the Provincials are preparing to exhibit, early in the spring, 'Measure for Measure.'"

The British officers, like all soldiers by profession, endeavored to while away the time by every amusement within their reach; but, in truth, the condition of the besieged town was daily becoming more and more distressing. The inhabitants were without flour, pulse, or vegetables; the troops were nearly as destitute. There was a lack of fuel, too, as well as food. The smallpox broke out, and it was necessary to inoculate the army. Men, women and children either left the city voluntarily, or were sent out of it; yet the distress increased. Several houses were broken open and plundered; others were demolished by the soldiery for fuel. General Howe resorted to the sternest measures to put a stop to these excesses. The provost was ordered to go the rounds with the hangman, and hang up the first man he should detect in the fact, without waiting for further proof for trial. Offenders were punished with four hundred, six hundred, and even one thousand lashes. The wife of a private soldier, convicted of receiving stolen goods, was sentenced to one hundred lashes on her bare back, at the cart's tail, in different parts of the town, and an imprisonment of three months.

Meanwhile, Washington was incessantly goaded by the impatient murmurs of the public, as we may judge by his letters to Mr. Reed. "I know the integrity of my own heart," writes he, on the 10th of February; "but to declare it, unless to a friend, may be an argument of vanity. I know the unhappy predicament I stand in; I know that much is expected of me; I know that, without men, without arms, without ammunition, without any thing fit for the accommodation of a soldier, little is to be done; and, what is mortifying, I know that I cannot stand justified to the world without exposing my own weakness, and injuring the cause, by declaring my wants; which I am determined not to do, further than unavoidable necessity brings every man acquainted with them.

"My own situation is so irksome to me at times, that, if I did not consult the public good more than my own tranquillity, I should long ere this have put every thing on the cast of a die. So far from my having an army of twenty thousand men, well armed, I have been here with less than one half of that number, including sick, furloughed, and on command; and those neither armed nor clothed as they should be. In short, my situation has been such, that I have been obliged to use art, to conceal it from my own officers."

How precious are those letters! And how fortunate that the absence of Mr. Reed from camp, should have procured for us such confidential outpourings of Washington's heart at this time of its great trial.

He still adhered to his opinion in favor of an attempt upon the town. He was aware that it would be attended with considerable loss, but believed it would be successful if the men should behave well. Within a few days after the date of this letter, the bay became sufficiently frozen for the transportation of troops. "This," writes he to Reed, "I thought, knowing the ice would not last, a favorable opportunity to make an assault upon the troops in town. I proposed it in council; but behold, though we had been waiting all the year for this favorable event, the enterprise was thought too dangerous. Perhaps it was; perhaps the irksomeness of my situation led me to undertake more than could be warranted by prudence. I did not think so, and I am sure yet that the enterprise, if it had been undertaken with resolution, must have succeeded; without it, any would fail."

His proposition was too bold for the field-officers assembled in council (Feb. 16th), who objected that there was not force, nor arms and ammunition sufficient in camp for such an attempt. Washington acquiesced in the decision, it being almost unanimous; yet he felt the irksomeness of his situation. "To have the eyes of the whole continent," said he, "fixed with anxious expectation of hearing of some great event, and to be restrained in every military operation for want of the necessary means of carrying it on, is not very pleasing, especially as the means used to conceal my weakness from the enemy, conceal it also from our friends, and add to their wonder."

In the council of war above mentioned, a cannonade and bombardment were considered advisable, as soon as there should be a sufficiency of powder; in the mean time, preparations might be made for taking possession of Dorchester Heights, and Noddle's Island.

At length the camp was rejoiced by the arrival of Colonel Knox, with his long train of sledges drawn by oxen, bringing more than fifty cannon, mortars, and howitzers, beside supplies of lead and flints. The zeal and perseverance which he had displayed in his wintry expedition across frozen lakes and snowy wastes, and the intelligence with which he had fulfilled his instructions, won him the entire confidence of Washington. His conduct in this enterprise was but an earnest of that energy and ability which he displayed throughout the war.

Further ammunition being received from the royal arsenal at New York, and other quarters, and a reinforcement of ten regiments of militia, Washington no longer met with opposition to his warlike measures. Lechmere Point, which Putnam had fortified, was immediately to be supplied with mortars and heavy cannon, so as to command Boston on the north; and Dorchester Heights, on the south of the town, were forthwith to be taken possession of. "If any thing," said Washington, "will induce the enemy to hazard an engagement, it will be our attempting to fortify those heights, as, in that event taking place, we shall be able to command a great part of the town, and almost the whole harbor." Their possession, moreover, would enable him to push his works to Nook's Hill, and other points opposite Boston, whence a cannonade and bombardment must drive the enemy from the city.

The council of Massachusetts, at his request, ordered the militia of the towns contiguous to Dorchester and Roxbury, to hold themselves in readiness to repair to the lines at those places with arms, ammunition and accoutrements, on receiving a preconcerted signal.

Washington felt painfully aware how much depended upon the success of this attempt. There was a cloud of gloom and distrust lowering upon the public mind. Danger threatened on the north and on the south. Montgomery had fallen before the walls of Quebec. The army in Canada was shattered. Tryon and the tories were plotting mischief in New York. Dunmore was harassing the lower part of Virginia, and Clinton and his fleet were prowling along the coast, on a secret errand of mischief.

Washington's general orders evince the solemn and anxious state of his feelings. In those of the 26th of February, he forbade all playing at cards and other games of chance. "At this time of public distress," writes he, "men may find enough to do in the service of God and their country, without abandoning themselves to vice and immorality. * * * * It is a noble cause we are engaged in; it is the cause of virtue and mankind; every advantage and comfort to us and our posterity depend upon the vigor of our exertions; in short, freedom or slavery must be the result of our conduct; there can, therefore, be no greater inducement to men to behave well. But it may not be amiss to the troops to know, that, if any man in action shall presume to skulk, hide himself, or retreat from the enemy without the orders of his commanding officer, he will be instantly shot down as an example of cowardice; cowards having too frequently disconcerted the best formed troops by their dastardly behavior."

In the general plan it was concerted, that, should the enemy detach a large force to dislodge our men from Dorchester Heights, as had been done in the affair of Bunker's Hill, an attack upon the opposite side of the town should forthwith be made by General Putnam. For this purpose he was to have four thousand picked men in readiness, in two divisions, under Generals Sullivan and Greene. At a concerted signal from Roxbury, they were to embark in boats near the mouth of Charles River, cross under cover of the fire of three floating batteries, land in two places in Boston, secure its strong posts, force the gates and works at the Neck, and let in the Roxbury troops.

CHAPTER XVIII.

THE AFFAIR OF DORCHESTER HEIGHTS—AMERICAN AND ENGLISH LETTERS RE-
SPECTING IT—A LABORIOUS NIGHT—REVELATIONS AT DAYBREAK—HOWE IN
A PERPLEXITY—A NIGHT ATTACK MEDITATED—STORMY WEATHER—THE
TOWN TO BE EVACUATED—NEGOTIATIONS AND ARRANGEMENTS—PREPARA-
TIONS TO EMBARK—EXCESSES OF THE TROOPS—BOSTON EVACUATED—SPEECH
OF THE DUKE OF MANCHESTER ON THE SUBJECT—A MEDAL VOTED BY CON-
GRESS.

THE evening of Monday, the 4th of March, was fixed upon for
the occupation of Dorchester Heights. The ground was frozen
too hard to be easily intrenched; fascines, therefore, and gabions,
and bundles of screwed hay, were collected during the two preceding nights, with which to form breastworks and redoubts.
During these two busy nights the enemy's batteries were cannonaded and bombarded from opposite points, to occupy their
attention, and prevent their noticing these preparations. They
replied with spirit, and the incessant roar of artillery thus kept
up, covered completely the rumbling of waggons and ordnance.

How little the enemy were aware of what was impending, we
may gather from the following extract of a letter from an officer
of distinction in the British army in Boston to his friend in London, dated on the 3d of March:

"For these last six weeks or near two months, we have been

better amused than could possibly be expected in our situation. We had a theatre, we had balls, and there is actually a subscription on foot for a masquerade. England seems to have forgot us, and we have endeavored to forget ourselves. But we were roused to a sense of our situation last night, in a manner unpleasant enough. The rebels have been for some time past erecting a bomb battery, and last night began to play upon us. Two shells fell not far from me. One fell upon Colonel Monckton's house, but luckily did not burst until it had crossed the street. Many houses were damaged, but no lives lost. The rebel army," adds he, " is not brave, I believe, but it is agreed on all hands that their artillery officers are at least equal to ours." *

The wife of John Adams, who resided in the vicinity of the American camp, and knew that a general action was meditated, expresses in a letter to her husband the feelings of a patriot woman during the suspense of these nights.

" I have been in a constant state of anxiety, since you left me," writes she on Saturday. " It has been said to-morrow, and to-morrow for this month, and when the dreadful to-morrow will be, I know not. But hark! The house this instant shakes with the roar of cannon. I have been to the door, and find it is a cannonade from our army. Orders, I find, are come, for all the remaining militia to repair to the lines Monday night, by twelve o'clock. No sleep for me to-night."

On Sunday the letter is resumed. " I went to bed after twelve, but got no rest; the cannon continued firing, and my heart kept pace with them all night. We have had a pretty quiet day, but what to-morrow will bring forth, God only knows."

* Am. Archives, 4th Series, v. 425.

On Monday, the appointed evening, she continues: "I have just returned from Penn's Hill, where I have been sitting to hear the amazing roar of cannon, and from whence I could see every shell which was thrown. The sound, I think, is one of the grandest in nature, and is of the true species of the sublime. 'Tis now an incessant roar; but oh, the fatal ideas which are connected with the sound! How many of our dear countrymen must fall!

"I went to bed about twelve, and rose again a little after one. I could no more sleep than if I had been in the engagement; the rattling of the windows, the jar of the house, the continual roar of twenty-four pounders, and the bursting of shells, give us such ideas, and realize a scene to us of which we could scarcely form any conception. I hope to give you joy of Boston, even if it is in ruins, before I send this away."

On the Monday evening thus graphically described, as soon as the firing commenced, the detachment under General Thomas set out on its cautious and secret march from the lines of Roxbury and Dorchester. Every thing was conducted as regularly and quietly as possible. A covering party of eight hundred men preceded the carts with the intrenching tools; then came General Thomas with the working party, twelve hundred strong, followed by a train of three hundred waggons, laden with fascines, gabions, and hay screwed into bundles of seven or eight hundred weight. A great number of such bundles were ranged in a line along Dorchester Neck on the side next the enemy, to protect the troops, while passing, from being raked by the fire of the enemy. Fortunately, although the moon, as Washington writes, was shining in its full lustre, the flash and roar of cannonry from opposite points, and the bursting of bombshells high in the air, so engaged and diverted the attention of the enemy, that the detachment reached the heights about eight o'clock, without being heard or perceived.   The covering party then divided; one half proceeded to the point nearest Boston, the other to the one nearest to Castle Williams.   The working party commenced to fortify, under the directions of Gridley, the veteran engineer, who had planned the works on Bunker's Hill.   It was severe labor, for the earth was frozen eighteen inches deep; but the men worked with more than their usual spirit; for the eye of the commander-in-chief was upon them.   Though not called there by his duties, Washington could not be absent from this eventful operation.   An eloquent orator has imagined his situation—"All around him intense movement; while nothing was to be heard excepting the tread of busy feet, and the dull sound of the mattock upon the frozen soil. Beneath him the slumbering batteries of the castle; the road-steads and harbor filled with the vessls of the royal fleet, motionless, except as they swung round at their moorings at the turn of the midnight tide; the beleaguered city occupied with a powerful army, and a considerable non-combatant population, startled into unnatural vigilance by the incessant and destructive cannonade, yet unobservant of the great operations in progress so near them; the surrounding country, dotted with a hundred rural settle-ments, roused from the deep sleep of a New England village, by the unwonted glare and tumult." *

The same plastic fancy suggests the crowd of visions, phan-toms of the past, which may have passed through Washington's mind, on this night of feverish excitement.   " His early training in the wilderness; his escape from drowning, and the deadly rifle

* Oration of the Hon. Edward Everett at Dorchester, July 4th, 1855.

of the savage in the perilous mission to Venango; the shower of iron hail through which he rode unharmed on Braddock's field; the early stages of the great conflict now brought to its crisis, and still more solemnly, the possibilities of the future for himself and for America—the ruin of the patriot cause if he failed at the outset; the triumphant consolidation of the Revolution if he prevailed. "

The labors of the night were carried on by the Americans with their usual activity and address. When a relief party arrived at four o'clock in the morning, two forts were in sufficient forwardness to furnish protection against small-arms and grape-shot; and such use was made of the fascines and bundles of screwed hay, that, at dawn, a formidable-looking fortress frowned along the height. We have the testimony of a British officer already quoted, for the fact. "This morning at daybreak we discovered two redoubts on Dorchester Point, and two smaller ones on their flanks. They were all raised during the last night, with an expedition equal to that of the genii belonging to Aladdin's wonderful lamp. From these hills they command the whole town, so that we must drive them from their post, or desert the place."

Howe gazed at the mushroom fortress with astonishment, as it loomed indistinctly, but grandly, through a morning fog. "The rebels," exclaimed he, "have done more work in one night, than my whole army would have done in one month."

Washington had watched, with intense anxiety, the effect of the revelation at daybreak. "When the enemy first discovered our works in the morning," writes he, "they seemed to be in great confusion, and from their movements, to intend an attack."

An American, who was on Dorchester Heights, gives a picture of the scene. A tremendous cannonade was commenced from the forts in Boston, and the shipping in the harbor. "Cannon shot," writes he, "are continually rolling and rebounding over the hill, and it is astonishing to observe how little our soldiers are terrified by them. The royal troops are perceived to be in motion, as if embarking to pass the harbor and land on Dorchester shore, to attack our works. The hills and elevations in this vicinity are covered with spectators, to witness deeds of horror in the expected conflict. His excellency, General Washington, is present, animating and encouraging the soldiers, and they in return manifest their joy; and express a warm desire for the approach of the enemy; each man knows his own place. Our breastworks are strengthened, and among the means of defence are a great number of barrels, filled with stones and sand, and arranged in front of our works, which are to be put in motion, and made to roll down the hill, to break the legs of the assailants as they advance."

General Thomas was reinforced with two thousand men. Old Putnam stood ready to make a descent upon the north side of the town, with his four thousand picked men, as soon as the heights on the south should be assailed: "All the forenoon," says the American above cited, "we were in momentary expectation of witnessing an awful scene; nothing less than the carnage of Breed's Hill battle was expected."

As Washington rode about the heights, he reminded the troops that it was the 5th of March, the anniversary of the Boston massacre, and called on them to revenge the slaughter of their brethren. They answered him with shouts. "Our officers and men," writes he, "appeared impatient for the appeal. The event,

I think, must have been fortunate; nothing less than success and victory on our side."

Howe, in the mean time, was perplexed between his pride and the hazards of his position. In his letters to the ministry, he had scouted the idea of "being in danger from the rebels." He had "hoped they would attack him." Apparently, they were about to fulfil his hopes, and with formidable advantages of position. He must dislodge them from Dorchester Heights, or evacuate Boston. The latter was an alternative too mortifying to be readily adopted. He resolved on an attack, but it was to be a night one.

"A body of light infantry, under the command of Major Mulgrave, and a body of grenadiers, are to embark to-night at seven," writes the gay British officer already quoted. "I think it likely to be a general affair. Adieu balls, masquerades, &c., for this may be looked upon as the opening of the campaign."

In the evening the British began to move. Lord Percy was to lead the attack. Twenty-five hundred men were embarked in transports, which were to convey them to the rendezvous at Castle William. A violent storm set in from the east. The transports could not reach their place of destination. The men-of-war could not cover and support them. A furious surf beat on the shore where the boats would have to land. The attack was consequently postponed until the following day.

That day was equally unpropitious. The storm continued, with torrents of rain. The attack was again postponed. In the mean time, the Americans went on strengthening their works; by the time the storm subsided, General Howe deemed them too strong to be easily carried; the attempt, therefore, was relinquished altogether.

What was to be done? The shells thrown from the heights into the town, proved that it was no longer tenable. The fleet was equally exposed. Admiral Shuldham, the successor to Graves, assured Howe that if the Americans maintained possession of the heights, his ships could not remain in the harbor. It was determined, therefore, in a council of war, to evacuate the place as soon as possible. But now came on a humiliating perplexity. The troops, in embarking, would be exposed to a destructive fire. How was this to be prevented? General Howe's pride would not suffer him to make capitulations; he endeavored to work on the fears of the Bostonians, by hinting that if his troops were molested while embarking, he might be obliged to cover their retreat, by setting fire to the town.

The hint had its effect. Several of the principal inhabitants communicated with him through the medium of General Robertson. The result of the negotiation was, that a paper was concocted and signed by several of the "select men" of Boston, stating the fears they had entertained of the destruction of the place, but that those fears had been quieted by General Howe's declaration that it should remain uninjured, provided his troops were unmolested while embarking; the select men, therefore, begged "some assurance that so dreadful a calamity might not be brought on, by any measures from without."

This paper was sent out from Boston, on the evening of the 8th, with a flag of truce, which bore it to the American lines at Roxbury. There it was received by Colonel Learned, and carried by him to head-quarters. Washington consulted with such of the general officers as he could immediately assemble. The paper was not addressed to him, nor to any one else. It was not authenticated by the signature of General Howe; nor was there any other act obliging that commander to fulfil the promise, asserted to have been made by him. It was deemed proper, therefore, that Washington should give no answer to the paper; but that Colonel Learned should signify in a letter, his having laid it before the commander-in-chief, and the reasons assigned for not answering it.

With this uncompromising letter, the flag returned to Boston. The Americans suspended their fire, but continued to fortify their positions. On the night of the 9th, a detachment was sent to plant a battery on Nook's Hill, an eminence at Dorchester, which lies nearest to Boston Neck. A fire kindled behind the hill, revealed the project. It provoked a cannonade from the British, which was returned with interest from Cobble Hill, Lechmere Point, Cambridge, and Roxbury. The roar of cannonry and bursting of bombshells prevailed from half after eight at night, until six in the morning. It was another night of terror to the people of Boston; but the Americans had to desist, for the present, from the attempt to fortify Nook's Hill. Among the accidents of the bombardment, was the bursting of Putnam's vaunted mortar, " the Congress."

Daily preparations were now made by the enemy for departure. By proclamation, the inhabitants were ordered to deliver up all linen and woollen goods, and all other goods, that, in possession of the rebels, would aid them in carrying on the war. Crean Bush, a New York tory, was authorized to take possession of such goods, and put them on board of two of the transports. Under cover of his commission, he and his myrmidons broke open stores, and stripped them of their contents. Marauding gangs from the fleet and army followed their example, and extended their depredations to private houses. On the 14th, Howe, in a general order, declared that the first soldier caught plundering should be hanged on the spot. Still on the 16th houses were broken open, goods destroyed, and furniture defaced by the troops. Some of the furniture, it is true, belonged to the officers, and was destroyed because they could neither sell it nor carry it away.

The letter of a British officer gives a lively picture of the hurried preparations for retreat. "Our not being burdened with provisions, permitted us to save some stores and ammunition, the light field-pieces, and such things as were most convenient of carriage. The rest, I am sorry to say, we were obliged to leave behind; such of the guns as by dismounting we could throw into the sea was so done. The carriages were disabled, and every precaution taken that our circumstances would permit; for our retreat was by agreement. The people of the town who were friends to government, took care of nothing but their merchandise, and found means to employ the men belonging to the transports in embarking their goods, so that several of the vessels were entirely filled with private property, instead of the king's stores. By some unavoidable accident, the medicines, surgeons' chests, instruments, and necessaries, were left in the hospital. The confusion unavoidable to such a disaster, will make you conceive how much must be forgot, where every man had a private concern. The necessary care and distress of the women, children, sick, and wounded, required every assistance that could be given. It was not like breaking up a camp, where every man knows his duty; it was like departing your country with your wives, your servants, your household furniture, and all your incumbrances. The officers, who felt the disgrace of their retreat, did their utmost to keep up appearances. The men, who thought they were changing for the better, strove to take advantage of the present times, and were kept from plunder and drink with difficulty." *

For some days the embarkation of the troops was delayed by adverse winds. Washington, who was imperfectly informed of affairs in Boston, feared that the movements there might be a feint. Determined to bring things to a crisis, he detached a force to Nook's Hill on Saturday, the 16th, which threw up a breastwork in the night regardless of the cannonading of the enemy. This commanded Boston Neck, and the south part of the town, and a deserter brought a false report to the British that a general assault was intended.

The embarkation, so long delayed, began with hurry and confusion at four o'clock in the morning. The harbor of Boston soon presented a striking and tumultuous scene. There were seventy-eight ships and transports casting loose for sea, and eleven or twelve thousand men, soldiers, sailors, and refugees, hurrying to embark; many, especially of the latter, with their families and personal effects. The refugees, in fact, labored under greater disadvantages than the king's troops, being obliged to man their own vessels, as sufficient seamen could not be spared from the king's transports. Speaking of those "who had taken upon themselves the style and title of government men" in Boston, and acted an unfriendly part in this great contest, Washington observes: "By all accounts there never existed a more miserable set of beings than these wretched creatures now are. Taught to believe that the power of Great Britain was superior to all opposition, and that foreign aid, if not, was at hand, they were even higher and more insulting in their opposition than the

* Remembrancer, vol. iii. p. 108.

Regulars. When the order issued, therefore, for embarking the troops in Boston, no electric shock—no sudden clap of thunder, —in a word, the last trump could not have struck them with greater consternation. They were at their wits' end, and conscious of their black ingratitude, chose to commit themselves, in the manner I have above described, to the mercy of the waves at a tempestuous season, rather than meet their offended countrymen." *

While this tumultuous embarkation was going on, the Americans looked on in silence from their batteries on Dorchester Heights, without firing a shot. "It was lucky for the inhabitants now left in Boston, that they did not," writes a British officer; "for I am informed every thing was prepared to set the town in a blaze, had they fired one cannon." †

At an early hour of the morning, the troops stationed at Cambridge and Roxbury had paraded, and several regiments under Putnam had embarked in boats, and dropped down Charles River, to Sewall's Point, to watch the movements of the enemy by land and water. About nine o'clock a large body of troops was seen marching down Bunker's Hill, while boats full of soldiers were putting off for the shipping. Two scouts were sent from the camp to reconnoitre. The works appeared still to be occupied, for sentries were posted about them with shouldered muskets. Observing them to be motionless, the scouts made nearer scrutiny, and discovered them to be mere effigies, set up to delay the advance of the Americans. Pushing on, they found the works deserted, and gave signal of the fact; whereupon, a detachment was sent from the camp to take possession.

* Letter to John A. Washington, Am. Arch. 4th Series, v. 560.
† Frothingham, Siege of Boston, 310.

Part of Putnam's troops were now sent back to Cambridge; a part were ordered forward to occupy Boston. General Ward, too, with five hundred men, made his way from Roxbury, across the neck, about which the enemy had scattered caltrops or crow's feet,* to impede invasion. The gates were unbarred and thrown open, and the Americans entered in triumph, with drums beating and colors flying.

By ten o'clock the enemy were all embarked and under way: Putnam had taken command of the city, and occupied the important points, and the flag of thirteen stripes, the standard of the Union, floated above all the forts.

On the following day, Washington himself entered the town, where he was joyfully welcomed. He beheld around him sad traces of the devastation caused by the bombardment, though not to the extent that he had apprehended. There were evidences, also, of the haste with which the British had retreated— five pieces of ordnance with their trunnions knocked off; others hastily spiked; others thrown off the wharf. "General Howe's retreat," writes Washington, "was precipitate beyond any thing I could have conceived. The destruction of the stores at Dunbar's camp, after Braddock's defeat, was but a faint image of what may be seen at Boston; artillery carts cut to pieces in one place, gun carriages in another; shells broke here, shots buried there, and every thing carrying with it the face of disorder and confusion, as also of distress." †

To add to the mortification of General Howe, he received, we are told, while sailing out of the harbor, despatches from the ministry, approving the resolution he had so strenuously ex-

* Iron balls, with four sharp points, to wound the feet of men or horses.
† Lee's Memoirs, p. 162.

pressed, of maintaining his post until he should receive reinforcements.

As the smallpox prevailed in some parts of the town, precautions were taken by Washington for its purification; and the main body of the army did not march in until the 20th. "The joy manifested in the countenances of the inhabitants," says an observer, "was overcast by the melancholy gloom caused by ten tedious months of siege;" but when, on the 22d, the people from the country crowded into the town, "it was truly interesting," writes the same observer, "to witness the tender interviews and fond embraces of those who had been long separated under circumstances so peculiarly distressing." *

Notwithstanding the haste with which the British army was embarked, the fleet lingered for some days in Nantucket Road. Apprehensive that the enemy, now that their forces were collected in one body, might attempt by some blow to retrieve their late disgrace, Washington hastily threw up works on Fort Hill, which commanded the harbor, and demolished those which protected the town from the neighboring country. The fleet at length disappeared entirely from the coast, and the deliverance of Boston was assured.

The eminent services of Washington throughout this arduous siege, his admirable management, by which, "in the course of a few months, *an undisciplined band of husbandmen* became soldiers, and were enabled to invest, for nearly a year, and finally to expel a brave army of veterans, commanded by the most experienced generals," drew forth the enthusiastic applause of the nation. No higher illustration of this great achievement need be

* Thacher's Mil. Journal, p. 50.

given, than the summary of it contained in the speech of a British statesman, the Duke of Manchester, in the House of Lords. "The army of Britain," said he, "equipped with every possible essential of war; a chosen army, with chosen officers, backed by the power of a mighty fleet, sent to correct revolted subjects; sent to chastise a resisting city; sent to assert Britain's authority;—has, for many tedious months, been imprisoned within that town by the Provincial army; who, their watchful guards, permitted them no inlet to the country; who braved all their efforts, and defied all their skill and ability in war could ever attempt. One way, indeed, of escape was left; the fleet is yet respected; to the fleet the army has recourse; and British generals, whose name never met with a blot of dishonor, are forced to quit that town which was the first object of the war, the immediate cause of hostilities, the place of arms, which has cost this nation more than a million to defend."

We close this eventful chapter of Washington's history, with the honor decreed to him by the highest authority of his country. On motion of John Adams, who had first moved his nomination as commander-in-chief, a unanimous vote of thanks to him was passed in Congress; and it was ordered that a gold medal be struck, commemorating the evacuation of Boston, bearing the effigy of Washington as its deliverer.

CHAPTER XIX.

THE British fleet bearing the army from Boston, had disappeared
from the coast. "Whither they are bound, and where they next
will pitch their tents," writes Washington, "I know not." He
conjectured their destination to be New York, and made his
arrangements accordingly; but he was mistaken. General Howe
had steered for Halifax, there to await the arrival of strong reinforcements from England, and the fleet of his brother, Admiral
Lord Howe; who was to be commander-in-chief of the naval
forces on the North American station.

It was thought these brothers would co-operate admirably
in the exercise of their relative functions on land and water.
Yet they were widely different in their habits and dispositions.
Sir William, easy, indolent, and self-indulgent, "hated business," we are told, "and never did any. Lord Howe loved it,

dwelt upon it, never could leave it." Beside his nautical commands, he had been treasurer of the navy, member of the board of admiralty, and had held a seat in Parliament; where, according to Walpole, he was "silent as a rock," excepting when naval affairs were under discussion; when he spoke briefly and to the point. "My Lord Howe," said George II., "your life has been a continued series of services to your country." He was now about fifty-one years of age, tall, and well proportioned like his brother; but wanting his ease of deportment. His complexion was dark, his countenance grave and strongly marked, and he had a shy reserve, occasionally mistaken for haughtiness. As a naval officer, he was esteemed resolute and enterprising, yet cool and firm. In his younger days he had contracted a friendship for Wolfe; "it was like the union of cannon and gunpowder," said Walpole. Howe, strong in mind, solid in judgment, firm of purpose, was said to be the cannon; Wolfe, quick in conception, prompt in execution, impetuous in action—the gunpowder.*
The bravest man, we are told, could not wish for a more able, or more gallant commander than Howe, and the sailors used to say of him, "Give us Black Dick, and we fear nothing."

Such is his lordship's portrait as sketched by English pencils; we shall see hereafter how far his conduct conforms to it. At present we must consider the state of the American army, in the appointments and commands of which various changes had recently taken place.

It was presumed the enemy, in the ensuing campaign, would direct their operations against the Middle and Southern colonies. Congress divided those colonies into two departments; one, com-

* Barrow's Life of Earl Howe, p. 400.

prehending New York, New Jersey, Pennsylvania, Delaware and Maryland, was to be under the command of a major-general, and two brigadier-generals; the other, comprising Virginia, the Carolinas and Georgia, to be under the command of a major-general, and four brigadiers.

In this new arrangement, the orders destining General Lee to Canada, were superseded, and he was appointed to the command of the Southern department, where he was to keep watch upon the movements of Sir Henry Clinton. He was somewhat dissatisfied with the change in his destination. "As I am the only general officer on the continent," writes he to Washington, "who can speak or think in French, I confess I think it would have been more prudent to have sent me to Canada; but I shall obey with alacrity, and I hope with success."

In reply, Washington observes, "I was just about to congratulate you on your appointment to the command in Canada, when I received the account that your destination was altered. As a Virginian, I must rejoice at the change, but as an American, I think you would have done more essential service to the common cause in Canada. For, besides the advantage of speaking and thinking in French, an officer who is acquainted with their manners and customs, and has travelled in their country, must certainly take the strongest hold of their affection and confidence."

The command in Canada was given to General Thomas, who had distinguished himself at Roxbury, and was promoted to the rank of major-general. It would have been given to Schuyler, but for the infirm state of his health; still Congress expressed a reliance on his efforts to complete the work "so conspicuously begun and well conducted" under his orders, in the last campaign; and, as not merely the success but the very existence of the army in Canada would depend on supplies sent from these colonies across the lakes, he was required, until further orders, to fix his head-quarters at Albany, where, without being exposed to the fatigue of the camp until his health was perfectly restored, he would be in a situation to forward supplies; to superintend the operations necessary for the defence of New York and the Hudson River, and the affairs of the whole middle department.

Lee set out for the South on the 7th of March, carrying with him his bold spirit, his shrewd sagacity, and his whimsical and splenetic humors. The following admirably impartial sketch is given of him by Washington, in a letter to his brother Augustine: "He is the first in military knowledge and experience we have in the whole army. He is zealously attached to the cause; honest and well meaning, but rather fickle and violent, I fear, in his temper. However, as he possesses an uncommon share of good sense and spirit, I congratulate my countrymen on his appointment to that department."*

We give by anticipation a few passages from Lee's letters, illustrative of his character and career. The news of the evacuation of Boston reached him in Virginia. In a letter to Washington, dated Williamsburg, April 5, he expresses himself on the subject with generous warmth. "My dear general," writes he, "I most sincerely congratulate you; I congratulate the public, on the great and glorious event, your possession of Boston. It will be a most bright page in the annals of America, and a most abominable black one in those of the beldam Britain. Go on, my dear general; crown yourself with glory, and establish the liber-

---

* Force's Am. Archives, 4th Series, v. 562.

ties and lustre of your country on a foundation more permanent than the Capitol rock."

Then reverting to himself, his subacid humors work up, and he shows that he had been as much annoyed in Williamsburg, by the interference of committees, as he had been in New York. " My situation," writes he, " is just as I expected. I am afraid I shall make a shabby figure, without any real demerits of my own. I am like a dog in a dancing-school; I know not where to turn myself, where to fix myself. The circumstances of the country, intersected with navigable rivers ; the uncertainty of the enemy's designs and motions, who can fly in an instant to any spot they choose, with their canvas wings, throw me, or would throw Julius Cæsar into this inevitable dilemma; I may possibly be in the North, when, as Richard says, I should serve my sovereign in the West. I can only act from surmise, and have a very good chance of surmising wrong. I am sorry to grate your ears with a truth, but must, at all events, assure you, that the Provincial Congress of New York are angels of decision, when compared with your countrymen, the committee of safety assembled at Williamsburg. Page, Lee, Mercer and Payne, are, indeed, exceptions; but from Pendleton, Bland, the Treasurer and Co.—*Libera nos domine !* "

Lee's letters from Virginia, written at a later date, were in a better humor. "There is a noble spirit in this province pervading all orders of men; if the same becomes universal, we shall be saved. I am, fortunately for my own happiness, and, I think, for the well-being of the community, on the best terms with the senatorial part, as well as the people at large. I shall endeavor to preserve their confidence and good opinion." *

* Force's Am. Archives, 4th Series, vol. v. 792.

And in a letter to Washington:

"I have formed two companies of grenadiers to each regiment, and with spears thirteen feet long. Their rifles (for they are all riflemen) sling over their shoulders, their appearance is formidable, and the men are conciliated to the weapon.   *   *   *   I am likewise furnishing myself with four-ounced rifled amusettes, which will carry an infernal distance; the two-ounced hit a half sheet of paper, at five hundred yards distance."

On Lee's departure for the South, Brigadier-general Lord Stirling had remained in temporary command at New York. Washington, however, presuming that the British fleet had steered for that port, with the force which had evacuated Boston, hastened detachments thither under Generals Heath and Sullivan, and wrote for three thousand additional men to be furnished by Connecticut. The command of the whole he gave to General Putnam, who was ordered to fortify the city and the passes of the Hudson, according to the plans of General Lee. In the mean time, Washington delayed to come on himself, until he should have pushed forward the main body of his army by divisions.

Lee's anticipations that laxity and confusion would prevail after his departure, were not realized. The veteran Putnam, on taking command, put the city under rigorous military rule. The soldiers were to retire to their barracks and quarters at the beating of the tattoo, and remain there until the reveille in the morning. The inhabitants were subjected to the same rule. None would be permitted to pass a sentry, without the countersign, which would be furnished to them on applying to any of the brigade majors. All communication between the "ministerial fleet" and shore was stopped; the ships were no longer to be fur-

nished with provisions. Any person taken in the act of holding
communication with them would be considered an enemy, and
treated accordingly.

We have a lively picture of the state of the city, in letters
written at the time, and already cited. "When you are informed
that New York is deserted by its old inhabitants, and filled with
soldiers from New England, Philadelphia, Jersey, &c., you will
naturally conclude the environs of it are not very safe from so
undisciplined a multitude as our Provincials are represented to
be; but I do believe there are very few instances of so great a
number of men together, with so little mischief done by them.
They have all the simplicity of ploughmen in their manners, and
seem quite strangers to the vices of older soldiers: they have
been employed in creating fortifications in every part of the town.
* * * Governor Tryon loses his credit with the people here
prodigiously; he has lately issued a proclamation, desiring the
deluded people of this colony to return to their obedience,
promising a speedy support to the friends of government, declaring a door of mercy open to the penitent, and a rod for the dis-
obedient, &c. The friends of government were provoked at
being so distinguished, and the friends to liberty hung him in
effigy, and printed a dying speech for him. A letter, too, was intercepted from him, hastening Lord Howe to New York, as the
rebels were fortifying. These have entirely lost him the good
will of the people. * * * You cannot think how sorry I am
the governer has so lost himself, a man once so much beloved.
O Lucifer, once the son of morn, how fallen! General Washington is expected hourly; General Putnam is here, with several
other generals, and some of their ladies. * * * The variety of
reports keeps one's mind always in agitation. Clinton and Howe

have set the continent a racing from Boston to Carolina. Clinton came into our harbor: away flew the women, children, goods and chattels, and in came the soldiers flocking from every part. No sooner was it known that he was not going to land here, than expresses were sent to Virginia and Carolina, to put them on their guard; his next expedition was to Virginia; there they were ready to receive him; from thence without attempting to land, he sailed to Carolina. Now General Howe is leading us another dance." *

Washington came on by the way of Providence, Norwich and New London, expediting the embarkation of troops from these posts, and arrived at New York on the 13th of April. Many of the works which Lee had commenced were by this time finished; others were in progress. It was apprehended the principal operations of the enemy would be on Long Island, the high grounds of which, in the neighborhood of Brooklyn, commanded the city. Washington saw that an able and efficient officer was needed at that place. Greene was accordingly stationed there, with a division of the army. He immediately proceeded to complete the fortifications of that important post, and to make himself acquainted with the topography, and the defensive points of the surrounding country.

The aggregate force distributed at several extensive posts in New York and its environs, and on Long Island, Staten Island and elsewhere, amounted to little more than ten thousand men; some of those were on the sick list, others absent on command, or on furlough; there were but about eight thousand available and fit for duty. These, too, were without pay; those recently en-

* Remembrancer, vol. iii. p. 85.

listed, without arms, and no one could say where arms were to be procured.

Washington saw the inadequacy of the force to the purposes required, and was full of solicitude about the security of a place, the central point of the Confederacy, and the grand deposit of ordnance and military stores. He was aware too, of the disaffection to the cause among many of the inhabitants; and apprehensive of treachery. The process of fortifying the place had induced the ships of war to fall down into the outer bay, within the Hook, upwards of twenty miles from the city; but Governor Tryon was still on board of one of them, keeping up an active correspondence with the tories on Staten and Long Islands, and in other parts of the neighborhood.

Washington took an early occasion to address an urgent letter to the committee of safety, pointing out the dangerous, and even treasonable nature of this correspondence. He had more weight and influence with that body than had been possessed by General Lee, and procured the passage of a resolution prohibiting, under severe penalties, all intercourse with the king's ships.

Head-quarters, at this time, was a scene of incessant toil on the part of the commander-in-chief, his secretaries and aides-de-camp. "I give in to no kind of amusements myself," writes he, "and consequently those about me can have none, but are confined from morning until evening, hearing and answering applications and letters." The presence of Mrs. Washington was a solace in the midst of these stern military cares, and diffused a feminine grace and decorum, and a cheerful spirit over the domestic arrangements of head-quarters, where every thing was conducted with simplicity and dignity. The wives of some of the other generals and officers rallied around Mrs. Washington, but social intercourse was generally at an end. "We all live here," writes a lady of New York, "like nuns shut up in a nunnery. No society with the town, for there are none there to visit; neither can we go in or out after a certain hour without the countersign."

In addition to his cares about the security of New York, Washington had to provide for the perilous exigencies of the army in Canada. Since his arrival in the city, four regiments of troops, a company of riflemen and another of artificers had been detached under the command of Brigadier-general Thompson, and a further corps of six regiments under Brigadier-general Sullivan, with orders to join General Thomas as soon as possible.

Still Congress inquired of him, whether further reinforcements to the army in Canada would not be necessary, and whether they could be spared from the army in New York. His reply shows the peculiar perplexities of his situation, and the tormenting uncertainty in which he was kept, as to where the next storm of war would break. "With respect to sending more troops to that country, I am really at a loss what to advise, as it is impossible, at present, to know the designs of the enemy. Should they send the whole force under General Howe up the river St. Lawrence, to relieve Quebec and recover Canada, the troops gone and now going, will be insufficient to stop their progress; and, should they think proper to send that, or an equal force, this way from Great Britain, for the purpose of possessing this city and securing the navigation of Hudson's River, the troops left here will not be sufficient to oppose them; and yet, for any thing we know, I think it not improbable they may attempt both; both being of the greatest importance to them, if they have men. I could wish, indeed, that the army in Canada should be more powerfully reinforced; at the same time, I am conscious that the trusting of this important post, which is now become the grand magazine of America, to the handful of men remaining here, is running too great a risk. The securing of this post and Hudson's River is to us also of so great importance, that I cannot, at present, advise the sending any more troops from hence; on the contrary, the general officers now here, whom I thought it my duty to consult, think it absolutely necessary to increase the army at this place with at least ten thousand men; especially when it is considered, that from this place only the army in Canada must draw its supplies of ammunition, provisions, and most probably of men."

Washington at that time was not aware of the extraordinary expedients England had recently resorted to, against the next campaign. The Duke of Brunswick, the Landgrave of Hesse Cassel, and the Hereditary Prince of Cassel, Count of Hanau, had been subsidized to furnish troops to assist in the subjugation of her colonies. Four thousand three hundred Brunswick troops, and nearly thirteen thousand Hessians, had entered the British service. Beside the subsidy exacted by the German princes, they were to be paid seven pounds four shillings and four pence sterling for every soldier furnished by them, and as much more for every one slain.

Of this notable arrangement, Washington, as we observed, was not yet aware. "The designs of the enemy," writes he, "are too much behind the curtain for me to form any accurate opinion of their plan of operations for the summer's campaign. We are left to wander, therefore, in the field of conjecture." *

* Letter to the President of Congress, 5th May.

Within a few days afterwards, he had vague accounts of "Hessians and Hanoverian troops coming over;" but it was not until the 17th of May, when he received letters from General Schuyler, inclosing others from the commanders in Canada, that he knew in what direction some of these bolts of war were launched; and this calls for some further particulars of the campaign on the banks of the St. Lawrence; which we shall give to the reader in the ensuing chapter.

CHAPTER XX.

ARNOLD BLOCKADES QUEBEC—HIS DIFFICULTIES—ARRIVAL OF GENERAL WOOS-
TER—OF GENERAL THOMAS—ABORTIVE ATTEMPT ON QUEBEC—PREPARA-
TIONS FOR RETREAT—SORTIE OF CARLETON—RETREAT OF THE AMERICANS
—HALT AT POINT DESCHAMBAULT—ALARM IN THE COLONIES AT THE RE-
TREAT OF THE ARMY—POPULAR CLAMOR AGAINST SCHUYLER—SLANDERS
REFUTED.

In a former chapter, we left Arnold before the walls of Quebec,
wounded, crippled, almost disabled, yet not disheartened; block-
ading that "proud town" with a force inferior, by half, in number
to that of the garrison. For his gallant services, Congress promoted him in January to the rank of brigadier-general.

Throughout the winter he kept up the blockade with his shattered army; though had Carleton ventured upon a sortie, he
might have been forced to decamp. That cautious general, however, remained within his walls. He was sure of reinforcements
from England in the spring, and, in the mean time, trusted to the
elements of dissolution at work in the besieging army.

Arnold, in truth, had difficulties of all kinds to contend with.
His military chest was exhausted; his troops were in want of
necessaries; to procure supplies, he was compelled to resort to
the paper money issued by Congress, which was uncurrent among

the Canadians; he issued a proclamation making the refusal to take it in payment a penal offence. This only produced irritation and disgust. As the terms of their enlistment expired, his men claimed their discharge and returned home. Sickness also thinned his ranks; so that, at one time, his force was reduced to five hundred men, and for two months, with all his recruitments of raw militia, did not exceed seven hundred.

The failure of the attack on Quebec had weakened the cause among the Canadians; the peasantry had been displeased by the conduct of the American troops; they had once welcomed them as deliverers; they now began to regard them as intruders. The seigneurs, or noblesse, also, feared to give further countenance to an invasion, which, if defeated, might involve them in ruin.

Notwithstanding all these discouragements, Arnold still kept up a bold face; cut off supplies occasionally, and harassed the place with alarms. Having repaired his batteries, he opened a fire upon the town, but with little effect; the best part of the artillerists, with Lamb, their capable commander, were prisoners within the walls.

On the 1st day of April, General Wooster arrived from Montreal, with reinforcements, and took the command. The day after his arrival, Arnold, by the falling of his horse, again received an injury on the leg recently wounded, and was disabled for upwards of a week. Considering himself slighted by General Wooster, who did not consult him in military affairs, he obtained leave of absence until he should be recovered from his lameness, and repaired to Montreal, where he took command.

General Thomas arrived at the camp in the course of April, and found the army in a forlorn condition, scattered at different posts, and on the island of Orleans. It was numerically increased to upwards of two thousand men, but several hundred were unfit for service. The smallpox had made great ravages. They had inoculated each other. In their sick and debilitated state, they were without barracks, and almost without medicine. A portion, whose term of enlistment had expired, refused to do duty, and clamored for their discharge.

The winter was over, the river was breaking up, reinforcements to the garrison might immediately be expected, and then the case would be desperate. Observing that the river about Quebec was clear of ice, General Thomas determined on a bold effort. It was, to send up a fire-ship with the flood, and, while the ships in the harbor were in flames, and the town in confusion, to scale the walls.

Accordingly, on the third of May, the troops turned out with scaling ladders; the fire-ship came up the river under easy sail, and arrived near the shipping before it was discovered. It was fired into. The crew applied a slow match to the train and pulled off. The ship was soon in a blaze, but the flames caught and consumed the sails; her way was checked, and she drifted off harmlessly with the ebbing tide. The rest of the plan was, of course, abandoned.

Nothing now remained but to retreat before the enemy should be reinforced. Preparations were made in all haste, to embark the sick and the military stores. While this was taking place, five ships made their way into the harbor, on the 6th of May, and began to land troops. Thus reinforced, General Carleton sallied forth, with eight hundred or a thousand men. We quote his own letter for an account of his sortie. "As soon as part of the 29th regiment with the marines, in all about two hundred, were landed, they, with the greatest part of the garri-

son, by this time much improved, and in high spirts, marched out
of the ports of St. Louis and St. Johns, to see what these mighty
boasters were about.   They were found very busy in their preparations for a retreat.   A few shots being exchanged, the line
marched forward, and the place was soon cleared of these plun-
derers."

By his own account, however, these "mighty boasters" had
held him and his garrison closely invested for five months; had
burnt the suburbs; battered the walls; thrown red-hot shot
among the shipping; made repeated and daring attempts to carry
the place by assault and stratagem, and rendered it necessary for
soldiers, sailors, marines, and even judges and other civil officers
to mount guard.*   One officer declares, in a letter, that for
eighty successive nights he slept in his clothes, to be ready in case
of alarm.

All this, too, was effected by a handful of men, exposed in
open encampments to the rigors of a Canadian winter.   If in
truth they were boasters, it must be allowed their deeds were
equal to their words.

The Americans were in no condition to withstand Carleton's
unlooked-for attack.   They had no intrenchments, and could not
muster three hundred men at any point.   A precipitate retreat
was the consequence, in which baggage, artillery, every thing was
abandoned.   Even the sick were left behind; many of whom
crawled away from the camp hospitals, and took refuge in the
woods, or among the Canadian peasantry.

General Carleton did not think it prudent to engage in a pursuit with his newly-landed troops.   He treated the prisoners with

* Carleton to Lord George Germaine, May 14.

great humanity, and caused the sick to be sought out in their hiding-places, and brought to the general hospitals; with assurances, that, when healed, they should have liberty to return to their homes.

General Thomas came to a halt at Point Deschambault, about sixty miles above Quebec, and called a council of war to consider what was to be done. The enemy's ships were hastening up the St. Lawrence; some were already but two or three leagues distant. The camp was without cannon; powder, forwarded by General Schuyler, had fallen into the enemy's hands; there were not provisions enough to subsist the army for more than two or three days; the men-of-war, too, might run up the river, intercept all their resources, and reduce them to the same extremity they had experienced before Quebec. It was resolved, therefore, to ascend the river still further.

General Thomas, however, determined to send forward the invalids, but to remain at Point Deschambault with about five hundred men, until he should receive orders from Montreal, and learn whether such supplies could be forwarded immediately as would enable him to defend his position.*

The despatches of General Thomas, setting forth the disastrous state of affairs, had a disheartening effect on Schuyler, who feared the army would be obliged to abandon Canada. Washington, on the contrary, spoke cheeringly on the subject. " We must not despair. A manly and spirited opposition only can insure success, and prevent the enemy from improving the advantage they have obtained."†

He regretted that the troops had not been able to make a stand

* General Thomas to Washington, May 8th.
† Washington to Schuyler, May 17.

at Point Deschambault, but hoped they would maintain a post as far down the river as possible. The lower it was, the more important would be the advantages resulting from it, as all the country above would be favorable, and furnish assistance and support; while all below would necessarily be in the power of the enemy.

The tidings of the reverses in Canada and the retreat of the American army, had spread consternation throughout the New Hampshire Grants, and the New England frontiers, which would now be laid open to invasion. Committees of towns and districts assembled in various places, to consult on the alarming state of affairs. In a time of adversity, it relieves the public mind to have some individual on whom to charge its disasters. General Schuyler, at present, was to be the victim. We have already noticed the prejudice and ill will, on the part of the New England people, which had harassed him throughout the campaign, and nearly driven him from the service. His enemies now stigmatized him as the cause of the late reverses. He had neglected, they said, to forward reinforcements and supplies to the army in Canada. His magnanimity in suffering Sir John Johnson to go at large, while in his power, was again misconstrued into a crime: he had thus enabled that dangerous man to renew his hostilities. Finally, it was insinuated that he was untrue to his country, if not positively leagued with her enemies.

These imputations were not generally advanced; and when advanced, were not generally countenanced; but a committee of King's County appears to have given them credence, addressing a letter to the commander-in-chief on the subject, accompanied by documents.

Washington, to whom Schuyler's heart had been laid open

throughout all its trials, and who knew its rectitude, received the letter and documents with indignation and disgust, and sent copies of them to the general. " From these," said he, " you will readily discover the diabolical and insidious arts and schemes carrying on by the tories and friends of government to raise distrust, dissensions, and divisions among us. Having the utmost confidence in your integrity, and the most incontestable proof of your great attachment to our common country and its interest, I could not but look upon the charge against you with an eye of disbelief, and sentiments of detestation and abhorrence; nor should I have troubled you with the matter, had I not been informed that copies were sent to different committees, and to Governor Trumbull, which I conceived would get abroad, and that you, should you find I had been furnished with them, would consider my suppressing them as an evidence of my belief, or at best of my doubts, of the charges." *

We will go forward, and give the sequel of this matter. While the imputations in question had merely floated in public rumor, Schuyler had taken no notice of them; "but it is now," writes he in reply to Washington, "a duty which I owe myself and my country, to detect the scoundrels, and the only means of doing this is by requesting that an immediate inquiry be made into the matter; when I trust it will appear that it was more a scheme calculated to ruin me, than to disunite and create jealousies in the friends of America. Your Excellency will, therefore, please to order a court of inquiry the soonest possible; for I cannot sit easy under such an infamous imputation; since on this extensive continent, numbers of the most respectable charac-

* Washington to Schuyler, May 21.

ters may not know what your Excellency and Congress do of my principles and exertions in the common cause."

He further adds: "I am informed by persons of good credit, that about one hundred persons, living on what are commonly called the New Hampshire Grants, have had a design to seize me as a tory, and perhaps still have. There never was a man so infamously scandalized and ill-treated as I am."

We need only add, that the Berkshire committees which, in a time of agitation and alarm, had hastily given countenance to these imputations, investigated them deliberately in their cooler moments, and acknowledged, in a letter to Washington, that they were satisfied their suspicions respecting General Schuyler were wholly groundless. "We sincerely hope," added they, "his name may be handed down, with immortal honor, to the latest posterity, as one of the great pillars of the American cause."

CHAPTER XXI.

As the reverses in Canada would affect the fortunes of the Revolution elsewhere, Washington sent General Gates to lay the despatches concerning them, before Congress. "His military experience," said he, "and intimate acquaintance with the situation of our affairs, will enable him to give Congress the fullest satisfaction about the measures necessary to be adopted at this alarming crisis; and, with his zeal and attachment to the cause of America, he will have a claim to their notice and favors."

Scarce had Gates departed on his mission (May 19th), when Washington himself received a summons to Philadelphia, to advise with Congress concerning the opening campaign. He was informed also that Gates, on the 16th of May, had been promoted to the rank of major-general, and Mifflin to that of brigadier-general, and a wish was intimated that they might take the command of Boston.

Washington prepared to proceed to Philadelphia. His general orders issued on the 19th of May, show the anxious situation of affairs at New York.   In case of an alarm the respective regiments were to draw up opposite to their encampments or quarters, until ordered to repair to the alarm posts.   The alarm signals for regulars, militia, and the inhabitants of the city, were, in the day-time—two cannon fired from the rampart at Fort George, and a flag hoisted on the top of Washington's headquarters.   In the night—two cannon fired as above, and two lighted lanterns hoisted on the top of head-quarters.*

In his parting instructions to Putnam, who, as the oldest major-general in the city, would have the command during his absence, Washington informed him of the intention of the Provincial Congress of New York to seize the principal tories, and disaffected persons in the city, and the surrounding country, especially on Long Island, and authorized him to afford military aid, if required, to carry the same into execution.   He was also to send Lord Stirling, Colonel Putnam the engineer, and Colonel Knox, if he could be spared, up to the Highlands, to examine the state of the forts and garrisons, and report what was necessary to put them in a posture of defence.   Their garrisons were chiefly

---

* The following statement of the batteries at New York, we find dated May 22d.

The *Grand Battery*, on the south part of the town.

Fort George, immediately above it.

White Hall Battery, on the left of the Grand Battery.

Oyster Battery, behind General Washington's head-quarters.

Grenadier Battery, near the Brew House on the North River.

Jersey Battery, on the left of the Grenadier Battery.

Bayard's Hill Redoubt, on Bayard's Hill.

Spencer's Redoubt, on the hill where his brigade is encamped.

Waterbury's Battery (fascines), on a wharf below this hill.

Badlam's Redoubt, on a hill near the Jews' burying ground.

composed of parts of a regiment of New York troops, commanded
by Colonel James Clinton, of Ulster County, and were said to be
sufficient.

The general, accompanied by Mrs. Washington, departed from
New York on the 21st of May, and they were invited by Mr.
Hancock, the President of Congress, to be his guests during their
sojourn at Philadelphia.

Lee, when he heard of Washington's visit there, augured good
effects from it. " I am extremely glad, dear general," writes he,
" that you are in Philadelphia, for their councils sometimes lack a
little of military electricity."

Washington, in his conferences with Congress, appears to have
furnished this electricity. He roundly expressed his conviction,
that no accommodation could be effected with Great Britain, on
acceptable terms. Ministerialists had declared in Parliament,
that, the sword being drawn, the most coercive measures would be
persevered in, until there was complete submission. The recent
subsidizing of foreign troops was a part of this policy, and indicated unsparing hostility. A protracted war, therefore, was inevitable; but it would be impossible to carry it on successfully,
with the scanty force actually embodied, and with transient
enlistments of militia.

In consequence of his representations, resolutions were passed
in Congress that soldiers should be enlisted for three years, with
a bounty of ten dollars for each recruit; that the army at New
York should be reinforced until the 1st of December, with thirteen thousand eight hundred militia; that gondolas and fire-rafts
should be built, to prevent the men-of-war and enemy's ships
from coming into New York Bay, or the Narrows; and that a
flying camp of ten thousand militia, furnished by Pennsylvania,

Delaware and Maryland, and likewise engaged until the 1st December, should be stationed in the Jerseys for the defence of the Middle colonies. Washington was, moreover, empowered, in case of emergency, to call on the neighboring colonies for temporary aid with their militia.

Another important result of his conferences with Congress was the establishment of a war office. Military affairs had hitherto been referred in Congress to committees casually appointed, and had consequently been subject to great irregularity and neglect. Henceforth a permanent committee, entitled the Board of War and Ordnance, was to take cognizance of them. The first board was composed of five members; John Adams, Colonel Benjamin Harrison, Roger Sherman, James Wilson, and Edward Rutledge; with Richard Peters as secretary. It went into operation on the 12th of June.

While at Philadelphia, Washington had frequent consultations with George Clinton, one of the delegates from New York, concerning the interior defences of that province, especially those connected with the security of the Highlands of the Hudson, where part of the regiment of Colonel James Clinton, the brother of the delegate, was stationed. The important part which these brothers were soon to act in the military affairs of that province, and ultimately in its political history, entitles them to a special notice.

They were of the old Clinton stock of England; being descended from General James Clinton, an adherent of royalty in the time of the civil wars, but who passed over to Ireland, after the death of Charles I. Their father, Charles Clinton, grandson of the general, emigrated to America in 1729, and settled in Ulster, now Orange County, just above the Highlands of the Hudson.

Though not more than fifty miles from the city of New York, it was at that time on the borders of a wilderness, where every house had at times to be a fortress. Charles Clinton, like most men on our savage frontier in those days, was a warrior by necessity, if not by choice. He took an active part in Indian and French wars, commanded a provincial regiment stationed at Fort Herkimer, joined in the expedition under General Bradstreet, when it passed up the valley of the Mohawk, and was present at the capture of Fort Frontenac. His sons, James and George, one twenty, the other seventeen years of age, served in the same campaign, the one as captain, the other as lieutenant; thus taking an early lesson in that school of American soldiers, the French war.

James, whose propensities were always military, continued in the provincial army until the close of that war; and afterwards, when settled on an estate in Ulster County, was able and active in organizing its militia. George applied himself to the law, and became successful at the bar, in the same county. Their father, having laid aside the sword, occupied for many years, with discernment and integrity, the honorable station of Judge of the Court of Common Pleas. He died in Ulster County, in 1773, in the eighty-third year of his age, "in full view of that revolution in which his sons were to act distinguished parts." With his latest breath he charged them "to stand by the liberties of their country."

They needed no such admonition. From the very first, they had been heart and hand in the cause. George had championed it for years in the New York legislature, signalizing himself by his zeal as one of an intrepid minority in opposing ministerial op-

pression. He had but recently taken his seat as delegate to
the Continental Congress.

James Clinton, appointed colonel on the 30th of June, 1775,
had served with his regiment of New York troops under Montgomery at the siege of St. Johns, and the capture of Montreal,
after which he had returned home. He had subsequently been
appointed to the command of a regiment in one of the four battalions raised for the defence of New York. We shall soon have
occasion to speak further of these patriot brothers.

The prevalence of the small-pox had frequently rendered
Washington uneasy on Mrs. Washington's account during her
visits to the army; he was relieved, therefore, by her submitting
to inoculation during their sojourn in Philadelphia, and having a
very favorable time.

He was gratified, also, by procuring the appointment of his
late secretary, Joseph Reed, to the post of adjutant-general,
vacated by the promotion of General Gates, thus placing him
once more by his side.

CHAPTER XXII.

DESPATCHES from Canada continued to be disastrous. General
Arnold, who was in command at Montreal, had established a post
on the St. Lawrence, about forty miles above that place, on a
point of land called the Cedars; where he had stationed Colonel
Bedel, with about four hundred men, to prevent goods being
sent to the enemy, in the upper country, and to guard against
surprise from them, or their Indians.

In the latter part of May, Colonel Bedel received intelligence that a large body of British, Canadians, and Indians,
under the command of Captain Forster, were coming down from
Oswegatchie, to attack him. Leaving Major Butterfield in command of the post, he hastened down to Montreal to obtain reinforcements. Arnold immediately detached one hundred men,
under Major Shelburne, and prepared to follow in person, with
a much greater force. In the mean time, the post at the Cedars
had been besieged, and Major Butterfield intimidated into a surrender, by a threat from Captain Forster, that resistance would

provoke a massacre of his whole garrison by the Indians. The reinforcements under Major Shelburne were assailed within four miles of the Cedars, by a large party of savages, and captured after a sharp skirmish, in which several were killed on both sides.

Arnold received word of these disasters while on the march. He instantly sent forward some Caughnawaga Indians, to overtake the savages, and demand a surrender of the prisoners; with a threat that, in case of a refusal, and that any of them were murdered, he would sacrifice every Indian who fell into his hands, and would follow the offenders to their towns, and destroy them by fire and sword. He now embarked four hundred of his men in bateaux, and pushed on with the remainder by land. Arriving at St. Ann's, above the rapids of the St. Lawrence, he discovered several of the enemy's bateaux, taking the prisoners off from an island, a league distant. It was a tormenting sight, as it was not in his power to relieve them. His bateaux were a league behind, coming up the rapids very slowly. He sent several expresses to hurry them. It was sunset before they arrived and he could embark all his people; in the mean time, his Caughnawaga messengers returned with an answer from the savages. They had five hundred prisoners collected together, they said, at Quinze Chiens, where they were posted; should he offer to land and attack them, they would kill every prisoner, and give no quarter to any who should fall into their hands thereafter.

"Words cannot express my feelings," writes Arnold, "at the delivery of this message. Torn by the conflicting passions of revenge and humanity; a sufficient force to take ample revenge, raging for action, urged me on one hand; and humanity for five hundred unhappy wretches, who were on the point of being sacrificed, if our vengeance was not delayed, pleaded equally strong on the other." In this situation, he ordered the boats to row immediately for the island, whither he had seen the enemy taking their prisoners. Before he reached it, the savages had conveyed them all away, excepting five, whom he found naked, and almost starved, and one or two, whom, being unwell, they had butchered. Arnold now pushed for Quinze Chiens, about four miles distant, on the mainland. Here was the whole force of the enemy, civilized and savage, intrenched and fortified. As Arnold approached, they opened a fire upon his boats, with small arms, and two brass six-pounders. He rowed near the land, without returning a shot. By this time it was too dark to distinguish any thing on shore, and being unacquainted with the ground, he judged it prudent to return to St. Johns.

Here he called a council of war, and it was determined to attack the enemy early in the morning. In the course of the night, a flag was sent by Captain Forster, with articles for an exchange of prisoners, which had been entered into by him and Major Sherburne. As the terms were not equal, they were objected to by Arnold, and a day passed before they were adjusted. A cartel was then signed, by which the prisoners, consisting of two majors, nine captains, twenty subalterns, and four hundred and forty-three privates, were to be exchanged for an equal number of British prisoners of the same rank, and were to be sent to the south shore of the St. Lawrence, near Caughnawaga, whence to return to their homes. Nine days were allowed for the delivery of the prisoners, during which time hostilities should be suspended.

Arnold, in a letter to the commissioners of Congress then at Montreal, giving an account of this arrangement, expressed his indignation at the conduct of the king's officers, in employing savages to screen their butcheries, and suffering their prisoners to be killed in cold blood. "I intend being with you this evening," added he, "to consult on some effectual measures to take with these savages, and still more savage British troops, who are still at Quinze Chiens. As soon as our prisoners are released, I hope it will be in our power to take ample vengeance, or nobly fall in the attempt." *

The accounts which reached Washington of these affairs were vague and imperfect, and kept him for some days in painful suspense. The disasters at the Cedars were attributed entirely to the base and cowardly conduct of Bedel and Butterworth, and he wrote to Schuyler to have good courts appointed, and bring them, and every other officer guilty of misconduct, to trial.

"The situation of our affairs in Canada," observes he, "is truly alarming. I sincerely wish the next letters from the northward may not contain the melancholy advices of General Arnold's defeat, and the loss of Montreal. The most vigorous exertions will be necessary to retrieve our circumstances there, and I hope you will strain every nerve for that purpose. Unless it can be done now, Canada will be lost to us for ever."

While his mind was agitated by these concerns, letters from Schuyler showed that mischief was brewing in another quarter.

Colonel Guy Johnson, accompanied by the Sachem Brant and the Butlers, had been holding councils with the Indians, and designed, it was said, to come back to the Mohawk country, at the head of a British and savage force. A correspondence was carried on between him and his cousin, Sir John Johnson, who

---

* Arnold to the Commis. of Cong. 27th May.

was said to be preparing to co-operate with his Scotch dependants and Indian allies.

Considering this a breach of Sir John's parole, Schuyler had sent Colonel Elias Dayton with a force to apprehend him. Sir John, with a number of his armed tenants, retreated for refuge among the Indians, on the borders of the lakes. Dayton took temporary possession of Johnson Hall, placed guards about it, seized upon Sir John's papers, and read them in presence of Lady Johnson, and subsequently conveyed her ladyship as a kind of hostage to Albany.

Shortly afterwards came further intelligence of the designs of the Johnsons. Sir John, with his Scotch warriors and Indian allies, was said to be actually coming down the valley of the Mohawk, bent on revenge, and prepared to lay every thing waste; and Schuyler collecting a force at Albany to oppose him. Washington instantly wrote to Schuyler, to detach Colonel Dayton with his regiment on that service, with instructions to secure a post where Fort Stanwix formerly stood, in the time of the French war. As to Schuyler himself, Washington, on his own responsibility, directed him to hold a conference with the Six Nations, and with any others whom he and his brother commissioners on Indian affairs might think necessary, and secure their active services, without waiting further directions from Congress; that body having recently resolved to employ Indian allies in the war, the enemy having set the example.

"We expect a bloody summer in New York and Canada," writes Washington to his brother Augustine, "and I am sorry to say that we are not, either in men or arms, prepared for it. However, it is to be hoped, that, if our cause is just, as I most religiously believe it, the same Providence which has in many instances appeared for us, will still go on to afford its aid."

Lord Stirling, who, by Washington's orders, had visited and inspected the defences in the Highlands, rendered a report of their condition, of which we give the purport. Fort Montgomery, at the lower part of the Highlands, was on the west bank of the river, north of Dunderberg (or Thunder Hill). It was situated on a bank one hundred feet high. The river at that place was about half a mile wide. Opposite the fort was the promontory of Anthony's Nose, many hundred feet high, accessible only to goats, or men expert in climbing. A body of riflemen stationed here, might command the decks of vessels. Fort Montgomery appeared to Lord Stirling the proper place for a guard post.

Fort Constitution was about six miles higher up the river, on a rocky island of the same name, at a narrow strait where the Hudson, shouldered by precipices, makes a sudden bend round West Point. A redoubt, in the opinion of Lord Stirling, would be needed on the point, not only for the preservation of Fort Constitution, but for its own importance.

The garrison of that fort consisted of two companies of Colonel James Clinton's regiment, and Captain Wisner's company of minute men, in all one hundred and sixty rank and file. Fort Montgomery was garrisond by three companies of the same regiment, about two hundred rank and file. Both garrisons were miserably armed. The direction of the works of both forts was in the hands of commissioners appointed by the Provincial Congress of New York. The general command of the posts required to be adjusted. Several persons accused of being "notorious tories," had recently been sent into Fort Montgomery by the district committees of the counties of Albany, Dutchess and Westchester, with directions to the commanding officers, to keep them at hard labor until their further order. They were employed upon the fortifications.

In view of all these circumstances, Washington, on the 14th of June, ordered Colonel James Clinton to take command of both posts, and of all the troops stationed at them. He seemed a fit custodian for them, having been a soldier from his youth; brought up on a frontier subject to Indian alarms and incursions, and acquainted with the strong points and fastnesses of the Highlands.

King's Bridge, and the heights adjacent, considered by General Lee of the utmost importance to the communication between New York and the mainland, and to the security of the Hudson, were reconnoitred by Washington on horseback, about the middle of the month; ordering where works should be laid out. Breast-works were to be thrown up for the defence of the bridge, and an advanced work (subsequently called Fort Independence) was to be built beyond it, on a hill commanding Spyt den Duivel Creek, as that inlet of the Hudson is called, which links it with the Harlaem River.

A strong work, intended as a kind of citadel, was to crown a rocky height between two and three miles south of the bridge, commanding the channel of the Hudson; and below it were to be redoubts on the banks of the river at Jeffrey's Point. In honor of the general, the citadel received the name of Fort Washington.

Colonel Rufus Putnam was the principal engineer, who had the direction of the works. General Mifflin encamped in their vicinity, with part of the two battalions from Pennsylvania, to be employed in their construction, aided by the militia.

While these preparations were made for the protection of the Hudson, the works about Brooklyn on Long Island were carried on with great activity, under the superintendence of General Greene.   In a word, the utmost exertions were made at every point, to put the city, its environs, and the Hudson River, in a state of defence, before the arrival of another hostile armament.

CHAPTER XXIII.

RETREAT OF GENERAL THOMAS—HIS DEATH—GENERAL SULLIVAN IN COMMAND
—SCENE ON THE SOREL—SANGUINE EXPECTATIONS OF SULLIVAN—WASHING-
TON'S OPINION OF SULLIVAN'S CHARACTER—GATES APPOINTED TO THE COM-
MAND IN CANADA—REINFORCEMENTS OF THE ENEMY—REVERSES—THOMPSON
CAPTURED—RETREAT OF SULLIVAN—CLOSE OF THE INVASION OF CANADA.

OPERATIONS in Canada were drawing to a disastrous close. General Thomas, finding it impossible to make a stand at Point
Deschambault, had continued his retreat to the mouth of the
Sorel, where he found General Thompson with part of the troops
detached by Washington, from New York, who were making some
preparations for defence. Shortly after his arrival, he was taken
ill with the small-pox, and removed to Chamblee. He had
prohibited inoculation among his troops, because it put too many
of their scanty number on the sick list; he probably fell a victim
to his own prohibition, as he died of that malady on the 2d of
June.

On his death, General Sullivan, who had recently arrived with
the main detachment of troops from New York, succeeded to the
command; General Wooster having been recalled. He advanced
immediately with his brigade to the mouth of the Sorel, where he
found General Thompson with but very few troops to defend that

post, having detached Colonel St. Clair, with six or seven hundred
men, to Three Rivers, about fifty miles down the St. Lawrence,
to give check to an advanced corps of the enemy of about eight
hundred regulars and Canadians, under the veteran Scot, Colonel
Maclean. In the mean time General Thompson, who was left
with but two hundred men to defend his post, was sending off his
sick and his heavy baggage, to be prepared for a retreat, if necessary. "It really was affecting," writes Sullivan to Washington,
"to see the banks of the Sorel lined with men, women and children, leaping and clapping their hands for joy, to see me arrive;
it gave no less joy to General Thompson, who seemed to be wholly
forsaken, and left to fight against an unequal force or retreat
before them."

Sullivan proceeded forthwith to complete the works on the
Sorel; in the mean time he detached General Thompson with
additional troops to overtake St. Clair, and assume command of
the whole party, which would then amount to two thousand men.
He was by no means to attack the encampment at Three Rivers,
unless there was great prospect of success, as his defeat might
prove the total loss of Canada. "I have the highest opinion of
the bravery and resolution of the troops you command," says
Sullivan in his instructions, "and doubt not but, under the direction of a kind Providence, you will open the way for our recover-
ing that ground which former troops have so shamefully lost."

Sullivan's letter to Washington, written at the same time, is
full of sanguine anticipation. It was his fixed determination to
gain post at Deschambault, and fortify it so as to make it inac-
cessible. "The enemy's ships are now above that place," writes
he; "but if General Thompson succeeds at Three Rivers, I will

soon remove the ships below Richelieu Falls, and after that, approach Quebec as fast as possible."

" Our affairs here," adds he, " have taken a strange turn since our arrival. The Canadians are flocking by hundreds to take a part with us. The only reason of their disaffection was, because our exertions were so feeble that they doubted much of our success, and even of our ability to protect them.

" I venture to assure you, and the Congress, that I can in a few days reduce the army to order, and with the assistance of a kind Providence, put a new face to our affairs here, which a few days since seemed almost impossible."

The letter of Sullivan gave Washington an unexpected gleam of sunshine. " Before it came to hand," writes he in reply, " I almost dreaded to hear from Canada, as my advices seemed to promise nothing favorable, but rather further misfortunes. But I now hope that our affairs, from the confused, distracted, and almost forlorn state in which you found them, will change, and assume an aspect of order and success." Still his sagacious mind perceived a motive for this favorable coloring of affairs. Sullivan was aiming at the command in Canada; and Washington soberly weighed his merits for the appointment, in a letter to the President of Congress. " He is active, spirited, and zealously attached to the cause. He has his wants, and he has his foibles. The latter are manifested in his little tincture of vanity, and in an over-desire of being popular, which now and then lead him into embarrassments. His wants are common to us all. He wants experience to move upon a grand scale; for the limited and contracted knowledge, which any of us have in military matters, stands in very little stead." This want was overbalanced, on the part of General Sullivan, by sound judgment, some acquaintance with men and books, and an enterprising genius.

"As the security of Canada is of the last importance to the well-being of these colonies," adds Washington, "I should like to know the sentiments of Congress, respecting the nomination of any officer to that command. The character I have drawn of General Sullivan is just, according to my ideas of him. Congress will therefore determine upon the propriety of continuing him in Canada, or sending another, as they shall see fit." *

Scarce had Washington despatched this letter, when he received one from the President of Congress, dated the 18th of June, informing him that Major-general Gates had been appointed to command the forces in Canada, and requesting him to expedite his departure as soon as possible. The appointment of Gates has been attributed to the influence of the Eastern delegates, with whom he was a favorite; indeed, during his station at Boston, he had been highly successful in cultivating the good graces of the New England people. He departed for his command on the 26th of June, vested with extraordinary powers for the regulation of affairs in that "distant, dangerous, and shifting scene." "I would fain hope," writes Washington, "his arrival there will give our affairs a complexion different from what they have worn for a long time past, and that many essential benefits will result from it."

Despatches just received from General Sullivan, had given a different picture of affairs in Canada from that contained in his previous letter. In fact, when he wrote that letter, he was ignorant of the actual force of the enemy in Canada, which had

---

* Washington to the President of Congress, July 12, 1776.

recently been augmented to about 13,000 men; several regiments having arrived from Ireland, one from England, another from General Howe, and a body of Brunswick troops under the Baron Reidesel. Of these, the greater part were on the way up from Quebec in divisions, by land and water, with Generals Carleton, Burgoyne, Philips and Reidesel; while a considerable number under General Frazer had arrived at Three Rivers, and others, under General Nesbit, lay near them on board of transports.

Sullivan's despatch, dated on the 8th of June, at the mouth of the Sorel, began in his former sanguine vein, anticipating the success of General Thompson's expedition to Three Rivers. "He has proceeded in the manner proposed, and made his attack at daylight, for at that time a very heavy cannonading began, which lasted with some intervals to twelve o'clock. It is now near one P. M.; the firing has ceased, except some irregular firing with cannon, at a considerable distance of time one from the other. At eight o'clock a very heavy firing of small-arms was heard even here, at the distance of forty-five miles. I am almost certain that victory has declared in our favor, as the irregular firing of the cannon for such a length of time after the small-arms ceased, shows that our men are in possession of the ground."

The letter was kept open to give the particulars of this supposed victory; it closed with a dismal reverse. General Thompson had coasted in bateaux along the right bank of the river at that expanse called Lake St. Pierre, and arrived at Nicolete, where he found St. Clair and his detachment. He crossed the river in the night, and landed a few miles above Three Rivers, intending to surprise the enemy before daylight; he was not aware at the time that additional troops had arrived under General Burgoyne.

After landing, he marched with rapidity toward Three Rivers, but was led by treacherous guides into a morass, and obliged to return back nearly two miles. Day broke, and he was discovered from the ships. A cannonade was opened upon his men as they made their way slowly for an hour and a half through a swamp. At length they arrived in sight of Three Rivers, but it was to find a large force drawn up in battle array, under General Frazer, by whom they were warmly attacked, and after a brief stand thrown in confusion. Thompson attempted to rally his troops, and partly succeeded, until a fire was opened upon them in rear by Nesbit, who had landed from his ships. Their rout now was complete. General Thompson, Colonel Irvine, and about two hundred men were captured, twenty-five were slain, and the rest pursued for several miles through a deep swamp. After great fatigues and sufferings, they were able to get on board of their boats, which had been kept from falling into the hands of the enemy. In these they made their way back to the Sorel, bringing General Sullivan a sad explanation of all the firing he had heard, and the alarming intelligence of the overpowering force that was coming up the river.

"This, my dear general," writes Sullivan, in the conclusion of his letter, "is the state of this unfortunate enterprise. What you will next hear I cannot say. I am every moment informed of the vast number of the enemy which have arrived. I have only two thousand five hundred and thirty-three rank and file. Most of the officers seem discouraged, and, of course, their men. I am employed day and night in fortifying and securing my camp, and am determined to hold it as long as a person will stick by me."

He had, indeed, made the desperate resolve to defend the mouth of the Sorel, but was induced to abandon it by the unanimous opinion of his officers, and the evident unwillingness of his troops. Dismantling his batteries, therefore, he retreated with his artillery and stores, just before the arrival of the enemy, and was followed, step by step along the Sorel, by a strong column under General Burgoyne.

On the 18th of June, he was joined by General Arnold with three hundred men, the garrison of Montreal, who had crossed at Longueil just in time to escape a large detachment of the enemy. Thus reinforced, and the evacuation of Canada being determined on in a council of war, Sullivan succeeded in destroying every thing at Chamblee and St. Johns that he could not carry away, breaking down bridges, and leaving forts and vessels in flames, and continued his retreat to the Isle aux Noix, where he made a halt for some days, until he should receive positive orders from Washington or General Schuyler. In a letter to Washington, he observes, " I am extremely sorry it was not in my power to fulfil your Excellency's wishes, by leading on our troops to victory." After stating the reason of his failure, he adds, " I think we shall secure all the public stores and baggage of the army, and secure our retreat with very little loss. Whether we shall have well men enough to carry them on, I much doubt, if we don't remove quickly ; unless Heaven is pleased to restore health to this wretched army, now, perhaps, the most pitiful one that ever was formed."

The low, unhealthy situation of the Isle aux Noix, obliged him soon to remove his camp to the Isle la Motte, whence, on receiving orders to that effect from General Schuyler, he ultimately embarked with his forces, sick and well, for Crown Point.

Thus ended this famous invasion; an enterprise bold in its conceptions, daring and hardy in its execution; full of ingenious expedients, and hazardous exploits; and which, had not unforeseen circumstances counteracted its well-devised plans, might have added all Canada to the American confederacy.

CHAPTER XXIV.

DESIGNS OF THE ENEMY AGAINST NEW YORK AND THE HUDSON—PLOT OF TRYON
AND THE TORIES—ARRIVAL OF A FLEET—ALARM POSTS—TREACHERY UP THE
HUDSON—FRESH ARRIVALS—GENERAL HOWE AT STATEN ISLAND—WASHING-
TON'S PREPARATIONS.

THE great aim of the British, at present, was to get possession of
New York and the Hudson, and make them the basis of military
operations. This they hoped to effect on the arrival of a powerful armament, hourly expected, and designed for operations on
the seaboard.

At this critical juncture there was an alarm of a conspiracy
among the tories in the city and on Long Island, suddenly to
take up arms and co-operate with the British troops on their
arrival. The wildest reports were in circulation concerning it.
Some of the tories were to break down King's Bridge, others
were to blow up the magazines, spike the guns, and massacre all
the field-officers. Washington was to be killed or delivered up to
the enemy. Some of his own body-guard were said to be in the
plot.

Several publicans of the city were pointed out, as having aided
or abetted the plot. One was landlord of the Highlander, at the
corner of Beaver Street and Broadway. Another dispensed

liquor under the sign of Robin Hood.   Another named Lowry, described as a "fat man in a blue coat," kept tavern in a low house opposite the Oswego market.   Another, James Houlding, kept a beer house in Tryon Row, opposite the gates of the upper barracks.   It would seem as if a network of corruption and treachery had been woven throughout the city by means of these liquor dealers.   One of the most noted, however, was Corbie, whose tavern was said to be "to the south-east of General Washington's house, to the westward of Bayard's Woods, and north of Lispenard's Meadows," from which it would appear that, at that time, the general was quartered at what was formerly called Richmond Hill; a mansion surrounded by trees, at a short distance from the city, in rather an isolated situation.

A committee of the New York Congress, of which John Jay was chairman, traced the plot up to Governor Tryon, who, from his safe retreat on shipboard, acted through agents on shore. The most important of these was David Matthews, the tory mayor of the city.   He was accused of disbursing money to enlist men, purchase arms, and corrupt the soldiery.

Washington was authorized and requested by the committee, to cause the mayor to be apprehended, and all his papers secured. Matthews was at that time residing at Flatbush on Long Island, at no great distance from General Greene's encampment.   Washington transmitted the warrant of the committee to the general on the 21st, with directions that it should "be executed with precision, and exactly by one o'clock of the ensuing morning, by a careful officer."

Precisely at the hour of one, a detachment from Greene's brigade surrounded the house of the mayor, and secured his person; but no papers were found, though diligent search was made.

Numerous other arrests took place, and among the number, some of Washington's body-guard. A great dismay fell upon the tories. Some of those on Long Island who had proceeded to arm themselves, finding the plot discovered, sought refuge in woods and morasses. Washington directed that those arrested, who belonged to the army, should be tried by a court-martial, and the rest handed over to the secular power.

According to statements made before the committee, five guineas bounty was offered by Governor Tryon to each man who should enter the king's service; with a promise of two hundred acres of land for himself, one hundred for his wife, and fifty for each child. The men thus recruited were to act on shore, in co-operation with the king's troops when they came.

Corbie's tavern, near Washington's quarters, was a kind of rendezvous of the conspirators. There one Gilbert Forbes, a gunsmith, "a short, thick man, with a white coat," enlisted men, gave them money, and "swore them on the book to secrecy." From this house a correspondence was kept up with Governor Tryon on shipboard, through a "mulatto-colored negro, dressed in blue clothes." At this tavern it was supposed Washington's body-guards were tampered with. Thomas Hickey, one of the guards, a dark-complexioned man, five feet six inches high, and well set, was said not only to be enlisted, but to have aided in corrupting his comrades; among others, Greene the drummer, and Johnson the fifer.

It was further testified before the committee, that one Sergeant Graham, an old soldier, formerly of the royal artillery, had been employed by Governor Tryon to prowl round and survey the grounds and works about the city, and on Long Island, and that, on information thus procured, a plan of operations had been

concerted.   On the arrival of the fleet, a man-of-war should cannonade the battery at Red Hook; while that was doing, a detachment of the army should land below with cannon, and by a circuitous march surprise and storm the works on Long Island.   The
shipping then, with the remainder of the army, were to divide,
one part to run up the Hudson, the other up the East River;
troops were to land above New York, secure the pass at King's
Bridge, and cut off all communication between the city and
country.*

Much of the evidence given was of a dubious kind.   It was
certain that persons had secretly been enlisted, and sworn to
hostile operations, but Washington did not think that any regular
plan had been digested by the conspirators.   "The matter,"
writes he, "I am in hopes, by a timely discovery, will be suppressed." †

According to the mayor's own admission before the committee, he had been cognizant of attempts to enlist tories and corrupt
Washington's guards, though he declared that he had discountenanced them.   He had on one occasion, also, at the request of
Governor Tryon, paid money for him to Gilbert Forbes, the gunsmith, for rifles and round-bored guns which he had already furnished, and for others which he was to make.   He had done so,
however (according to his account), with great reluctance, and
after much hesitation and delay, warning the gunsmith that he
would be hanged if found out.   The mayor, with a number of
others, were detained in prison to await a trial.

Thomas Hickey, the individual of Washington's guard, was
tried before a court-martial.   He was an Irishman, and had been

* Am. Archives, 5th Series, vi. 1177.
† Washington to the President of Congress, June 28.

a deserter from the British army. The court-martial found him guilty of mutiny and sedition, and treacherous correspondence with the enemy, and sentenced him to be hanged.

The sentence was approved by Washington, and was carried promptly into effect, in the most solemn and impressive manner, to serve as a warning and example in this time of treachery and danger. On the morning of the 28th, all the officers and men off duty, belonging to the brigades of Heath, Spencer, Stirling and Scott, assembled under arms at their respective parades at 10 o'clock, and marched thence to the ground. Twenty men from each brigade, with bayonets fixed, guarded the prisoner to the place of execution, which was a field near the Bowery Lane. There he was hanged in the presence, we are told, of near twenty thousand persons.

While the city was still brooding over this doleful spectacle, four ships-of-war, portentous visitants, appeared off the Hook, stood quietly in at the Narrows, and dropped anchor in the bay.

In his orderly book, Washington expressed a hope that the unhappy fate of Thomas Hickey, executed that day for mutiny, sedition, and treachery, would be a warning to every soldier in the line, to avoid the crimes for which he suffered.*

---

* As a specimen of the reports which circulated throughout the country, concerning this conspiracy, we give an extract from a letter, written from Wethersfield, in Connecticut, 9th of July, 1776, by the Reverend John Marsh.

"You have heard of the infernal plot that has been discovered. About ten days before any of the conspirators were taken up, a woman went to the general and desired a private audience. He granted it to her, and she let him know that his life was in danger, and gave him such an account of the conspiracy as gained his confidence. He opened the matter to a few friends, on whom he could depend. A strict watch was kept night and day, until a favorable opportunity occurred; when the general went to bed as usual, arose

On the 29th of June, an express from the look-out on Staten Island, announced that forty sail were in sight. They were, in fact, ships from Halifax, bringing between nine and ten thousand of the troops recently expelled from Boston; together with six transports filled with Highland troops, which had joined the fleet at sea. At sight of this formidable armament standing into the harbor, Washington instantly sent notice of its arrival to Colonel James Clinton, who had command of the posts in the Highlands, and urged all possible preparations to give the enemy a warm reception should they push their frigates up the river.

According to general orders issued from head-quarters on the following day (June 30), the officers and men, not on duty, were to march from their respective regimental parades to their alarm posts, at least once every day, that they might become well acquainted with them. They were to go by routes least exposed to a fire from the shipping, and all the officers, from the highest to the lowest, were to make themselves well acquainted with the grounds. Upon a signal of the enemy's approach, or upon any

---

about two o'clock, told his lady he was a going, with some of the Provincial Congress, to order some tories seized—desired she would make herself easy, and go to sleep. He went off without any of his aides-de-camp, except the captain of his life-guard, was joined by a number of chosen men, with lanterns, and proper instruments to break open houses, and before six o'clock next morning, had forty men under guard at the City Hall, among whom was the mayor of the city, several merchants, and five or six of his own life-guard. Upon examination, one Forbes confessed that the plan was to assassinate the general, and as many of the superior officers as they could, and to blow up the magazine upon the appearance of the enemy's fleet, and to go off in boats prepared for that purpose to join the enemy. Thos. Hickey, who has been executed, went from this place. He came from Ireland a few years ago. What will be done with the mayor is uncertain. He can't be tried by court-martial, and, it is said, there is no law of that colony by which he can be condemned. May he have his deserts."

alarm, all fatigue parties were immediately to repair to their respective corps with their arms, ammunition and accoutrements, ready for instant action.

It was ascertained that the ramifications of the conspiracy lately detected, extended up the Hudson. Many of the disaffected in the upper counties were enlisted in it. The committee of safety at Cornwall, in Orange County, sent word to Colonel James Clinton, Fort Constitution, of the mischief that was brewing. James Haff, a tory, had confessed before them, that he was one of a number who were to join the British troops as soon as they should arrive. It was expected the latter would push up the river and land at Verplanck's Point; whereupon the guns at the forts in the Highlands were to be spiked by soldiers of their own garrisons; and the tories throughout the country were to be up in arms.*

Clinton received letters, also, from a meeting of committees in the precincts of Newburgh, apprising him that persons dangerous to the cause were lurking in that neighborhood, and requesting him to detach twenty-five men under a certain lieutenant acquainted with the woods, " to aid in getting some of these rascals apprehended and secured."

While city and country were thus agitated by apprehensions of danger, internal and external, other arrivals swelled the number of ships in the bay of New York to one hundred and thirty, men-of-war and transports. They made no movement to ascend the Hudson, but anchored off Staten Island, where they landed their troops, and the hill sides were soon whitened with their tents.

* Extracts from minutes of the committee, Am. Archives, 4th S. vi. 1112.

In the frigate Greyhound, one of the four ships which first arrived, came General Howe. He had preceded the fleet, in order to confer with Governor Tryon, and inform himself of the state of affairs. In a letter to his government he writes: " I met with Governor Tryon on board of a ship at the Hook, and many gentlemen, fast friends of government, attending him, from whom I have the fullest information of the state of the rebels. * * * * * We passed the Narrows with three ships-of-war, and the first division of transports, landed the grenadiers and light infantry, as the ships came up, on this island, to the great joy of a most loyal people, long suffering on that account under the oppression of the rebels stationed among them; who precipitately fled on the approach of the shipping. * * * * * * There is great reason to expect a numerous body of the inhabitants to join the army from the province of York, the Jerseys and Connecticut, who, in this time of universal oppression, only wait for opportunities to give proofs of their loyalty and zeal." *

Washington beheld the gathering storm with an anxious eye, aware that General Howe only awaited the arrival of his brother, the admiral, to commence hostile operations. He wrote to the President of Congress, urging a call on the Massachusetts govern-

* Governor Tryon, in a letter dated about this time from on board of the Duchess of Gordon, off Staten Island, writes: "The testimony given by the inhabitants of the island, of loyalty to his majesty, and attachment to his government, I flatter myself will be general throughout the province, as soon as the army gets the main body of the rebels between them and the sea; which will leave all the back country open to the command of the king's friends, and yield a plentiful resource of provisions for the army, and place them in a better situation to cut off the rebels' retreat when forced from their strong hold."—*Am. Arch. 5th S.* i. 122.

ment for its quota of continental troops; and the formation of a flying camp of ten thousand men, to be stationed in the Jerseys as a central force, ready to act in any direction as circumstances might require.

On the 2d of July, he issued a general order, calling upon the troops to prepare for a momentous conflict which was to decide their liberties and fortunes. Those who should signalize themselves by acts of bravery, would be noticed and rewarded; those who proved craven would be exposed and punished. No favor would be shown to such as refused or neglected to do their duty at so important a crisis.

CHAPTER XXV.

ABOUT this time, we have the first appearance in the military
ranks of the Revolution, of one destined to take an active and
distinguished part in public affairs; and to leave the impress of
his genius on the institutions of the country.

As General Greene one day, on his way to Washington's
head-quarters, was passing through a field,—then on the outskirts
of the city, now in the heart of its busiest quarter, and known as
"the Park,"—he paused to notice a provincial company of artillery, and was struck with its able performances, and with the tact
and talent of its commander.   He was a mere youth, apparently
about twenty years of age; small in person and stature, but
remarkable for his alert and manly bearing.   It was Alexander
Hamilton.

Greene was an able tactician, and quick to appreciate any dis-
play of military science; a little conversation sufficed to convince
him that the youth before him had a mind of no ordinary grasp
and quickness.   He invited him to his quarters, and from that
time, cultivated his friendship.

Hamilton was a native of the island of Nevis, in the West Indies, and at a very early age had been put in a counting-house at Santa Cruz. His nature, however, was aspiring. " I contemn the grovelling condition of a clerk to which my fortune condemns me," writes he to a youthful friend, " and would willingly risk my life, though not my character, to exalt my station. * * * I mean to prepare the way for futurity. I am no philosopher, and may be justly said to build castles in the air; yet we have seen such schemes succeed, when the projector is constant. I shall conclude by saying, I wish there was a war."

Still he applied himself with zeal and fidelity to the duties of his station, and such were the precocity of his judgment, and his aptness at accounts, that, before he was fourteen years of age, he was left for a brief interval, during the absence of the principal, at the head of the establishment. While his situation in the house gave him a practical knowledge of business, and experience in finance, his leisure hours were devoted to self-cultivation. He made himself acquainted with mathematics and chemistry, and indulged a strong propensity to literature. Some early achievements of his pen attracted attention, and showed such proof of talent, that it was determined to give him the advantage of a regular education. He was accordingly sent to Elizabethtown, in the Jerseys, in the autumn of 1772, to prepare, by a course of studies, for admission into King's (now Columbia) College, at New York. He entered the college as a private student, in the latter part of 1773, and endeavored, by diligent application, to fit himself for the medical profession.

The contentions of the colonies with the mother country gave a different direction and impulse to his ardent and aspiring mind. He soon signalized himself by the exercise of his pen, sometimes in a grave, sometimes in a satirical manner. On the 6th of July, 1774, there was a general meeting of the citizens in the "Fields," to express their abhorrence of the Boston Port Bill. Hamilton was present, and, prompted by his excited feelings and the instigation of youthful companions, ventured to address the multitude. The vigor and maturity of his intellect, contrasted with his youthful appearance, won the admiration of his auditors; even his diminutive size gave additional effect to his eloquence.

The war, for which in his boyish days he had sighed, was approaching. He now devoted himself to military studies, especially pyrotechnics and gunnery, and formed an amateur corps out of a number of his fellow students, and the young gentlemen of the city. In the month of March, 1776, he became captain of artillery, in a provincial corps, newly raised, and soon, by able drilling, rendered it conspicuous for discipline.

It was while exercising his artillery company that he attracted, as we have mentioned, the attention of General Greene. Further acquaintance heightened the general's opinion of his extraordinary merits, and he took an early occasion to introduce him to the commander-in-chief, by whom we shall soon find him properly appreciated.

A valuable accession to the army, at this anxious time, was Washington's neighbor, and former companion in arms, Hugh Mercer, the veteran of Culloden and Fort Duquesne. His military spirit was alert as ever; the talent he had shown in organizing the Virginia militia, and his zeal and efficiency as a member of the committee of safety, had been properly appreciated by Congress, and on the 5th of June he had received the commission of brigadier-general. He was greeted by Washington with the right hand of fellowship. The flying camp was about forming. The committee of safety of Pennsylvania were forwarding some of the militia of that province to the Jerseys, to perform the service of the camp until the militia levies, specified by Congress, should arrive. Washington had the nomination of some continental officer to the command. He gave it to Mercer, of whose merits he felt sure, and sent him over to Paulus Hook, in the Jerseys, to make arrangements for the Pennsylvania militia as they should come in; recommending him to Brigadier-general William Livingston, as an officer on whose experience and judgment great confidence might be reposed.

Livingston was a man inexperienced in arms, but of education, talent, sagacity and ready wit. He was of the New York family of the same name, but had resided for some time in the Jerseys, having a spacious mansion in Elizabethtown, which he had named Liberty Hall. Mercer and he were to consult together, and concert plans to repel invasions; the New Jersey militia, however, were distinct from the flying camp, and only called out for local defence. New Jersey's greatest danger of invasion was from Staten Island, where the British were throwing up works, and whence they might attempt to cross to Amboy. The flying camp was therefore to be stationed in the neighborhood of that place.

"The known disaffection of the people of Amboy," writes Washington, "and the treachery of those on Staten Island, who, after the fairest professions, have shown themselves our most inveterate enemies, have induced me to give directions that all persons of known enmity and doubtful character, should be removed from those places."

According to General Livingston's humorous account, his own village of Elizabethtown was not much more reliable, being peopled in those agitated times by "unknown, unrecommended strangers, guilty-looking tories, and very knavish whigs."

While danger was gathering round New York, and its inhabitants were in mute suspense and fearful anticipations, the General Congress at Philadelphia was discussing, with closed doors, what John Adams pronounced—"The greatest question ever debated in America, and as great as ever was or will be debated among men." The result was, a resolution passed unanimously, on the 2d of July, "that these United Colonies are, and of right ought to be, free and independent States."

"The 2d of July," adds the same patriotic statesman, "will be the most memorable epoch in the history of America. I am apt to believe that it will be celebrated by succeeding generations, as the great anniversary festival. It ought to be commemorated as the day of deliverance, by solemn acts of devotion to Almighty God. It ought to be solemnized with pomp and parade, with shows, games, sports, guns, bells, bonfires and illuminations, from one end of this continent to the other, from this time forth for evermore."

The glorious event has, indeed, given rise to an annual jubilee, but not on the day designated by Adams. The fourth of July is the day of national rejoicing, for on that day, the "Declaration of Independence," that solemn and sublime document, was adopted. Tradition gives a dramatic effect to its announcement. It was known to be under discussion, but the closed doors of Congress excluded the populace. They awaited, in throngs, an appointed signal. In the steeple of the state-house was a bell, imported twenty-three years previously from London by the Provincial Assembly of Pennsylvania. It bore the portentous text from scripture: "Proclaim liberty throughout all the land, unto all the inhabitants thereof." A joyous peal from that bell gave notice that the bill had been passed. It was the knell of British domination.

No one felt the importance of the event more deeply than John Adams, for no one had been more active in producing it. We quote his words written at the moment. "When I look back to the year 1761, and recollect the argument concerning writs of assistance in the superior court, which I have hitherto considered as the commencement of the controversy between Great Britain and America, and run through the whole period from that time to this, and recollect the series of political events, the chain of causes and effects; I am surprised at the suddenness, as well as the greatness of this Revolution; Great Britain has been filled with folly, America with wisdom."

His only regret was, that the declaration of independence had not been made sooner. "Had it been made seven months ago," said he, "we should have mastered Quebec, and been in possession of Canada, and might before this hour have formed alliances with foreign states. Many gentlemen in high stations, and of great influence, have been duped by the ministerial bubble of commissioners to treat, and have been slow and languid in promoting measures for the reduction of that province."

Washington hailed the declaration with joy. It is true, it was but a formal recognition of a state of things which had long existed, but it put an end to all those temporizing hopes of reconciliation which had clogged the military action of the country.

On the 9th of July, he caused it to be read at six o'clock in the evening, at the head of each brigade of the army. "The general hopes," said he in his orders, "that this important event will serve as a fresh incentive to every officer and soldier, to act

with fidelity and courage, as knowing that now the peace and
safety of his country depend, under God, solely on the success of
our arms; and that he is now in the service of a state, possessed
of sufficient power to reward his merit, and advance him to the
highest honors of a free country."

The excitable populace of New York were not content with the
ringing of bells to proclaim their joy. There was a leaden statue
of George III. in the Bowling Green, in front of the fort.
Since kingly rule is at an end, why retain its effigy? On the
same evening, therefore, the statue was pulled down amid the
shouts of the multitude, and broken up to be run into bullets
"to be used in the cause of independence."

Some of the soldiery having been implicated in this popular
effervescence, Washington censured it in general orders, as having
much the appearance of a riot and a want of discipline, and the
army was forbidden to indulge in any irregularities of the kind.
It was his constant effort to inspire his countrymen in arms with
his own elevated idea of the cause in which they were engaged,
and to make them feel that it was no ordinary warfare, admitting
of vulgar passions and perturbations. "The general hopes and
trusts," said he, "that every officer and man will endeavor so to
live and act as becomes a Christian soldier, defending the dearest
rights and liberties of his country." *

* Orderly book, July 9, Sparks, iii 456.

CHAPTER XXVI.

ARRIVAL OF MORE SHIPS—MOVEMENTS OF THE PHŒNIX AND THE ROSE—PANIC
IN THE CITY—HOSTILE SHIPS UP THE HUDSON—STIR OF WAR ALONG THE
RIVER—GENERAL GEORGE CLINTON, AND THE MILITIA OF ULSTER COUNTY—
FRESH AGITATION OF NEW YORK—ARRIVAL OF LORD HOWE.

THE exultation of the patriots of New York, caused by the
Declaration of Independence, was soon overclouded.   On the
12th of July, several ships stood in from sea, and joined the
naval force below.   Every nautical movement was now a matter
of speculation and alarm, and all the spy-glasses in the city were
incessantly reconnoitring the bay.

"The enemy are now in the harbor," writes an American
officer, "although they have not yet ventured themselves within
gunshot of the city, but we hourly expect to be called into
action.   The whole army is out between two and three every
morning, at their respective alarm posts, and remain there until
sunrise.   I am morally certain that it will not be long before we
have an engagement."

Scarce had this letter been penned, when two ships-of-war
were observed getting under way, and standing toward the city.
One was the Phœnix, of forty guns; the other the Rose, of
twenty guns, commanded by Captain Wallace, of unenviable

renown, who had marauded the New England coast, and domineered over Rhode Island. The troops were immediately at their alarm posts. It was about half-past three o'clock in the afternoon, as the ships and three tenders came sweeping up the bay with the advantage of wind and tide, and shaped their course up the Hudson. The batteries of the city and of Paulus Hook on the opposite Jersey shore, opened a fire upon them. They answered it with broadsides. There was a panic throughout the city. Women and children ran hither and thither about the streets, mingling their shrieks and cries with the thundering of the cannon. "The attack has begun! The city is to be destroyed! What will become of us?"

The Phœnix and the Rose continued their course up the Hudson. They had merely fired upon the batteries as they passed; and on their own part had sustained but little damage, their decks having ramparts of sand-bags. The ships below remained in sullen quiet at their anchors, and showed no intention of following them. The firing ceased. The fear of a general attack upon the city died away, and the agitated citizens breathed more freely.

Washington, however, apprehended this movement of the ships might be with a different object. They might be sent to land troops and seize upon the passes of the Highlands. Forts Montgomery and Constitution were far from complete, and were scantily manned. A small force might be sufficient to surprise them. The ships might intend, also, to distribute arms among the tories in the river counties, and prepare them to co-operate in the apprehended attack upon New York.

Thus thinking, the moment Washington saw these ships standing up the river, he sent off an express to put General

Mifflin on the alert, who was stationed with his Philadelphia troops at Fort Washington and King's Bridge. The same express carried a letter from him to the New York Convention, at that time holding its sessions at White Plains in Westchester County, apprising it of the impending danger. His immediate solicitude was for the safety of Forts Constitution and Montgomery.

Fortunately George Clinton, the patriotic legislator, had recently been appointed brigadier-general of the militia of Ulster and Orange counties. Called to his native State by his military duties in this time of danger, he had only remained in Congress to vote for the declaration of independence, and then hastened home. He was now at New Windsor, in Ulster County, just above the Highlands. Washington wrote to him on the afternoon of the 12th, urging him to collect as great a force as possible of the New York militia, for the protection of the Highlands against this hostile irruption, and to solicit aid, if requisite, from the western parts of Connecticut. "I have the strongest reason to believe," added he, "it will be absolutely necessary, if it were only to prevent an insurrection of your own tories."

Long before the receipt of Washington's letter, Clinton had been put on the alert. About nine o'clock in the morning of the 13th, an alarm gun from his brother at Fort Constitution, thundered through the echoing defiles of the mountains. Shortly afterwards, two river sloops came to anchor above the Highlands before the general's residence. Their captains informed him that New York had been attacked on the preceding afternoon. They had seen the cannonade from a distance, and judged from the subsequent firing, that the enemy's ships were up the river as far as King's Bridge.

Clinton was as prompt a soldier as he had been an intrepid legislator. The neighboring militia were forthwith put in motion. Three regiments were ordered out; one was to repair to Fort Montgomery; another to Fort Constitution; the third to rendezvous at Newburgh, just above the Highlands, ready to hasten to the assistance of Fort Constitution, should another signal be given. All the other regiments under his command were to be prepared for service at a moment's notice. In ordering these hasty levies, however, he was as considerate as he was energetic. The colonels were directed to leave the frontier companies at home, to protect the country against the Indians, and some men out of each company to guard against internal enemies.

Another of his sagacious measures was to send expresses to all the owners of sloops and boats twenty miles up the west side of the river, to haul them off so as to prevent their grounding. Part of them were to be ready to carry over the militia to the forts; the rest were ordered down to Fort Constitution, where a chain of them might be drawn across the narrowest part of the river, to be set on fire, should the enemy's ships attempt to pass.

Having made these prompt arrangements, he proceeded early in the afternoon of the same day, with about forty of his neighbors, to Fort Constitution; whence, leaving some with his brother, he pushed down on the same evening to Fort Montgomery, where he fixed his head-quarters, as being nearer the enemy and better situated to discover their motions.

Here, on the following day (July 14th), he received Washington's letter, written two days previously; but by this time he had anticipated its orders, and stirred up the whole country. On that same evening, two or three hundred of the hardy Ulster yeomanry, roughly equipped, part of one of the regiments he had ordered out, marched into Fort Montgomery, headed by their colonel (Woodhull). Early the next morning five hundred of another regiment arrived, and he was told that parts of two other regiments were on the way.

"The men," writes he to Washington, "turn out of their harvest fields to defend their country with surprising alacrity. The absence of so many of them, however, at this time, when their harvests are perishing for want of the sickle, will greatly distress the country. I could wish, therefore, that a less number might answer the purpose."

On no one could this prompt and brave gathering of the yeomanry produce a more gratifying effect, than upon the commander-in-chief; and no one could be more feelingly alive, in the midst of stern military duties, to the appeal in behalf of the peaceful interests of the husbandman.

While the vigilant Clinton was preparing to defend the passes of the Highlands, danger was growing more imminent at the mouth of the Hudson.

New York has always been a city prone to agitations. That into which it was thrown on the afternoon of the 12th of July, by the broadsides of the Phœnix and the Rose, was almost immediately followed by another. On the same evening there was a great booming of cannon, with clouds of smoke, from the shipping at anchor at Staten Island. Every spy-glass was again in requisition. The British fleet were saluting a ship of the line, just arrived from sea. She advanced grandly, every man-of-war thundering a salute as she passed. At her foretop mast-head she bore St. George's flag. "It is the admiral's ship!" cried the nautical men on the look-out at the Battery. "It is the admiral's ship!" was echoed from mouth to mouth, and the word soon flew throughout the city, "Lord Howe is come!"

CHAPTER XXVII.

PRECAUTIONS AGAINST TORIES—SECRET COMMITTEES—DECLARATION OF LORD
HOWE—HIS LETTER TO THE COLONIAL GOVERNORS—HIS LETTER TO WASH-
INGTON REJECTED—INTERVIEW BETWEEN THE BRITISH ADJUTANT-GENERAL
AND COLONEL REED—RECEPTION OF THE ADJUTANT-GENERAL BY WASH-
INGTON—THE PHŒNIX AND ROSE IN THE TAPPAN SEA AND HAVERSTRAW
BAY—ARMING OF THE RIVER YEOMANRY—GEORGE CLINTON AT THE GATES
OF THE HIGHLANDS.

LORD HOWE was indeed come, and affairs now appeared to be
approaching a crisis. In consequence of the recent conspiracy,
the Convention of New York, seated at White Plains in Westchester County, had a secret committee stationed in New York
for the purpose of taking cognizance of traitorous machinations.
To this committee Washington addressed a letter the day after
his lordship's arrival, suggesting the policy of removing from
the city and its environs, "all persons of known disaffection and
enmity to the cause of America;" especially those confined in
jail for treasonable offences; who might become extremely dangerous in case of an attack and alarm. He took this step with
great reluctance; but felt compelled to it by circumstances.
The late conspiracy had shown him that treason might be lurking in his camp. And he was well aware that the city and
the neighboring country, especially Westchester County, and

Queens and Suffolk counties on Long Island, abounded with "tories," ready to rally under the royal standard whenever backed by a commanding force.

In consequence of his suggestion, thirteen persons in confinement for traitorous offences, were removed to the jail of Litchfield in Connecticut. Among the number was the late mayor; but as his offence was not of so deep a dye as those whereof the rest stood charged, it was recommended by the president of the Convention that he should be treated with indulgence.

The proceedings of Lord Howe soon showed the policy of these precautions. His lordship had prepared a declaration, addressed to the people at large, informing them of the powers vested in his brother and himself as commissioners for restoring peace; and inviting communities as well as individuals, who, in the tumult and disasters of the times, had deviated from their allegiance to the crown, to merit and receive pardon by a prompt return to their duty. It was added, that proper consideration would be had of the services of all who should contribute to the restoration of public tranquillity.

His lordship really desired peace. According to a contemporary, he came to America " as a mediator, not as a destroyer," * and had founded great hopes in the efficacy of this document in rallying back the people to their allegiance; it was a sore matter of regret to him, therefore, to find that, in consequence of his tardy arrival, his invitation to loyalty had been forestalled by the Declaration of Independence.

Still it might have an effect in bringing adherents to the royal standard; he sent a flag on shore, therefore, bearing a cir-

* Letter of Mr. Dennis de Berdt, to Mr. Joseph Reed. Am. Archives, 5th Series, i. 372.

cular letter, written in his civil and military capacity, to the colonial governor, requesting him to publish his address to the people as widely as possible.

We have heretofore shown the tenacity with which Washington, in his correspondence with Generals Gage and Howe, exacted the consideration and deference due to him as commander-in-chief of the American armies; he did this not from official pride and punctilio, but as the guardian of American rights and dignities. A further step of the kind was yet to be taken. The British officers, considering the Americans in arms rebels without valid commissions, were in the habit of denying them all military title. Washington's general officers had urged him not to submit to this tacit indignity, but to reject all letters directed to him without a specification of his official rank.

An occasion now presented itself for the adjustment of this matter. Within a day or two an officer of the British navy, Lieutenant Brown, came with a flag from Lord Howe, seeking a conference with Washington. Colonel Reed, the adjutant-general, embarked in a barge, and met him half way between Governor's and Staten Islands. The lieutenant informed him that he was the bearer of a letter from Lord Howe to *Mr*. Washington. Colonel Reed replied, that he knew no such person in the American army. The lieutenant produced and offered the letter. It was addressed to George Washington, Esquire. He was informed that it could not be received with such a direction. The lieutenant expressed much concern. The letter, he said, was of a civil, rather than a military nature—Lord Howe regretted he had not arrived sooner—he had great powers—it was much to be wished the letter could be received.

While the lieutenant was embarrassed and agitated, Reed

maintained his coolness, politely declining to receive the letter, as inconsistent with his duty. They parted; but after the lieutenant had been rowed some little distance, his barge was put about, and Reed waited to hear what further he had to say. It was to ask by what title *General*—but, catching himself, *Mr.* Washington chose to be addressed.

Reed replied that the general's station in the army was well known; and they could not be at a loss as to the proper mode of addressing him, especially as this matter had been discussed in the preceding summer, of which, he presumed, the admiral could not be ignorant. The lieutenant again expressed his disappointment and regret, and their interview closed.

On the 19th, an aide-de-camp of General Howe came with a flag, and requested to know, as there appeared to be an obstacle to a correspondence between the two generals, whether Colonel Patterson, the British adjutant-general, could be admitted to an interview with General Washington. Colonel Reed, who met the flag, consented in the name of the general, and pledged his honor for the safety of the adjutant-general during the interview, which was fixed for the following morning.

At the appointed time, Col. Reed and Colonel Webb, one of Washington's aides, met the flag in the harbor, took Colonel Patterson into their barge, and escorted him to town, passing in front of the grand battery. The customary precaution of blindfolding was dispensed with; and there was a lively and sociable conversation the whole way. Washington received the adjutant-general at head-quarters with much form and ceremony, in full military array, with his officers and guards about him.

Colonel Patterson, addressing him by the title of *your excellency*, endeavored to explain the address of the letter as consistent with propriety, and founded on a similar address in the previous summer, to General Howe. That General Howe did not mean to derogate from the respect or rank of General Washington, but conceived such an address consistent with what had been used by ambassadors or plenipotentiaries where difficulties of rank had arisen. He then produced, but did not offer, a letter addressed to George Washington, Esquire, &c. &c., hoping that the et ceteras, which implied every thing, would remove all impediments.

Washington replied, that it was true, the et ceteras implied every thing, but they also implied any thing. His letter alluded to, of the previous summer, was in reply to one addressed in like manner. A letter, he added, addressed to a person acting in a public character, should have some inscriptions to designate it from a mere private letter; and he should absolutely decline any letter addressed to himself as a private person, when it related to his public station.

Colonel Patterson, finding the letter would not be received, endeavored, as far as he could recollect, to communicate the scope of it in the course of a somewhat desultory conversation. What he chiefly dwelt upon was, that Lord Howe and his brother had been specially nominated commissioners for the promotion of peace, which was esteemed a mark of favor and regard to America; that they had great powers, and would derive the highest pleasure from effecting an accommodation; and he concluded by adding, that he wished his visit to be considered as making the first advance toward that desirable object.

Washington replied that, by what had appeared (alluding, no doubt, to Lord Howe's circular), their powers, it would seem, were only to grant pardons. Now those who had committed no fault needed no pardon; and such was the case with the Americans, who were only defending what they considered their indisputable rights.

Colonel Patterson avoided a discussion of this matter, which, he observed, would open a very wide field; so here the conference, which had been conducted on both sides with great courtesy, terminated. The colonel took his leave, excusing himself from partaking of a collation, having made a late breakfast, and was again conducted to his boat. He expressed himself highly sensible of the courtesy of his treatment, in having the usual ceremony of blindfolding dispensed with.

Washington received the applause of Congress and of the public for sustaining the dignity of his station. His conduct in this particular was recommended as a model to all American officers in corresponding with the enemy; and Lord Howe informed his government that, thenceforward, it would be politic to change the superscription of his letters.

In the mean time the irruption of the Phœnix and the Rose into the waters of the Hudson had roused a belligerent spirit along its borders. The lower part of that noble river is commanded on the eastern side by the bold woody heights of Manhattan Island and Westchester County, and on the western side by the rocky cliffs of the Palisades. Beyond those cliffs, the river expands into a succession of what may almost be termed lakes; first the Tappan Sea, then Haverstraw Bay, then the Bay of Peekskill; separated from each other by long stretching points, or high beetling promontories, but affording ample sea room and safe anchorage. Then come the redoubtable Highlands, that strait, fifteen miles in length, where the river bends its course, narrow and deep, between rocky, forest-clad mountains.

"He who has command of that grand defile," said an old navigator, "may at any time throttle the Hudson."

The New York Convention, aware of the impending danger, despatched military envoys to stir up the yeomanry along the river, and order out militia. Powder and ball were sent to Tarrytown, before which the hostile ships were anchored, and yeoman troops were stationed there and along the neighboring shores of the Tappan Sea. In a little while the militia of Dutchess County and Cortlandt's Manor were hastening, rudely armed, to protect the public stores at Peekskill, and mount guard at the entrance of the Highlands.

No one showed more zeal in this time of alarm, than Colonel Pierre Van Cortlandt, of an old colonial family, which held its manorial residence at the mouth of the Croton. With his regiment he kept a dragon watch along the eastern shore of the Tappan Sea and Haverstraw Bay; while equal vigilance was maintained night and day along the western shore, from Nyack quite up to the Donderberg, by Colonel Hay and his regiment of Haverstraw. Sheep and cattle were driven inland, out of the reach of maraud. Sentinels were posted to keep a look-out from heights and headlands and give the alarm should any boats approach the shore, and rustic marksmen were ready to assemble in a moment, and give them a warm reception.

The ships-of-war which caused this alarm and turmoil, lay quietly anchored in the broad expanses of the Tappan Sea and Haverstraw Bay; shifting their ground occasionally, and keeping out of musket shot of the shore, apparently sleeping in the summer sunshine, with awnings stretched above their decks; while their boats were out taking soundings quite up to the Highlands, evidently preparing for further operations. At night, too, their barges were heard rowing up and down the river on mysterious errands; perriaugers, also, paid them furtive visits occasionally; it was surmised, with communications and supplies from tories on shore.

While the ships were anchored in Haverstraw Bay, one of the tenders stood into the Bay of Peekskill, and beat up within long shot of Fort Montgomery, where General George Clinton was ensconced with six hundred of the militia of Orange and Ulster counties. As the tender approached, a thirty-two pounder was brought to range upon her. The ball passed through her quarter; whereupon she put about, and ran round the point of the Donderberg, where the boat landed, plundered a solitary house at the foot of the mountain, and left it in flames. The marauders, on their way back to the ships, were severely galled by rustic marksmen, from a neighboring promontory.

The ships, now acquainted with the channel, moved up within six miles of Fort Montgomery. General Clinton apprehended they might mean to take advantage of a dark night, and slip by him in the deep shadows of the mountains. The shores were high and bold, the river was deep, the navigation of course safe and easy. Once above the Highlands, they might ravage the country beyond, and destroy certain vessels of war which were being constructed at Poughkeepsie.

To prevent this, he stationed a guard at night on the furthest point in view, about two miles and a half below the fort, prepared to kindle a blazing fire should the ships appear in sight. Large piles of dry brushwood mixed with combustibles, were prepared at various places up and down the shore opposite to the fort, and men stationed to set fire to them as soon as a signal should be given from the lower point. The fort, therefore, while it remained in darkness, would have a fair chance with its batteries as the ships passed between it and these conflagrations.

A private committee sent up by the New York Convention, had a conference with the general, to devise further means of obstructing the passage of ships up the river. Fire rafts were to be brought from Poughkeepsie and kept at hand ready for action. These were to be lashed two together, with chains, between old sloops filled with combustibles, and sent down with a strong wind and tide, to drive upon the ships. An iron chain, also, was to be stretched obliquely across the river from Fort Montgomery to the foot of Anthony's Nose, thus, as it were, chaining up the gate of the Highlands.

For a protection below the Highlands, it was proposed to station whale-boats about the coves and promontories of Tappan Sea and Haverstraw Bay; to reconnoitre the enemy, cruise about at night, carry intelligence from post to post, seize any river craft that might bring the ships supplies, and cut off their boats when attempting to land. Galleys, also, were prepared, with nine-pounders mounted at the bows.

Colonel Hay of Haverstraw, in a letter to Washington, rejoices that the national Congress are preparing to protect this great highway of the country, and anticipates that the banks of the Hudson were about to become the chief theatre of the war.

NOTE.

THE VAN CORTLANDT FAMILY.—Two members of this old and honorable family were conspicuous patriots throughout the Revolution. Pierre Van Cortlandt, the father, at this time about 56 years of age, a stanch friend and ally of George Clinton, was member of the first Provincial Congress, and president of the Committee of Public Safety. Governor Tryon had visited him in his old manor house at the mouth of the Croton, in 1774, and made him offers of royal favors, honors, grants of land, &c., if he would abandon the popular cause. His offers were nobly rejected. The Cortlandt family suffered in consequence, being at one time obliged to abandon their manorial residence : but the head remained true to the cause, and subsequently filled the office of Lieutenant-governor with great dignity.

His son Pierre, mentioned in the above chapter, and then about 27 years of age, had likewise resisted the overtures of Tryon, destroying a major's commission in the Cortlandt militia, which he sent him. Congress, in 1775, made him lieutenant-colonel in the Continental service, in which capacity we now find him, acquitting himself with zeal and ability.

CHAPTER XXVIII.

QUESTION OF COMMAND BETWEEN GATES AND SCHUYLER—CONDITION OF THE
ARMY AT CROWN POINT—DISCONTENT AND DEPARTURE OF SULLIVAN—
FORTIFICATIONS AT TICONDEROGA—THE QUESTION OF COMMAND ADJUSTED
—SECRET DISCONTENTS—SECTIONAL JEALOUSIES IN THE ARMY—SOUTHERN
TROOPS—SMALLWOOD'S MACARONI BATTALION—CONNECTICUT LIGHT-HORSE.

WHILE the security of the Hudson from invading ships was
claiming the attention of Washington, he was equally anxious
to prevent an irruption of the enemy from Canada. He was
grieved, therefore, to find there was a clashing of authorities
between the generals who had charge of the Northern frontier.
Gates, on his way to take command of the army in Canada, had
heard with surprise in Albany, of its retreat across the New
York frontier. He still considered it under his orders, and was
proceeding to act accordingly; when General Schuyler observed,
that the resolution of Congress, and the instructions of Washington, applied to the army only while in Canada; the moment it
retreated within the limits of New York, it came within his
(Schuyler's) command. A letter from Schuyler to Washington,
written at the time, says: "If Congress intended that General
Gates should command the Northern army, wherever it may be,
as he assures me they did, it ought to have been signified to me,

and I should then have immediately resigned the command to him; but until such intention is properly conveyed to me, I never can. I must, therefore, entreat your Excellency to lay this letter before Congress, that they may clearly and explicitly signify their intentions, to avert the dangers and evils that may arise from a disputed command."

That there might be no delay in the service at this critical juncture, the two generals agreed to refer the question of command to Congress, and in the mean time to act in concert. They accordingly departed together for Lake Champlain, to prepare against an anticipated invasion by Sir Guy Carleton. They arrived at Crown Point on the 6th of July, and found there the wrecks of the army recently driven out of Canada. They had been harassed in their retreat by land; their transportation on the lake had been in leaky boats, without awnings, where the sick, suffering from smallpox, lay on straw, exposed to a burning July sun; no food but salt pork, often rancid, hard biscuit or unbaked flour, and scarcely any medicine. Not more than six thousand men had reached Crown Point, and half of those were on the sick list; the shattered remains of twelve or fifteen very fine battalions. Some few were sheltered in tents, some under sheds, and others in huts hastily formed of bushes; scarce one of which but contained a dead or dying man. Two thousand eight hundred were to be sent to a hospital recently established at the south end of Lake George, a distance of fifty miles; when they were gone, with those who were to row them in boats, there would remain but the shadow of an army.*

In a council of war, it was determined that, under present

* Col. John Trumbull's Autobiography, p. 285, Appendix.

circumstances, the post of Crown Point was not tenable; neither was it capable of being made so this summer, without a force greatly superior to any they might reasonably expect; and that, therefore, it was expedient to fall back, and take a strong position at Ticonderoga.

General Sullivan had been deeply hurt that Gates, his former inferior in rank, should have been appointed over him to the command of the army in Canada; considering it a tacit intimation that Congress did not esteem him competent to the trust which had devolved upon him. He now, therefore, requested leave of absence, in order to wait on the commander-in-chief. It was granted with reluctance. Before departing, he communicated to the army, through General Schuyler, his high and grateful sense of their exertions in securing a retreat from Canada, and the cheerfulness with which his commands had been received and obeyed.

On the 9th of July, Schuyler and Gates returned to Ticonderoga, accompanied by Arnold. Instant arrangements were made to encamp the troops, and land the artillery and stores as fast as they should arrive. Great exertions, also, were made to strengthen the defences of the place. Colonel John Trumbull, who was to have accompanied Gates to Canada, as adjutant-general, had been reconnoitring the neighborhood of Ticonderoga, and had pitched upon a place for a fortification on the eastern side of the lake, directly opposite the east point of Ticonderoga, where Fort Independence was subsequently built. He also advised the erection of a work on a lofty eminence, the termination of a mountain ridge, which separates Lake George from Lake Champlain. His advice was unfortunately disregarded. The eminence, subsequently called Mount Defiance, looked down upon and commanded the narrow parts of both lakes. We shall hear more of it hereafter.

Preparations were made, also, to augment the naval force on the lakes. Ship carpenters from the Eastern States were employed at Skenesborough, to build the hulls of galleys and boats, which, when launched, were to be sent down to Ticonderoga for equipment and armament, under the superintendence of General Arnold.

Schuyler soon returned to Albany, to superintend the general concerns of the Northern department. He was indefatigable in procuring and forwarding the necessary materials and artillery for the fortification of Ticonderoga.

The question of command between him and Gates, was apparently at rest. A letter from the President of Congress, dated July 8th, informed General Gates, that according to the resolution of that body under which he had been appointed, his command was totally independent of General Schuyler, *while the army was in Canada,* but no longer. Congress had no design to divest General Schuyler of the command while the troops were *on this side of Canada.*"

To Schuyler, under the same date, the president writes : " The Congress highly approve of your patriotism and magnanimity in not suffering any difference of opinion to hurt the public service.

" A mutual confidence and good understanding are at this time essentially necessary, so that I am persuaded they will take place on all occasions between yourself and General Gates."

Gates professed himself entirely satisfied with the explanation he had received, and perfectly disposed to obey the commands of Schuyler. " I am confident," added he, " we shall, as the Congress wish, go hand in hand to promote the public welfare."

Schuyler, too, assured both Congress and Washington, "that the difference in opinion between Gates and himself had not caused the least ill-will, nor interrupted that harmony necessary to subsist between their officers."

Samuel Adams, however, who was at that time in Congress, had strong doubts in the matter.

"Schuyler and Gates are to command the troops," writes he, "the former while they are without, the latter while they are within, the bounds of Canada. Admitting these generals to have the accomplishments of a Marlborough, or a Eugene, I cannot conceive that such a disposition of them will be attended with any good effects, unless harmony subsists between them. Alas, I fear this is not the case. Already disputes have arisen, which they have referred to Congress; and, although they affect to treat each other with a politeness becoming their rank, in my mind, altercations between commanders who have pretensions nearly equal (I mean in point of command), forebode a repetition of misfortune. I sincerely wish my apprehensions may prove groundless." *

We have a letter before us, also, written to Gates, by his friend Joseph Trumbull, commissary-general, on whose appointment of a deputy, the question of command had arisen. Trumbull's letter was well calculated to inflame the jealousy of Gates. "I find you are in a cursed situation," writes he; "your authority at an end; and commanded by a person who will be willing

* S. Adams to R. H. Lee. Am. Arch. 5th Series, i. 347.

to have you knocked in the head, as General Montgomery was, if he can have the money chest in his power."

Governor Trumbull, too, the father of the commissary-general, observes subsequently : " It is justly to be expected that General Gates is discontented with his situation, finding himself limited and removed from the command, to be a wretched spectator of the ruin of the army, without power of attempting to save them." * We shall have frequent occasion hereafter to notice the discord in the service caused by this rankling discontent.

As to General Sullivan, who repaired to Philadelphia and tendered his resignation, the question of rank which had aggrieved him was explained in a manner that induced him to continue in service. It was universally allowed that his retreat had been ably conducted through all kinds of difficulties and disasters.

A greater source of solicitude to Washington than this jealousy between commanders, was the sectional jealousy springing up among the troops. In a letter to Schuyler (July 17th), he says, " I must entreat your attention to do away the unhappy and pernicious distinctions and jealousies between the troops of different governments. Enjoin this upon the officers, and let them inculcate and press home to the soldiery, the necessity of order and harmony among those who are embarked in one common cause, and mutually contending for all that freemen hold dear."

Nowhere were these sectional jealousies more prevalent than in the motley army assembled from distant quarters under Washington's own command. Reed, the adjutant-general, speaking on

* Gov. Trumbull to Mr. William Williams.

this subject, observes: "The Southern troops, comprising the regiments south of the Delaware, looked with very unkind feelings on those of New England; especially those from Connecticut, whose peculiarities of deportment made them the objects of ill-disguised derision among their fellow-soldiers." *

Among the troops thus designated as Southern, were some from Virginia under a Major Leitch; others from Maryland, under Colonel Smallwood; others from Delaware led by Colonel Haslet. There were four Continental battalions from Pennsylvania, commanded by Colonels Shee, St. Clair, Wayne, and Magaw; and provincial battalions, two of which were severally commanded by Colonels Miles and Atlee. The Continental battalion under Colonel Shee, was chiefly from the city of Philadelphia, especially the officers; among whom were Lambert Cadwalader and William Allen, members of two of the principal, and most aristocratic families, and Alexander Graydon, to whose memoirs we are indebted for some graphic pictures of the times.

These Pennsylvania troops were under the command of Brigadier-general Mifflin, who, in the preceding year, had acted as Washington's aide-de-camp, and afterwards as quartermaster-general. His townsman and intimate, Graydon, characterizes him as a man of education and cultivated manners, with a great talent at haranguing; highly animated in his appearance, full of activity and apparently of fire; but rather too much of a bustler, harassing his men unnecessarily. "He assumed," adds Graydon, "a little of the veteran, from having been before Boston." His troops were chiefly encamped near King's Bridge, and employed in constructing works at Fort Washington.

* Life of Reed, vol. i. p. 239.

Smallwood's Maryland battalion was one of the brightest in point of equipment. The scarlet and buff uniforms of those Southerners contrasted vividly with the rustic attire of the yeoman battalions from the East. Their officers, too, looked down upon their Connecticut compeers, who could only be distinguished from their men by wearing a cockade. " There were none," says Graydon, " by whom an unofficer-like appearance and deportment could be tolerated less than by a city-bred Marylander; who, at this time, was distinguished by the most fashionable cut coat, the most *macaroni* cocked-hat, and hottest blood in the Union." Alas, for the homespun-clad officers from Connecticut River!

The Pennsylvania regiment under Shee, according to Graydon, promoted balls and other entertainments, in contradistinction to the fast-days and sermons borrowed from New England. There was nothing of the puritanical spirit among the Pennsylvanian soldiery.

In the same sectional spirit, he speaks of the Connecticut light-horse : " Old-fashioned men, truly irregulars ; whether their clothing, equipments, or caparisons were regarded, it would have been difficult to have discovered any circumstance of uniformity. Instead of carbines and sabres, they generally carried fowling-pieces, some of them very long, such as in Pennsylvania are used for shooting ducks. Here and there one appeared in a dingy regimental of scarlet, with a triangular, tarnished, laced hat. These singular dragoons were volunteers, who came to make a tender of their services to the commander-in-chief. But they staid not long in New York. As such a body of cavalry had not been counted upon, there was in all probability a want of forage for their *jades*, which, in the spirit of ancient knight-hood, they absolutely refused to descend from ; and as the general had no use for cavaliers in his insular operations, they were forthwith dismissed, with suitable acknowledgments for their truly chivalrous ardor." *

The troops thus satirized, were a body of between four and five hundred Connecticut light-horse, under Colonel Thomas Seymour. On an appeal for aid to the governor of their State, they had voluntarily hastened on in advance of the militia, to render the most speedy succor. Supposing, from the suddenness and urgency of the call upon their services, that they were immediately to be called into action and promptly to return home, they had come off in such haste, that many were unprovided even with a blanket or a change of clothing.

Washington speaks of them as being for the most part, if not all, men of reputation and property. They were, in fact, mostly farmers. As to their sorry *jades*, they were rough country horses, such as farmers keep, not for show, but service. As to their dingy regimentals, we quote a word in their favor from a writer of that day. " Some of these worthy soldiers assisted in their present uniforms at the reduction of Louisburg, and their ' lank cheeks and war-worn coats,' are viewed with more veneration by their honest countrymen, than if they were glittering nabobs from India, or bashaws with nine tails." †

On arriving, their horses, from scarcity of forage, had to be pastured about King's Bridge. In fact, Washington informed them that, under present circumstances, they could not be of use as horsemen ; on which they concluded to stay, and do duty on foot till the arrival of the new levies. ‡ In a letter to Governor Trumbull (July 11), Washington observes : " The officers and

* Graydon's Memoirs, p. 155.   † Am. Archives, 5th Series, i. 175.
‡ Webb to Gov. Trumbull.

men of that corps have manifested so firm an attachment to the cause we are engaged in, that they have consented to remain here, till such a body of troops are marched from your colony as will be a sufficient reinforcement, so as to admit of their leaving this city with safety. * * * * They have the additional merit of determining to stay, even if they are obliged to maintain their horses at their own expense." *

In a very few days, however, the troopers, on being requested to mount guard like other soldiers, grew restless and uneasy. Colonel Seymour and his brother field-officers, therefore, addressed a note to Washington, stating that, by the positive laws of Connecticut, the light-horse were expressly exempted from staying in garrison, or doing duty on foot, apart from their horses; and that they found it impossible to detain their men any longer under that idea, they having come " without the least expectation or preparation for such services." They respectfully, therefore, asked a dismission in form. Washington's brief reply, shows that he was nettled by their conduct.

" Gentlemen: In answer to yours of this date, I can only repeat to you what I said last night, and that is, that if your men think themselves exempt from the common duty of a soldier—will not mount guard, do garrison duty, or service separate from their horses—they can no longer be of any use here, where horses cannot be brought to action, and I do not care how soon they are dismissed."

In fact, the assistance of these troops was much needed; yet he apprehended the exemption from fatigue and garrison duty which they demanded as a right, would, if granted, set a

---

* Am. Archives, 5th Series, i. 192.

dangerous example to others, and be productive of many evil consequences.

In the hurry of various concerns he directed his aide-de-camp, Colonel Webb, to write in his name to Governor Trumbull on the subject.

Colonel Seymour, on his return home, addressed a long letter to the governor explanatory of his conduct. "I can't help remarking to your honor," adds he, "that it may with truth be said, General Washington is a gentleman of extreme care and caution : that his requisitions for men are fully equal to the necessities of the case. * * * I should have stopped here, but am this moment informed that Mr. Webb, General Washington's aide-de-camp, has written to your honor something dishonorable to the light-horse. Whatever it may be I know not, but this I do know, that it is a general observation both in camp and country, if the butterflies and coxcombs were away from the army, we should not be put to so much difficulty in obtaining men of common sense to engage in the defence of their country." *

As to the Connecticut infantry which had been furnished by Governor Trumbull in the present emergency, they likewise were substantial farmers, whose business, he observed, would require their return, when the necessity of their further stay in the army should be over. They were all men of simple rural manners, from an agricultural State, where great equality of condition prevailed; the officers were elected by the men out of their own ranks, they were their own neighbors, and every way their equals. All this, as yet, was but little understood or appreci-

* Am. Archives, 5th Series, i. 513.

ated by the troops from the South, among whom military rank
was more defined and tenaciously observed, and where the officers
were men of the cities, and of more aristocratic habits.

We have drawn out from contemporary sources these few
particulars concerning the sectional jealousies thus early springing up among the troops from the different States, to show the
difficulties with which Washington had to contend at the outset,
and which formed a growing object of solicitude throughout the
rest of his career.

John Adams, speaking of the violent passions, and discordant
interests at work throughout the country, from Florida to Canada, observes: "It requires more serenity of temper, a deeper
understanding, and more courage than fell to the lot of Marlborough, to ride in this whirlwind." *

* Am. Archives, 4th Series, v. 1112.

CHAPTER XXIX.

SOUTHERN CRUISE OF SIR HENRY CLINTON—FORTIFICATIONS AT CHARLESTON
—ARRIVAL THERE OF GENERAL LEE—BATTLE AT SULLIVAN'S ISLAND—
WASHINGTON ANNOUNCES THE RESULT TO THE ARMY.

LETTERS from General Lee gave Washington intelligence of the
fate of Sir Henry Clinton's expedition to the South; that expedition which had been the subject of so much surmise and perplexity. Sir Henry in his cruise along the coast had been repeatedly foiled by Lee. First, as we have shown, when he looked
in at New York; next, when he paused at Norfolk in Virginia;
and lastly, when he made a bold attempt at Charleston in South
Carolina; for scarce did his ships appear off the bar of the harbor,
than the omnipresent Lee was marching his troops into the city.

Within a year past, Charleston had been fortified at various
points. Fort Johnson, on James Island, three miles from the
city, and commanding the breadth of the channel, was garrisoned
by a regiment of South Carolina regulars under Colonel Gadsden.
A strong fort had recently been constructed nearly opposite, on
the south-west point of Sullivan's Island, about six miles below
the city. It was mounted with twenty-six guns, and garrisoned
by three hundred and seventy-five regulars and a few militia, and
commanded by Colonel William Moultrie, of South Carolina,

who had constructed it. This fort, in connection with that on James Island, was considered the key of the harbor.

Cannon had also been mounted on Haddrell's Point on the mainland, to the north-west of Sullivan's Island, and along the bay in front of the town.

The arrival of General Lee gave great joy to the people of Charleston, from his high reputation for military skill and experience. According to his own account in a letter to Washington, the town on his arrival was "utterly defenceless." He was rejoiced therefore, when the enemy, instead of immediately attacking it, directed his whole force against the fort on Sullivan's Island. "He has lost an opportunity," said Lee, "such as I hope will never occur again, of taking the town."

The British ships, in fact, having passed the bar with some difficulty, landed their troops on Long Island, situated to the east of Sullivan's Island, and separated from it by a small creek called the Breach. Sir Henry Clinton meditated a combined attack with his land and naval forces on the fort commanded by Moultrie; the capture of which, he thought, would insure the reduction of Charleston.

The Americans immediately threw up works on the north-eastern extremity of Sullivan's Island, to prevent the passage of the enemy over the Breach, stationing a force of regulars and militia there, under Colonel Thompson. General Lee encamped on Haddrell's Point, on the mainland, to the north of the island, whence he intended to keep up a communication by a bridge of boats, so as to be ready at any moment to aid either Moultrie or Thompson.

Sir Henry Clinton, on the other hand, had to construct batteries on Long Island, to oppose those of Thompson, and cover the passage of his troops by boats or by the ford. Thus time was consumed, and the enemy were, from the 1st to the 28th of June, preparing for the attack; their troops suffering from the intense heat of the sun on the burning sands of Long Island, and both fleet and army complaining of brackish water and scanty and bad provisions.

At length on the 28th of June, the Thunder Bomb commenced the attack, throwing shells at the fort as the fleet, under Sir Peter Parker, advanced. About eleven o'clock the ships dropped their anchors directly before the front battery. "I was at this time in a boat," writes Lee, "endeavoring to make the island; but the wind and tide being violently against us, drove us on the main. They immediately commenced the most furious fire I ever heard or saw. I confess I was in pain, from the little confidence I reposed in our troops; the officers being all boys, and the men raw recruits. What augmented my anxiety was, that we had no bridge finished for retreat or communication; and the creek or cove which separates it from the continent is near a mile wide. I had received, likewise, intelligence that their land troops intended at the same time to land and assault. I never in my life felt myself so uneasy; and what added to my uneasiness was, that I knew our stock of ammunition was miserably low. I had once thought of ordering the commanding officer to spike his guns, and, when his ammunition was spent, to retreat with as little loss as possible. However, I thought proper previously to send to town for a fresh supply, if it could possibly be procured, and ordered my aide-de-camp, Mr. Byrd (who is a lad of magnanimous courage), to pass over in a small canoe, and report the state of the spirit of the garrison. If it had been low, I should have abandoned all thoughts of defence. His report was flattering.

I then determined to maintain the post at all risks, and passed the creek or cove in a small boat, in order to animate the garrison in propria personâ; but I found they had no occasion for such an encouragement.

"They were pleased with my visit, and assured me they never would abandon the post but with their lives. The cool courage they displayed astonished and enraptured me, for I do assure you, my dear general, I never experienced a better fire. Twelve full hours it was continued without intermission. The noble fellows who were mortally wounded, conjured their brethren never to abandon the standard of liberty. Those who lost their limbs deserted not their posts. Upon the whole, they acted like Romans in the third century."

Much of the foregoing is corroborated by the statement of a British historian. "While the continued fire of our ships," writes he, "seemed sufficient to shake the fierceness of the bravest enemy, and daunt the courage of the most veteran soldier, the return made by the fort could not fail calling for the respect, as well as of highly incommoding the brave seamen of Britain. In the midst of that dreadful roar of artillery, they stuck with the greatest constancy and firmness to their guns; fired deliberately and slowly, and took a cool and effective aim. The ships suffered accordingly, they were torn almost to pieces, and the slaughter was dreadful. Never did British valor shine more conspicuous, and never did our marine in an engagement of the same nature with any foreign enemy experience so rude an encounter." *

The fire from the ships did not produce the expected effect.

* Hist. Civil War in America.   Dublin, 1779.   Annual Register.

The fortifications were low, composed of earth and palmetto wood, which is soft, and makes no splinters, and the merlons were extremely thick. At one time there was a considerable pause in the American fire, and the enemy thought the fort was abandoned. It was only because the powder was exhausted. As soon as a supply could be forwarded from the mainland by General Lee, the fort resumed its fire with still more deadly effect. Through unskilful pilotage, several of the ships ran aground, where one, the frigate Actæon, remained; the rest were extricated with difficulty. Those which bore the brunt of the action were much cut up. One hundred and seventy-five men were killed, and nearly as many wounded. Captain Scott, commanding the Experiment, of fifty guns, lost an arm, and was otherwise wounded. Captain Morris, commanding the Actæon, was slain. So also was Lord Campbell, late governor of the province, who served as a volunteer on board of the squadron.

Sir Henry Clinton, with two thousand troops and five or six hundred seamen, attempted repeatedly to cross from Long Island, and co-operate in the attack upon the fort, but was as often foiled by Colonel Thompson, with his battery of two cannons, and a body of South Carolina rangers and North Carolina regulars. "Upon the whole," says Lee, "the South and North Carolina troops and Virginia rifle battalion we have here, are admirable soldiers."

The combat slackened before sunset, and ceased before ten o'clock. Sir Peter Parker, who had received a severe contusion in the engagement, then slipped his cables, and drew off his shattered ships to Five Fathom Hole. The Actæon remained aground.

On the following morning Sir Henry Clinton made another

attempt to cross from Long Island to Sullivan's Island; but was again repulsed, and obliged to take shelter behind his breast-works. Sir Peter Parker, too, giving up all hope of reducing the fort in the shattered condition of his ships, ordered that the Actæon should be set on fire and abandoned. The crew left her in flames, with the guns loaded, and the colors flying. The Americans boarded her in time to haul down her colors, and secure them as a trophy, discharge her guns at one of the enemy's ships, and load three boats with stores. They then abandoned her to her fate, and in half an hour she blew up.

Within a few days the troops were re-embarked from Long Island; the attempt upon Charleston was for the present abandoned, and the fleet once more put to sea.

In this action, one of the severest in the whole course of the war, the loss of the Americans in killed and wounded, was but thirty-five men. Colonel Moultrie derived the greatest glory from the defence of Sullivan's Island; though the thanks of Congress were voted as well to General Lee, Colonel Thompson, and those under their command.

"For God's sake, my dear general," writes Lee to Washington, "urge the Congress to furnish me with a thousand cavalry. With a thousand cavalry I could insure the safety of these Southern provinces; and without cavalry, I can answer for nothing. From want of this species of troops we had infallibly lost this capital, but the dilatoriness and stupidity of the enemy saved us."

The tidings of this signal repulse of the enemy came most opportunely to Washington, when he was apprehending an attack upon New York. He writes in a familiar vein to Schuyler on the subject. "Sir Peter Parker and his fleet got a severe drubbing in an attack upon our works on Sullivan's Island, just by Charleston in South Carolina; a part of their troops, at the same time, in attempting to land, were repulsed." He assumed a different tone in announcing it to the army in a general order of the 21st July. "This generous example of our troops under the like circumstances with us, the general hopes, will animate every officer and soldier to imitate, and even outdo them, when the enemy shall make the same attempt on us. With such a bright example before us of what can be done by brave men fighting in defence of their country, we shall be loaded with a double share of shame and infamy if we do not acquit ourselves with courage, and manifest a determined resolution to conquer or die."

CHAPTER XXX.

GENERAL PUTNAM, beside his bravery in the field, was somewhat
of a mechanical projector. The batteries at Fort Washington
had proved ineffectual in opposing the passage of hostile ships up
the Hudson. He was now engaged on a plan for obstructing the
channel opposite the fort, so as to prevent the passing of any
more ships. A letter from him to General Gates (July 26th) ex-
plains his project. " We are preparing chevaux-de-frise, at which
we make great despatch by the help of ships, which are to be
sunk—a scheme of mine which you may be assured is very simple; a plan of which I send you. The two ships' sterns lie towards each other, about seventy feet apart. Three large logs,
which reach from ship to ship, are fastened to them. The two

ships and logs stop the river two hundred and eighty feet. The ships are to be sunk, and when hauled down on one side, the pricks will be raised to a proper height, and they must inevitably stop the river, if the enemy will let us sink them."

It so happened that one Ephraim Anderson, adjutant to the second Jersey battalion, had recently submitted a project to Congress for destroying the enemy's fleet in the harbor of New York. He had attempted an enterprise of the kind against the British ships in the harbor of Quebec during the siege, and, according to his own account, would have succeeded, had not the enemy discovered his intentions, and stretched a cable across the mouth of the harbor, and had he not accidentally been much burnt.

His scheme was favorably entertained by Congress, and Washington, by a letter dated July 10th, was instructed to aid him in carrying it into effect. Anderson, accordingly, was soon at work at New York constructing fire-ships, with which the fleet was to be attacked. Simultaneous with the attack, a descent was to be made on the British camp on Staten Island, from the nearest point of the Jersey shore, by troops from Mercer's flying camp, and by others stationed at Bergen under Major Knowlton, Putnam's favorite officer for daring enterprises.

Putman entered into the scheme as zealously as if it had been his own. Indeed, by the tenor of his letter to Gates, already quoted, he seemed almost to consider it so. "The enemy's fleet," writes he, "now lies in the bay, close under Staten Island. Their troops possess no land here but the island. Is it not strange that those invincible troops, who were to lay waste all this country with their fleets and army, are so fond of islands and peninsulas, and dare not put their feet on the main? But I hope, by the blessing of God, and good friends, we shall pay them a visit on their island. For that end we are preparing fourteen fire-ships to go into their fleet, some of which are ready charged and fitted to sail, and I hope soon to have them all fixed."

Anderson, also, on the 31st July, writes from New York to the President of Congress: "I have been for some time past very assiduous in the preparation of fire-ships. Two are already complete, and hauled off into the stream; two more will be off to-morrow, and the residue in a very short time. In my next, I hope to give you a particular account of a general conflagration, as every thing in my power shall be exerted for the demolition of the enemy's fleet. I expect to take an active part, and be an instrument for that purpose. I am determined (God-willing) to make a conspicuous figure among them, by being a 'burning and shining light,' and thereby serve my country, and have the honor of meeting the approbation of Congress." *

Projectors are subject to disappointments. It was impossible to construct a sufficient number of fire-ships and galleys in time. The flying camp, too, recruited but slowly, and scarcely exceeded three thousand men; the combined attack by fire and sword had therefore to be given up, and the " burning and shining light " again failed of conflagration.

Still, a partial night attack on the Staten Island encampment was concerted by Mercer and Knowlton, and twice attempted. On one occasion, they were prevented from crossing the strait by tempestuous weather, on another by deficiency of boats.

In the course of a few days arrived a hundred sail, with large reinforcements, among which were one thousand Hessians, and as many more were reported to be on the way. The troops were disembarked on Staten Island, and fortifications thrown up on some of the most commanding hills.

All projects of attack upon the enemy were now out of the question. Indeed, some of Washington's ablest advisers questioned the policy of remaining in New York, where they might be entrapped as the British had been in Boston. Reed, the adjutant-general, observed that, as the communication by the Hudson was interrupted, there was nothing now to keep them at New York but a mere point of honor; in the mean time, they endangered the loss of the army and its military stores. Why should they risk so much in defending a city, while the greater part of its inhabitants were plotting their destruction? His advice was, that, when they could defend the city no longer, they should evacuate, and burn it, and retire from Manhattan Island; should avoid any general action, or indeed any action, unless in view of great advantages; and should make it a war of posts.

During the latter part of July, and the early part of August, ships of war with their tenders continued to arrive, and Scotch Highlanders, Hessians, and other troops to be landed on Staten Island. At the beginning of August, the squadron with Sir Henry Clinton, recently repulsed at Charleston, anchored in the bay. "His coming," writes Colonel Reed, "was as unexpected as if he had dropped from the clouds." He was accompanied by Lord Cornwallis, and brought three thousand troops.

In the mean time, Putnam's contrivances for obstructing the channel had reached their destined place. A letter dated Fort Washington, August 3d, says: "Four ships chained and boomed, with a number of amazing large chevaux-de-frise, were sunk close by the fort under command of General Mifflin, which fort mounts thirty-two pieces of heavy cannon. We are thoroughly sanguine that they [the ships up the river] never will be able to join the British fleet, nor assistance from the fleet be afforded to them; so that we may set them down as our own."

Another letter, written at the same date from Tarrytown, on the borders of the Tappan Sea, gives an account of an attack made by six row galleys upon the Phœnix and the Rose. They fought bravely for two hours, hulling the ships repeatedly, but sustaining great damage in return; until their commodore, Colonel Tupper, gave the signal to draw off. "Never," says the writer, "did men behave with more firm, determined spirit, than our little crews. One of our tars being mortally wounded, cried to his companions: 'I am a dying man; revenge my blood, my boys, and carry me alongside my gun, that I may die there.' We were so preserved by a gracious Providence, that in all our galleys we had but two men killed and fourteen wounded, two of which are thought dangerous. We hope to have another touch at those pirates before they leave our river; which God prosper!"

Such was the belligerent spirit prevailing up the Hudson.

The force of the enemy collected in the neighborhood of New York was about thirty thousand men; that of the Americans a little more than seventeen thousand, but was subsequently increased to twenty thousand, for the most part, raw and undisciplined. One fourth were on the sick list with bilious and putrid fevers and dysentery; others were absent on furlough or command; the rest had to be distributed over posts and stations fifteen miles apart.

The sectional jealousies prevalent among them, were more and more a subject of uneasiness to Washington. In one of his general orders he observes: "It is with great concern that the general understands that jealousies have arisen among the troops from the different provinces, and reflections are frequently thrown out which can only tend to irritate each other, and injure the noble cause in which we are engaged, and which we ought to support with one hand and one heart.   The general most earnestly entreats the officers and soldiers to consider the consequences; that they can no way assist our enemies more effectually than by making divisions among ourselves; that the honor and success of the army, and the safety of our bleeding country, depend upon harmony and good agreement with each other; that the provinces are all united to oppose the common enemy, and all distinctions sunk in the name of an American.   To make this name honorable, and to preserve the liberty of our country, ought to be our only emulation; and he will be the best soldier and the best patriot, who contributes most to this glorious work, whatever be his station, or from whatever part of the continent he may come.   Let all distinction of nations, countries and provinces, therefore, be lost in the generous contest, who shall behave with the most courage against the enemy, and the most kindness and good-humor to each other.   If there be any officers or soldiers so lost to virtue and a love of their country, as to continue in such practices after this order, the general assures them, and is authorized by Congress to declare to the whole army, that such persons shall be severely punished, and dismissed from the service with disgrace."

The urgency of such a general order is apparent in that early period of our confederation, when its various parts had not as yet been sufficiently welded together to acquire a thorough feeling of nationality; yet what an enduring lesson does it furnish for every stage of our Union!

We subjoin another of the general orders issued in this time
of gloom and anxiety :

"That the troops may have an opportunity of attending
public worship, as well as to take some rest after the great fatigue
they have gone through, the general, in future, excuses them
from fatigue duty on Sundays, except at the ship-yards, or on
special occasions, until further orders. The general is sorry to
be informed, that the foolish and wicked practice of profane
cursing and swearing, a vice heretofore little known in an American army, is growing into fashion. He hopes the officers will, by
example as well as influence, endeavor to check it, and that both
they and the men will reflect, that we can have little hope of the
blessing of Heaven on our arms, if we insult it by our impiety
and folly. Added to this, it is a vice so mean and low, without
any temptation, that every man of sense and character detests
and despises it." *

While Washington thus endeavored to elevate the minds of
his soldiery to the sanctity of the cause in which they were engaged, he kept the most watchful eye upon the movements of the
enemy. Beside their great superiority in point of numbers as well
as discipline, to his own crude and scanty legions, they possessed
a vast advantage in their fleet. "They would not be half the
enemy they are," observed Colonel Reed, "if they were once
separated from their ships." Every arrival and departure of
these, therefore, was a subject of speculation and conjecture.
Aaron Burr, at that time in New York, aide-de-camp to General
Putnam, speaks in a letter to an uncle, of thirty transports,

---

* Orderly Book, Aug. 3, as cited by Sparks. Writings of Washington,
vol. iv. p. 28.

which, under convoy of three frigates, had put to sea on the 7th of August, with the intention of sailing round Long Island and coming through the Sound, and thus investing the city by the North and East Rivers. " They are then to land on both sides of the island," writes he, " join their forces, and draw a line across, which will hem us in, and totally cut off all communication; after which, they will have their own fun." He adds: " They hold us in the utmost contempt. Talk of forcing all our lines without firing a gun. The bayonet is their pride. They have forgot Bunker's Hill." *

In this emergency, Washington wrote to General Mercer for 2,000 men from the flying camp. Colonel Smallwood's battalion was immediately furnished, as a part of them. The Convention of the State ordered out hasty levies of country militia, to form temporary camps on the shore of the Sound, and on that of the Hudson above King's Bridge, to annoy the enemy, should they attempt to land from their ships on either of these waters. Others were sent to reinforce the posts on Long Island. As Kings County on Long Island was noted for being a stronghold of the disaffected, the Convention ordered that, should any of the militia of that county refuse to serve, they should be disarmed and secured, and their possessions laid waste.

Many of the yeomen of the country, thus hastily summoned from the plough, were destitute of arms, in lieu of which they were ordered to bring with them a shovel, spade, or pickaxe, or a scythe straightened and fastened to a pole. This rustic array may have provoked the thoughtless sneers of city scoffers, such as those cited by Graydon; but it was in truth one of the glori-

* Am. Archives, 5th Series, i. 887.

ous features of the Revolution, to be thus aided in its emergencies by "hasty levies of husbandmen." *

By the authority of the New York Convention, Washington had appointed General George Clinton to the command of the levies on both sides of the Hudson. He now ordered him to hasten down with them to the fort just erected on the north side of King's Bridge; leaving two hundred men under the command of a brave and alert officer to throw up works at the pass of Anthony's Nose, where the main road to Albany crosses that mountain. Troops of horse also were to be posted by him along the river to watch the motions of the enemy.

Washington now made the last solemn preparations for the impending conflict. All suspected persons, whose presence might promote the plans of the enemy, were removed to a distance. All papers respecting affairs of State were put up in a large case, to be delivered to Congress. As to his domestic arrangements,

---

* General orders, Aug. 8th, show the feverish state of affairs in the city. "As the movements of the enemy, and intelligence by deserters, give the utmost reason to believe that the great struggle in which we are contending for every thing dear to us and our posterity is near at hand, the general most earnestly recommends the closest attention to the state of the men's arms, ammunition, and flints; that if we should be suddenly called to action, nothing of this kind may be to provide. And he does most anxiously exhort both officers and soldiers not to be out of their quarters or encampments, especially in the morning, or upon the tide of flood.

"A flag in the daytime, or a light at night, in the fort on Bayard's Hill, with three guns from the same place fired quick but distinct, is to be considered as a signal for the troops to repair to their alarm posts, and prepare for action. And that the alarm may be more effectually given, the drums are immediately to beat to arms upon the signal being given from Bayard's Hill. This order is not to be considered as countermanding the firing two guns at Fort George, as formerly ordered. That is also to be done on an alarm, but the flag will not be hoisted at the old head-quarters in Broadway."—*Am. Archives, 5th Series,* i. 912.

Mrs. Washington had some time previously gone to Philadelphia, with the intention of returning to Virginia, as there was no prospect of her being with him any part of the summer, which threatened to be one of turmoil and danger. The other ladies, wives of general officers, who used to grace and enliven head-quarters, had all been sent out of the way of the storm which was lowering over this devoted city.

Accounts of deserters, and other intelligence, informed Washington, on the 17th, that a great many of the enemy's troops had gone on board of the transports; that three days' provisions had been cooked, and other steps taken indicating an intention of leaving Staten Island. Putnam, also, came up from below with word that at least one fourth of the fleet had sailed. There were many conjectures at head-quarters as to whither they were bound, or whether they had not merely shifted their station. Every thing indicated, however, that affairs were tending to a crisis.

The "hysterical alarms" of the peaceful inhabitants of New York, which had provoked the soldierlike impatience and satirical sneers of Lee, inspired different sentiments in the benevolent heart of Washington, and produced the following letter to the New York Convention:

"When I consider that the city of New York will, in all human probability, very soon be the scene of a bloody conflict, I cannot but view the great numbers of women, children, and infirm persons remaining in it, with the most melancholy concern. When the men-of-war (the Phœnix and Rose) passed up the river, the shrieks and cries of these poor creatures, running every way with their children, were truly distressing, and I fear they will have an unhappy effect upon the ears and minds of our young and inexperienced soldiery. Can no method be devised for their removal?"

How vividly does this call to mind the compassionate sensibility of his younger days, when commanding at Winchester, in Virginia, in time of public peril; and melted to "deadly sorrow" by the "supplicating tears of the women, and moving petitions of the men." As then, he listened to the prompt suggestions of his own heart; and, without awaiting the action of the Convention, issued a proclamation, advising the inhabitants to remove, and requiring the officers and soldiery to aid the helpless and the indigent. The Convention soon responded to his appeal, and appointed a committee to effect these purposes in the most humane and expeditious manner.

A gallant little exploit at this juncture, gave a fillip to the spirits of the community. Two of the fire-ships recently constructed, went up the Hudson to attempt the destruction of the ships which had so long been domineering over its waters. One succeeded in grappling the Phœnix, and would soon have set her in flames, but in the darkness got to leeward, and was cast loose without effecting any damage. The other, in making for the Rose, fell foul of one of the tenders, grappled and burnt her. The enterprise was conducted with spirit, and though it failed of its main object, had an important effect. The commanders of the ships determined to abandon those waters, where their boats were fired upon by the very yeomanry whenever they attempted to land; and where their ships were in danger from midnight incendiaries, while riding at anchor. Taking advantage of a brisk wind, and favoring tide, they made all sail early on the morning of the 18th of August, and stood down the river, keeping close under the eastern shore, where they supposed the guns from

Mount Washington could not be brought to bear upon them. Notwithstanding this precaution, the Phœnix was thrice hulled by shots from the fort, and one of the tenders once. The Rose, also, was hulled once by a shot from Burdett's Ferry. The men on board were kept close, to avoid being picked off by a party of riflemen posted on the river bank. The ships fired grape-shot as they passed, but without effecting any injury. Unfortunately, a passage had been left open in the obstructions on which General Putnam had calculated so sanguinely; it was to have been closed in the course of a day or two. Through this they made their way, guided by a deserter; which alone, in Putnam's opinion, saved them from being checked in their career, and utterly destroyed by the batteries.

CHAPTER XXXI.

THE BATTLE OF LONG ISLAND.

THE movements of the British fleet, and of the camp on Staten Island, gave signs of a meditated attack; but, as the nature of that attack was uncertain, Washington was obliged to retain the greater part of his troops in the city for its defence, holding them ready, however, to be transferred to any point in the vicinity. General Mifflin, with about five hundred of the Pennsylvania troops, of Colonels Shee and Magaw's regiments, were at King's Bridge, ready to aid at a moment's notice. "They are the best disciplined of any troops that I have yet seen in the army," said General Heath, who had just reviewed them. General George Clinton was at that post, with about fourteen hundred of his yeomanry of the Hudson. As the Phœnix and Rose had explored the shores, and taken the soundings as far as they had gone up the river, General Heath thought Howe might attempt an attack somewhere above King's Bridge, rather than in the face of the many and strong works erected in and around the city. "Should his inclination lead him this way," adds he, "nature has done much for us, and we shall, as fast as possible, add the strength of art. We are pushing our works with great diligence." *

* Heath to Washington, Aug. 17–18.

Reports from different quarters, gave Washington reason to apprehend that the design of the enemy might be to land part of their force on Long Island, and endeavor to get possession of the heights of Brooklyn, which overlooked New York; while another part should land above the city, as General Heath suggested. Thus, various disconnected points, distant from each other, and a great extent of intervening country, had to be defended by raw troops, against a superior force, well disciplined, and possessed of every facility for operating by land and water.

General Greene, with a considerable force, was stationed at Brooklyn. He had acquainted himself with all the localities of the island, from Hell Gate to the Narrows, and made his plan of defence accordingly. His troops were diligently occupied in works which he laid out, about a mile beyond the village of Brooklyn, and facing the interior of the island, whence a land attack might be attempted.

Brooklyn was immediately opposite to New York. The Sound, commonly called the East River, in that place about three quarters of a mile in width, swept its rapid tides between them. The village stood on a kind of peninsula, formed by the deep inlets of Wallabout Bay on the north, and Gowanus Cove on the south. A line of intrenchments and strong redoubts extended across the neck of the peninsula, from the bay to a swamp and creek emptying into the cove. To protect the rear of the works from the enemy's ships, a battery was erected at Red Hook, the south-west corner of the peninsula, and a fort on Governor's Island, nearly opposite.

About two miles and a half in front of the line of intrench-ments and redoubts, a range of hills, densely wooded, extended from south-west to north-east, forming a natural barrier across the

island. It was traversed by three roads. One, on the left of
the works, stretched eastwardly to Bedford, and then by a pass
through the Bedford Hills to the village of Jamaica; another,
central and direct, led through the woody heights to Flatbush; a
third, on the right of the lines, passed by Gowanus Cove to the
Narrows and Gravesend Bay.

The occupation of this range of hills, and the protection of
its passes, had been designed by General Greene; but unfortunately, in the midst of his arduous toils, he was taken down by a
raging fever, which confined him to his bed; and General Sullivan, just returned from Lake Champlain, had the temporary
command.

Washington saw that to prevent the enemy from landing on
Long Island would be impossible, its great extent affording so
many places favorable for that purpose, and the American works
being at the part opposite to New York. "However," writes he
to the President of Congress, "we shall attempt to harass them
as much as possible, which is all that we can do."

On the 21st came a letter, written in all haste by Brigadier-
general William Livingston, of New Jersey. Movements of the
enemy on Staten Island had been seen from his camp. He had
sent over a spy at midnight, who brought back the following
intelligence. Twenty thousand men had embarked to make an
attack on Long Island, and up the Hudson. Fifteen thousand
remained on Staten Island, to attack Bergen Point, Elizabethtown Point, and Amboy. The spy declared that he had heard
orders read, and the conversation of the generals. "They appear
very determined," added he, "and will put all to the sword!"

Washington sent a copy of the letter to the New York Convention. On the following morning (August 22d) the enemy

appeared to be carrying their plans into execution.   The reports of cannon and musketry were heard from Long Island, and columns of smoke were descried rising above the groves and orchards at a distance.   The city, as usual, was alarmed, and had reason to be so; for word soon came that several thousand men, with artillery and light-horse, were landed at Gravesend; and that Colonel Hand, stationed there with the Pennsylvania rifle regiment, had retreated to the lines, setting fire to stacks of wheat, and other articles, to keep them from falling into the enemy's hands.

Washington apprehended an attempt of the foe by a forced march, to surprise the lines at Brooklyn.   He immediately sent over a reinforcement of six battalions.   It was all that he could spare, as with the next tide the ships might bring up the residue of the army, and attack the city.   Five battalions more, however, were ordered to be ready as a reinforcement, if required.   " Be cool, but determined," was the exhortation given to the departing troops.   " Do not fire at a distance, but wait the commands of your officers.   It is the general's express orders, that if any man attempt to skulk, lie down, or retreat without orders, he be instantly shot down for an example."

In justice to the poor fellows, most of whom were going for the first time on a service of life and death, Washington observes, that " they went off in high spirits," and that the whole capable of duty evinced the same cheerfulness.*

Nine thousand of the enemy had landed, with forty pieces of cannon.   Sir Henry Clinton had the chief command, and led the first division.   His associate officers were the Earls of

* Washington to the President of Congress.

Cornwallis and Percy, General Grant, and General Sir William Erskine. As their boats approached the shore, Colonel Hand, stationed, as has been said, in the neighborhood with his rifle regiment, retreated to the chain of wooded hills, and took post on a height commanding the central road leading from Flatbush. The enemy having landed without opposition, Lord Cornwallis was detached with the reserve to Flatbush, while the rest of the army extended itself from the ferry at the Narrows through Utrecht and Gravesend, to the village of Flatland.

Lord Cornwallis, with two battalions of light-infantry, Colonel Donop's corps of Hessians, and six field-pieces, advanced rapidly to seize upon the central pass through the hills. He found Hand and his riflemen ready to make a vigorous defence. This brought him to a halt, having been ordered not to risk an attack should the pass be occupied. He took post for the night, therefore, in the village of Flatbush.

It was evidently the aim of the enemy to force the lines at Brooklyn, and get possession of the heights. Should they succeed, New York would be at their mercy. The panic and distress of the inhabitants went on increasing. Most of those who could afford it, had already removed to the country. There was now a new cause of terror. It was rumored that, should the American army retreat from the city, leave would be given for any one to set it on fire. The New York Convention apprised Washington of this rumor. "I can assure you, gentlemen," writes he in reply, "that this report is not founded on the least authority from me. On the contrary, I am so sensible of the value of such a city, and the consequences of its destruction to many worthy citizens and their families, that nothing but the last necessity, and that such as would justify me to the whole world, would induce me to give orders to that purpose."

In this time of general alarm, head-quarters were besieged by applicants for safeguard from the impending danger; and Washington was even beset in his walks by supplicating women with their children. The patriot's heart throbbed feelingly under the soldier's belt. Nothing could surpass the patience and benignant sympathy with which he listened to them, and endeavored to allay their fears. Again he urged the Convention to carry out their measures for the removal of these defenceless beings. " There are many," writes he, " who anxiously wish to remove, but have not the means."

On the 24th he crossed over to Brooklyn, to inspect the lines and reconnoitre the neighborhood. In this visit he felt sensibly the want of General Greene's presence, to explain his plans and point out the localities.

The American advanced posts were in the wooded hills. Colonel Hann, with his riflemen, kept watch over the central road, and a strong redoubt had been thrown up in front of the pass, to check any advance of the enemy from Flatbush. Another road leading from Flatbush to Bedford, by which the enemy might get round to the left of the works at Brooklyn, was guarded by two regiments, one under Colonel Williams, posted on the north side of the ridge, the other by a Pennsylvanian rifle regiment, under Colonel Miles, posted on the south side. The enemy were stretched along the country beyond the chain of hills.

As yet, nothing had taken place but skirmishing and irregular firing between the outposts. It was with deep concern Washington noticed a prevalent disorder and confusion in the camp. There was a want of system among the officers, and co-operation among the troops, each corps seeming to act independently of the rest. Few of the men had any military experience, except, perchance, in bush-fighting with the Indians. Unaccustomed to discipline and the restraint of camps, they sallied forth whenever they pleased, singly or in squads, prowling about and firing upon the enemy, like hunters after game.

Much of this was no doubt owing to the protracted illness of General Greene.

On returning to the city, therefore, Washington gave the command on Long Island to General Putnam, warning him, however, in his letter of instructions, to summon the officers together, and enjoin them to put a stop to the irregularities which he had observed among the troops. Lines of defence were to be formed round the encampment, and works on the most advantageous ground. Guards were to be stationed on the lines, with a brigadier of the day constantly at hand to see that orders were executed. Field-officers were to go the rounds and report the situation of the guards, and no one was to pass beyond the lines without a special permit in writing. At the same time, partisan and scouting parties, under proper officers, and with regular license, might sally forth to harass the enemy, and prevent their carrying off the horses and cattle of the country people.

Especial attention was called to the wooded hills between the works and the enemy's camp. The passes through them were to be secured by *abatis*, and defended by the best troops, who should, at all hazards, prevent the approach of the enemy. The militia being the least tutored and experienced, might man the interior works.

Putnam crossed with alacrity to his post. "He was made

happy," writes Colonel Reed, "by obtaining leave to go over. The brave old man was quite miserable at being kept here."

In the mean time, the enemy were augmenting their forces on the island. Two brigades of Hessians, under Lieutenant-general De Heister, were transferred from the camp on Staten Island on the 25th. This movement did not escape the vigilant eye of Washington. By the aid of his telescope, he had noticed that from time to time tents were struck on Staten Island, and portions of the encampment broken up; while ship after ship weighed anchor, and dropped down to the Narrows.

He now concluded that the enemy were about to make a push with their main force for the possession of Brooklyn Heights. He accordingly sent over additional reinforcements, and among them Colonel John Haslet's well equipped and well disciplined Delaware regiment; which was joined to Lord Stirling's brigade, chiefly composed of Southern troops, and stationed outside of the lines. These were troops which Washington regarded with peculiar satisfaction, on account of their soldierlike appearance and discipline.

On the 26th, he crossed over to Brooklyn, accompanied by Reed, the adjutant-general. There was much movement among the enemy's troops, and their number was evidently augmented. In fact, General De Heister had reached Flatbush with his Hessians, and taken command of the centre; whereupon Sir Henry Clinton, with the right wing, drew off to Flatlands, in a diagonal line to the right of De Heister, while the left wing, commanded by General Grant, extended to the place of landing on Gravesend Bay.

Washington remained all day, aiding General Putnam with his counsels, who, new to the command, had not been able to make himself well acquainted with the fortified posts beyond the lines. In the evening, Washington returned to the city, full of anxious thought. A general attack was evidently at hand. Where would it be made? How would his inexperienced troops stand the encounter? What would be the defence of the city if assailed by the ships? It was a night of intense solicitude, and well might it be; for during that night a plan was carried into effect, fraught with disaster to the Americans.

The plan to which we allude was concerted by General Howe, the commander-in-chief. Sir Henry Clinton, with the vanguard, composed of the choicest troops, was, by a circuitous march in the night, to throw himself into the road leading from Jamaica to Bedford, seize upon a pass through the Bedford Hills, within three miles of that village, and thus turn the left of the American advanced posts. It was preparatory to this nocturnal march, that Sir Henry during the day had fallen back with his troops from Flatbush to Flatlands, and caused that stir and movement which had attracted the notice of Washington.

To divert the attention of the Americans from this stealthy march on their left, General Grant was to menace their right flank toward Gravesend before daybreak, and General De Heister to cannonade their centre, where Colonel Hand was stationed. Neither, however, was to press an attack until the guns of Sir Henry Clinton should give notice that he had effected his purpose, and turned the left flank of the Americans; then the latter were to be assailed at all points with the utmost vigor.

About nine o'clock in the evening, of the 26th, Sir Henry Clinton began his march from Flatlands with the vanguard, composed of light infantry. Lord Percy followed with the grenadiers, artillery, and light dragoons, forming the centre. Lord

Cornwallis brought up the rear-guard with the heavy ordnance. General Howe accompanied this division.

It was a silent march, without beat of drum or sound of trumpet, under guidance of a Long Island tory, along by-roads traversing a swamp by a narrow causeway, and so across the country to the Jamaica road. About two hours before daybreak, they arrived within half a mile of the pass through the Bedford Hills, and halted to prepare for an attack. At this juncture they captured an American patrol, and learnt, to their surprise, that the Bedford pass was unoccupied. In fact, the whole road beyond Bedford, leading to Jamaica, had been left unguarded, excepting by some light volunteer troops. Colonels Williams and Miles, who were stationed to the left of Colonel Hand, among the wooded hills, had been instructed to send out parties occasionally to patrol the road, but no troops had been stationed at the Bedford pass. The road and pass may not have been included in General Greene's plan of defence, or may have been thought too far out of the way to need special precaution. The neglect of them, however, proved fatal.

Sir Henry Clinton immediately detached a battalion of light infantry to secure the pass; and, advancing with his corps at the first break of day, possessed himself of the heights. He was now within three miles of Bedford, and his march had been undiscovered. Having passed the heights, therefore, he halted his division for the soldiers to take some refreshment, preparatory to the morning's hostilities.

There we will leave them, while we note how the other divisions performed their part of the plan.

About midnight General Grant moved from Gravesend Bay, with the left wing, composed of two brigades and a regiment of regulars, a battalion of New York loyalists, and ten field-pieces. He proceeded along the road leading past the Narrows and Gowanus Cove, toward the right of the American works. A picket guard of Pennsylvanian and New York militia, under Colonel Atlee, retired before him fighting to a position on the skirts of the wooded hills.

In the mean time, scouts had brought in word to the American lines that the enemy were approaching in force upon the right. General Putnam instantly ordered Lord Stirling to hasten with the two regiments nearest at hand, and hold them in check. These were Haslet's Delaware, and Smallwood's Maryland regiments; the latter the *macaronis*, in scarlet and buff, who had outshone, in camp, their yoeman fellow-soldiers in homespun. They turned out with great alacrity, and Stirling pushed forward with them on the road toward the Narrows. By the time he had passed Gowanus Cove, daylight began to appear. Here, on a rising ground, he met Colonel Atlee with his Pennsylvania Provincials, and learned that the enemy were near. Indeed, their front began to appear in the uncertain twilight. Stirling ordered Atlee to place himself in ambush in an orchard on the left of the road, and await their coming up, while he formed the Delaware and Maryland regiments along a ridge from the road, up to a piece of woods on the top of the hill.

Atlee gave the enemy two or three volleys as they approached, and then retreated and formed in the wood on Lord Stirling's left. By this time his lordship was reinforced by Kichline's riflemen, part of whom he placed along a hedge at the foot of the hill, and part in front of the wood. General Grant threw his light troops in the advance, and posted them in an orchard and behind hedges, extending in front of the Americans, and about one hundred and fifty yards distant.

It was now broad daylight. A rattling fire commenced between the British light troops and the American riflemen, which continued for about two hours, when the former retired to their main body. In the mean time, Stirling's position had been strengthened by the arrival of Captain Carpenter with two field-pieces. These were placed on the side of the hill, so as to command the road and the approach for some hundred yards. General Grant, likewise, brought up his artillery within three hundred yards, and formed his brigades on opposite hills, about six hundred yards distant. There was occasional cannonading on both sides, but neither party sought a general action.

Lord Stirling's object was merely to hold the enemy in check; and the instructions of General Grant, as we have shown, were not to press an attack until aware that Sir Henry Clinton was on the left flank of the Americans.

During this time, De Heister had commenced his part of the plan by opening a cannonade from his camp at Flatbush, upon the redoubt, at the pass of the wooded hills, where Hand and his riflemen were stationed. On hearing this, General Sullivan, who was within the lines, rode forth to Colonel Hand's post to reconnoitre. De Heister, however, according to the plan of operations, did not advance from Flatbush, but kept up a brisk fire from his artillery on the redoubt in front of the pass, which replied as briskly. At the same time, a cannonade from a British ship upon the battery at Red Hook, contributed to distract the attention of the Americans.

In the mean time terror reigned in New York. The volleying of musketry and the booming of cannon at early dawn, had told of the fighting that had commenced. As the morning advanced, and platoon firing and the occasional discharge of a field-piece were heard in different directions, the terror increased. Washington was still in doubt whether this was but a part of a general attack, in which the city was to be included. Five ships of the line were endeavoring to beat up the bay. Were they to cannonade the city, or to land troops above it? Fortunately, a strong head-wind baffled their efforts; but one vessel of inferior force got up far enough to open the fire already mentioned upon the fort at Red Hook.

Seeing no likelihood of an immediate attack upon the city, Washington hastened over to Brooklyn in his barge, and galloped up to the works. He arrived there in time to witness the catastrophe for which all the movements of the enemy had been concerted.

The thundering of artillery in the direction of Bedford, had given notice that Sir Henry had turned the left of the Americans. De Heister immediately ordered Colonel Count Donop to advance with his Hessian regiment, and storm the redoubt, while he followed with his whole division. Sullivan did not remain to defend the redoubt. Sir Henry's cannon had apprised him of the fatal truth, that his flank was turned, and he in danger of being surrounded. He ordered a retreat to the lines, but it was already too late. Scarce had he descended from the height, and emerged into the plain, when he was met by the British light infantry, and dragoons, and driven back into the woods. By this time De Heister and his Hessians had come up, and now commenced a scene of confusion, consternation, and slaughter, in which the troops under Williams and Miles were involved. Hemmed in and untrapped between the British and Hessians, and driven from one to the other, the Americans fought for a time bravely, or rather desperately. Some were cut down and trampled by the cavalry, others bayoneted without mercy by the Hessians. Some rallied in groups, and made a brief stand with their rifles from rocks or behind trees. The whole pass was a scene of carnage, resounding with the clash of arms, the tramp of horses, the volleying of fire-arms and the cries of the combatants, with now and then the dreary braying of the trumpet. We give the words of one who mingled in the fight, and whom we have heard speak with horror of the sanguinary fury with which the Hessians plied the bayonet. At length some of the Americans, by a desperate effort, cut their way through the host of foes, and effected a retreat to the lines, fighting as they went. Others took refuge among the woods and fastnesses of the hills, but a great part were either killed or taken prisoners. Among the latter was General Sullivan.

Washington, as we have observed, arrived in time to witness this catastrophe, but was unable to prevent it. He had heard the din of the battle in the woods, and seen the smoke rising from among the trees; but a deep column of the enemy was descending from the hills on the left; his choicest troops were all in action, and he had none but militia to man the works. His solicitude was now awakened for the safety of Lord Stirling and his corps, who had been all the morning exchanging cannonades with General Grant. The forbearance of the latter in not advancing, though so superior in force, had been misinterpreted by the Americans. According to Colonel Haslet's statement, the Delawares and Marylanders, drawn up on the side of the hill, " stood upwards of four hours, with a firm and determined countenance, in close array, their colors flying, the enemy's artillery playing on them all the while, *not daring to advance and attack them*, though six times their number, and nearly surrounding them." [*]

Washington saw the danger to which these brave fellows were exposed, though they could not. Stationed on a hill within the lines, he commanded, with his telescope, a view of the whole field, and saw the enemy's reserve, under Cornwallis, marching down by a cross-road to get in their rear, and thus place them between two fires. With breathless anxiety he watched the result.

The sound of Sir Henry Clinton's cannon apprised Stirling that the enemy was between him and the lines. General Grant, too, aware that the time had come for earnest action, was closing up, and had already taken Colonel Atlee prisoner. His lordship now thought to effect a circuitous retreat to the lines, by crossing the creek which empties into Gowanus Cove, near what was called the Yellow Mills. There was a bridge and mill-dam, and the creek might be forded at low water, but no time was to be lost, for the tide was rising.

Leaving part of his men to keep face toward General Grant, Stirling advanced with the rest to pass the creek, but was suddenly checked by the appearance of Cornwallis and his grenadiers.

Washington, and some of his officers on the hill, who watched every movement, had supposed that Stirling and his troops, finding the case desperate, would surrender in a body, without firing. On the contrary, his lordship boldly attacked Cornwallis with half of Smallwood's battalion, while the rest of his troops retreated across the creek. Washington wrung his hands in agony

---

[*] Atlee to Col. Rodney.   Sparks, iv. 516.

at the sight. "Good God!" cried he, "what brave fellows I must this day lose!"*

It was, indeed, a desperate fight; and now Smallwood's *macaronis* showed their game spirit. They were repeatedly broken, but as often rallied, and renewed the fight. "We were on the point of driving Lord Cornwallis from his station," writes Lord Stirling, "but large reinforcements arriving, rendered it impossible to do more than provide for safety."

"Being thus surrounded, and no probability of a reinforcement," writes a Maryland officer, "his lordship ordered me to retreat with the remaining part of our men, and force our way to our camp. We soon fell in with a party of the enemy, who clubbed their firelocks, and waved their hats to us as if they meant to surrender as prisoners; but on our advancing within sixty yards, they presented their pieces and fired, which we returned with so much warmth that they soon quitted their post, and retired to a large body that was lying in ambuscade." †

The enemy rallied, and returned to the combat with additional force. Only five companies of Smallwood's battalion were now in action. There was a warm and close engagement for nearly ten minutes. The struggle became desperate on the part of the Americans. Broken and disordered, they rallied in a piece of woods, and made a second attack. They were again overpowered with numbers. Some were surrounded and bayoneted in a field of Indian corn; others joined their comrades who were retreating across the marsh. Lord Stirling had encouraged and animated his young soldiers by his voice and example, but

* Letter from an American officer. Am. Archives, 5th Series, ii. 108.
† Letter from a Marylander. Idem, 5th Series, i. 1232.

when all was lost, he sought out General De Heister, and surrendered himself as his prisoner.

More than two hundred and fifty brave fellows, most of them of Smallwood's regiment, perished in this deadly struggle, within sight of the lines of Brooklyn. That part of the Delaware troops who had first crossed the creek and swamp, made good their retreat to the lines with a trifling loss, and entered the camp covered with mud and drenched with water, but bringing with them twenty-three prisoners, and their standard tattered by grapeshot.

The enemy now concentrated their forces within a few hundred yards of the redoubts. The grenadiers were within musket shot. Washington expected they would storm the works, and prepared for a desperate defence. The discharge of a cannon and volleys of musketry from the part of the lines nearest to them, seemed to bring them to a pause.

It was, in truth, the forbearance of the British commander that prevented a bloody conflict. His troops, heated with action and flushed with success, were eager to storm the works; but he was unwilling to risk the loss of life that must attend an assault, when the object might be attained at a cheaper rate, by regular approaches. Checking the ardor of his men, therefore, though with some difficulty, he drew them off to a hollow way, in front of the lines, but out of reach of the musketry, and encamped there for the night. *

The loss of the Americans in this disastrous battle has been variously stated, but is thought in killed, wounded and prisoners, to have been nearly two thousand; a large number, considering

---

* General Howe to Lord G. Germaine. Remembrancer, iii. 347.

that not above five thousand were engaged. The enemy acknowledgd a loss of 380 killed and wounded.*

The success of the enemy was attributed, in some measure, to the doubt in which Washington was kept as to the nature of the intended attack, and at what point it would chiefly be made. This obliged him to keep a great part of his forces in New York, and to distribute those at Brooklyn over a wide extent of country, and at widely distant places. In fact, he knew not the superior number of the enemy encamped on Long Island, a majority of them having been furtively landed in the night, some days after the debarkation of the first division.

Much of the day's disaster has been attributed, also, to a confusion in the command, caused by the illness of General Greene. Putnam, who had supplied his place in the emergency after the enemy had landed, had not time to make himself acquainted with the post, and the surrounding country. Sullivan, though in his letters he professes to have considered himself subordinate to General Putnam within the lines, seems still to have exercised somewhat of an independent command, and to have acted at his own discretion : while Lord Stirling was said to have command of all the troops outside of the works.

The fatal error, however, and one probably arising from all these causes, consisted in leaving the passes through the wooded hills too weakly fortified and guarded; and especially in neglecting the eastern road, by which Sir Henry Clinton got in the rear of the advanced troops, cut them off from the lines, and subjected them to a cross fire of his own men and De Heister's Hessians.

* Howe states the prisoners at 1094, and computes the whole American loss at 3,300.

This able and fatal scheme of the enemy might have been thwarted, had the army been provided with a few troops of light-horse, to serve as videttes. With these to scour the roads and bring intelligence, the night march of Sir Henry Clinton, so decisive of the fortunes of the day, could hardly have failed to be discovered and reported. The Connecticut horsemen, therefore, ridiculed by the Southerners for their homely equipments, sneered at as useless, and dismissed for standing on their dignity and privileges as troopers, might, if retained, have saved the army from being surprised and severed, its advanced guards routed, and those very Southern troops cut up, captured, and almost annihilated.

CHAPTER XXXII.

THE RETREAT FROM LONG ISLAND.

THE night after the battle was a weary, yet almost sleepless one to the Americans. Fatigued, dispirited, many of them sick and wounded, yet they were, for the most part, without tent or other shelter. To Washington it was a night of anxious vigil. Every thing boded a close and deadly conflict. The enemy had pitched a number of tents about a mile distant. Their sentries were but a quarter of a mile off, and close to the American sentries. At four o'clock in the morning, Washington went the round of the works, to see that all was right, and to speak words of encouragement. The morning broke lowering and dreary. Large encampments were gradually descried; to appearance, the enemy were twenty thousand strong. As the day advanced, their ordnance began to play upon the works. They were proceeding to intrench themselves, but were driven into their tents by a drenching rain.

Early in the morning General Mifflin arrived in camp, with part of the troops which had been stationed at Fort Washington and King's Bridge. He brought with him Shee's prime Phila-delphia regiment, and Magaw's Pennsylvania regiment, both well disciplined and officered, and accustomed to act together. They were so much reduced in number, however, by sickness, that they

did not amount in the whole, to more than eight hundred men.
With Mifflin came also Colonel Glover's Massachusetts regiment,
composed chiefly of Marblehead fishermen and sailors, hardy,
adroit, and weather-proof; trimly clad in blue jackets and trowsers. The detachment numbered, in the whole, about thirteen
hundred men, all fresh and full of spirits. Every eye brightened
as they marched briskly along the line with alert step and cheery
aspect. They were posted at the left extremity of the intrenchments towards the Wallabout.

There were skirmishes throughout the day, between the riflemen on the advanced posts and the British "irregulars," which
at times were quite severe; but no decided attack was attempted.
The main body of the enemy kept within their tents until the
latter part of the day; when they began to break ground at
about five hundred yards distance from the works, as if preparing to carry them by regular approaches.

On the 29th, there was a dense fog over the island, that
wrapped every thing in mystery. In the course of the morning,
General Mifflin, with Adjutant-general Reed, and Colonel Grayson of Virginia, one of Washington's aides-de-camp, rode to the
western outposts, in the neighborhood of Red Hook. While they
were there, a light breeze lifted the fog from a part of the New
York Bay, and revealed the British ships at their anchorage opposite Staten Island. There appeared to be an unusual bustle
among them. Boats were passing to and from the admiral's ship,
as if seeking or carrying orders. Some movement was apparently in agitation. The idea occurred to the reconnoitring
party that the fleet was preparing, should the wind hold and the
fog clear away, to come up the bay at the turn of the tide, silence
the feeble batteries at Red Hook and the city, and anchor in the

East River. In that case the army on Long Island would be completely surrounded and entrapped.

Alarmed at this perilous probability, they spurred back to head-quarters, to urge the immediate withdrawal of the army. As this might not be acceptable advice, Reed, emboldened by his intimacy with the commander-in-chief, undertook to give it. Washington instantly summoned a council of war. The difficulty was already apparent, of guarding such extensive works with troops fatigued and dispirited, and exposed to the inclemencies of the weather. Other dangers now presented themselves. Their communication with New York might be cut off by the fleet from below. Other ships had passed round Long Island, and were at Flushing Bay on the Sound. These might land troops on the east side of Harlem River, and make themselves masters of King's Bridge; that key of Manhattan Island. Taking all these things into consideration, it was resolved to cross with the troops to the city that very night.

Never did retreat require greater secrecy and circumspection. Nine thousand men, with all the munitions of war, were to be withdrawn from before a victorious army, encamped so near, that every stroke of spade and pickaxe from their trenches could be heard. The retreating troops, moreover, were to be embarked and conveyed across a strait three quarters of a mile wide, swept by rapid tides. The least alarm of their movement would bring the enemy upon them, and produce a terrible scene of confusion and carnage at the place of embarkation.

Washington made the preparatory arrangements with great alertness, yet profound secrecy. Verbal orders were sent to Colonel Hughes, who acted as quartermaster-general, to impress all water craft, large and small, from Spyt den Duivel on the

Hudson round to Hell Gate on the Sound, and have them on the east side of the city by evening. The order was issued at noon, and so promptly executed, that, although some of the vessels had to be brought a distance of fifteen miles, they were all at Brooklyn at eight o'clock in the evening, and put under the management of Colonel Glover's amphibious Marblehead regiment.

To prepare the army for a general movement without betraying the object, orders were issued for the troops to hold themselves in readiness for a night attack upon the enemy. The orders caused surprise, for the poor fellows were exhausted, and their arms rendered nearly useless by the rain; all, however, prepared to obey; but several made nuncupative wills; as is customary among soldiers on the eve of sudden and deadly peril.

According to Washington's plan of retreat, to keep the enemy from discovering the withdrawal of the Americans until their main body should have embarked in the boats and pushed off from the shore, General Mifflin was to remain at the lines with his Pennsylvania troops, and the gallant remains of Haslet, Smallwood and Hand's regiments, with guards posted and sentinels alert, as if nothing extraordinary was taking place; when the main embarkation was effected, they were themselves to move off quietly, march briskly to the ferry, and embark. In case of any alarm that might disconcert the arrangements, Brooklyn church was to be the rallying place, whither all should repair, so as unitedly to resist any attack.

It was late in the evening when the troops began to retire from the breastworks. As one regiment quietly withdrew from their station on guard, the troops on the right and left moved up and filled the vacancy. There was a stifled murmur in the camp, unavoidable in a movement of the kind; but it gradually died away in the direction of the river, as the main body moved on in silence and order. The youthful Hamilton, whose military merits had won the favor of General Greene, and who had lost his baggage and a field-piece in the battle, brought up the rear of the retreating party. In the dead of the night, and in the midst of this hushed and anxious movement, a cannon went off with a tremendous roar. "The effect," says an American who was present, " was at once alarming and sublime. If the explosion was within our lines, the gun was probably discharged in the act of spiking it, and could have been no less a matter of speculation to the enemy than to ourselves." *

"What with the greatness of the stake, the darkness of the night, the uncertainty of the design, and the extreme hazard of the issue," adds the same writer, " it would be difficult to conceive a more deeply solemn and interesting scene."

The meaning of this midnight gun was never ascertained; fortunately, though it startled the Americans, it failed to rouse the British camp.

In the mean time the embarkation went on with all possible despatch, under the vigilant eye of Washington, who stationed himself at the ferry, superintending every movement. In his anxiety for despatch, he sent back Colonel Scammel, one of his aides-de-camp, to hasten forward all the troops that were on the march. Scammel blundered in executing his errand, and gave the order to Mifflin likewise. The general instantly called in his pickets and sentinels, and set off for the ferry.

By this time the tide had turned; there was a strong wind from the north-east; the boats with oars were insufficient to con-

* Graydon's Memoirs, edited by I. S. Littell, p. 167.

vey the troops; those with sails could not make headway against wind and tide. There was some confusion at the ferry, and in the midst of it, General Mifflin came down with the whole covering party; adding to the embarrassment and uproar.

"Good God! General Mifflin!" cried Washington, "I am afraid you have ruined us by so unseasonably withdrawing the troops from the lines."

"I did so by your order," replied Mifflin with some warmth. "It cannot be!" exclaimed Washington. "By G—, I did!" was the blunt rejoinder. "Did Scammel act as aide-de-camp for the day, or did he not?" "He did." "Then," said Mifflin, "I had orders through him." "It is a dreadful mistake," rejoined Washington, "and unless the troops can regain the lines before their absence is discovered by the enemy, the most disastrous consequences are to be apprehended."

Mifflin led back his men to the lines, which had been completely deserted for three quarters of an hour. Fortunately, the dense fog had prevented the enemy from discovering that they were unoccupied. The men resumed their former posts, and remained at them until called off to cross the ferry. "Whoever has seen troops in a similar situation," writes General Heath, "or duly contemplates the human heart in such trials, will know how to appreciate the conduct of these brave men on this occasion."

The fog which prevailed all this time, seemed almost providential. While it hung over Long Island, and concealed the movements of the Americans, the atmosphere was clear on the New York side of the river. The adverse wind, too, died away, the river became so smooth that the row-boats could be laden almost to the gunwale; and a favoring breeze sprang up for the sail-boats. The whole embarkation of troops, artillery, ammunition, provisions, cattle, horses and carts, was happily effected, and by daybreak the greater part had safely reached the city, thanks to the aid of Glover's Marblehead men. Scarce any thing was abandoned to the enemy, excepting a few heavy pieces of artillery. At a proper time, Mifflin with his covering party left the lines, and effected a silent retreat to the ferry. Washington, though repeatedly entreated, refused to enter a boat until all the troops were embarked; and crossed the river with the last.

A Long Island tradition tells how the British camp became aware of the march which had been stolen upon it.* Near the ferry, resided a Mrs. Rapelye, whose husband, suspected of favoring the enemy, had been removed to the interior of New Jersey. On seeing the embarkation of the first detachment, she, out of loyalty or revenge, sent off a black servant to inform the first British officer he could find, of what was going on. The negro succeeded in passing the American sentinels, but arrived at a Hessian outpost, where he could not make himself understood, and was put under guard as a suspicious person. There he was kept until daybreak, when an officer visiting the post, examined him, and was astounded by his story. An alarm was given, the troops were called to arms; Captain Montresor, aide-de-camp of General Howe, followed by a handful of men, climbed cautiously over the crest of the works and found them deserted. Advanced parties were hurried down to the ferry. The fog had cleared away, sufficiently for them to see the rear boats of the retreating army half way across the river. One boat, still within musket-shot, was compelled to return; it was manned by three vagabonds, who had lingered behind to plunder.

* Hist. Long Island, p. 258.

This extraordinary retreat, which, in its silence and celerity, equalled the midnight fortifying of Bunker's Hill, was one of the most signal achievements of the war, and redounded greatly to the reputation of Washington, who, we are told, for forty-eight hours preceding the safe extricating of his army from their perilous situation, scarce closed his eyes, and was the greater part of the time on horseback. Many, however, who considered the variety of risks and dangers which surrounded the camp, and the apparently fortuitous circumstances which averted them all, were disposed to attribute the safe retreat of the patriot army to a peculiar Providence.

CHAPTER XXXIII.

LONG ISLAND IN POSSESSION OF THE ENEMY—DISTRESSED SITUATION OF THE AMERICAN ARMY AT NEW YORK—QUESTION OF ABANDONING THE CITY—LETTERS FROM EITHER CAMP—ENEMY'S SHIPS IN THE SOUND—REMOVAL OF WOMEN AND CHILDREN FROM THE CITY—YEARNING FOR HOME AMONG THE MILITIA—TOLERANT IDEAS OF WASHINGTON AND GREENE—FORT CONSTITUTION—CONFERENCE OF LORD HOWE WITH A COMMITTEE FROM CONGRESS.

THE enemy had now possession of Long Island. British and Hessian troops garrisoned the works at Brooklyn, or were distributed at Bushwick, Newtown, Hell Gate and Flushing. Admiral Howe came up with the main body of the fleet, and anchored close to Governor's Island, within cannon shot of the city.

" Our situation is truly distressing," writes Washington to the President of Congress, on the 2d of September. "The check our detachment sustained on the 27th ultimo, has dispirited too great a proportion of our troops, and filled their minds with apprehension and despair. The militia, instead of calling forth their utmost efforts to a brave and manly opposition in order to repair our losses, are dismayed, intractable, and impatient to return. Great numbers of them have gone off; in some instances almost by whole regiments, by half ones, and by companies, at a time. * * * * With the deepest concern, I am obliged to confess my want of confidence in the generality of the troops. * * * Our number of men at present fit for duty is under twenty thousand. I have ordered General Mercer to send the men intended for the flying camp to this place, about a thousand in number, and to try with the militia, if practicable, to make a diversion upon Staten Island. Till of late, I had no doubt in my own mind of defending this place; nor should I have yet, if the men would do their duty, but this I despair of.

"If we should be obliged to abandon the town, ought it to stand as winter quarters for the enemy? They would derive great conveniences from it, on the one hand, and much property would be destroyed on the other. It is an important question, but will admit of but little time for deliberation. At present, I dare say the enemy mean to preserve it if they can. If Congress, therefore, should resolve upon the destruction of it, the resolution should be a profound secret, as the knowledge will make a capital change in their plans."

Colonel Reed, writing on the same day to his wife, says, " I have only time to say I am alive and well; as to spirits, but middling. * * * * My country will, I trust, yet be free, whatever may be our fate who are cooped up, or are in danger of so being, on this tongue of land, where we ought never to have been."*

We turn to cite letters of the very same date from British officers on Long Island, full of rumors and surmises. "I have just heard," writes an English field-officer, "there has been a most dreadful fray in the town of New York. The New Englanders insisted on setting the town on fire and retreating. This

* Force's Am. Archives, 5th Series, ii. 123.

was opposed by the New Yorkers, who were joined by the Pennsylvanians, and a battle has been the consequence, in which many have lost their lives. By the steps our general is taking, I imagine he will effectually cut off their retreat at King's Bridge, by which the island of New York is joined to the continent."

An English officer of the guards, writing from camp on the same day, varies the rumor. The Pennsylvanians, according to his version, joined with the New Englanders in the project to set fire to the town; both had a battle with the New Yorkers on the subject, and then withdrew themselves from the city—which, "with other favorable circumstances," gave the latter writer a lively "hope that this distressful business would soon be brought to a happy issue."

Another letter gives a different version. "In the night of the 2d instant, three persons escaped from the city in a canoe and informed our general that Mr. Washington had ordered three battalions of New York Provincials to leave New York, and that they should be replaced by an equal number of Connecticut troops; but the former, assured that the Connecticutians would burn and destroy all the houses, peremptorily refused to give up their city, declaring that no cause of exigency whatever should induce them to intrust the defence of it to any other than her own inhabitants. This spirited and stubborn resolution prevailed over the order of their commander, and the New Yorkers continue snugly in possession of the place." *

" Matters go on swimmingly," writes another officer. " I don't doubt the next news we send you, is, that New York is ours, though in ashes, for the rebel troops have vowed to put it in flames if the tory troops get over."

* Force's Am. Archives, 5th Series, ii. 168.

An American officer writes to an absent New Yorker, in a different tone. "I fear we shall evacuate your poor city. The very thought gives me the horrors!" Still he indulges a vague hope of succor from General Lee, who was returning, all glorious, from his successes at the South. "General Lee," writes he, "is hourly expected, as if from heaven,—with a legion of flaming swordsmen." It was, however, what Lee himself would have termed a mere *brutum fulmen.*

These letters show the state of feeling in the opposite camps, at this watchful moment, when matters seemed hurrying to a crisis.

On the night of Monday (Sept. 2d), a forty gun ship, taking advantage of a favorable wind and tide, passed between Governor's Island and Long Island, swept unharmed by the batteries which opened upon her, and anchored in Turtle Bay, above the city. In the morning, Washington despatched Major Crane of the artillery, with two twelve-pounders and a howitzer to annoy her from the New York shore. They hulled her several times, and obliged her to take shelter behind Blackwell's Island. Several other ships-of-war, with transports and store-ships, had made their appearance in the upper part of the Sound, having gone round Long Island.

As the city might speedily be attacked, Washington caused all the sick and wounded to be conveyed to Orangetown, in the Jerseys, and such military stores and baggage as were not immediately needed, to be removed, as fast as conveyances could be procured, to a post partially fortified at Dobbs' Ferry, on the eastern bank of the Hudson, about twenty-two miles above the city.

Reed, in his letters to his wife, talks of the dark and mysterious motions of the enemy, and the equally dark and intricate councils of Congress, by which the army were disheartened and perplexed. "We are still here," writes he on the 6th, "in a posture somewhat awkward; we think (at least I do) that we cannot stay, and yet we do not know how to go, so that we may be properly said to be between hawk and buzzard."

The "shameful and scandalous desertions," as Washington termed them, continued. In a few days the Connecticut militia dwindled down from six to less than two thousand. "The impulse for going home was so irresistible," writes he, "that it answered no purpose to oppose it. Though I would not discharge them, I have been obliged to acquiesce."

Still his considerate mind was tolerant of their defection. "Men," said he, "accustomed to unbounded freedom, cannot brook the restraint which is indispensably necessary to the good order and government of an army." And again, "Men just dragged from the tender scenes of domestic life, unaccustomd to the din of arms, totally unacquainted with every kind of military skill (which is followed by a want of confidence in themselves, when opposed to troops regularly trained, superior in knowledge, and superior in arms), are timid and ready to fly from their own shadows. Besides, the sudden change in their manner of living, brings on an unconquerable desire to return to their homes."

Greene, also, who coincided so much with Washington in opinions and sentiments, observes: "People coming from home with all the tender feelings of domestic life, are not sufficiently fortified with natural courage to stand the shocking scenes of war. To march over dead men, to hear without concern the groans of the wounded—I say few men can stand such scenes unless steeled by habit or fortified by military pride."

Nor was this ill-timed yearning for home confined to the yeomanry of Connecticut, who might well look back to their humble farms, where they had left the plough standing in the furrow, and where every thing might go to ruin, and their family to want, in their absence. Some of the gentlemen volunteers from beyond the Delaware, who had made themselves merry at the expense of the rustic soldiery of New England, were likewise among the first to feel the homeward impulse. "When I look around," said Reed, the adjutant-general, "and see how few of the numbers who talked so loudly of death and honor are around me, I am lost in wonder and surprise. Some of our Philadelphia gentlemen who came over on visits, upon the first cannon, went off in a most violent hurry. Your noisy sons of liberty, are, I find, the quietest on the field." *

Present experience induced Washington to reiterate the opinion he had repeatedly expressed to Congress, that little reliance was to be placed on militia enlisted for short periods. The only means of protecting the national liberties from great hazard, if not utter loss, was, he said, an army enlisted for the war.

The thousand men ordered from the flying camp were furnished by General Mercer. They were Maryland troops under Colonels Griffith and Richardson, and were a seasonable addition to his effective forces; but the ammunition carried off by the disbanding militia, was a serious loss at this critical juncture.

A work had been commenced on the Jersey shore, opposite Fort Washington, to aid in protecting Putnam's chevaux-de-frise which had been sunk between them. This work had received the name of Fort Constitution (a name already borne by one of

* Life of Reed, i. 231.

the forts in the Highlands.) Troops were drawn from the flying camp to make a strong encampment in the vicinity of the fort, with an able officer to command it and a skilful engineer to strengthen the works. It was hoped, by the co-operation of these opposite forts and the chevaux-de-frise, to command the Hudson, and prevent the passing and repassing of hostile ships.

The British, in the mean time, forbore to press further hostilities. Lord Howe was really desirous of a peaceful adjustment of the strife between the colonies and the mother country, and supposed this a propitious moment for a new attempt at pacification. He accordingly sent off General Sullivan on parole, charged with an overture to Congress. In this he declared himself empowered and disposed to compromise the dispute between Great Britain and America, on the most favorable terms, and, though he could not treat with Congress as a legally organized body, he was desirous of a conference with some of its members. These, for the time, he should consider only as private gentlemen, but if in the conference any probable scheme of accommodation should be agreed upon, the authority of Congress would afterwards be acknowledged, to render the compact complete.*

The message caused some embarrassment in Congress. To accede to the interview might seem to waive the question of independence; to decline it was to shut the door on all hope of conciliation, and might alienate the co-operation of some worthy whigs who still clung to that hope. After much debate, Congress, on the 5th September, replied, that, being the representatives of the free and independent States of America, they could not send any members to confer with his lordship in their private

* Civil War, vol. i. p. 190.

characters, but that, ever desirous of establishing peace on reasonable terms, they would send a committee of their body to ascertain what authority he had to treat with persons authorized by Congress, and what propositions he had to offer.

A committee was chosen on the 6th of September, composed of John Adams, Edward Rutledge, and Doctor Franklin. The latter, in the preceding year, during his residence in England, had become acquainted with Lord Howe, at the house of his lordship's sister, the Honorable Mrs. Howe, and they had held frequent conversations on the subject of American affairs, in the course of which, his lordship had intimated the possibility of his being sent commissioner to settle the differences in America.

Franklin had recently adverted to this in a letter to Lord Howe. "Your lordship may possibly remember the tears of joy that wet my cheek, when, at your good sister's in London, you gave me expectations that a reconciliation might soon take place. I had the misfortune to find those expectations disappointed.

* * * * * * * * *

"The well-founded esteem, and, permit me to say, affection, which I shall always have for your lordship, makes it painful for me to see you engaged in conducting a war, the great ground of which, as expressed in your letter, is 'the necessity of preventing the American trade from passing into foreign channels.' * * * I know your great motive in coming hither, was the hope of being instrumental in a reconciliation; and I believe that when you find *that* impossible on any terms given to you to propose, you will relinquish so odious a command, and return to a more honorable private station."

"I can have no difficulty to acknowledge," replied Lord Howe, "that the powers I am invested with were never calculated to negotiate a reunion with America, under any other description than as subject to the crown of Great Britain. But I do esteem these powers competent, not only to confer and negotiate with any gentlemen of influence in the colonies upon the terms, but also to effect a lasting peace and reunion between the two countries, were the tempers of the colonies such as professed in the last petition of Congress to the king." *

A hope of the kind lingered in the breast of his lordship when he sought the proposed conference. It was to take place on the 11th, at a house on Staten Island, opposite to Amboy; at which latter place the veteran Mercer was stationed with his flying camp. At Amboy, the committee found Lord Howe's barge waiting to receive them; with a British officer of rank, who was to remain within the American lines during their absence, as a hostage. This guarantee of safety was promptly declined, and the parties crossed together to Staten Island. The admiral met them on their landing, and conducted them through his guards to his house.

On opening the conference, his lordship again intimated that he could not treat with them as a committee of Congress, but only confer with them as private gentlemen of influence in the colonies, on the means of restoring peace between the two countries.

The commissioners replied that, as their business was to hear, he might consider them in what light he pleased; but that they should consider themselves in no other character than that in which they were placed by order of Congress.

Lord Howe then entered into a discourse of considerable

* Franklin's Writings, v. 103.

length, but made no explicit proposition of peace, nor promise of redress of grievances, excepting on condition that the colonies should return to their allegiance.

This, the commissioners replied, was not now to be expected. Their repeated humble petitions to the king and parliament having been treated with contempt, and answered by additional injuries, and war having been declared against them, the colonies had declared their independence, and it was not in the power of Congress to agree for them that they should return to their former dependent state.*

His lordship expressed his sorrow that no accommodation was likely to take place; and, on breaking up the conference, assured his old friend, Dr. Franklin, that he should suffer great pain in being obliged to distress those for whom he had so much regard.

"I feel thankful to your lordship for your regard," replied Franklin good-humoredly; "the Americans, on their part, will endeavor to lessen the pain you may feel, by taking good care of themselves."

The result of this conference had a beneficial effect. It showed that his lordship had no power but what was given by the act of Parliament; and put an end to the popular notion that he was vested with secret powers to negotiate an adjustment of grievances.

* Report of the Comm. to Cong., Sept. 13, 1776.

CHAPTER XXXIV.

MOVEMENTS OF THE ENEMY—COUNCILS OF WAR—QUESTION OF THE ABANDON-
MENT OF THE CITY—DISTRIBUTION OF THE ARMY—SHIPS IN THE EAST RIVER
—THE ENEMY AT HELL GATE—SKIRMISH AT TURTLE BAY—PANIC OF THE
CONNECTICUT MILITIA—RAGE AND PERSONAL PERIL OF WASHINGTON—PUT-
NAM'S PERILOUS RETREAT FROM THE CITY—BRITISH REGALE AT MURRAY
HILL.

SINCE the retreat from Brooklyn, Washington had narrowly
watched the movements of the enemy to discover their further
plans. Their whole force, excepting about four thousand men,
had been transferred from Staten to Long Island. A great part
was encamped on the peninsula between Newtown Inlet and
Flushing Bay. A battery had been thrown up near the extremity of the peninsula, to check an American battery at Horen's
Hook opposite, and to command the mouth of Harlem River.
Troops were subsequently stationed on the islands about Hell
Gate. " It is evident," writes Washington, " the enemy mean to
enclose us on the island of New York, by taking post in our rear,
while the shipping secures the front, and thus, by cutting off our
communication with the country, oblige us to fight them on their
own terms, or surrender at discretion ; or by a brilliant stroke
endeavor to cut this army in pieces, and secure the collection of

arms and stores, which, they well know, we shall not be able soon
to replace." *

The question was, how could their plans be most successfully
opposed ?   On every side, he saw a choice of difficulties; every
measure was to be formed with some apprehension that all the
troops would not do their duty.   History, experience, the opinions of able friends in Europe, the fears of the enemy, even the
declarations of Congress, all concurred in demonstrating that the
war on the American side should be defensive; a war of posts;
that, on all occasions, a general action should be avoided, and
nothing put at risk unnecessarily.   "With these views," said
Washington, "and being fully persuaded that it would be pre-
sumption to draw out our young troops into open ground against
their superiors, both in number and discipline, I have never
spared the spade and pickaxe."

In a council of war, held on the 7th of September, the question was discussed, whether the city should be defended or evacuated.   All admitted that it would not be tenable, should it be
cannonaded and bombarded.   Several of the council, among
whom was General Putnam, were for a total and immediate removal from the city; urging that one part of the army might be
cut off before the other could support it; the extremities being
at least sixteen miles apart, and the whole, when collected, being
inferior to the enemy.   By removing, they would deprive the
enemy of the advantage of their ships; they would keep them at
bay; put nothing at hazard; keep the army together to be recruited another year, and preserve the unspent stores and the
heavy artillery.   Washington himself inclined to this opinion.
Others, however, were unwilling to abandon a place which had

* Letter to the President of Congress.

been fortified with great cost and labor, and seemed defensible;
and which, by some, had been considered the key to the northern
country; it might dispirit the troops, and enfeeble the cause.
General Mercer, who was prevented by illness from attending the
council, communicated his opinion by letter. "We should keep
New York if possible," said he, "as the acquiring of it will give
eclat to the arms of Great Britain, afford the soldiers good quarters, and furnish a safe harbor for the fleet."

General Greene, also, being still unwell, conveyed his opinion
in a letter to Washington, dated Sept. 5th. He advised that the
army should abandon both city and island, and post itself at
King's Bridge and along the Westchester shore. That there
was no object to be obtained by holding any position below
King's Bridge. The enemy might throw troops on Manhattan
Island, from their camps on Long Island, and their ships on the
Hudson, and form an intrenched line across it, between the city
and the middle division of the army, and support the two flanks
of the line by their shipping. In such case, it would be necessary to fight them on disadvantageous terms or submit.

The city and island, he observed, were objects not to be put
in competition with the general interests of America. Two
thirds of the city and suburbs belonged to tories, there was no
great reason, therefore, to run any considerable risk in its defence. The honor and interest of America required a general
and speedy retreat. But as the enemy, once in possession, could
never be dislodged without a superior naval force; as the place
would furnish them with excellent winter quarters and barrack
room, and an abundant market, he advised to burn both city and
suburbs before retreating.*

* Force's Am. Archives, 5th Series, ii. 182.

Well might the poor, harassed citizens feel hysterical, threatened as they were by sea and land, and their very defenders debating the policy of burning their houses over their heads. Fortunately for them, Congress had expressly forbidden that any harm should be done to New York, trusting, that though the enemy might occupy it for a time, it would ultimately be regained.

After much discussion a middle course was adopted. Putnam, with five thousand men, was to be stationed in the city. Heath, with nine thousand, was to keep guard on the upper part of the island, and oppose any attempt of the enemy to land. His troops, among whom were Magaw's, Shee's, Hand's, and Miles's Pennsylvanian battalions, and Haslet's Delaware regiment, were posted about King's Bridge and its vicinity.

The third division, composed principally of militia, was under the command of Generals Greene and Spencer, the former of whom, however, was still unwell. It was stationed about the centre of the island, chiefly along Turtle Bay and Kip's Bay, where strong works had been thrown up, to guard against any landing of troops from the ships or from the encampments on Long Island. It was also to hold itself ready to support either of the other divisions. Washington himself had his head-quarters at a short distance from the city. A resolution of Congress, passed the 10th of September, left the occupation or abandonment of the city entirely at Washington's discretion. Nearly the whole of his officers, too, in a second council of war, retracted their former opinion, and determined that the removal of his army was not only prudent, but absolutely necessary. Three members of the council, however, Generals Spencer, Heath, and George Clinton, tenaciously held to the former decision.

Convinced of the propriety of evacuation, Washington prepared for it by ordering the removal of all stores, excepting such as were indispensable for the subsistence of the troops while they remained. A letter from a Rhode Island officer, on a visit to New York, gives an idea of its agitations. "On the 13th of September, just after dinner, three frigates and a forty-gun ship sailed up the East River with a gentle breeze, toward Hell Gate, and kept up an incessant fire, assisted by the cannon at Governor's Island. The batteries of the city returned the ships the like salutation. Three men agape, idle spectators, had the misfortune of being killed by one cannon ball. One shot struck within six feet of General Washington, as he was on horseback, riding into the fort." [*]

On the 14th, Washington's baggage was removed to King's Bridge, whither head-quarters were to be transferred the same evening; it being clear that the enemy were preparing to encompass him on the island. "It is now a trial of skill whether they will or not," writes Colonel Reed, "and every night we lie down with the most anxious fears for the fate of to-morrow." [†]

About sunset of the same day, six more ships, two of them men-of-war, passed up the Sound and joined those above. Within half an hour came expresses spurring to head-quarters, one from Mifflin at King's Bridge, the other from Colonel Sargent at Horen's Hook. Three or four thousand of the enemy were crossing at Hell Gate to the islands at the mouth of Harlem River, where numbers were already encamped. An immediate landing at Harlem, or Morrisania, was apprehended. Washington was instantly in the saddle, spurring to Harlem Heights. The night,

[*] Col. Babcock to Gov. Cooke. Am. Archives, 5th Series, ii. 443.
[†] Reed to Mrs. Reed.

however, passed away quietly. In the morning the enemy commenced operations. Three ships of war stood up the Hudson, "causing a most tremendous firing, assisted by the cannons of Governor's Island, which firing was returned from the city as well as the scarcity of heavy cannon would allow." * The ships anchored opposite Bloomingdale, a few miles above the city, and put a stop to the removal by water of stores and provisions to Dobbs' Ferry. About eleven o'clock, the ships in the East River commenced a heavy cannonade upon the breastworks between Turtle Bay and the city. At the same time two divisions of the troops encamped on Long Island, one British, under Sir Henry Clinton, the other Hessian, under Colonel Donop, emerged in boats from the deep, woody recesses of Newtown Inlet, and under cover of the fire from the ships, began to land at two points between Turtle and Kip's Bays. The breastworks were manned by militia who had recently served at Brooklyn. Disheartened by their late defeat, they fled at the first advance of the enemy. Two brigades of Putnam's Connecticut troops (Parsons' and Fellows') which had been sent that morning to support them, caught the panic, and regardless of the commands and entreaties of their officers, joined in the general scamper.

At this moment Washington, who had mounted his horse at the first sound of the cannonade, came galloping to the scene of confusion ; riding in among the fugitives, he endeavored to rally and restore them to order. All in vain. At the first appearance of sixty or seventy red coats, they broke again without firing a shot, and fled in headlong terror. Losing all self-command at the sight of such dastardly conduct, he dashed his hat upon the

* Letter of Col. Babcock to Gov. Cooke.

ground in a transport of rage. "Are these the men," exclaimed he, "with whom I am to defend America!" In a paroxysm of passion and despair he snapped his pistols at some of them, threatened others with his sword, and was so heedless of his own danger, that he might have fallen into the hands of the enemy, who were not eighty yards distant, had not an aide-de-camp seized the bridle of his horse, and absolutely hurried him away.*

It was one of the rare moments of his life, when the vehement element of his nature was stirred up from its deep recesses. He soon recovered his self-possession, and took measures against the general peril. The enemy might land another force about Hell Gate, seize upon Harlem Heights, the strong central portion of the island, cut off all retreat of the lower divisions, and effectually sever his army. In all haste, therefore, he sent off an express to the forces encamped above, directing them to secure that position immediately; while another express to Putnam, ordered an immediate retreat from the city to those heights.

It was indeed a perilous moment. Had the enemy followed up their advantage, and seized upon the heights, before thus occupied; or had they extended themselves across the island, from the place where they had effected a landing, the result might have been most disastrous to the Americans. Fortunately, they contented themselves for the present with sending a strong detachment down the road along the East River, leading to the city, while the main body, British and Hessians, rested on their arms.

* Graydon's Memoirs, Littell's ed., p. 174. General Greene, in a letter to a friend, writes : " We made a miserable, disorderly retreat from New York, owing to the conduct of the militia, who ran at the appearance of the enemy's advanced guard. Fellows' and Parsons' brigades ran away from about fifty men, and left his excellency on the ground, within eighty yards of the enemy, so vexed at the infamous conduct of his troops, that he sought death rather than life."

In the mean time, Putnam, on receiving Washington's express, called in his pickets and guards, and abandoned the city in all haste, leaving behind him a large quantity of provisions and military stores, and most of the heavy cannon. To avoid the enemy he took the Bloomingdale road, though this exposed him to be raked by the enemy's ships anchored in the Hudson. It was a forced march, on a sultry day, under a burning sun and amid clouds of dust. His army was encumbered with women and children and all kinds of baggage. Many were overcome by fatigue and thirst, some perished by hastily drinking cold water; but Putnam rode backward and forward, hurrying every one on.

Colonel Humphreys, at that time a volunteer in his division, writes: "I had frequent opportunities that day of beholding him, for the purpose of issuing orders and encouraging the troops, flying on his horse covered with foam, wherever his presence was most necessary. Without his extraordinary exertions, the guards must have been inevitably lost, and it is probable the entire corps would have been cut in pieces.

"When we were not far from Bloomingdale, an aide-de-camp came to him at full speed, to inform him that a column of British infantry was descending upon our right. Our rear was soon fired upon, and the colonel of our regiment, whose order was just communicated for the front to file off to the left, was killed upon the spot. With no other loss, we joined the army after dark upon the heights of Harlem."[*]

Tradition gives a circumstance which favored Putnam's retreat. The British generals, in passing by Murray Hill, the country residence of a patriot of that name who was of the So-

[*] Peabody, Life of Putnam.   Sparks' Am. Biog., vii. 189.

ciety of Friends, made a halt to seek some refreshment. The proprietor of the house was absent; but his wife set cake and wine before them in abundance. So grateful were these refreshments in the heat of the day, that they lingered over their wine, quaffing and laughing, and bantering their patriotic hostess about the ludicrous panic and discomfiture of her countrymen. In the mean time, before they were roused from their regale, Putnam and his forces had nearly passed by, within a mile of them. All the loss sustained by him in his perilous retreat, was fifteen killed, and about three hundred taken prisoners. It became, adds the tradition, a common saying among the American officers, that Mrs. Murray saved Putnam's division of the army.*

* Thacher's Military Journal, p. 70.

CHAPTER XXXV.

FORTIFIED CAMP AT KING'S BRIDGE—AMERICAN AND BRITISH LINES—THE MOR-
RIS HOUSE—ALEXANDER HAMILTON—THE ENEMY ADVANCE—SUCCESSFUL
SKIRMISH—DEATH OF KNOWLTON—GREAT FIRE IN NEW YORK—REORGAN-
IZATION OF THE ARMY—EXCHANGE OF PRISONERS—DANIEL MORGAN RE-
GAINED—DE LANCEY'S TORY BRIGADE—ROBERT ROGERS, THE PARTISAN—
HIS RANGERS—THE ROEBUCK, PHŒNIX, AND TARTAR IN THE HUDSON—MILI-
TARY MOVEMENTS BY LAND AND WATER—LETTER OF JOHN JAY.

THE fortified camp, where the main body of the army was now
assembled, was upon that neck of land several miles long, and for
the most part not above a mile wide, which forms the upper part
of Manhattan or New York Island. It forms a chain of rocky
heights, and is separated from the mainland by Harlem River, a
narrow strait, extending from Hell Gate on the Sound, to Spyt
den Duivel, a creek or inlet of the Hudson. Fort Washington
occupied the crest of one of the rocky heights above mentioned,
overlooking the Hudson, and about two miles north of it was
King's Bridge, crossing Spyt den Duivel Creek, and forming at
that time the only pass from Manhattan Island to the mainland.

About a mile and a half south of the fort, a double row of
lines extended across the neck from Harlem River to the Hudson. They faced south towards New York, were about a quarter
of a mile apart, and were defended by batteries.

VOL. II.—15

There were strong advanced posts, about two miles south of the outer line; one on the left of Harlem, commanded by General Spencer, the other on the right, at what was called Mc-Gowan's Pass, commanded by General Putnam. About a mile and a half beyond these posts the British lines extended across the island from Horen's Hook to the Hudson, being a continuous encampment, two miles in length, with both flanks covered by shipping. An open plain intervened between the hostile camps.

Washington had established his head-quarters about a quarter of a mile within the inner line; at a country-seat, the owners of which were absent. It belonged in fact to Colonel Roger Morris, his early companion in arms in Braddock's campaign, and his successful competitor for the hand of Miss Mary Philipse. Morris had remained in America, enjoying the wealth he had acquired by his marriage; but had adhered to the royal party, and was a member of the council of the colony. It is said that at this time he was residing in the Highlands at Beverley, the seat of his brother-in-law, Washington's old friend, Beverley Robinson.*

While thus posted, Washington was incessantly occupied in fortifying the approaches to his camp by redoubts, *abatis*, and deep intrenchments. "Here," said he, "I should hope the enemy, in case of attack, would meet a defeat, if the generality of our troops would behave with tolerable bravery; but experience, to my extreme affliction, has convinced me that it is rather to be wished than expected. However, I trust there are many who will act like men worthy of the blessings of freedom." The late disgraceful scene at Kip's Bay was evidently rankling in his mind.

---

* The portrait of Miss Mary Philipse is still to be seen in the possession of Frederick Phillips, Esquire, at the Grange, on the Highlands opposite West Point.

In the course of his rounds of inspection, he was struck with the skill and science displayed in the construction of some of the works, which were thrown up under the direction of a youthful captain of artillery. It proved to be the same young officer, Alexander Hamilton, whom Greene had recommended to his notice. After some conversation with him, Washington invited him to his marquee, and thus commenced that intercourse which has indissolubly linked their memories together.

On the morning of the 16th, word was brought to head-quarters that the enemy were advancing in three large columns. There had been so many false reports, that Reed, the adjutant-general, obtained leave to sally out and ascertain the truth. Washington himself soon mounted his horse and rode towards the advanced posts. On arriving there he heard a brisk firing. It was kept up for a time with great spirit. There was evidently a sharp conflict. At length Reed came galloping back with information. A strong detachment of the enemy had attacked the most advanced post, which was situated on a hill skirted by a wood. It had been bravely defended by Lieutenant-colonel Knowlton, Putnam's favorite officer, who had distinguished himself at Bunker's Hill; he had under him a party of Connecticut rangers, volunteers from different regiments. After skirmishing for a time, the party had been overpowered by numbers and driven in, and the outpost was taken possession of by the enemy. Reed supposed the latter to be about three hundred strong, but they were much stronger, the main part having been concealed behind a rising ground in the wood. They were composed of a battalion of light infantry, another of Royal Highlanders, and three companies of Hessian riflemen; all under the command of General Leslie.

Reed urged that troops should be sent to support the brave fellows who had behaved so well. While he was talking with Washington, " the enemy," he says, "appeared in open view, and sounded their bugles in the most insulting manner, as usual after a fox-chase. I never," adds he, "felt such a sensation before; it seemed to crown our disgrace."

Washington, too, was stung by the taunting note of derision; it recalled the easy triumph of the enemy at Kip's Bay. Resolved that something should be done to wipe out that disgrace, and rouse the spirits of the army, he ordered out three companies from Colonel Weedon's regiment just arrived from Virginia, and sent them under Major Leitch, to join Knowlton's rangers. The troops thus united were to get in the rear of the enemy, while a feigned attack was made upon them in front.

The plan was partially successful. As the force advanced to make the false attack, the enemy ran down the hill, and took what they considered an advantageous position behind some fences and bushes which skirted it. A firing commenced between them and the advancing party, but at too great distance to do much harm on either side. In the mean time, Knowlton and Leitch, ignorant of this change in the enemy's position, having made a circuit, came upon them in flank instead of in rear. They were sharply received. A vivid contest took place, in which Connecticut vied with Virginia in bravery. In a little while Major Leitch received three bullets in his side, and was borne off the field. Shortly afterward, a wound in the head from a musket ball, brought Knowlton to the ground. Colonel Reed placed him on his horse, and conveyed him to a distant redoubt. The men, undismayed by the fall of their leaders, fought with unflinching resolution under the command of their captains.

The enemy were reinforced by a battalion of Hessians and a company of chasseurs. Washington likewise sent reinforcements of New England and Maryland troops. The action waxed hotter and hotter; the enemy were driven from the wood into the plain, and pushed for some distance; the Americans were pursuing them with ardor, when Washington, having effected the object of this casual encounter, and being unwilling to risk a general action, ordered a retreat to be sounded.

It was with difficulty, however, his men could be called off, so excited were they by the novelty of pursuing an enemy. They retired in good order; and, as it subsequently appeared, in good season, for the main body of the enemy were advancing at a rapid rate, and might have effectually reversed the scene.

Colonel Knowlton did not long survive the action. "When gasping in the agonies of death," says Colonel Reed, "all his inquiry was whether he had driven in the enemy." He was anxious for the tarnished honor of Connecticut. He had the dying satisfaction of knowing that his men had behaved bravely, and driven the enemy in an open field-fight. So closed his gallant career.

The encounter thus detailed was a small affair in itself, but important in its effects. It was the first gleam of success in the campaign, and revived the spirits of the army. Washington sought to turn it to the greatest advantage. In his general orders, he skilfully distributed praise and censure. The troops under Leitch were thanked for being the first to advance upon the enemy; and the New England troops for gallantly supporting them, and their conduct was honorably contrasted with that of the recreant troops at Kip's Bay. Of Knowlton, who had fallen while gloriously fighting, he spoke as "one who would have done honor to any country."

The name of Leitch was given by him for the next day's parole. That brave officer died of his wounds on the 1st of October, soothed in his last moments by that recompense so dear to a soldier's heart, the encomium of a beloved commander.

In the dead of the night, on the 20th September, a great light was beheld by the picket guards, looming up from behind the hills in the direction of the city. It continued throughout the night, and was at times so strong that the heavens in that direction appeared to them, they said, as if in flames. At daybreak huge columns of smoke were still rising. It was evident there had been a great conflagration in New York.

In the course of the morning Captain Montresor, aide-de-camp to General Howe, came out with a flag, bearing a letter to Washington on the subject of an exchange of prisoners. According to Montresor's account a great part of the city had been burnt down, and as the night was extremely windy, the whole might have been so, but for the exertions of the officers and men of the British army. He implied it to be the act of American incendiaries, several of whom, he informed Colonel Reed, had been caught in the fact and instantly shot. General Howe, in his private correspondence, makes the same assertion, and says they were detected, and killed on the spot by the enraged troops in garrison.

Enraged troops, with weapons in their hands, are not apt, in a time of confusion and alarm, to be correct judges of fact, or dispensers of justice. The act was always disclaimed by the Americans, and it is certain their commanders knew nothing about it. We have shown that the destruction of the city was at one time discussed in a council of war as a measure of policy, but never adopted, and was expressly forbidden by Congress.

The enemy were now bringing up their heavy cannon, preparatory to an attack upon the American camp by the troops and by the ships. What was the state of Washington's army? The terms of engagement of many of his men would soon be at an end, most of them would terminate with the year, nor did Congress hold out offers to encourage re-enlistments. "We are now, as it were, upon the eve of another dissolution of the army," writes he, "and unless some speedy and effectual measures are adopted by Congress, our cause will be lost." Under these gloomy apprehensions, he borrowed, as he said, "a few moments from the hours allotted to sleep," and on the night of the 24th of September, penned an admirable letter to the President of Congress, setting forth the total inefficiency of the existing military system, the total insubordination, waste, confusion, and discontent produced by it among the men, and the harassing cares and vexations to which it subjected the commanders. Nor did he content himself with complaining, but, in his full, clear, and sagacious manner, pointed out the remedies. To the achievements of his indefatigable pen, we may trace the most fortunate turns in the current of our revolutionary affairs. In the present instance his representations, illustrated by sad experience, produced at length a reorganization of the army, and the establishment of it on a permanent footing. It was decreed that eighty-eight battalions should be furnished in quotas, by the different States, according to their abilities. The pay of the officers was raised. The troops which engaged to serve throughout the war were to receive a bounty of twenty dollars and one hundred acres of land, besides a yearly suit of clothes while in service. Those who enlisted for but three years, received no bounty in land. The bounty to officers was on a higher ratio. The States were to send commissioners to the army, to arrange with the commander-in-chief as to the appointment of officers in their quotas; but, as they might occasionally be slow in complying with this regulation, Washington was empowered to fill up all vacancies.

All this was a great relief to his mind. He was gratified, also, by effecting, after a long correspondence with the British commander, an exchange of prisoners, in which those captured in Canada were included. Among those restored to the service were Lord Stirling and Captain Daniel Morgan. The latter, in reward of his good conduct in the expedition with Arnold, and of "his intrepid behavior in the assault upon Quebec where the brave Montgomery fell," was recommended to Congress by Washington for the command of a rifle regiment about to be raised. We shall see how eminently he proved himself worthy of this recommendation.

About this time information was received that the enemy were enlisting great numbers of the loyalists of Long Island, and collecting large quantities of stock for their support. Oliver De Lancey, a leading loyalist of New York, member of a wealthy family of honorable Huguenot descent, was a prime agent in the matter. He had recently been appointed brigadier-general in the royal service, and authorized by General Howe to raise a brigade of provincials; and was actually at Jamaica, on Long Island, offering commissions of captain, lieutenant and ensign, to any respectable pesron who should raise a company of seventy men; the latter to receive British pay.

A descent upon Long Island, to counteract these projects, was concerted by General George Clinton of New York, and

General Lincoln of Massachusetts, but men and water craft were wanting to carry it into effect, and the " tory enlistments continued." They were not confined to Long Island, but prevailed more or less on Staten Island, in the Jerseys, up the Hudson as far as Dutchess County, and in Westchester County more especially. Many of the loyalists, it must be acknowledged, were honorable men, conscientiously engaged in the service of their sovereign, and anxious to put down what they sincerely regarded as an unjustifiable rebellion ; and among these may be clearly classed the De Lanceys. There were others, however, of a different stamp, the most notorious of whom, at this juncture, was one Robert Rogers of New Hampshire. He had been a worthy comrade of Putnam and Stark, in some of their early enterprises during the French war, and had made himself famous as major of a partisan corps called Rogers' Rangers. Governor Trumbull described him as a " famous scouter and wood-hunter, skilled in waylaying, ambuscade, and sudden attack." His feats of arms had evidently somewhat of the Indian character. He had since been Governor of Michilimackinac (1766), and accused of a plot to plunder his own fort and join the French. At the outbreak of the Revolution he played a skulking, equivocal part, and appeared ready to join either party. In 1775, Washington had received notice that he was in Canada, in the service of Carleton, and had been as a spy, disguised as an Indian, through the American camp at St. Johns.

Recently, on learning that he was prowling about the country under suspicious circumstances, Washington had caused him to be arrested. On examination, he declared that he was on his way to offer his secret services to Congress. He was accordingly sent on to that body, in custody of an officer. Congress liberated him on his pledging himself in writing, " on the honor of a gentleman," not to bear arms against the American United Colonies in any manner whatever, during the contest with Great Britain.

Scarcely was he liberated when he forfeited his parole, offered his services to the enemy, received a colonel's commission, and was now actually raising a tory corps to be called the Queen's Rangers. All such as should bring recruits to his standard were promised commissions, portions of rebel lands, and privileges equal to any of his majesty's troops.

Of all Americans of note enlisted under the royal standard, this man had rendered himself the most odious. He was stigmatized as an arrant renegade, a perfect Judas Iscariot; and his daring, adventurous spirit and habits of Indian warfare rendered him a formidable enemy.

Nothing perplexed Washington at this juncture more than the conduct of the enemy. He beheld before him a hostile army, armed and equipped at all points, superior in numbers, thoroughly disciplined, flushed with success, and abounding in the means of pushing a vigorous campaign, yet suffering day after day to elapse unimproved. What could be the reason of this supineness on the part of Sir William Howe? He must know the depressed and disorganized state of the American camp; the absolute chaos that reigned there. Did he meditate an irruption into the Jerseys? A movement towards Philadelphia? Did he intend to detach a part of his forces for a winter's campaign against the South?

In this uncertainty, Washington wrote to General Mercer, of the flying camp, to keep a vigilant watch from the Jersey shore on the movements of the enemy, by sea and land, and to station videttes on the Neversink Heights, to give immediate intelligence should any of the British fleet put to sea. At the same time he himself practised unceasing vigilance, visiting the different parts of his camp on horseback. Occasionally he crossed over to Fort Constitution, on the Jersey shore, of which General Greene had charge, and, accompanied by him, extended his reconnoitrings down to Paulus Hook, to observe what was going on in the city and among the enemy's ships. Greene had recently been promoted to the rank of major-general, and now had command of all the troops in the Jerseys. He had liberty to shift his quarters to Baskingridge or Bergen, as circumstances might require; but was enjoined to keep up a communication with the main army, east of the Hudson, so as to secure a retreat in case of necessity.

The security of the Hudson was at this time an object of great solicitude with Congress, and much reliance was placed on Putnam's obstructions at Fort Washington. Four galleys, mounted with heavy guns and swivels, were stationed at the chevaux-de-frise, and two new ships were at hand, which, filled with stones, were to be sunk where they would block up the channel. A sloop was also at anchor, having on board a machine, invented by a Mr. Bushnell, for submarine explosion, with which to blow up the men-of-war; a favorite scheme with General Putnam. The obstructions were so commanded by batteries on each shore, that it was thought no hostile ship would be able to pass.

On the 9th of October, however, the Roebuck and Phœnix, each of forty-four guns, and the Tartar of twenty guns, which had been lying for some time opposite Bloomingdale, got under way with their three tenders, at eight o'clock in the morning, and came standing up the river with an easy southern breeze. At their approach, the galleys and the two ships intended to be sunk, got under way with all haste, as did a schooner laden with rum, sugar, and other supplies for the American army, and the sloop with Bushnell's submarine machine.

The Roebuck, Phœnix and Tartar, broke through the vaunted barriers as through a cobweb. Seven batteries kept up a constant fire upon them, yet a gentleman was observed walking the deck of the second ship as coolly as if nothing were the matter.* Washington, indeed, in a letter to Schuyler, says "they passed without any kind of damage or interruption;" but Lord Howe reports to the admiralty that they suffered much in their masts and rigging, and that a lieutenant, two midshipmen, and six men were killed, and eighteen wounded.

The hostile ships kept on their course, the American vessels scudding before them. The schooner was overhauled and captured; a well-aimed shot sent the sloop and Bushnell's submarine engine to the bottom of the river. The two new ships would have taken refuge in Spyt den Duivel Creek, but fearing there might not be water enough, they kept on and drove ashore at Philips' Mills at Yonkers. Two of the galleys got into a place of safety, where they were protected from the shore; the other two trusted to outsail their pursuers. The breeze freshened, and the frigates gained on them fast; at 11 o'clock began to fire on them with their bow-chasers, and at 12 o'clock overreached them, which caused them to bear in shore; at half past one the galleys ran aground just above Dobbs' Ferry, and lay exposed to a shower of grape-shot. The crews, without stopping to burn or bilge them, swam on shore, and the enemy took possession of the

* Col. Ewing to the Maryland Comm. of Safety.

two galleys, which were likely to be formidable means of annoyance in their hands.

One express after another brought Washington word of these occurrences. First, he sent off a party of rifle and artillery men, with two twelve-pounders, to secure the new ships which had run aground at Yonkers. Next, he ordered Colonel Sargent to march up along the eastern shore with five hundred infantry, a troop of light-horse, and a detachment of artillery, to prevent the landing of the enemy. Before the troops arrived at Dobbs' Ferry the ships' boats had plundered a store there, and set it on fire.

To prevent, if possible, the men-of-war already up the river from coming down, or others from below joining them, Washington gave orders to complete the obstructions. Two hulks which lay in Spyt den Duivel Creek, were hastily ballasted by men from General Heath's division, and men were sent up to get off the ships which had run aground at Philips' Mills, that they might be brought down and sunk immediately.

It is difficult to give an idea of the excitement caused by this new irruption of hostile ships into the waters of the Hudson, or of the various conjectures as to their object. They might intend merely to interrupt navigation, and prevent supplies from coming down to the American army. They might be carrying arms and ammunition for domestic enemies skulking about the river, and only waiting an opportunity to strike a blow. They might have troops concealed on board with intent to surprise the posts in the Highlands, and cut off the intercourse between the American armies. To such a degree had the spirit of disaffection been increased in the counties adjacent to the river, since the descent of the Rose and Phœnix, by the retreats and evacuation which had take place; and so great had been the drain on the militia of those counties for the army of Washington, that, in case of insurrection, those who remained at home and were well affected, would be outnumbered, and might easily be overpowered, especially with the aid of troops landed from ships.

While this agitation prevailed below, fugitive river crafts carried the news up to the Highlands that the frigates were already before Tarrytown in the Tappan Sea. Word was instantly despatched to Peter R. Livingston, president of the Provincial Congress, and startled that deliberative body, which was then seated at Fishkill just above the Highlands. The committee of safety wrote, on the spur of the moment, to Washington. "Nothing," say they, "can be more alarming than the present situation of our State. We are daily getting the most authentic intelligence of bodies of men enlisted and armed in order to assist the enemy. We much fear that they, co-operating with the enemy, may seize such passes as will cut off the communication between the army and us, and prevent your supplies. * * * * We beg leave to suggest to your Excellency the propriety of sending a body of men to the Highlands or Peekskill, to secure the passes, prevent insurrection, and overawe the disaffected."

Washington transmitted the letter to the President of Congress on the 12th. "I have ordered up," writes he, "part of the militia from Massachusetts, under General Lincoln, to prevent, if possible, the consequences which they suggest may happen, and which there is reason to believe the conspirators have in contemplation. I am persuaded that they are on the eve of breaking out, and that they will leave nothing unessayed that will distress us, and favor the designs of the enemy, as soon as their schemes are ripe for it." In fact, it was said that the tories were arming and collecting in the Highlands under the direction of disguised officers, to aid the conspiracies formed by Governor Tryon and his adherents.

As a further precaution, an express was sent off by Washington to Colonel Tash, who, with a regiment of New Hampshire militia, was on his way from Hartford to the camp, ordering him to repair with all possible dispatch to Fishkill, and there hold himself at the disposition of the committee of safety.

James Clinton, also, who had charge of the posts in the Highlands, was put on the alert. That trusty officer was now a brigadier-general, having been promoted by Congress, on the 8th of August. He was charged to have all boats passing up and down the river rigidly searched, and the passengers examined. Beside the usual sentries, a barge, well manned, was to patrol the river opposite to each fort every night; all barges, row-boats, and other small craft, between the forts in the Highlands and the army, were to be secured in a place of safety, to prevent their falling into the enemy's hands and giving intelligence. Moreover, a French engineer was sent up to aid in strengthening and securing the passes. The commanding officers of the counties of Litchfield and Fairfield in Connecticut, had, likewise, orders to hold their militia in readiness to render assistance in case of insurrections in the State of New York.

So perilous appeared the condition of affairs to residents up the river, that John Jay, a member of the New York Convention, and one of the secret committee for the defence of the Hudson, applied for leave of absence, that he might remove his aged parents to a place of safety. A letter from him to Edward Rutledge, of the Board of War, contains this remarkable sentence: "I wish our army well stationed in the Highlands, and all the lower country desolated; we might then bid defiance to all the further efforts of the enemy in that quarter."

Nor was this a random or despairing wish. It shows a brave spirit of a leading civilian of the day, and the sacrifices that true patriots were disposed to make in the cause of independence.

But a few days previously he had held the following language to Gouverneur Morris, chairman of a special committee: "Had I been vested with absolute power in this State, I have often said, and still think, that I would last spring have desolated all *Long Island*, *Staten Island*, the city and county of *New York*, and all that part of the county of *Westchester* which lies below the mountains. I would then have stationed the main body of the army in the mountains on the east, and eight or ten thousand men in the Highlands on the west side of the river. I would have directed the river at *Fort Montgomery*, which is nearly at the southern extremity of the mountains, to be so shallowed as to afford only depth sufficient for an *Albany* sloop, and all the southern passes and defiles in the mountains to be strongly fortified. Nor do I think the shallowing of the river a romantic scheme. Rocky mountains rise immediately from the shores. The breadth is not very great, though the depth is. But what cannot eight or ten thousand men, well worked, effect? According to this plan of defence the State would be absolutely impregnable against all the world, on the seaside, and would have nothing to fear except from the way of the lake. Should the enemy gain the river, even below the mountains, I think I foresee that a retreat would become necessary, and I can't forbear wishing that a desire of saving a few acres may not lead us into difficulties." *

* Am. Archives, 5th Series, vol. ii. 921.

Three days after this remarkable letter was written, the enemy's ships did gain the river; and two days afterwards, October 11th, Reed, the adjutant-general, the confidant of Washington's councils, writes to his wife from Harlem Heights: "My most sanguine views do not extend further than keeping our ground here till this campaign closes. If the enemy incline to press us, it is resolved to risk an engagement, for, if we cannot fight them on this ground, we can on none in America. The ships are the only circumstances unfavorable to us here."

On the same day that this letter was written, a small vessel, sloop-rigged, with a topsail, was descried from Mount Washington, coming down the river with a fresh breeze. It was suspected by those on the look-out to be one of the British tenders, and they gave it a shot from a twelve-pounder. Their aim was unfortunately too true. Three of the crew were killed and the captain wounded. It proved to be Washington's yacht, which had run up the river previously to the enemy's ships, and was now on its return.*

* Heath's Memoirs.

CHAPTER XXXVI.

"IF General Lee should be in Philadelphia," writes John Jay to Rutledge, "pray hasten his departure—he is much wanted at New York." The successes of Lee at the South were contrasted by many with the defeat on Long Island, and evacuation of New York, and they began to consider him the main hope of the army. Hazard, the postmaster, writing from Harlem Heights to General Gates on the 11th, laments it as a misfortune that Lee should have been to the southward for several months past, but adds cheeringly, "he is expected here to-day."

Joseph Trumbull, the commissary-general, also writes to Gates under the same date: "General Lee is to be here this evening. He left Philadelphia on the 8th."

Lee, the object of so many hopes, was actually in the Jerseys, on his way to the camp. He writes from Amboy on the 12th, to the President of Congress, informing him, that the Hes sians, encamped opposite on Staten Island, had disappeared on the preceding night, quitting the island entirely, and some great measure was believed to be in agitation. "I am confident," writes he, "they will not attack General Washington's lines; such a measure is too absurd for a man of Mr. Howe's genius; and unless they have received flattering accounts from Burgoyne, that he will be able to effectuate a junction (which I conceive they have not), they will no longer remain kicking their heels at New York. They will put the place in a respectable state of defence, which, with their command of the waters, may be easily done, leave four or five thousand men, and direct their operations to a more decisive object. They will infallibly proceed either immediately up the river Delaware with their whole troops, or, what is more probable, land somewhere about South Amboy or Shrewsbury, and march straight to Trenton or Burlington. On the supposition that this will be the case, what are we to do? What force have we? What means have we to prevent their possessing themselves of Philadelphia? General Washington's army cannot possibly keep pace with them. The length of his route is not only infinitely greater, but his obstructions almost insuperable. In short, before he could cross Hudson River, they might be lodged and strongly fortified on both banks of the Delaware, * * For Heaven's sake, arouse yourselves! For Heaven's sake let ten thousand men be immediately assembled, and stationed somewhere about Trenton. In my opinion, your whole depends upon it. I set out immediately for head-quarters, where I shall communicate my apprehension that such will be the next operation of the enemy, and urge the expediency of sparing a part of his army (if he has any to spare) for this object." *

* Am. Archives, 5th Series, ii. 1008.

On the very morning that Lee was writing this letter at Amboy, Washington received intelligence by express from General Heath, stationed above King's Bridge, that the enemy were landing with artillery on Throg's Neck* in the Sound, about nine miles from the camp.   Washington surmised that Howe was pursuing his orginal plan of getting into the rear of the American army, cutting off its supplies, which were chiefly derived from the East, and interrupting its communication with the main country.   Officers were ordered to their alarm posts, and the troops to be ready, under arms, to act as occasion might require. Word, at the same time, was sent to General Heath to dispose of the troops on his side of King's Bridge, and of two militia regiments posted on the banks of Harlem River opposite the camp, in such manner as he should think necessary.

Having made all his arrangements as promptly as possible, Washington mounted his horse, and rode over towards Throg's Neck to reconnoitre.

Throg's Neck is a peninsula in Westchester County, stretching upwards of two miles into the Sound.   It was separated from the mainland by a narrow creek and a marsh, and was surrounded by water every high tide.   A bridge across a creek connecting with a ruined causeway across the marsh, led to the mainland, and the upper end of the creek was fordable at low water.   Early in the morning, eighty or ninety boats full of men had stood up the Sound from Montresor's Island, and Long Island, and had landed troops to the number of four thousand on Throg's Point, the extremity of the neck.   Thence their advance pushed forward toward the causeway and bridge, to secure that pass to the main-

* Properly Throck's Neck, from Throckmorton, the name of the original proprietor.

land. General Heath had been too rapid for them. Colonel Hand and his Philadelphia riflemen, the same who had checked the British advance on Long Island, had taken up the planks of the bridge, and posted themselves opposite the end of the causeway, whence they commenced firing with their rifles. They were soon reinforced by Colonel Prescott, of Bunker's Hill renown, with his regiment, and Lieutenant Bryant of the artillery, with a three-pounder. Checked at this pass, the British moved toward the head of the creek; here they found the Americans in possession of the ford, where they were reinforced by Colonel Graham, of the New York line, with his regiment, and Lieutenant Jackson of the artillery, with a six-pounder. These skilful dispositions of his troops by General Heath had brought the enemy to a stand. By the time Washington arrived in the vicinity, the British had encamped on the neck; the riflemen and yagers keeping up a scattering fire at each other across the marsh; and Captain Bryant now and then saluting the enemy with his field-piece.

Having surveyed the ground, Washington ordered works to be thrown up at the passes from the neck to the mainland. The British also threw up a work at the end of the causeway. In the afternoon nine ships, with a great number of schooners, sloops, and flat-bottomed boats full of men, passed through Hell Gate, towards Throg's Point; and information received from two deserters, gave Washington reason to believe that the greater part of the enemy's forces were gathering in that quarter. General McDougall's brigade, in which were Colonel Smallwood and the independent companies, was sent in the evening to strengthen Heath's division at King's Bridge, and to throw up works opposite the ford of Harlem River.

Greene, who had heard of the landing of the enemy at

Throg's Neck, wrote over to Washington, from Fort Constitution, informing him that he had three brigades ready to join him if required. "If the troops are wanted over your side," said he, "or likely to be so, they should be got over in the latter part of the night, as the shipping may move up from below, and impede, if not totally stop the troops from passing. The tents upon Staten Island," he added, "had all been struck, as far as could be ascertained." It was plain the whole scene of action was changing.

On the 14th, General Lee arrived in camp, where he was welcomed as the harbinger of good luck. Washington was absent, visiting the posts beyond King's Bridge, and the passes leading from Throg's Neck; Lee immediately rode forth to join him. No one gave him a sincerer greeting than the commander-in-chief; who, diffident of his own military knowledge, had a high opinion of that of Lee. He immediately gave him command of the troops above King's Bridge, now the greatest part of the army, but desired that he would not exercise it for a day or two, until he had time to acquaint himself with the localities and arrangements of the post; Heath, in the interim, held the command.

Lee was evidently elevated by his successes at the South, and disposed to criticise disparagingly the military operations of other commanders. In a letter, written on the day of his arrival to his old associate in arms, General Gates, he condemns the position of the army, and censures Washington for submitting to the dictation of Congress, whose meddlesome instructions had produced it. *Inter nos,*" writes he, " the Congress seem to stumble every step. I do not mean one or two of the cattle, but the whole stable. I have been very free in delivering my opinion to them. In my opinion General Washington is much to blame in not menacing 'em with resignation, unless they refrain from unhinging the army by their absurd interference.

"Keep us Ticonderoga; much depends upon it. We ought to have an army in the Delaware. I have roared it in the ears of Congress, but *carent auribus*. Adieu, my dear friend; if we do meet again—why, we shall smile." *

In the mean time, Congress, on the 11th of October, having heard of the ingress of the Phœnix, Roebuck and Tartar, passed a resolution that General Washington be desired, if it be practicable, by every art, and at whatever expense, to obstruct effectually the navigation of the North River between Fort Washington and Mount Constitution, as well to prevent the regress of the enemy's vessels lately gone up as to hinder them from receiving succors.

Under so many conflicting circumstances, Washington held a council of war on the 16th, at Lee's head-quarters, at which all the major-generals were present excepting Greene, and all the brigadiers, as well as Colonel Knox, who commanded the artillery. Letters from the Convention and from individual members of it were read, concerning the turbulence of the disaffected in the upper parts of the State; intelligence gained from deserters was likewise stated, showing the intention of the enemy to surround the camp. The policy was then discussed of remaining in their present position on Mahattan Island, and awaiting there the menaced attack: the strength of the position was urged; its being well fortified, and extremely difficult of access. Lee, in reply, scoffed at the idea of a position being good

---

* Am. Archives, 5th Series, ii. 1038.

merely because its approaches were difficult. How could they think of holding a position where the enemy were so strong in front and rear; where ships had the command of the water on each side, and where King's Bridge was their only pass by which to escape from being wholly enclosed? Had not their recent experience on Long Island and at New York taught them the danger of such positions? "For my part," said he, "I would have nothing to do with the islands to which you have been clinging so pertinaciously—I would give Mr. Howe a fee-simple of them."

"After much consideration and debate," says the record of the council, "the following question was stated: Whether (it having appeared that the obstructions in the North River have proved insufficient, and that the enemy's whole force is now in our rear on Frog Point) it is now deemed possible, in our situation, to prevent the enemy from cutting off the communication with the country, and compelling us to fight them at all disadvantages or surrender prisoners at discretion?"

All agreed, with but one dissenting voice, that it was not possible to prevent the communication from being cut off, and that one of the consequences mentioned in the question must follow.

The dissenting voice was that of General George Clinton, a brave downright man, but little versed in the science of warfare. He could not comprehend the policy of abandoning so strong a position; they were equal in number to the enemy, and, as they must fight them somewhere, could do it to more advantage there than any where else. Clinton felt as a guardian of the Hudson and the upper country, and wished to meet the enemy, as it were, at the very threshold.

As the resolve of Congress seemed imperative with regard to

Fort Washington, that post, it was agreed, should be "retained as long as possible."

A strong garrison was accordingly placed in it, composed chiefly of troops from Magaw's and Shee's Pennsylvania regiments, the latter under Lieutenant-colonel Lambert Cadwalader, of Philadelphia. Shee having obtained leave of absence, Colonel Magaw was put in command of the post, and solemnly charged by Washington to defend it to the last extremity. The name of the opposite post on the Jersey shore, where Greene was stationed, was changed from Fort Constitution to Fort Lee, in honor of the general. Lee, in fact, was the military idol of the day. Even the family of the commander in-chief joined in paying him homage. Colonel Tench Tilghman, Washington's aide-de-camp, in a letter to a friend, writes: "You ask if General Lee is in health, and our people bold. I answer both in the affirmative. His appearance amongst us has contributed not a little to the latter."

VOL. II.—16

CHAPTER XXXVII.

ARMY ARRANGEMENTS—WASHINGTON AT WHITE PLAINS—THE ENEMY AT THROG'S POINT—SKIRMISH OF COLONEL GLOVER—ATTEMPT TO SURPRISE ROGERS, THE RENEGADE—TROOPERS IN A ROUGH COUNTRY—ALARMS AT WHITE PLAINS—CANNONADING OF SHIPS AT FORT WASHINGTON—MARCH OF LEE—FORTIFIED CAMP AT WHITE PLAINS—RECONNOITRING—THE AFFAIR AT CHATTERTON HILL—RELATIVE SITUATION OF THE ARMIES—CHANGE OF POSITION—CONTRAST OF THE APPEARANCE OF THE TROOPS—GEORGE CLINTON'S IDEA OF STRATEGY—MOVEMENT OF THE BRITISH ARMY—INCENDIARIES AT WHITE PLAINS.

PREVIOUS to decamping from Manhattan Island, Washington formed four divisions of the army, which were respectively assigned to Generals Lee, Heath, Sullivan (recently obtained in exchange for General Prescott), and Lincoln. Lee was stationed on Valentine's Hill on the mainland, immediately opposite King's Bridge, to cover the transportation across it of the military stores and heavy baggage. The other divisions were to form a chain of fortified posts, extending about thirteen miles along a ridge of hills on the west side of the Bronx, from Lee's camp up to the village of White Plains.

Washington's head-quarters continued to be on Harlem Heights for several days, during which time he was continually in the saddle, riding about a broken, woody, and half wild country, forming posts, and choosing sites for breastworks and redoubts. By his skilful disposition of the army, it was protected in its whole length by the Bronx, a narrow but deep stream, fringed with trees, which ran along the foot of the ridge; at the same time his troops faced and outflanked the enemy, and covered the roads along which the stores and baggage had to be transported. On the 21st, he shifted his head-quarters to Valentine's Hill, and on the 23d to White Plains, where he stationed himself in a fortified camp.

While he was thus incessantly in action, General, now Sir William Howe (having recently, in reward for his services, been made a knight companion of the Bath), remained for six days passive in his camp on Throg's Point, awaiting the arrival of supplies and reinforcements, instead of pushing across to the Hudson, and throwing himself between Washington's army and the upper country. His inaction lost him a golden opportunity. By the time his supplies arrived, the Americans had broken up the causeway leading to the mainland, and taken positions too strong to be easily forced.

Finding himself headed in this direction, Sir William re-embarked part of his troops in flat boats on the 18th, crossed Eastchester Bay, and landed on Pell's Point, at the mouth of Hutchinson's River. Here he was joined in a few hours by the main body, with the baggage and artillery, and proceeded through the manor of Pelham towards New Rochelle; still with a view to get above Washington's army.

In their march, the British were waylaid and harassed by Colonel Glover of Massachusetts, with his own, Reed's, and Shepard's regiments of infantry. Twice the British advance guard were thrown into confusion and driven back with severe loss, by a sharp fire from behind stone fences. A third time they advanced in solid columns. The Americans gave them repeated volleys, and then retreated with the loss of eight killed and thirteen wounded, among whom was Colonel Shepard. Colonel Glover, and the officers and soldiers who were with him in this skirmish, received the public thanks of Washington for their merit and good behavior.

On the 21st, General Howe was encamped about two miles north of New Rochelle, with his outposts extending to Mamaroneck on the Sound. At the latter place was posted Colonel Rogers, the renegade, as he was called, with the Queen's Rangers, his newly-raised corps of loyalists.

Hearing of this, Lord Stirling resolved, if possible, to cut off this outpost and entrap the old hunter. Colonel Haslet, of his brigade, always prompt on such occasions, undertook the exploit at the head of seven hundred and fifty of the Delaware troops, who had fought so bravely on Long Island. With these he crossed the line of the British march; came undiscovered upon the post; drove in the guard; killed a lieutenant and several men, and brought away thirty-six prisoners, with a pair of colors, sixty stands of arms, and other spoils. He missed the main prize, however.—Rogers skulked off in the dark at the first fire. He was too old a partisan to be easily entrapped.

For this exploit, Colonel Haslet and his men were publicly thanked by Lord Stirling, on parade.

These, and other spirited and successful skirmishes, while they retarded the advance of the enemy, had the far more important effect of exercising and animating the American troops, and accustoming them to danger.

While in this neighborhood, Howe was reinforced by a second

division of Hessians under General Knyphausen, and a regiment
of Waldeckers, both of which had recently arrived in New York.
He was joined, also, by the whole of the seventeenth light-dra-
goons, and a part of the sixteenth, which had arrived on the 3d
instant from Ireland, with Lieutenant-colonel (afterwards Earl)
Harcourt. Some of their horses had been brought with them
across the sea, others had been procured since their arrival.

The Americans at first regarded these troopers with great
dread. Washington, therefore, took pains to convince them, that
in a rough, broken country, like the present, full of stone fences,
no troops were so inefficient as cavalry. They could be waylaid
and picked off by sharp-shooters from behind walls and thickets,
while they could not leave the road to pursue their covert foe.

Further to inspirit them against this new enemy, he proclaimed, in general orders, a reward of one hundred dollars for every
trooper brought in with his horse and accoutrements, and so on,
in proportion to the completeness of the capture.

On the 25th, about two o'clock in the afternoon, intelligence
was brought to head-quarters that three or four detachments of
the enemy were on the march, within four miles of the camp, and
the main army following in columns. The drums beat to arms;
the men were ordered to their posts; an attack was expected.
The day passed away, however, without any demonstration of the
enemy. Howe detached none of his force on lateral expeditions,
evidently meditating a general engagement. To prepare for it,
Washington drew all his troops from the posts along the Bronx
into the fortified camp at White Plains. Here every thing
remained quiet but expectant, throughout the 26th. In the
morning of the 27th, which was Sunday, the heavy booming of
cannon was heard from a distance, seemingly in the direction of

Fort Washington.   Scouts galloped off to gain intelligence.
We will anticipate their roport.

Two of the British frigates, at seven o'clock in the morning,
had moved up the Hudson, and come to anchor near Bourdett's
Ferry, below the Morris House, Washington's old head-quarters,
apparently with the intention of stopping the ferry, and cutting
off the communication between Fort Lee and Fort Washington.
At the same time, troops made their appearance on Harlem
Plains, where Lord Percy held command.   Colonel Morgan
immediately manned the lines with troops from the garrison of
Fort Washington.   The ships opened a fire to enfilade and dislodge them.   A barbette battery on the cliffs of the Jersey
shore, left of the ferry, fired down upon the frigate, but with little
effect.   Colonel Magaw got down an eighteen-pounder to the
lines near the Morris House, and fired fifty or sixty rounds, two
balls at a time.   Two eighteen-pounders were likewise brought
down from Fort Lee, and planted opposite the ships.   By the fire
from both shores they were hulled repeatedly.

It was the thundering of these cannonades which had reached
Washington's camp at White Plains, and even startled the Highlands of the Hudson.   The ships soon hoisted all sail.   The
foremost slipped her cable, and appeared to be in the greatest
confusion.   She could make no way, though towed by two boats.
The other ship seeing her distress, sent two barges to her assistance, and by the four boats she was dragged out of reach of the
American fire, her pumps going all the time.   "Had the tide been
flood one half hour longer," writes General Greene, "we should
have sunk her."

At the time that the fire from the ships began, Lord Percy
brought up his field-pieces and mortars, and made an attack upon

the lines. He was resolutely answered by the troops sent down from Fort Washington, and several Hessians were killed. An occasional firing was kept up until evening, when the ships fell down the river, and the troops which had advanced on Harlem Plains drew within their lines again.

"We take this day's movement to be only a feint," writes one of the garrison at Fort Lee; "at any rate, it is little honorable to the red coats." Its chief effect was to startle the distant camp, and astound a quiet country with the thundering din of war.

The celebrated Thomas Paine, author of "The Rights of Man," and other political works, was a spectator of the affair from the rocky summit of the Palisades, on the Jersey shore

While these things were passing at Fort Washington, Lee had struck his tents, and with the rear division, eight thousand strong, the baggage and artillery, and a train of waggons four miles long, laden with stores and ammunition, was lumbering along the rough country roads to join the main army. It was not until Monday morning, after being on the road all night, that he arrived at White Plains.

Washington's camp was situated on high ground, facing the east. The right wing stretched towards the south along a rocky hill, at the foot of which the Bronx, making an elbow, protected it in flank and rear. The left wing rested on a small, deep lake among the hills. The camp was strongly intrenched in front.

About a quarter of a mile to the right of the camp, and separated from the height on which it stood by the Bronx and a marshy interval, was a corresponding height called Chatterton's Hill. As this partly commmanded the right flank, and as the intervening bend of the Bronx was easily passable, Washington had stationed on its summit a militia regiment.

The whole encampment was a temporary one, to be changed as soon as the military stores collected there could be removed; and now that General Lee was arrived, Washington rode out with him, and other general officers who were off duty, to reconnoitre a height which appeared more eligible. When arrived at it, Lee pointed to another on the north, still more commanding. "Yonder," said he, "is the ground we ought to occupy." "Let us go, then, and view it," replied Washington. They were gently riding in that direction, when a trooper came spurring up his panting horse. "The British are in the camp, sir!" cried he. "Then, gentlemen," said Washington, "we have other business to attend to than reconnoitring." Putting spurs to his horse, he set off for the camp at full gallop, the others spurring after him.

Arrived at head-quarters, he was informed by Adjutant-general Reed, that the picket guards had all been driven in, and the enemy were advancing: but that the whole American army was posted in order of battle. "Gentlemen," said Washington, turning calmly to his companions, "you will return to your respective posts, and do the best you can."

Apprehensive that the enemy might attempt to get possession of Chatterton's Hill, he detached Colonel Haslet with his Delaware regiment, to reinforce the militia posted there. To these he soon added General McDougall's brigade, composed of Smallwood's Marylanders, Ritzema's New Yorkers, and two other regiments. These were much reduced by sickness and absence. General McDougall had command of the whole force upon the hill, which did not exceed 1,600 men.

These dispositions were scarcely made, when the enemy appeared glistening on the high grounds beyond the village of White Plains. They advanced in two columns, the right commanded by

Sir Henry Clinton, the left by the Hessian general, De Heister. There was also a troop of horse; so formidable in the inexperienced eyes of the Americans. " It was a brilliant but formidable sight," writes Heath in his memoirs. " The sun shone bright, their arms glittered; and perhaps troops never were shown to more advantage."

For a time they halted in a wheat field, behind a rising ground, and the general officers rode up in the centre to hold a consultation. Washington supposed they were preparing to attack him in front, and such indeed was their intention; but the commanding height of Chatterton's Hill had caught Sir William's eye, and he determined first to get possession of it.

Colonel Rahl was accordingly detached with a brigade of Hessians, to make a circuit southwardly round a piece of wood, cross the Bronx about a quarter of a mile below, and ascend the south side of the hill; while General Leslie, with a large force, British and Hessian, should advance directly in front, throw a bridge across the stream, and charge up the hill.

A furious cannonade was now opened by the British from fifteen or twenty pieces of artillery, placed on high ground opposite the hill; under cover of which, the troops of General Leslie hastened to construct the bridge. In so doing, they were severely galled by two field-pieces, planted on a ledge of rock on Chatterton's Hill, and in charge of Alexander Hamilton, the youthful captain of artillery. Smallwood's Maryland battalion, also, kept up a sharp fire of small arms.

As soon as the bridge was finished, the British and Hessians under Leslie rushed over it, formed, and charged up the hill to take Hamilton's two field-pieces. Three times the two field-pieces were discharged, ploughing the ascending columns from hill-top to river, while Smallwood's "blue and buff" Marylanders kept up their volleys of musketry.

In the mean time, Rahl and his Hessian brigade forded the Bronx lower down, pushed up the south side of the hill, and endeavored to turn McDougall's right flank. The militia gave the general but little support. They had been dismayed at the opening of the engagement by a shot from a British cannon, which wounded one of them in the thigh, and nearly put the whole to flight. It was with the utmost difficulty McDougall had rallied them, and posted them behind a stone wall. Here they did some service, until a troop of British cavalry, having gained the crest of the hill, came on, brandishing their sabres. At their first charge the militia gave a random, scattering fire, then broke, and fled in complete confusion.

A brave stand was made on the summit of the hill by Haslet, Ritzema, and Smallwood, with their troops. Twice they repulsed horse and foot, British and Hessians, until, cramped for room and greatly outnumbered, they slowly and sullenly retreated down the north side of the hill, where there was a bridge across the Bronx. Smallwood remained upon the ground for some time after the retreat had begun, and received two flesh wounds, one in the hip, the other through the arm. At the bridge over the Bronx, the retreating troops were met by General Putnam, who was coming to their assistance with Beall's brigade. In the rear of this they marched back into the camp.

The loss on both sides, in this short but severe action, was nearly equal. That of the Americans was between three and four hundred men, killed, wounded, and taken prisoners. At first it was thought to be much more, many of the militia and a few of the regulars being counted as lost, who had scattered themselves among the hills, but afterwards returned to head-quarters.

The British army now rested with their left wing on the hill they had just taken, and which they were busy intrenching. They were extending their right wing to the left of the American lines, so that their two wings and centre formed nearly a semicircle. It was evidently their design to outflank the American camp, and get in the rear of it. The day, however, being far advanced, was suffered to pass without any further attack; but the morrow was looked forward to for a deadly conflict. Washington availed himself of this interval to have the sick and wounded, and as much of the stores as possible, removed from the camp. "The two armies," says General Heath in his Memoirs, "lay looking at each other, within long cannon shot. In the night time the British lighted up a vast number of fires, the weather growing pretty cold. These fires, some on the level ground, some at the foot of the hills, and at all distances to their brows, some of which were lofty, seemed to the eye to mix with the stars. The American side doubtless exhibited to them a similar appearance."

During this anxious night, Washington was assiduously occupied throwing back his right wing to stronger ground; doubling his intrenchments and constructing three redoubts, with a line in front, on the summit of his post. These works were principally intended for defence against small arms, and were thrown up with a rapidity that to the enemy must have savored of magic. They were, in fact, made of the stalks of Indian corn or maize taken from a neighboring corn-field, and pulled up with the earth clinging in masses to the large roots. "The roots of the stalks," says Heath, "and earth on them placed in the face of the works, answered the purpose of sods and fascines. The tops being placed inwards, as the loose earth was thrown upon them, became as so many trees to the work, which was carried up with a despatch scarcely conceivable.

In the morning of the 29th, when Howe beheld how greatly Washington had improved his position and strengthened it, by what appeared to be solidly constructed works, he postponed his meditated assault, ordered up Lord Percy from Harlem with the fourth brigade and two battalions of the sixth, and proceeded to throw up lines and redoubts in front of the American camp, as if preparing to cannonade it. As the enemy were endeavoring to outflank him, especially on his right wing, Washington apprehended one of their objects might be to advance a part of their force, and seize on Pine's Bridge over Croton River, which would cut off his communication with the upper country. General Beall, with three Maryland regiments, was sent off with all expedition to secure that pass. It was Washington's idea that, having possession of Croton River and the passes in the Highlands, his army would be safe from further pursuit, and have time to repose after its late excessive fatigue, and would be fresh, and ready to harass the enemy should they think fit to winter up the country.

At present nothing could exceed the war-worn condition of the troops, unseasoned as they were to this kind of service. A scornful letter, written at this time by a British officer, to his friend in London, gives a picture of the ragged plight to which they were reduced, in this rainy and inclement season. " The rebel army are in so wretched a condition as to clothing and accoutrements, that I believe no nation ever saw such a set of tatterdemalions. There are few coats among them but what are out at elbows, and in a whole regiment there is scarce a pair of breeches. Judge, then, how they must be pinched by a winter's campaign. We, who are warmly clothed and well equipped, already feel it severely; for it is even now much colder than I ever felt it in England."

Alas for the poor half-naked, weather-beaten patriots, who had to cope with these well-fed, well-clad, well-appointed mercenaries! A letter written at the very same date (October 31), by General George Clinton, shows what, in their forlorn plight, they had to grapple with.

"We had reason," writes he, "to apprehend an attack last night, or by daylight this morning. Our lines were manned all night in consequence; and a most horrid night it was to lay in cold trenches. Uncovered as we are, daily on fatigue, making redoubts, fleches, abattis, and retreating from them and the little temporary huts made for our comfort before they are well finished, I fear will ultimately destroy our army without fighting."* "However," adds he, honestly, "I would not be understood to condemn measures. They may be right for aught I know. I do not understand much of the refined art of war; it is said to consist in stratagem and deception." In a previous letter to the same friend, in a moment of hurry and alarm, he writes, "Pray let Mrs. Clinton know that I am well, and that she need not be uneasy about me. It would be too much honor to die in so good a cause."

Clinton, as we have before intimated, was an honest and ardent patriot, of resolute spirit, and plain, direct good sense; but an inexperienced soldier. His main idea of warfare was

* George Clinton to John McKesson, Oct. 31. Am. Archives, 5th Series, ii. 1312.

straightforward fighting; and he was greatly perplexed by the continual strategy which Washington's situation required. One of the aides-de-camp of the latter had a truer notion on the subject. "The campaign hitherto," said he, "has been a fair trial of generalship, in which I flatter myself we have had the advantage. If we, with our motley army, can keep Mr. Howe and his grand appointment at bay, I think we shall make no contemptible military figure." *

On the night of the 31st, Washington made another of those moves which perplexed the worthy Clinton. In the course of the night he shifted his whole position, set fire to the barns and out-houses containing forage and stores, which there was no time to remove, and, leaving a strong rear-guard on the heights, and in the neighboring woods, retired with his main army a distance of five miles, among the high, rocky hills about Northcastle. Here he immediately set to work to intrench and fortify himself; his policy at this time being, as he used to say, " to fight with the spade and mattock."

General Howe did not attempt to dislodge him from this fastness. He at one time ordered an attack on the rear-guard, but a violent rain prevented it, and for two or three days he remained seemingly inactive. "All matters are as quiet as if the enemy were one hundred miles distant from us," writes one of Washington's aides on the 2d of November. During the night of the 4th, this quiet was interrupted. A mysterious sound was heard in the direction of the British camp; like the rumbling of waggons and artillery. At daybreak the meaning of it was discovered. The enemy were decamping. Long trains were observed,

* Tench Tilghman to William Duer, Oct. 31.

defiling across the hilly country, along the roads leading to
Dobbs' Ferry on the Hudson. The movement continued for
three successive days, until their whole force, British and Hessians, disappeared from White Plains.

The night after their departure a party of Americans, heated
with liquor, set fire to the court-house and other edifices in the
village, as if they had belonged to the enemy; an outrage which
called forth a general order from Washington, expressive of his
indignation, and threatening the perpetrators with signal punishment when detected. We notice this matter, because in British
accounts, the burning of those buildings had been charged upon
Washington himself; being, no doubt, confounded with the burning of the barns and out-houses ordered by him on shifting his
encampment.

CHAPTER XXXVIII.

CONJECTURES AS TO THE INTENTIONS OF THE ENEMY—CONSEQUENT PRECAUTIONS
—CORRESPONDENCE WITH GREENE RESPECTING FORT WASHINGTON—DIS-
TRIBUTION OF THE ARMY—LEE LEFT IN COMMAND AT NORTHCASTLE—IN-
STRUCTIONS TO HIM—WASHINGTON AT PEEKSKILL—VISITS TO THE POSTS
IN THE HIGHLANDS.

VARIOUS were the speculations at head-quarters on the sudden
movement of the enemy. Washington writes to General William
Livingston (now governor of the Jerseys): "They have gone
towards the North River and King's Bridge. Some suppose
they are going into winter quarters, and will sit down in New
York without doing more than investing Fort Washington. I
cannot subscribe wholly to this opinion myself. That they will
invest Fort Washington, is a matter of which there can be no
doubt; and I think there is a strong probability that General
Howe will detach a part of his force to make an incursion into
the Jerseys, provided he is going to New York. He must attempt something on account of his reputation, for what has he
done as yet, with his great army?"

In the same letter he expressed his determination, as soon as
it should appear that the present manœuvre was a real retreat,
and not a feint, to throw over a body of troops into the Jerseys

to assist in checking Howe's progress. He, moreover, recommended to the governor to have the militia of that State put on the best possible footing, and a part of them held in readiness to take the place of the State levies, whose term of service would soon expire. He advised, also, that the inhabitants contiguous to the water, should be prepared to remove their stock, grain, effects, and carriages, on the earliest notice.

In a letter of the same date, he charged General Greene, should Howe invest Fort Washington with part of his force, to give the garrison all possible assistance.

On the following day (Nov. 8), his aide-de-camp, Colonel Tilghman, writes to General Greene from head-quarters: "The enemy are at Dobbs' Ferry with a great number of boats, ready to go into Jersey, *or proceed up the river.*"

Greene doubted any intention of the enemy to cross the river; it might only be a feint to mislead; still, as a precaution, he had ordered troops up from the flying camp, and was posting them opposite Dobbs' Ferry, and at other passes where a landing might be attempted; the whole being under the command of General Mercer.

Affairs at Fort Washington soon settled the question of the enemy's intentions with regard to it. Lord Percy took his station with a body of troops before the lines to the south. Knyphausen advanced on the north. The Americans had previously abandoned Fort Independence, burnt its barracks, and removed the stores and cannon. Crossing King's Bridge, Knyphausen took a position between it and Fort Washington. The approach to the fort, on this side, was exceedingly steep and rocky; as, indeed, were all its approaches excepting that on the south, where the country was more open, and the ascent gradual. The fort could not hold within its walls above one thousand men; the rest of the troops were distributed about the lines and outworks. While the fort was thus menaced, the chevaux-de-frise had again proved inefficient. On the night of the 5th, a frigate and two transports, bound up to Dobbs' Ferry, with supplies for Howe's army, had broken through; though, according to Greene's account, not without being considerably shattered by the batteries.

Informed of these facts, Washington wrote to Greene on the 8th: "If we cannot prevent vessels from passing up the river, and the enemy are possessed of all the surrounding country, what valuable purpose can it answer to hold a post from which the expected benefit cannot be had? I am, therefore, inclined to think, that it will not be prudent to hazard the men and stores at Mount Washington; but, as you are on the spot, I leave it to you to give such orders as to evacuating Mount Washington as you may judge best, and so far revoking the orders given to Colonel Magaw, to defend it to the last."

Accounts had been received at head-quarters of a considerable movement on the preceding evening (Nov. 7th), among the enemy's boats at Dobbs' Ferry, with the intention, it was said, of penetrating the Jerseys, and falling down upon Fort Lee. Washington, therefore, in the same letter directed Greene to have all the stores not necessary to the defence removed immediately, and to destroy all the stock, the hay and grain, in the neighborhood, which the owners refused to remove. "Experience has shown," adds he, "that a contrary conduct is not of the least advantage to the poor inhabitants, from whom all their effects of every kind are taken without distinction and without the least satisfaction."

Greene, in reply (Nov. 9th), adhered with tenacity to the

policy of maintaining Fort Washington. "The enemy," said he, "must invest it with double the number of men required for its defence. They must keep troops at King's Bridge, to cut off all communication with the country, and in considerable force, for fear of an attack." He did not consider the fort in immediate danger. Colonel Magaw thought it would take the enemy until the end of December to carry it. In the mean time, the garrison could at any time be brought off, and even the stores removed, should matters grow desperate. If the enemy should not find it an object of importance, they would not trouble themselves about it; if they should, it would be a proof that they felt an injury from its being maintained. The giving it up would open for them a free communication with the country by the way of King's Bridge.*

It is doubtful when or where Washington received this letter, as he left the camp at Northcastle at eleven o'clock of the following morning. There being still considerable uncertainty as to the intentions of the enemy, all his arrangements were made accordingly. All the troops belonging to the States west of the Hudson, were to be stationed in the Jerseys, under command of General Putnam. Lord Stirling had already been sent forward with the Maryland and Virginia troops to Peekskill, to cross the river at King's Ferry. Another division composed of Connecticut and Massachusetts troops, under General Heath, was to co-operate with the brigade of New York militia under General George Clinton, in securing the Highland posts on both sides of the river.

The troops which would remain at Northcastle after the

* Am. Archives, 5th Series, iii. 618.

departure of Heath and his division, were to be commanded by Lee. Washington's letter of instructions to that general is characterized by his own modesty, and his deference for Lee's superior military experience. He suggests, rather than orders, yet his letter is sufficiently explicit. "A little time now," writes he, "must manifest the enemy's designs, and point out to you the measures proper to be pursued by that part of the army under your command. I shall give no directions, therefore, on this head, having the most entire confidence in your judgment and military exertions. One thing, however, I will suggest, namely, that the appearance of embarking troops for the Jerseys may be intended as a feint to weaken us, and render the post we now hold more vulnerable, or the enemy may find that troops are assembled with more expedition, and in greater numbers, than they expected, on the Jersey shore, to oppose them; and, as it is possible, from one or other of these motives, that they may yet pay the party under your command a visit, it will be unnecessary, I am persuaded, to recommend to you the propriety of putting this post, if you stay at it, into a proper posture of defence, and guarding against surprises. But I would recommend it to your consideration, whether, under the suggestion above, your retiring to Croton Bridge, and some strong post still more easterly (covering the passes through the Highlands), may not be more advisable than to run the hazard of an attack with unequal numbers. At any rate, I think all your baggage and stores, except such as are necessary for immediate use, ought to be to the northward of Croton River. * * * * You will consider the post at Croton's (or Pine's) Bridge as under your immediate care. * * * * If the enemy should remove the whole, or the greater part of their force to the west side of Hudson's River, I have no doubt of your following with all possible dispatch, leaving the militia and invalids to cover the frontiers of Connecticut in case of need."

We have been minute in stating these matters, from their bearing on subsequent operations.

On the 10th of November, Washington left the camp at North-castle, at 11 o'clock, and arrived at Peekskill at sunset; whither General Heath, with his division, had preceded him by a few hours. Lord Stirling was there, likewise, having effected the transportation of the Maryland and Virginia troops across the river, and landed them at the ferry south of Stony Point; though a better landing was subsequently found north of the point. His lordship had thrown out a scouting party in the advance, and a hundred men to take possession of a gap in the mountain, through which a road passed toward the Jerseys.

Washington was now at the entrance of the Highlands, that grand defile of the Hudson, the object of so much precaution and solicitude. On the following morning, accompanied by Gene-rals Heath, Stirling, James and George Clinton, Mifflin, and others, he made a military visit in boats to the Highland posts. Fort Montgomery was in a considerable state of forwardness, and a work in the vicinity was projected to co-operate with it. Fort Constitution commanded a sudden bend of the river, but Lord Stirling, in his report of inspection, had intimated that the fort itself was commanded by West Point opposite. A glance of the eye, without going on shore, was sufficient to convince Washington of the fact. A fortress subsequently erected on that point, has been considered the Key of the Highlands.

On the morning of the 12th, at an early hour, Washington rode out with General Heath to reconnoitre the east side of the Hudson, at the gorge of the Highlands.   Henry Wisner, in a report to the New York Convention, had mentioned a hill to the north of Peekskill, so situated, with the road winding along the side of it, that ten men on the top, by rolling down stones, might prevent ten thousand from passing.   " I believe," said he, " nothing more need be done than to keep great quantities of stones at the different places where the troops must pass, if they attempt penetrating the mountains."

Near Robinson's Bridge, in this vicinity, about two miles from Peekskill, Washington chose a place where troops should be stationed to cover the south entrance into the mountains; and here, afterwards, was established an important military depot called Continental Village.

On the same day (12th), he wrote to General Lee, inclosing a copy of resolutions just received from Congress, respecting levies for the new army, showing the importance of immediately begin‧ning the recruiting service.   If no commissioners arrived from Rhode Island, he was to appoint the officers recommended to tha State by General Greene.   " I cannot conclude," adds he, " without reminding you of the military and other stores about your encampment, and at Northcastle, and to press the removal of them above Croton Bridge, or such other places of security as you may think proper.   General Howe, having sent no part of his force to Jersey yet, makes the measure more necessary, as he may turn his views another way, and attempt their destruction."

It was evidently Washington's desire that Lee should post himself, as soon as possible, beyond the Croton, where he would be safe from surprise, and at hand to throw his troops promptly across the Hudson, should the Jerseys be invaded.

Having made all these surveys and arrangements, Washington

placed Heath in the general command of the Highlands, with written instructions to fortify the passes with all possible despatch, and directions how the troops were to be distributed on both sides of the river; and here we take occasion to give some personal notice of this trusty officer.

Heath was now in the fortieth year of his age. Like many of the noted officers of the Revolution, he had been brought up in rural life, on an hereditary farm near Boston; yet, according to his own account, though passionately fond of agricultural pursuits, he had also, almost from childhood, a great relish for military affairs, and had studied every treatise on the subject in the English language, so that he considered himself "fully acquainted with the *theory* of war, in all its branches and duties, from the private soldier to the commander-in-chief."

He describes himself to be of a middling stature, light complexion, very corpulent and bald-headed, so that the French officers who served in America, compared him, in person, to the Marquis of Granby.*

Such was the officer intrusted with the command of the High-land passes, and encamped at Peekskill, their portal. We shall find him faithful to his trust; scrupulous in obeying the letter of his instructions; but sturdy and punctilious in resisting any undue assumption of authority.

* Heath's Memoirs.

CHAPTER XXXIX.

DURING his brief and busy sojourn at Peekskill, Washington received important intelligence from the Northern army; especially that part of it on Lake Champlain, under the command of General Gates. A slight retrospect of affairs in that quarter is proper, before we proceed to narrate the eventful campaign in the Jerseys.

The preparations for the defence of Ticonderoga, and the nautical service on the lake, had met with difficulties at every step. At length, by the middle of August, a small flotilla was completed, composed of a sloop and schooner each of twelve guns (six and four pounders), two schooners mounting eight guns each, and five gondolas, each of three guns. The flotilla was subsequently augmented, and the command given by Gates to Arnold, in compliance with the advice of Washington; who had a high opinion of that officer's energy intrepidity, and fertility in expedients.

Sir Guy Carleton, in the mean time, was straining every nerve for the approaching conflict. The successes of the British forces on the seaboard, had excited the zealous rivalry of the forces in Canada. The commanders, newly arrived, were fearful the war might be brought to a close, before they could have an opportunity to share in the glory. Hence the ardor with which they encountered and vanquished obstacles which might otherwise have appeared insuperable. Vessels were brought from England in pieces and put together at St. Johns, boats of various kinds and sizes were transported over land, or dragged up the rapids of the Sorel. The soldiers shared with the seamen in the toil. The Canadian farmers, also, were taken from their agricultural pursuits, and compelled to aid in these, to them, unprofitable labors. Sir Guy was full of hope and ardor. Should he get the command of Lakes Champlain and George, the northern part of New York would be at his mercy; before winter set in he might gain possession of Albany. He would then be able to co-operate with General Howe in severing and subduing the northern and southern provinces, and bringing the war to a speedy and triumphant close.

In despite of every exertion, three months elapsed before his armament was completed. Winter was fast approaching. Before it arrived, the success of his brilliant plan required that he should fight his way across Lake Champlain; carry the strong posts of Crown Point and Ticonderoga; traverse Lake George, and pursue a long and dangerous march through a wild and rugged country, beset with forests and morasses, to Albany. That was the first post to the southward where he expected to find rest and winter quarters for his troops.*

* Civil War in America, vol. i. p. 212.

By the month of October, between twenty and thirty sail were afloat, and ready for action. The flag-ship (the Inflexible) mounted eighteen twelve-pounders; the rest were gunboats, a gondola and a flat-bottomed vessel called a radeau, and named the *Thunderer;* carrying a battery of six twenty-four and twelve six-pounders, besides howitzers. The gunboats mounted brass fieldpieces and howitzers. Seven hundred seamen navigated the fleet; two hundred of them were volunteers from the transports. The guns were worked by detachments from the corps of artillery. In a word, according to British accounts, " no equipment of the kind was ever better appointed or more amply furnished with every kind of provision necessary for the intended service." *

Captain Pringle conducted the armament, but Sir Guy Carleton was too full of zeal, and too anxious for the event, not to head the enterprise; he accordingly took his station on the deck of the flag-ship. They made sail early in October, in quest of the American squadron, which was said to be abroad upon the lake. Arnold, however, being ignorant of the strength of the enemy, and unwilling to encounter a superior force in the open lake, had taken his post under cover of Valcour Island, in the upper part of a deep channel, or strait between that island and the mainland. His force consisted of three schooners, two sloops, three galleys and eight gondolas; carrying in all seventy guns, many of them eighteen-pounders.

The British ships, sweeping past Cumberland Head with a fair wind and flowing sail on the morning of the 11th, had left the southern end of Valcour Island astern, when they discovered Arnold's flotilla anchored behind it, in a line extend-

* Civil war in America, i. 211.

ing across the strait so as not to be outflanked. They immediately hauled close to the wind, and tried to beat up into the channel. The wind, however, did not permit the largest of them to enter. Arnold took advantage of the circumstance. He was on board of the galley Congress, and, leaving the line, advanced with two other galleys and the schooner Royal Savage, to attack the smaller vessels as they entered before the large ones could come up. About twelve o'clock the enemy's schooner Carleton opened a brisk fire upon the Royal Savage and the galleys. It was as briskly returned. Seeing the enemy's gunboats approaching, the Americans endeavored to return to the line. In so doing, the Royal Savage ran aground. Her crew set her on fire and abandoned her. In about an hour the British brought all their gunboats in a range across the lower part of the channel, within musket shot of the Americans, the schooner Carleton in the advance. They landed, also, a large number of Indians on the island, to keep up a galling fire from the shore upon the Americans with their rifles. The action now became general, and was severe and sanguinary. The Americans, finding themselves thus hemmed in by a superior force, fought with desperation. Arnold pressed with his galley into the hottest of the fight. The Congress was hulled several times, received seven shots between wind and water, was shattered in mast and rigging, and many of the crew were killed or wounded. The ardor of Arnold increased with his danger. He cheered on his men by voice and example, often pointing the guns with his own hands. He was ably seconded by Brigadier-general Waterbury, in the Washington galley, which, like his own vessel, was terribly cut up. The contest lasted throughout the day. Carried on as it was within a narrow compass, and on a tranquil lake, almost every shot took effect. The fire of the Indians from the shore was less deadly than had been expected; but their whoops and yells, mingling with the rattling of the musketry, and the thundering of the cannon, increased the horrors of the scene. Volumes of smoke rose above the woody shores, which echoed with the unusual din of war, and for a time this lovely recess of a beautiful and peaceful lake was rendered a perfect pandemonium.

The evening drew nigh, yet the contest was undecided. Captain Pringle, after a consultation with Sir Guy Carleton, called off the smaller vessels which had been engaged, and anchored his whole squadron in a line as near as possible to the Americans, so as to prevent their escape; trusting to capture the whole of them when the wind should prove favorable, so that he could bring his large vessels into action.

Arnold, however, sensible that with his inferior and crippled force all resistance would be unavailing, took advantage of a dark cloudy night, and a strong north wind; his vessels slipped silently through the enemy's line without being discovered, one following a light on the stern of the other; and by daylight they were out of sight. They had to anchor, however, at Schuyler's Island, about ten miles up the lake, to stop leaks and make repairs. Two of the gondolas were here sunk, being past remedy. About noon the retreat was resumed, but the wind had become adverse; and they made little progress. Arnold's galley, the Congress, the Washington galley and four gondolas, all which had suffered severely in the late fight, fell astern of the rest of the squadron in the course of the night. In the morning, when the sun lifted a fog which had covered the lake, they beheld the enemy within a few miles of them in full chase, while their own comrades were nearly out of sight, making the best of their way for Crown Point.

It was now an anxious trial of speed and seamanship. Arnold, with the crippled relics of his squadron, managed by noon to get within a few leagues of Crown Point, when they were overtaken by the Inflexible, the Carleton, and the schooner Maria of 14 guns. As soon as they came up, they poured in a tremendous fire. The Washington galley, already shattered, and having lost most of her officers, was compelled to strike, and General Waterbury and the crew were taken prisoners. Arnold had now to bear the brunt of the action. For a long time he was engaged within musket shot with the Inflexible, and the two schooners, until his galley was reduced to a wreck and one third of the crew were killed. The gondolas were nearly in the same desperate condition; yet the men stood stoutly to their guns. Seeing resistance vain, Arnold determined that neither vessels nor crew should fall into the hands of the enemy. He ordered the gondolas to run on shore, in a small creek in the neighborhood, the men to set fire to them as soon as they grounded, to wade on shore with their muskets, and keep off the enemy until they were consumed. He did the same with his own galley; remaining on board of her until she was in flames, lest the enemy should get possession and strike his flag, which was kept flying to the last.

He now set off with his gallant crew, many of whom were wounded, by a road through the woods to Crown Point, where he arrived at night, narrowly escaping an Indian ambush. Two schooners, two galleys, one sloop and one gondola, the remnant which had escaped of this squadron, were at anchor at the Point, and General

Waterbury and most of his men arrived there the next day on parole. Seeing that the place must soon fall into the hands of the enemy, they set fire to the houses, destroyed every thing they could not carry away, and embarking in the vessels made sail for Ticonderoga.

The loss of the Americans in these two actions is said to have been between eighty and ninety men; that of the British about forty. It is worthy of mention, that among the young officers in Sir Guy Carleton's squadron, was Edward Pellew, who afterwards rose to renown as Admiral Viscount Exmouth; celebrated, among other things for his victory at Algiers.

The conduct of Arnold in these naval affairs gained him new laurels. He was extolled for the judgment with which he chose his position, and brought his vessels into action; for his masterly retreat, and for the self-sacrificing devotion with which he exposed himself to the overwhelming force of the enemy in covering the retreat of part of his flotilla.

Sir Guy Carleton took possession of the ruined works at Crown Point, where he was soon joined by the army. He made several movements by land and water, as if meditating an attack upon Ticonderoga; pushing strong detachments on both sides of the lake, which approached within a small distance of the fort, while one vessel appeared within cannon shot of a lower battery, sounding the depth of the channel, until a few shot obliged her to retire. General Gates, in the mean time, strengthened his works with incessant assiduity, and made every preparation for an obstinate defence. A strong easterly wind prevented the enemy's ships from advancing to attack the lines, and gave time for the arrival of reinforcements of militia to the garrison. It also afforded time for Sir Guy Carleton to cool in ardor, and calculate the chances and the value of success. The post, from its strength, and the apparent number and resolution of the garrison, could not be taken without great loss of life. If taken, the season was now too far advanced to think of passing Lake George, and exposing the army to the perils of a winter campaign in the inhospitable and impracticable wilds to the southward. Ticonderoga, too, could not be kept during the winter, so that the only result of the capture would be the reduction of the works and the taking of some cannon; all which damage the Americans could remedy before the opening of the summer campaign. If, however, the defence should be obstinate, the British army, even if successful, might sustain a loss sufficient to cripple its operations in the coming year.[*]

These, and other prudential reasons, induced Carleton to give up all attempt upon the fortress at present; wherefore, re-embarking his troops, he returned to St. Johns, and cantoned them in Canada for the winter. It was not until about the 1st of November, that a reconnoitring party, sent out from Ticonderoga by General Gates, brought him back intelligence that Crown Point was abandoned by the enemy, and not a hostile sail in sight. All apprehensions of an attack upon Ticonderoga during the present year were at an end, and many of the troops stationed there were already on their march toward Albany.

Such was the purport of the news from the north, received by Washington at Peekskill. It relieved him for the present from all anxiety respecting affairs on Lake Champlain, and gave him the prospect of reinforcements from that quarter.

---

[*] Civil War in America, vol. i. p. 214.

CHAPTER XL.

WASHINGTON CROSSES THE HUDSON—ARRIVES AT FORT LEE—AFFAIRS AT FORT
WASHINGTON—QUESTION ABOUT ITS ABANDONMENT—MOVEMENTS OF HOWE
—THE FORT SUMMONED TO SURRENDER—REFUSAL OF COLONEL MAGAW
—THE FORT ATTACKED—CAPTURE OF THE FORT AND GARRISON—COMMENTS
OF WASHINGTON ON THE STATE OF AFFAIRS.

ON the morning of the 12th of November, Washington crossed
the Hudson, to the ferry below Stony Point, with the residue
of the troops destined for the Jerseys. Far below were to be
descried the Phœnix, the Roebuck, and the Tartar, at anchor
in the broad waters of Haverstraw Bay and the Tappan Sea,
guarding the lower ferries. The army, thus shut out from the
nearer passes, was slowly winding its way by a circuitous route
through the gap in the mountains, which Lord Stirling had
secured. Leaving the troops which had just landed, to pursue
the same route to the Hackensack, Washington, accompanied by
Colonel Reed, struck a direct course for Fort Lee, being anxious
about affairs at Fort Washington. He arrived there on the following day, and found, to his disappointment, that General Greene
had taken no measures for the evacuation of that fortress; but
on the contrary, had reinforced it with a part of Colonel Durkee's
regiment, and the regiment of Colonel Rawlings, so that its

garison now numbered upwards of two thousand men; a great part, however, were militia. Washington's orders for its evacuation had, in fact, been discretionary, leaving the execution of them to Greene's judgment, " as being on the spot." The latter had differed in opinion as to the policy of such a measure; and Colonel Magaw, who had charge of the fortress, was likewise confident it might be maintained.

Colonel Reed was of opposite counsels; but then he was personally interested in the safety of the garrison. It was composed almost entirely of Pennsylvania troops under Magaw and Lambert Cadwalader; excepting a small detachment of Maryland riflemen commanded by Otho H. Williams. They were his friends and neighbors, the remnant of the brave men who had suffered so severely under Atlee and Smallwood.* The fort was now invested on all sides but one; and the troops under Howe which had been encamped at Dobbs' Ferry, were said to be moving down toward it. Reed's solicitude was not shared by the garrison itself. Colonel Magaw, its brave commander, still thought it was in no immediate danger.

Washington was much perplexed. The main object of Howe was still a matter of doubt with him. He could not think that Sir William was moving his whole force upon that fortress, to invest which, a part would be sufficient. He suspected an ulterior object, probably a Southern expedition, as he was told a large number of ships were taking in wood and water at New York. He resolved, therefore, to continue a few days in this neighborhood, during which he trusted the designs of the enemy would be more apparent; in the mean time he would distribute

* W. B. Reed's Life of Reed, i. 252.

troops at Brunswick, Amboy, Elizabethtown and Fort Lee, so as to be ready at these various points, to check any incursions into the Jerseys.

In a letter to the President of Congress he urged for an increase of ordnance and field-artillery. The rough, hilly country east of the Hudson, and the strongholds and fastnesses of which the Americans had possessed themselves, had prevented the enemy from profiting by the superiority of their artillery; but this would not be the case, should the scene of action change to an open champaign country, like the Jerseys.

Washington was mistaken in his conjecture as to Sir William Howe's design. The capture of Fort Washington was, at present, his main object; and he was encamped on Fordham Heights, not far from King's Bridge, until preliminary steps should be taken. In the night of the 14th, thirty flat-bottomed boats stole quietly up the Hudson, passed the American forts undiscovered, and made their way through Spyt den Duivel Creek into Harlem River. The means were thus provided for crossing that river and landing before unprotected parts of the American works.

On the 15th, General Howe sent in a summons to surrender, with a threat of extremities should he have to carry the place by assault. Magaw, in his reply, intimated a doubt that General Howe would execute a threat "so unworthy of himself and the British nation; but give me leave," added he, "to assure his Excellency, that, actuated by the most glorious cause that mankind ever fought in, I am determined to defend this post to the very last extremity."

Apprised by the Colonel of his peril, General Greene sent over reinforcements, with an exhortation to him to persist in his defence; and despatched an express to Washington, who was at

Hackensack, where the troops which had crossed from Peekskill were encamped. It was nightfall when Washington arrived at Fort Lee. Greene and Putnam were over at the besieged fortress. He threw himself into a boat, and had partly crossed the river, when he met those generals returning. They informed him of the garrison's having been reinforced, and assured him that it was in high spirits, and capable of making a good defence. It was with difficulty, however, they could prevail on him to return with them to the Jersey shore, for he was excessively excited.

Early the next morning (16th), Magaw made his dispositions for the expected attack. His forces, with the recent addition, amounted to nearly three thousand men. As the fort could not contain above a third of that number, most of them were stationed about the outworks.

Colonel Lambert Cadwalader, with eight hundred Pennsylvanians, was posted in the outer lines, about two miles and a half south of the fort, the side menaced by Lord Percy with sixteen hundred men. Colonel Rawlings, of Maryland, with a body of troops, many of them riflemen, was stationed by a three gun battery, on a rocky, precipitous hill, north of the fort, and between it and Spyt den Duivel Creek. Colonel Baxter, of Bucks County, Pennsylvania, with his regiment of militia, was posted east of the fort, on rough, woody heights, bordering the Harlem River, to watch the motions of the enemy, who had thrown up redoubts on high and commanding ground, on the opposite side of the river, apparently to cover the crossing and landing of troops

Sir William Howe had planned four simultaneous attacks; one on the north by Knyphausen, who was encamped on the York side of King's Bridge, within cannon shot of Fort Washington, but separated from it by high and rough hills, covered with almost impenetrable woods. He was to advance in two columns, formed by detachments made from the Hessians of his corps, the brigade of Rahl, and the regiment of Waldeckers. The second attack was to be by two battalions of light infantry, and two battalions of guards, under Brigadier-general Mathew, who was to cross Harlem River in flat-boats, under cover of the redoubts above mentioned, and to land on the right of the fort. This attack was to be supported by the first and second grenadiers, and a regiment of light infantry under command of Lord Cornwallis. The third attack, intended as a feint to distract the attention of the Americans, was to be by Colonel Sterling, with the forty-second regiment, who was to drop down the Harlem River in bateaux, to the left of the American lines, facing New York. The fourth attack was to be on the south, by Lord Percy, with the English and Hessian troops under his command, on the right flank of the American intrenchments.*

About noon, a heavy cannonade thundering along the rocky hills, and sharp volleys of musketry, proclaimed that the action was commenced. Knyphausen's division was pushing on from the north in two columns, as had been arranged. The right was led by Colonel Rahl, the left by himself. Rahl essayed to mount a steep, broken height called Cock Hill, which rises from Spyt den Duivel Creek, and was covered with woods. Knyphausen undertook a hill rising from the King's Bridge road, but soon found himself entangled in a woody defile, difficult to penetrate, and where his Hessians were exposed to the fire of the three-gun battery, and Rawlings' riflemen.

* Sir William Howe to Lord George Germaine.

While this was going on at the north of the fort, General Mathew, with his light infantry and guards, crossed the Harlem River in the flat-boats, under cover of a heavy fire from the redoubts.

He made good his landing, after being severely handled by Baxter and his men, from behind rocks and trees, and the breastworks thrown up on the steep river bank. A short contest ensued. Baxter, while bravely encouraging his men, was killed by a British officer. His troops, overpowered by numbers, retreated to the fort. General Mathew now pushed on with his guards and light infantry to cut off Cadwalader. That officer had gallantly defended the lines against the attack of Lord Percy, until informed that Colonel Sterling was dropping down Harlem River in bateaux to flank the lines, and take him in the rear. He sent off a detachment to oppose his landing. They did it manfully. About ninety of Sterling's men were killed or wounded in their boats, but he persevered, landed, and forced his way up a steep height, which was well defended, gained the summit, forced a redoubt, and took nearly two hundred prisoners. Thus doubly assailed, Cadwalader was obliged to retreat to the fort. He was closely pursued by Percy with his English troops and Hessians, but turned repeatedly on his pursuers. Thus he fought his way to the fort, with the loss of several killed and more taken prisoners; but marking his track by the number of Hessians slain.

The defence on the north side of the fort was equally obstinate and unsuccessful. Rawlings with his Maryland riflemen and the aid of the three-gun battery, had for some time kept the left column of Hessians and Waldeckers under Knyphausen at bay. At length Colonel Rahl, with the right column of the division, having forced his way directly up the north side of the steep hill at Spyt den Duivel Creek, came upon Rawlings' men, whose rifles, from frequent discharges, had become foul and almost useless, drove them from their strong post, and followed them until within a hundred yards of the fort, where he was joined by Knyphausen, who had slowly made his way through dense forest and over felled trees. Here they took post behind a large stone house, and sent in a flag, with a second summons to surrender.

Washington, surrounded by several of his officers, had been an anxious spectator of the battle from the opposite side of the Hudson. Much of it was hidden from him by intervening hills and forest; but the roar of cannonry from the valley of Harlem River, the sharp and incessant reports of rifles, and the smoke rising above the tree tops, told him of the spirit with which the assault was received at various points, and gave him for a time a hope that the defence might be successful. The action about the lines to the south lay open to him, and could be distinctly seen through a telescope; and nothing encouraged him more than the gallant style in which Cadwalader with an inferior force maintained his position. When he saw him, however, assailed in flank, the line broken, and his troops, overpowered by numbers, retreating to the fort, he gave up the game as lost. The worst sight of all, was to behold his men cut down and bayoneted by the Hessians while begging quarter. It is said so completely to have overcome him, that he wept " with the tenderness of a child."

Seeing the flag go into the fort from Knyphausen's division, and surmising it to be a summons to surrender, he wrote a note to Magaw, telling him that if he could hold out until evening, and the place could not be maintained, he would endeavor to bring off the garrison in the night. Captain Gooch, of Boston, a brave and daring man, offered to be the bearer of the note. "He ran down to the river, jumped into a small boat, pushed over the river, landed under the bank, ran up to the fort and delivered the message :—came out, ran and jumped over the broken ground, dodging the Hessians, some of whom struck at him with their pieces and others attempted to thrust him with their bayonets; escaping through them, he got to his boat and returned to Fort Lee." *

Washington's message arrived too late. "The fort was so crowded by the garrison, and the troops which had retreated into it, that it was difficult to move about. The enemy, too, were in possession of the little redoubts around, and could have poured in showers of shells and ricochet balls that would have made dreadful slaughter." It was no longer possible for Magaw to get his troops to man the lines; he was compelled, therefore, to yield himself and his garrison prisoners of war. The only terms granted them were, that the men should retain their baggage and the officers their swords.

The sight of the American flag hauled down, and the British flag waving in its place, told Washington of the surrender. His instant care was for the safety of the upper country, now that the lower defences of the Hudson were at an end. Before he knew any thing about the terms of capitulation, he wrote to General Lee, informing him of the surrender, and calling his attention to the passes of the Highlands and those which lay east of the river; begging him to have such measures adopted for their defence as his judgment should suggest to be necessary. "I do not mean," added he, " to advise abandoning your present post,

* Heath's Memoirs, p. 86.

contrary to your own opinion; but only to mention my own ideas of the importance of those passes, and that you cannot give too much attention to their security, by having works erected on the most advantageous places for that purpose."

Lee, in reply, objected to removing from his actual encampment at Northcastle. "It would give us," said he, "the air of being frightened; it would expose a fine, fertile country to their ravages; and I must add, that we are as secure as we could be in any position whatever." After stating that he should deposit his stores, &c., in a place fully as safe, and more central than Peekskill, he adds: "As to ourselves, light as we are, several retreats present themselves. In short, if we keep a good look-out, we are in no danger; but I must entreat your Excellency to enjoin the officers posted at Fort Lee, to give us the quickest intelligence, if they observe any embarkation on the North River." As to the affair of Fort Washington, all that Lee observed on the subject was: "Oh, general, why would you be over-persuaded by men of inferior judgment to your own? It was a cursed affair."

Lee's allusion to men of inferior judgment, was principally aimed at Greene, whose influence with the commander-in-chief seems to have excited the jealousy of other officers of rank. So Colonel Tilghman, Washington's aide-de-camp, writes on the 17th, to Robert R. Livingston of New York, "We were in a fair way of finishing the campaign with credit to ourselves, and, I think, to the disgrace of Mr. Howe; and, had the general followed his own opinion, the garrison would have been withdrawn immediately upon the enemy's falling down from Dobbs' Ferry. But General Greene was positive that our forces might at any time be drawn off under the guns of Fort Lee. Fatal experience has evinced the contrary." *

* Am. Archives, 5th Series, iii. 780.

Washington's own comments on the reduction of the fort, made in a letter to his brother Augustine, are worthy of special note. "This is a most unfortunate affair, and has given me great mortification; as we have lost, not only two thousand men,* that were there, but a good deal of artillery, and some of the best arms we had. And what adds to my mortification is, that this post, after the last ships went past it, was held contrary to my wishes and opinion, as I conceived it to be a hazardous one : but it having been determined on by a full council of general officers, and a resolution of Congress having been received, strongly expressive of their desire that the channel of the river which we had been laboring to stop for a long time at that place, might be obstructed, if possible; and knowing that this could not be done, unless there were batteries to protect the obstructions, I did not care to give an absolute order for withdrawing the garrison, till I could get round and see the situation of things; and then it became too late, as the place was invested. Upon the passing of the last ships, I had given it as my opinion to General Greene, under whose care it was, that it would be best to evacuate the place; but, as the order was discretionary, and his opinion differed from mine, it was unhappily delayed too long; to my great grief."

The correspondence of Washington with his brother, is full of gloomy anticipations. "In ten days from this date, there will not be above two thousand men, if that number, of the fixed established regiments on this side of Hudson River, to oppose Howe's whole army; and very little more on the other, to secure

---

* The number of prisoners, as returned by Sir William Howe, was 2,818 of whom 2,607 were privates. They were marched off to New York at midnight.

the eastern colonies, and the important passes leading through the Highlands to Albany, and the country about the lakes. In short it is impossible for me, in the compass of a letter, to give you any idea of our situation, of my difficulties, and of the constant perplexities I meet with, derived from the unhappy policy of short enlistments, and delaying them too long. Last fall, or winter, before the army, which was then to be raised, was set about, I represented in clear and explicit terms the evils which would arise from short enlistments, the expense which must attend the raising an army every year, and the futility of such an army when raised; and if I had spoken with a prophetic spirit, I could not have foretold the evils with more accuracy than I did. All the year since, I have been pressing Congress to delay no time in engaging men upon such terms as would insure success, telling them that the longer it was delayed, the more difficult it would prove. Bnt the measure was not commenced until it was too late to be effected. * * * I am wearied almost to death with the retrograde motion of things; and I solemnly protest, that a pecuniary reward of twenty thousand pounds a year would not induce me to undergo what I do, and, after all, perhaps to lose my character; as it is impossible, under such a variety of distressing circumstances, to conduct matters agreeably to public expectation."

CHAPTER XLI.

THE ENEMY CROSS THE HUDSON—RETREAT OF THE GARRISON FROM FORT LEE
—THE CROSSING OF THE HACKENSACK—LEE ORDERED TO MOVE TO THE
WEST SIDE OF THE RIVER—REED'S LETTER TO HIM—SECOND MOVE OF THE
ARMY BEYOND THE PASSAIC—ASSISTANCE SOUGHT FROM VARIOUS QUARTERS
—CORRESPONDENCES AND SCHEMES OF LEE—HEATH STANCH TO HIS INSTRUC-
TIONS—ANXIETY OF GEORGE CLINTON FOR THE SAFETY OF THE HUDSON—
CRITICAL SITUATION OF THE ARMY—DISPARAGING CORRESPONDENCE BE-
TWEEN LEE AND REED—WASHINGTON RETREATS ACROSS THE RARITAN—AR-
RIVES AT TRENTON—REMOVES HIS BAGGAGE ACROSS THE DELAWARE—
DISMAY AND DESPONDENCY OF THE COUNTRY—PROCLAMATION OF LORD HOWE
—EXULTATION OF THE ENEMY—WASHINGTON'S RESOLVE IN CASE OF EX-
TREMITY.

WITH the capture of Fort Washington, the project of obstructing
the navigation of the Hudson, at that point, was at an end.
Fort Lee, consequently, became useless, and Washington ordered
all the ammunition and stores to be removed, preparatory to its
abandonment. This was effected with the whole of the ammunition, and a part of the stores, and every exertion was making to
hurry off the remainder, when, early in the morning of the 20th,
intelligence was brought that the enemy, with two hundred boats,
had crossed the river and landed a few miles above. General
Greene immediately ordered the garrison under arms, sent out
troops to hold the enemy in check, and sent off an express to
Washington, at Hackensack.

The enemy had crossed the Hudson, on a very rainy night, in two divisions, one diagonally upward from King's Bridge, landing on the west side, about eight o'clock; the other marched up the east bank, three or four miles, and then crossed to the opposite shore. The whole corps, six thousand strong, and under the command of Lord Cornwallis, were landed, with their cannon, by ten o'clock, at a place called Closter Dock, five or six miles above Fort Lee, and under that line of lofty and perpendicular cliffs known as the Palisades. "The seamen," says Sir William Howe, "distinguished themselves remarkably on this occasion, by their readiness to drag the cannon up a very narrow road, for nearly half a mile to the top of a precipice, which bounds the shore for some miles on the west side." *

Washington arrived at the fort in three quarters of an hour. Being told that the enemy were extending themselves across the country, he at once saw that they intended to form a line from the Hudson to the Hackensack, and hem the whole garrison in between the two rivers. Nothing would save it but a prompt retreat to secure the bridge over the Hackensack. No time was to be lost. The troops sent out to check the enemy were recalled. The retreat commenced in all haste. There was a want of horses and waggons; a great quantity of baggage, stores and provisions, therefore, was abandoned. So was all the artillery excepting two twelve-pounders. Even the tents were left standing, and camp-kettles on the fire. With all their speed they did not reach the Hackensack River before the vanguard of the ene-

* Some writers have stated that Cornwallis crossed on the 18th. They have been misled by a letter of Sir William Howe, which gives that date. Lord Howe, in a letter to the Secretary of the Admiralty, gives the date we have stated (the 20th), which is the true one.

my was close upon them. Expecting a brush, the greater part hurried over the bridge, others crossed at the ferry, and some higher up. The enemy, however, did not dispute the passage of the river; but Cornwallis stated in his despatches, that, had not the Americans been apprised of his approach, he would have surrounded them at the fort. Some of his troops that night occupied the tents they had abandoned.

From Hackensack, Colonel Grayson, one of Washington's aides-de-camp, wrote instantly, by his orders, to General Lee; informing him that the enemy had crossed into the Jerseys, and, as was reported, *in great numbers*. "His Excellency," adds Grayson, "thinks it would be advisable in you to remove the troops under your command on this side of the North River, and there wait for further commands."

Washington himself wrote to Lee on the following day (Nov. 21st). "I am of opinion," said he, "and the gentlemen about me concur in it, that the public interest requires your coming over to this side of the Hudson with the Continental troops. * * * * The enemy is evidently changing the seat of war to this side of the North River, and the inhabitants of this country will expect the Continental army to give them what support they can; and failing in that, they will cease to depend upon, or support a force from which no protection is to be derived. It is, therefore, of the utmost importance, that at least an appearance of force should be made, to keep this province in connection with the others."

In this moment of hurry and agitation, Colonel Reed, also, Washington's *fidus Achates*, wrote to Lee, but in a tone and spirit that may surprise the reader, knowing the devotion he had hitherto manifested for the commander-in-chief. After express ing the common wish that Lee should be at the principal scene of action, he adds : " I do not mean to flatter or praise you, at the expense of any other ; but I do think it is entirely owing to you, that this army, and the liberties of America, so far as they are dependent on it, are not entirely cut off. You have decision, a quality often wanting in minds otherwise valuable, and I ascribe to this our escape from York Island, King's Bridge, and the Plains ; and I have no doubt, had you been here, the garrison of Mount Washington would now have composed a part of this army ; and from all these circumstances, I confess, I do ardently wish to see you removed from a place where there will be so little call for your judgment and experience, to the place where they are likely to be so necessary. Nor am I singular in my opinion ; every gentleman of the family, the officers and soldiers generally, have a confidence in you. The enemy constantly inquire where you are, and seem to be less confident when you are present."

Then alluding to the late affair at Fort Washington, he continues : " General Washington's own judgment, seconded by representations from us, would, I believe, have saved the men, and their arms ; but, unluckily, General Greene's judgment was contrary. This kept the general's mind in a state of suspense, till the stroke was struck. Oh, general! An indecisive mind is one of the greatest misfortunes that can befall an army ; how often have I lamented it this campaign. All circumstances considered, we are in a very awful and alarming situation ; one that requires the utmost wisdom, and firmness of mind. As soon as the season will admit, I think yourself and some others, should go to Congress, and form the plan of the new army. * * * * I must conclude, with my clear and explicit opinion, that your presence is of the last importance." *

Well might Washington apprehend that his character and conduct, in the perplexities in which he was placed, would be liable to be misunderstood by the public, when the friend of his bosom could so misjudge him.

Reed had evidently been dazzled by the daring spirit and unscrupulous policy of Lee, who, in carrying out his measures, heeded but little the counsels of others, or even the orders of government; Washington's respect for both, and the caution with which he hesitated in adopting measures in opposition to them, was stamped by the bold soldier and his admirers as indecision.

At Hackensack the army did not exceed three thousand men, and they were dispirited by ill success, and the loss of tents and baggage. They were without intrenching tools, in a flat country, where there were no natural fastnesses. Washington resolved, therefore, to avoid any attack from the enemy, though, by so doing, he must leave a fine and fertile region open to their ravages; or a plentiful storehouse, from which they would draw voluntary supplies. A second move was necessary, again to avoid the danger of being enclosed between two rivers. Leaving three regiments, therefore, to guard the passes of the Hackensack, and serve as covering parties, he again decamped, and threw himself on the west bank of the Passaic, in the neighborhood of Newark.

His army, small as it was, would soon be less. The term of enlistment of those under General Mercer, from the flying-camp, was nearly expired; and it was not probable that, disheartened

* Memoirs of Reed, i. 255.

as they were by defeats and losses, exposed to inclement weather, and unaccustomed to military hardships, they would longer forego the comforts of their homes, to drag out the residue of a ruinous campaign.

In addition, too, to the superiority of the force that was following him, the rivers gave the enemy facilities, by means of their shipping, to throw troops in his rear. In this extremity he cast about in very direction for assistance. Colonel Reed, on whom he relied as on a second self, was despatched to Burlington, with a letter to Governor William Livingston, describing his hazardous situation, and entreating him to call out a portion of the New Jersey militia; and General Mifflin was sent to Philadelphia to implore immediate aid from Congress, and the local authorities.

His main reliance for prompt assistance, however, was upon Lee. On the 24th came a letter from that general, addressed to Colonel Reed. Washington opened it, as he was accustomed to do, in the absence of that officer, with letters addressed to him on the business of the army. Lee was at his old encampment at Northcastle. He had no means, he said, of crossing at Dobbs' Ferry, and the round by King's Ferry would be so great, that he could not get there in time to answer any purpose. "I have therefore," added he, "ordered General Heath, who is close to the only ferry which can be passed, to detach two thousand men to apprise his Excellency, and await his further orders; a mode which I flatter myself will answer better what I conceive to be the spirit of the orders, than should I move the corps from hence. Withdrawing our troops from hence would be attended with some very serious consequences, which at present would be tedious to enumerate; as to myself," adds he, "I hope to set out to-morrow."

A letter of the same date (Nov. 23d), from Lee to James Bowdoin, president of the Massachusetts council, may throw some light on his motives for delaying to obey the orders of the commander-in-chief. "Before the unfortunate affair of Fort Washington," writes he, "it was my opinion that the two armies—that on the east, and that on the west side of the North River—must rest each on its own bottom; that the idea of detaching and reinforcing from one side to the other, on every motion of the enemy, was chimerical; but to harbor such a thought in our present circumstances, is absolute insanity. In this invasion, should the enemy alter the present direction of their operations, and attempt to open the passage of the Highlands, or enter New England, I should never entertain the thought of being succored by the western army. I know it is impossible. We must, therefore, depend upon ourselves. To Connecticut and Massachusetts, I shall look for assistance. * * * * * * I hope the cursed job of Fort Washington will occasion no dejection : the place itself was of no value. For my own part, I am persuaded that if we only act with common sense, spirit, and decision, the day must be our own."

In another letter to Bowdoin, dated on the following day, and enclosing an extract from Washington's letter of Nov. 21st, he writes : "Indecision bids fair for tumbling down the goodly fabric of American freedom, and, with it, the rights of mankind. 'Twas indecision of Congress prevented our having a noble army, and on an excellent footing. 'Twas indecision in our military councils which cost us the garrison of Fort Washington, the consequence of which must be fatal, unless remedied in time by a contrary spirit. Enclosed I send you an extract of a letter from the general, on which you will make your comments; and I have no

doubt you will concur with me in the necessity of raising immediately an army to save us from perdition.   Affairs appear in so important a crisis, that I think the resolves of the Congress must no
longer too nicely weigh with us.   We must save the community, in
spite of the ordinances of the legislature.   There are times when
we must commit treason against the laws of the State, for the sal
vation of the State.   The present crisis demands this brave, virtuous kind of treason."   He urges President Bowdoin, therefore,
to waive all formalities, and not only complete the regiments prescribed to the province, but to add four companies to each regiment.   " We must not only have a force sufficient to cover your
province, and all these fertile districts, from the insults and irruptions of the tyrant's troops, but sufficient to drive 'em out of all
their quarters in the Jerseys, or all is lost.   *   *   *   In the mean
time, send up a formidable body of militia, to supply the place of
the Continental troops, which I am ordered to convey over the
river.   Let your people be well supplied with blankets, and warm
clothes, as I am determined, by the help of God, to unnest 'em,
even in the dead of winter. "*

It is evident Lee considered Washington's star to be on the
decline, and his own in the ascendant.   The " affair of Fort
Washington," and the " indecision of the commander-in-chief,"
were apparently his watchwords.

On the following day (24th), he writes to Washington from
Northcastle, on the subject of removing troops across the Hudson.   " I have received your orders, and shall endeavor to put
them in execution, but question whether I shall be able to carry
with me any considerable number; not so much from a want of

---

* Am. Archives, 5th Series, iii. 811.

zeal in the men, as from their wretched condition with respect to shoes, stockings, and blankets, which the present bad weather renders more intolerable. I sent Heath orders to transport two thousand men across the river, apprise the general, and wait for further orders; but that great man (as I might have expected) intrenched himself within the letter of his instructions, and refused to part with a single file, though I undertook to replace them with a part of my own." He concludes by showing that, so far from hurrying to the support of his commander-in-chief, he was meditating a side blow of his own devising. " I should march this day with Glover's brigade; but have just received intelligence that Rogers' corps, a part of the light-horse, and another brigade lie in so exposed a situation, as to present us the fairest opportunity of carrying them off. If we succeed, it will have a great effect, and amply compensate for two days' delay."

Scarce had Lee sent this letter, when he received one from Washington, informing him that he had mistaken his views in regard to the troops required to cross the Hudson; it was his (Lee's) division that he wanted to have over. The force under Heath must remain to guard the posts and passes through the Highlands, the importance of which was so infinitely great, that there should not be the least possible risk of losing them. In the same letter Washington, who presumed Lee was by this time at Peekskill, advised him to take every precaution to come by a safe route, and by all means to keep between the enemy and the mountains, as he understood they were taking measures to intercept his march.

Lee's reply was still from Northcastle. He explained that his idea of detaching troops from Heath's division was merely for expedition's sake, intending to replace them from his own.

The want of carriages and other causes had delayed him. From the force of the enemy remaining in Westchester County, he did not conceive the number of them in the Jerseys to be near so great as Washington was taught to believe. He had been making a sweep of the country to clear it of the tories. Part of his army had now moved on, and he would set out on the following day. He concluded with the assurance, "I shall take care to obey your Excellency's orders, in regard to my march, as exactly as possible."

On the same day, he vents his spleen in a tart letter to Heath. "I perceive," writes he, "that you have formed an idea, that should General Washington remove to the Straits of Magellan, the instructions he left with you, upon a particular occasion, have, to all intents and purposes, invested you with a command separate from, and independent of any other superiors. *   *   *   * That General Heath is by no means to consider himself obliged to obey the second in command." He concluded by informing him that, as the commander-in-chief was now separated from them, he (Lee) commanded, of course, on this side of the water, and for the future would, and must be obeyed.

Before receiving this letter, Heath, doubtful whether Washington might not be pressed, and desirous of having his troops across the Hudson, had sent off an express to him for explicit instructions on that point, and, in the mean time, had kept them ready for a move.

General George Clinton, who was with him, and had the safety of the Hudson at heart, was in an agony of solicitude. "We have been under marching orders these three days past," writes he, "and only wait the directions of General Washington. Should they be to move, all's over with the river this season, and, I fear, for ever. General Lee, four or five days ago, had orders to move with his division across the river. Instead of so doing, he ordered General Heath to march his men through, and he would replace them with so many of his. General Heath could not do this consistent with his instructions, but put his men under marching orders to wait his Excellency's orders." Honest George Clinton was still perplexed and annoyed by these marchings and counter-marchings; and especially with these incessant retreats. " A strange way of cooking business ! " writes he. " We have no particular accounts yet from head-quarters, *but I am apt to believe retreating is yet fashionable.*"

The return of the express sent to Washington, relieved Clinton's anxiety about the Highlands; reiterating the original order, that the division under Heath should remain for the protection of the passes.

Washington was still at Newark when, on the 27th, he received Lee's letter of the 24th, speaking of his scheme of capturing Rogers the partisan. Under other circumstances it might have been a sufficient excuse for his delay, but higher interests were at stake; he immediately wrote to Lee as follows : " My former letters were so full and explicit, as to the necessity of your marching as early as possible, that it is unnecessary to add more on that head. I confess I expected you would have been sooner in motion. The force here, when joined by yours, will not be adequate to any great opposition; at present it is weak, and it has been more owing to the badness of the weather that the enemy's progress has been checked, than any resistance we could make. They are now pushing this way,—part of 'em have passed the Passaic. Their plan is not entirely unfolded, but I shall not be surprised if Philadelphia should turn out the object of their movement."

The situation of the little army was daily becoming more perilous. In a council of war, several of the members urged a move to Morristown, to form a junction with the troops expected from the Northern army. Washington, however, still cherished the idea of making a stand at Brunswick on the Raritan, or, at all events, of disputing the passage of the Delaware; and in this intrepid resolution he was warmly seconded by Greene.

Breaking up his camp once more, therefore, he continued his retreat towards New Brunswick; but so close was Cornwallis upon him, that his advance entered one end of Newark, just as the American rear-guard had left the other.

From Brunswick, Washington wrote on the 29th to William Livingston, governor of the Jerseys, requesting him to have all boats and river craft, for seventy miles along the Delaware, removed to the western bank out of the reach of the enemy, and put under guard. He was disappointed in his hope of making a stand on the banks of the Raritan. All the force he could muster at Brunswick, including the New Jersey militia, did not exceed four thousand men. Colonel Reed had failed in procuring aid from the New Jersey legislature. That body, shifting from place to place, was on the eve of dissolution. The term of the Maryland and New Jersey troops in the flying camp had expired. General Mercer endeavored to detain them, representing the disgrace of turning their back upon the cause when the enemy was at hand: his remonstrances were fruitless. As to the Pennsylvania levies, they deserted in such numbers, that guards were stationed on the roads and ferries to intercept them.

At this moment of care and perplexity, a letter, forwarded

by express, arrived at head-quarters. It was from General Lee, dated from his camp at Northcastle, to Colonel Reed, and was in reply to the letter written by that officer from Hackensack on the 21st, which we have already laid before the reader. Supposing that it related to official business, Washington opened it, and read as follows:

My dear Reed:—I received your most obliging, flattering letter; lament with you that fatal indecision of mind, which in war is a much greater disqualification than stupidity, or even want of personal courage. Accident may put a decisive blunderer in the right; but eternal defeat and miscarriage must attend the man of the best parts, if cursed with indecision. The General recommends in so pressing a manner as almost to amount to an order, to bring over the continental troops under my command, which recommendation, or order, throws me into the greatest dilemma from several considerations." After stating these considerations, he adds: " My reason for not having marched already is, that we have just received intelligence that Rogers' corps, the light-horse, part of the Highlanders, and another brigade, lie in so exposed a situation as to give the fairest opportunity of being carried. I should have attempted it last night, but the rain was too violent, and when our pieces are wet, you know our troops are *hors du combat*. This night I hope will be better. * * * * * * I only wait myself for this business of Rogers and company being over. I shall then fly to you; for, to confess a truth, I really think our chief will do better with me than without me."

A glance over this letter sufficed to show Washington that, at this dark moment, when he most needed support and sympathy, his character and military conduct were the subject of disparaging comments, between the friend in whom he had so implicitly confided, and a sarcastic and apparently self-constituted rival. Whatever may have been his feelings of wounded pride and outraged friendship, he restrained them, and enclosed the letter to Reed, with the following chilling note:

"DEAR SIR:—The enclosed was put into my hands by an express from White Plains. Having no idea of its being a private letter, much less suspecting the tendency of the correspondence, I opened it; as I have done all other letters to you from the same place, and Peekskill, upon the business of your office, as I conceived, and found them to be. This, as it is the truth, must be my excuse for seeing the contents of a letter, which neither inclination nor intention would have prompted me to," &c.

The very calmness and coldness of this note must have had a greater effect upon Reed, than could have been produced by the most vehement reproaches. In subsequent communications, he endeavored to explain away the offensive paragraphs in Lee's letter, declaring there was nothing in his own inconsistent with the respect and affection he had ever borne for Washington's person and character.

Fortunately for Reed, Washington never saw that letter. There were passages in it beyond the reach of softening explanation. As it was, the purport of it, as reflected in Lee's reply, had given him a sufficient shock. His magnanimous nature, however, was incapable of harboring long resentments; especially in matters relating solely to himself. His personal respect for Colonel Reed continued; he invariably manifested a high sense of his merits, and consulted him, as before, on military affairs; but his hitherto affectionate confidence in him, as a sympathizing friend, had received an incurable wound. His letters, before so frequent, and such perfect outpourings of heart and mind, became few and far between, and confined to matters of business.

It must have been consoling to Washington at this moment of bitterness, to receive the following letter (dated Nov. 27th) from William Livingston, the intelligent and patriotic governor of New Jersey. It showed that while many misjudged him, and friends seemed falling from his side, others appreciated him truly, and the ordeal he was undergoing.

" I can easily form some idea of the difficulties under which you labor," writes Livingston, "particularly of one for which the public can make no allowance, because your prudence, and fidelity to the cause, will not suffer you to reveal it to the public; an instance of magnanimity, superior, perhaps, to any that can be shown in battle. But depend upon it, my dear sir, the impartial world will do you ample justice before long. May God support you under the fatigue, both of body and mind, to which you must be constantly exposed." *

Washington lingered at Brunswick until the 1st of December, in the vain hope of being reinforced. The enemy, in the mean time, advanced through the country, impressing waggons and horses, and collecting cattle and sheep, as if for a distant march. At length their vanguard appeared on the opposite side

---

* We cannot dismiss this painful incident in Washington's life, without a prospective note on the subject. Reed was really of too generous and intelligent a nature not to be aware of the immense value of the friendship he had put at hazard. He grieved over his mistake, especially as after events showed more and more the majestic greatness of Washington's character. A letter in the following year, in which he sought to convince Washington of his sincere and devoted attachment, is really touching in its appeals. We are happy to add, that it appears to have been successful, and to have restored, in a great measure, their relations of friendly confidence.

of the Raritan. Washington immediately broke down the end of the bridge next the village, and after nightfall resumed his retreat. In the mean time, as the river was fordable, Captain Alexander Hamilton planted his field-pieces on high, commanding ground, and opened a spirited fire, to check any attempt of the enemy to cross.

At Princeton, Washington left twelve hundred men in two brigades, under Lord Stirling and General Adam Stephen, to cover the country, and watch the motions of the enemy. Stephen was the same officer that had served as a colonel under Washington in the French war, as second in command of the Virginia troops, and had charge of Fort Cumberland. In consideration of his courage and military capacity, he had, in 1764, been intrusted with the protection of the frontier. He had recently brought a detachment of Virginia troops to the army, and received from Congress, in September, the commission of brigadier-general.

The harassed army reached Trenton on the 2d of December. Washington immediately proceeded to remove his baggage and stores across the Delaware. In his letters from this place to the President of Congress, he gives his reasons for his continued retreat. "Nothing but necessity obliged me to retire before the enemy, and leave so much of the Jerseys unprotected. Sorry am I to observe that the frequent calls upon the militia of this State, the want of exertion in the principal gentlemen of the country, and a fatal supineness and insensibility of danger, till it is too late to prevent an evil that was not only foreseen, but foretold, have been the causes of our late disgraces.

"If the militia of this State had stepped forth in season (and timely notice they had), we might have prevented the enemy's crossing the Hackensack. We might, with equal possibility of success, have made a stand at Brunswick on the Raritan. But as both these rivers were fordable in a variety of places, being knee deep only, it required many men to guard the passes, and these we had not."

In excuse for the people of New Jersey, it may be observed, that they inhabited an open, agricultural country, where the sound of war had never been heard. Many of them looked upon the Revolution as rebellion; others thought it a ruined enterprise; the armies engaged in it had been defeated and broken up. They beheld the commander-in-chief retreating through their country with a handful of men, weary, wayworn, dispirited; without tents, without clothing, many of them barefooted, exposed to wintry weather, and driven from post to post, by a well-clad, well-fed, triumphant force, tricked out in all the glittering bravery of war. Could it be wondered at, that peaceful husbandmen, seeing their quiet fields thus suddenly overrun by adverse hosts, and their very hearthstones threatened with outrage, should, instead of flying to arms, seek for the safety of their wives and little ones, and the protection of their humble means, from the desolation which too often marks the course even of friendly armies?

Lord Howe and his brother sought to profit by this dismay and despondency. A proclamation, dated 30th of November, commanded all persons in arms against his majesty's government, to disband and return home, and all Congresses to desist from treasonable acts: offering a free pardon to all who should comply within fifty days.

Many who had been prominent in the cause, hastened to take advantage of this proclamation. Those who had most property to lose, were the first to submit. The middle ranks remained generally steadfast in this time of trial.*

The following extract of a letter from a field-officer in New York, dated Dec. 2d, to his friend in London, gives the British view of affairs. " The rebels continue flying before our army. Lord Cornwallis took the fort opposite Brunswick, plunged into Raritan River, and seized the town. Mr. Washington had orders from the Congress to rally and defend that post, but he sent them word he could not. He was seen retreating with two brigades to Trenton, where they talk of resisting; but such a panic has seized the rebels, that no part of the Jerseys will hold them, and I doubt whether Philadelphia itself will stop their career. The Congress have lost their authority. * * * * They are in such consternation that they know not what to do. The two Adamses are in New England; Franklin gone to France; Lynch has lost his senses; Rutledge has gone home disgusted; Dana is persecuting at Albany, and Jay's in the country playing as bad a part; so that the fools have lost the assistance of the knaves. However, should they embrace the enclosed proclamation, they may yet escape the halter. * * * Honest David Mathew, the mayor, has made his escape from them, and arrived here this day." †

In this dark day of peril to the cause, and to himself, Washington remained firm and undaunted. In casting about for some stronghold where he might make a desperate stand for the liberties of his country, his thoughts reverted to the mountain regions of his early campaigns. General Mercer was at hand, who had shared his perils among these mountains, and his presence may

---

* Gordon's Hist. Am. War, ii. p. 129.
† Am. Archives, 5th Series, iii. 1037.

have contributed to bring them to his mind. "What think you," said Washington; "if we should retreat to the back parts of Pennsylvania, would the Pennsylvanians support us?"

"If the lower counties give up, the back counties will do the same," was the discouraging reply.

"We must then retire to Augusta County in Virginia," said Washington. "Numbers will repair to us for safety, and we will try a predatory war. If overpowered, we must cross the Alleganies."

Such was the indomitable spirit, rising under difficulties, and buoyant in the darkest moment, that kept our tempest-tost cause from foundering.

CHAPTER XLII.

NOTWITHSTANDING the repeated and pressing orders and entreaties of the commander-in-chief, Lee did not reach Peekskill until
the 30th of November. In a letter of that date to Washington,
who had complained of his delay, he simply alleged difficulties,
which he would explain *when both had leisure*. His scheme to
entrap Rogers, the renegade, had failed; the old Indian hunter
had been too much on the alert; he boasted, however, to have
rendered more service by his delay, than he would have done had
he moved sooner. His forces were thereby augmented, so that
he expected to enter the Jerseys with four thousand firm and
willing men, who would make *a very important diversion*.

"The day after to-morrow," added he, "we shall pass the
river, when I should be glad to receive your instructions; but I
could wish you would bind me as little as possible; not from any
opinion, I do assure you, of my own parts, but from a persuasion

that detached generals cannot have too great latitude, unless they are very incompetent indeed."

Lee had calculated upon meeting no further difficulty in obtaining men from Heath. He rode to that general's quarters in the evening, and was invited by him to alight and take tea. On entering the house, Lee took Heath aside, and alluding to his former refusal to supply troops as being inconsistent with the orders of the commander-in-chief, "in point of *law*," said he, "you are right, but in point of policy I think you are wrong. I am going into the Jerseys for the salvation of America; I wish to take with me a larger force than I now have, and request you to order two thousand of your men to march with me."

Heath answered that he could not spare that number. He was then asked to order one thousand; to which he replied, that the business might be as well brought to a point at once—that not a single man should march from the post by *his* order. "Then," exclaimed Lee, "I will order them myself." "That makes a wide difference," rejoined Heath. "You are my senior, but I have received positive written instructions from him who is superior to us both, and I will not *myself* break those orders." In proof of his words, Heath produced the recent letter received from Washington, repeating his former orders that no troops should be removed from that post. Lee glanced over the letter. "The commander-in-chief is now at a distance, and does not know what is necessary here so well as I do." He asked a sight of the return book of the division. It was brought by Major Huntington, the deputy adjutant-general. Lee ran his eye over it, and chose two regiments. "You will order them to march early to-morrow morning to join me," said he to the major. Heath, ruffling with the pride of military law, turned to the major with an air of authority. "Issue such orders at your peril!" exclaimed he: then addressing Lee, "Sir," said he, "if you come to this post, and mean to issue orders here which will break the positive ones I have received, I pray you do it completely yourself, and through your own deputy adjutant-general who is present, and not draw me or any of my family in as partners in the guilt."

"It is right," said Lee; "Colonel Scammel, do you issue the order." It was done accordingly; but Heath's punctilious scruples were not yet satisfied. "I have one more request to make, sir," said he to Lee, "and that is, that you will be pleased to give me a certificate that you *exercise command* at this post, and order from it these regiments."

Lee hesitated to comply, but George Clinton, who was present, told him he could not refuse a request so reasonable. He accordingly wrote, "For the satisfaction of General Heath, and at his request, I do certify that I am commanding officer, at this present writing, in this post, and that I have, in that capacity, ordered Prescott's and Wyllis's regiments to march."

Heath's military punctilio was satisfied, and he smoothed his ruffled plumes. Early the next morning the regiments moved from their cantonments ready to embark, when Lee again rode up to his door. "Upon further consideration," said he, "I have concluded not to take the two regiments with me—you may order them to return to their former post."

"This conduct of General Lee," adds Heath in his memoirs, "appeared not a little extraordinary, and one is almost at a loss to account for it. He had been a soldier from his youth, had a perfect knowledge of service in all its branches, but was rather obstinate in his temper, and could scarcely brook being crossed in any thing in the line of his profession." *

It was not until the 4th of December, that Lee crossed the Hudson and began a laggard march, though aware of the imminent peril of Washington and his army—how different from the celerity of his movements in his expedition to the South!

In the mean time, Washington, who was at Trenton, had profited by a delay of the enemy at Brunswick, and removed most of the stores and baggage of the army across the Delaware; and, being reinforced by fifteen hundred of the Pennsylvania militia, procured by Mifflin, prepared to face about, and march back to Princeton with such of his troops as were fit for service, there to be governed by circumstances, and the movements of General Lee. Accordingly, on the 5th of December he sent about twelve hundred men in the advance, to reinforce Lord Stirling, and the next day set off himself with the residue.

"The general has gone forward to Princeton," writes Colonel Reed, "where there are about three thousand men, with which, I fear, he will not be able to make any stand." †

While on the march, Washington received a letter from Greene, who was at Princeton, informing him of a report that Lee was "at the heels of the enemy." "I should think," adds Greene, "he had better keep on the flanks than the rear, unless it were possible to concert an attack at the same instant of time in front and rear. * * * I think General Lee must be confined within the lines of some general plan, or else his operations will be independent of yours. His own troops, General St. Clair's, and the militia, must form a respectable army."

* The above scene is given almost literally from General Heath's Memoirs.
† Reed to the President of Congress.

Lee had no idea of conforming to a general plan; he had an independent plan of his own, and was at that moment at Pompton, indulging speculations on military greatness, and the lamentable want of it in his American contemporaries. In a letter from that place to Governor Cooke of Rhode Island, he imparts his notions on the subject. "Theory joined to practice, or a heaven-born genius, can alone constitute a general. As to the latter, God Almighty indulges the modern world very rarely with the spectacle; and I do not know, from what I have seen, that he has been more profuse of this ethereal spirit to the Americans, than to other nations."

While Lee was thus loitering and speculating, Cornwallis, knowing how far he was in the rear, and how weak was the situation of Washington's army, and being himself strongly reinforced, made a forced march from Brunswick, and was within two miles of Princeton. Stirling, to avoid being surrounded, immediately set out with two brigades for Trenton. Washington, too, receiving intelligence by express of these movements, hastened back to that place, and caused boats to be collected from all quarters, and the stores and troops transported across the Delaware. He himself crossed with the rear-guard on Sunday morning, and took up his quarters about a mile from the river; causing the boats to be destroyed, and troops to be posted opposite the fords. He was conscious, however, as he said, that with his small force he could make no great opposition, should the enemy bring boats with them. Fortunately they did not come thus provided.

The rear-guard, says an American account, had barely crossed the river, when Lord Cornwallis "came marching down with all the pomp of war, in great expectation of getting boats, and immediately pursuing." Not one was to be had there or elsewhere;

for Washington had caused the boats, for an extent of seventy miles up and down the river, to be secured on the right bank. His lordship was effectually brought to a stand. He made some moves with two columns, as if he would cross the Delaware above and below, either to push on to Philadelphia, or to entrap Washington in the acute angle made by the bend of the river opposite Bordentown. An able disposition of American troops along the upper part of the river, and of a number of galleys below, discouraged any attempt of the kind. Cornwallis, therefore, gave up the pursuit, distributed the German troops in cantonments along the left bank of the river, and stationed his main force at Brunswick, trusting to be able before long to cross the Delaware on the ice.

On the 8th, Washington wrote to the President of Congress: "There is not a moment's time to be lost in assembling such a force as can be collected, as the object of the enemy cannot now be doubted in the smallest degree. Indeed, I shall be out in my conjecture, for it is only conjecture, if the late embarkation at New York is not for Delaware River, to co-operate with the army under General Howe, who, I am informed from good authority, is with the British troops, and his whole force upon this route. I have no certain intelligence of General Lee, although I have sent expresses to him, and lately a Colonel Humpton, to bring me some accurate accounts of his situation. I last night despatched another gentleman to him (Major Hoops), desiring he would hasten his march to the Delaware, on which I would provide boats near a place called Alexandria, for the transportation of his troops. I cannot account for the slowness of his march."

In further letters to Lee, Washington urged the peril of Philadelphia. "Do come on," writes he; "your arrival may be fortunate, and, if it can be effected without delay, it may be the means of preserving a city, whose loss must prove of the most fatal consequence to the cause of America."

Putnam was now detached to take command of Philadelphia, and put it in a state of defence, and General Mifflin to have charge of the munitions of war deposited there. By their advice Congress hastily adjourned on the 12th of December, to meet again on the 20th, at Baltimore.

Washington's whole force at this time, was about five thousand five hundred men; one thousand of them Jersey militia, fifteen hundred militia from Philadelphia, and a battalion of five hundred of the German yeomanry of Pennsylvania. Gates, however, he was informed, was coming on with seven regiments detached by Schuyler from the Northern department; reinforced by these, and the troops under Lee, he hoped to be able to attempt a stroke upon the enemy's forces, which lay a good deal scattered, and to all appearances, in a state of security. "A lucky blow in this quarter," writes he, "would be fatal to them, and would most certainly raise the spirits of the people, which are quite sunk by our late misfortunes." *

While cheering himself with these hopes, and trusting to speedy aid from Lee, that wayward commander, though nearly three weeks had elapsed since he had received Washington's orders and entreaties to join him with all possible despatch, was no farther on his march than Morristown, in the Jerseys; where, with militia recruits, his force was about four thousand men. In a letter written by him on the 8th of December to a committee of Congress, he says: "If I was not taught to think the army with

* Washington to Gov. Trumbull, 14th Dec.

General Washington had been considerably reinforced, I should immediately join him; but as I am assured he is very strong, I should imagine we can make a better impression by beating up and harassing their detached parties in their rear, for which purpose, a good post at Chatham seems the best calculated. It is a happy distance from Newark, Elizabethtown, Woodbridge and Boundbrook. We shall, I expect, annoy, distract, and consequently weaken them in a desultory war." *

On the same day he writes from Chatham, in reply to Washington's letter by Major Hoops, just received: "I am extremely shocked to hear that your force is so inadequate to the necessity of your situation, as I had been taught to think you had been considerably reinforced. Your last letters proposing a plan of surprises and forced marches, convinced me that there was no danger of your being obliged to pass the Delaware; in consequence of which proposals, I have put myself in a position the most convenient to co-operate with you by attacking their rear. I cannot persuade myself that Philadelphia is their object at present. * * * It will be difficult, I am afraid, to join you; but cannot I do you more service by attacking their rear?"

This letter, sent by a light-horseman, received an instant reply from Washington. "Philadelphia, beyond all question, is the object of the enemy's movements, and nothing less than our utmost exertions will prevent General Howe from possessing it. The force I have is weak, and utterly incompetent to that end. I must, therefore, entreat you to push on with every possible succor you can bring." †

On the 9th, Lee, who was at Chatham, receives information

---

* Am. Archives, 5th Series, iii. 1121.
† Am. Archives, 5th Series, iii. 1138.

from Heath, that three of the regiments detached under Gates from the Northern army, had arrived from Albany at Peekskill. He instantly writes to him to forward them, without loss of time, to Morristown: "I am in hopes," adds he, "to reconquer (if I may so express myself) the Jerseys. It was really in the hands of the enemy before my arrival."

On the 11th, Lee writes to Washington from Morristown, where he says his troops had been obliged to halt two days for want of shoes. He now talked of crossing the great Brunswick post-road, and, by a forced night's march, making his way to the ferry above Burlington, where boats should be sent up from Philadelphia to receive him.

"I am much surprised," writes Washington in reply, "that you should be in any doubt respecting the route you should take, after the information you have received upon that head. A large number of boats was procured, and is still retained at Tinicum, under a strong guard, to facilitate your passage across the Delaware. I have so frequently mentioned our situation, and the necessity of your aid, that it is painful for me to add a word on the subject. * * * Congress have directed Philadelphia to be defended to the last extremity. The fatal consequences that must attend its loss, are but too obvious to every one; your arrival may be the means of saving it."

In detailing the close of General Lee's march, so extraordinary for its tardiness, we shall avail ourselves of the memoir already cited of General Wilkinson, who was at that time a brigade major, about twenty-two years of age, and was accompanying General Gates, who had been detached by Schuyler with seven regiments to reinforce Washington. Three of these regiments, as we have shown, had descended the Hudson to Peekskill, and

were ordered by Lee to Morristown. Gates had embarked with
the remaining four, and landed with them at Esopus, whence he
took a back route by the Delaware and the Minisink.

On the 11th of December, he was detained by a heavy snow
storm, in a sequestered valley near the Wallpeck in New Jersey.
Being cut off from all information respecting the adverse armies, he detached Major Wilkinson to seek Washington's camp,
with a letter, stating the force under his command, and inquiring
what route he should take. Wilkinson crossed the hills on
horseback to Sussex court-house, took a guide, and proceeded
down the country. Washington, he soon learnt, had passed the
Delaware several days before; the boats, he was told, had been
removed from the ferries, so that he would find some difficulty in
getting over, but Major-general Lee was at Morristown. Finding such obstacles in his way to the commander-in-chief, he determined to seek the second in command, and ask orders from
him for General Gates. Lee had decamped from Morristown on
the 12th of December, but had marched no further than Vealtown, barely eight miles distant. There he left General Sullivan
with the troops, while he took up his quarters three miles off, at
a tavern, at Baskingridge. As there was not a British cantonment within twenty miles, he took but a small guard for his
protection, thinking himself perfectly secure.

About four o'clock in the morning, Wilkinson arrived at his
quarters. He was presented to the general as he lay in bed, and
delivered into his hands the letter of General Gates. Lee, observing it was addressed to Washington, declined opening it, until
apprised by Wilkinson of its contents, and the motives of his
visit. He then broke the seal, and recommended Wilkinson to
take repose. The latter lay down on his blanket, before a com-

fortable fire, among the officers of his suite; "for we were not encumbered in those days," says he, "with beds or baggage."

Lee, naturally indolent, lingered in bed until eight o'clock. He then came down in his usual slovenly style, half-dressed, in slippers and blanket coat, his collar open, and his linen apparently of some days' wear. After some inquiries about the campaign in the North, he gave Wilkinson a brief account of the operations of the main army, which he condemned in strong terms, and in his usual sarcastic way. He wasted the morning in altercation with some of the militia, particularly the Connecticut light-horse; "several of whom," says Wilkinson, "appeared in large, full-buttoned perukes, and were treated very irreverently. One wanted forage, another his horse shod, another his pay, a fourth provisions, &c.; to which the general replied, ' Your wants are numerous; but you have not mentioned the last,—you want to go home, and shall be indulged; for d— you, you do no good here.' "

Colonel Scammel, the adjutant-general, called from General Sullivan for orders concerning the morning's march. After musing a moment or two, Lee asked him if he had a manuscript map of the country. It was produced, and spread upon a table. Wilkinson observed Lee trace with his finger the route from Vealtown to Pluckamin, thence to Somerset court-house, and on, by Rocky Hill, to Princeton; he then returned to Pluckamin, and traced the route in the same manner by Boundbrook to Brunswick, and after a close inspection carelessly said to Scammel, "Tell General Sullivan to move down towards Pluckamin; that I will soon be with him." This, observes Wilkinson, was off his route to Alexandria on the Delaware, where he had been ordered to cross, and directly on that towards Brunswick and

Princeton. He was convinced, therefore, that Lee meditated an attack on the British post at the latter place.

From these various delays they did not sit down to breakfast before ten o'clock. After breakfast Lee sat writing a reply to General Gates, in which, as usual, he indulged in sarcastic comments on the commander-in-chief. " The ingenious manœuvre of Fort Washington," writes he, " has completely unhinged the goodly fabric we had been building. There never was so d—d a stroke; *entre nous*, a certain great man is most damnably deficient. He has thrown me into a situation where I have my choice of difficulties: if I stay in this province I risk myself and army; and if I do not stay, the province is lost for ever. * * * * * As to what relates to yourself, if you think you can be in time to aid the general, I would have you by all means go; you will at least save your army," &c.*

While Lee was writing, Wilkinson was looking out of a window down a lane, about a hundred yards in length, leading from the house to the main road. Suddenly a party of British dragoons turned a corner of the avenue at a full charge. " Here, sir, are the British cavalry!" exclaimed Wilkinson. " Where ?" replied Lee, who had just signed his letter. " Around the house !"—for they had opened file and surrounded it. " Where is the guard? d— the guard, why dont they fire?" Then after a momentary pause—" Do, sir, see what has become of the guard."

The guards, alas, unwary as their general, and chilled by the air of a frosty morning, had stacked their arms, and repaired to the south side of a house on the opposite side of the road to sun

* Am. Archives, 5th Series, iii. 1201.

themselves, and were now chased by the dragoons in different directions. In fact, a tory, who had visited the general the evening before, to complain of the loss of a horse taken by the army, having found where Lee was to lodge and breakfast, had ridden eighteen miles in the night to Brunswick and given the information, and had piloted back Colonel Harcourt with his dragoons.*

The women of the house would fain have concealed Lee in a bed, but he rejected the proposition with disdain. Wilkinson, according to his own account, posted himself in a place where only one person could approach at a time, and there took his stand, a pistol in each hand, resolved to shoot the first and second assailant, and then appeal to his sword. While in this "unpleasant situation," as he terms it, he heard a voice declare, "If the general does not surrender in five minutes, I will set fire to the house!" After a short pause the threat was repeated, with a solemn oath. Within two minutes he heard it proclaimed, "Here is the general, he has surrendered."

There was a shout of triumph, but a great hurry to make sure of the prize before the army should arrive to the rescue. A trumpet sounded the recall to the dragoons, who were chasing the scattered guards. The general, bareheaded, and in his slippers and blanket coat, was mounted on Wilkinson's horse, which stood at the door, and the troop clattered off with their prisoner to Brunswick. In three hours the booming of cannon in that direction told the exultation of the enemy.† They boasted of having taken the American Palladium; for they considered Lee the most scientific and experienced of the rebel generals.

On the departure of the troops, Wilkinson, finding the coast

* Jos. Trumbull to Gov. Trumbull.—*Am. Archives,* 5th Series, iii. 1265.
† Idem.

clear, ventured from his stronghold, repaired to the stable, mounted the first horse he could find, and rode full speed in quest of General Sullivan, whom he found under march toward Pluckamin. He handed him the letter to Gates, written by Lee the moment before his capture, and still open. Sullivan having read it, returned it to Wilkinson, and advised him to rejoin General Gates without delay : for his own part, being now in command, he changed his route, and pressed forward to join the commander-in-chief.

The loss of Lee was a severe shock to the Americans; many of whom, as we have shown, looked to him as the man who was to rescue them from their critical, and well-nigh desperate situation. With their regrets, however, were mingled painful doubts, caused by his delay in obeying the repeated summons of his commander-in-chief, when the latter was in peril; and by his exposing himself so unguardedly in the very neighborhood of the enemy. Some at first suspected that he had done so designedly, and with collusion ; but this was soon disproved by the indignities attending his capture, and his rigorous treatment subsequently by the British; who affected to consider him a deserter, from his having formerly served in their army.

Wilkinson, who was at that time conversant with the cabals of the camp, and apparently in the confidence of some of the leaders, points out what he considers the true secret of Lee's conduct. His military reputation, originally very high, had been enhanced of late, by its being generally known that he had been opposed to the occupation of Fort Washington; while the fall of that fortress and other misfortunes of the campaign, though beyond the control of the commander-in-chief, had quickened the discontent which, according to Wilkinson, had been generated against him at Cambridge, and raised a party against him in Congress. "It was confidently asserted at the time," adds he, " but is not worthy of credit, that a motion had been made in that body tending to supersede him in the command of the army. In this temper of the times, if General Lee had antici- pated General Washington in cutting the cordon of the enemy between New York and the Delaware, the commander-in-chief would probably have been superseded. In this case, Lee would have succeeded him."

What an unfortunate change would it have been for the country ! Lee was undoubtedly a man of brilliant talents, shrewd sagacity, and much knowledge and experience in the art of war ; but he was wilful and uncertain in his temper, self-indulgent in his habits, and an egoist in warfare; boldly dashing for a soldier's glory rather than warily acting for a country's good. He wanted those great moral qualities which, in addition to military capacity, inspired such universal confidence in the wisdom, rectitude and patriotism of Washington, enabling him to direct and control legislative bodies as well as armies ; to harmonize the jarring pasions and jealousies of a wide and imperfect confederacy, and to cope with the varied exigencies of the Revolution.

The very retreat which Washington had just effected through the Jerseys bore evidence to his generalship. Thomas Paine, who had accompanied the army " from Fort Lee to the edge of Pennsylvania," thus speaks in one of his writings published at the time : " With a handful of men we sustained an orderly retreat for near an hundred miles, brought off our ammunition, all our field-pieces, the greatest part of our stores, and had four rivers to pass. None can say that our retreat was precipitate, for we were three weeks in performing it, that the country might have time to come in. Twice we marched back to meet the enemy, and remained out until dark. The sign of fear was not seen in our camp; and had not some of the cowardly and disaffected inhabitants spread false alarms through the country, the Jerseys had never been ravaged."

And this is his testimony to the moral qualities of the commander-in-chief, as evinced in this time of perils and hardships. "Voltaire has remarked, that King William never appeared to full advantage but in difficulties and in action. The same remark may be made of General Washington, for the character fits him. There is a natural firmness in some minds, which cannot be unlocked by trifles; but which, when unlocked, discovers a cabinet of fortitude; and I reckon it among those kinds of public blessings which we do not immediately see, that God hath blessed him with uninterrupted health, and given him a mind that can even flourish upon care." *

* American Crisis, No. 1.

CHAPTER XLIII.

WASHINGTON CLOTHED WITH ADDITIONAL POWERS—RECRUITMENT OF THE ARMY
—INCREASED PAY—COLONEL JOHN CADWALADER—ARRIVAL OF SULLIVAN—
—GATES—WILKINSON—A COUP DE MAIN MEDITATED—POSTURE OF AFFAIRS
AT TRENTON—GATES DECLINES TO TAKE A PART—HIS COMMENTS ON WASH-
INGTON'S PLANS—PREPARATIONS FOR THE COUP DE MAIN—CROSSING OF THE
DELAWARE—ATTACK ON THE ENEMY'S FORCES AT TRENTON—DEATH OF
RAHL—HIS CHARACTER.

"BEFORE you receive this letter," writes Washington to his
brother Augustine, "you will undoubtedly have heard of the cap-
tivity of General Lee. This is an additional misfortune; and the
more vexatious, as it was by his own folly and imprudence, and
without a view to effect any good that he was taken. As he went
to lodge three miles out of his own camp, and within twenty miles
of the enemy, a rascally tory rode in the night to give notice of
it to the enemy, who sent a party of light-horse that seized him,
and carried him off with every mark of triumph and indignity."

This is the severest comment that the magnanimous spirit of
Washington permitted him to make on the conduct and fortunes
of the man who would have supplanted him; and this is made in
his private correspondence with his brother. No harsh strictures
on them appear in his official letters to Congress or the Board of
War; nothing but regret for his capture, as a loss to the service.

In the same letter he speaks of the critical state of affairs: " If every nerve is not strained to recruit the army with all possible expedition, I think the game is pretty nearly up. 　*　*　* You can form no idea of the perplexity of my situation. No man I believe ever had a greater choice of evils and less means to extricate himself from them. However, under a full persuasion of the justice of our cause, I cannot entertain an idea that it will finally sink, though it may remain for some time under a cloud."

Fortunately, Congress, prior to their adjournment, had resolved that " until they should otherwise order, General Washington should be possessed of all power to order and direct all things relative to the department and to the operations of war." Thus empowered, he proceeded immediately to recruit three battalions of artillery. To those whose terms were expiring, he promised an augmentation of twenty-five per cent. upon their pay, and a bounty of ten dollars to the men for six weeks' service. " It was no time," he said, " to stand upon expense ; nor in matters of self-evident exigency, to refer to Congress at the distance of a hundred and thirty or forty miles." " If any good officers will offer to raise men upon continental pay and establishment in this quarter, I shall encourage them to do so, and regiment them when they have done it. It may be thought that I am going a good deal out of the line of my duty, to adopt these measures, or to advise thus freely. A character to lose, an estate to forfeit, the inestimable blessings of liberty at stake, and a life devoted, must be my excuse."*

The promise of increased pay and bounties, had kept together

* Letter to the President of Congress.

for a time the dissolving army. The local militia began to turn out freely. Colonel John Cadwalader, a gentleman of gallant spirit, and cultivated mind and manners, brought a large volunteer detachment, well equipped, and composed principally of Philadelphia troops. Washington, who held Cadwalader in high esteem, assigned him an important station at Bristol, with Colonel Reed, who was his intimate friend, as an associate. They had it in charge to keep a watchful eye upon Count Donop's Hessians, who were cantoned along the opposite shore from Bordentown to the Black Horse.

On the 20th of December arrived General Sullivan in camp, with the troops recently commanded by the unlucky Lee. They were in a miserable plight; destitute of almost every thing; many of them fit only for the hospital, and those whose terms were nearly out, thinking of nothing but their discharge. About four hundred of them, who were Rhode Islanders, were sent down under Colonel Hitchcock to reinforce Cadwalader; who was now styled brigadier-general by courtesy, lest the Continental troops might object to act under his command.

On the same day arrived General Gates, with the remnants of four regiments from the Northern army. With him came Wilkinson, who now resumed his station as brigade-major in St. Clair's brigade, to which he belonged. To his Memoirs we are indebted for notices of the commander-in-chief. "When the divisions of Sullivan and Gates joined General Washington," writes Wilkinson, "he found his numbers increased, yet his difficulties were not sensibly diminished; ten days would disband his corps and leave him 1,400 men, miserably provided in all things. I saw him in that gloomy period; dined with him, and attentively marked his aspect; always grave and thoughtful, he appeared at that time pensive and solemn in the extreme."

There were vivid schemes forming under that solemn aspect. The time seemed now propitious for the *coup de main* which Washington had of late been meditating. Every thing showed careless confidence on the part of the enemy. Howe was in winter quarters at New York. His troops were loosely cantoned about the Jerseys, from the Delaware to Brunswick, so that they could not readily be brought to act in concert on a sudden alarm. The Hessians were in the advance, stationed along the Delaware, facing the American lines, which were along the west bank. Cornwallis, thinking his work accomplished, had obtained leave of absence, and was likewise at New York, preparing to embark for England. Washington had now between five and six thousand men fit for service; with these he meditated to cross the river at night, at different points, and make simultaneous attacks upon the Hessian advance posts.

He calculated upon the eager support of his troops, who were burning to revenge the outrages on their homes and families, committed by these foreign mercenaries. They considered the Hessians mere hirelings; slaves to a petty despot, fighting for sordid pay, and actuated by no sentiment of patriotism or honor. They had rendered themselves the horror of the Jerseys, by rapine, brutality, and heartlessness. At first, their military discipline had inspired awe, but of late they had become careless and unguarded, knowing the broken and dispirited state of the Americans, and considering them incapable of any offensive enterprise.

A brigade of three Hessian regiments, those of Rahl,* Loss-

* Seldom has a name of so few letters been spelled so many ways as that of this commander. We find it written Rall in the military journals before us; yet we adhere to the one hitherto adopted by us, apparently on good authority.

berg, and Knyphausen, was stationed at Trenton.   Colonel Rahl had the command of the post at his own solicitation, and in consequence of the laurels he had gained at White Plains and Fort Washington.   We have before us journals of two Hessian lieutenants and a corporal, which give graphic particulars of the colonel and his post.   According to their representations, he, with all his bravery, was little fitted for such an important command.   He lacked the necessary vigilance and forecast.

One of the lieutenants speaks of him in a sarcastic vein, and evidently with some degree of prejudice.   According to his account, there was more bustle than business at the post.   The men were harassed with watches, detachments, and pickets, without purpose and without end.   The cannon must be drawn forth every day from their proper places, and paraded about the town, seemingly only to make a stir and uproar.

The lieutenant was especially annoyed by the colonel's passion for music.   Whether his men when off duty were well or ill clad, whether they kept their muskets clean and bright, and their ammunition in good order, was of little moment to the colonel, he never inquired about it;—but the music ! that was the thing ! the hautboys—he never could have enough of them.   The main guard was at no great distance from his quarters, and the music could not linger there long enough.   There was a church close by, surrounded by palings ; the officer on guard must march round and round it, with his men and musicians, looking, says the lieutenant, like a Catholic procession, wanting only the cross and the banner, and chanting choristers.

According to the same authority, Rahl was a boon companion ; made merry until a late hour in the night, and then lay in bed until nine o'clock in the morning.   When the officers came to parade between ten end eleven o'clock, and presented themselves at head-quarters, he was often in his bath, and the guard must be kept waiting half an hour longer. On parade, too, when any other commander would take occasion to talk with his staff officers and others upon duty about the concerns of the garrison, the colonel attended to nothing but the music—he was wrapped up in it to the great disgust of the testy lieutenant.

And then, according to the latter, he took no precautions against the possibility of being attacked. A veteran officer, Major Von Dechow, proposed that some works should be thrown up, where the cannon might be placed, ready against any assault. "Works!—pooh—pooh:"—the colonel made merry with the very idea—using an unseemly jest, which we forbear to quote. "An assault by the rebels! Let them come! We'll at them with the bayonet."

The veteran Dechow gravely persisted in his counsel. "Herr Colonel," said he, respectfully, "it costs almost nothing; if it does not help, it does not harm." The pragmatical lieutenant, too, joined in the advice, and offered to undertake the work. The jovial colonel only repeated his joke, went away laughing at them both, and no works were thrown up.

The lieutenant, sorely nettled, observes sneeringly: "He believed the name of Rahl more fearful and redoubtable than all the works of Vauban and Cohorn, and that no rebel would dare to encounter it. A fit man truly to command a corps! and still more to defend a place lying so near an enemy having a hundred times his advantages. Every thing with him was done heedlessly and without forecast." *

* Tagebuch eines Hessischen officiers.—MS.

Such is the account given of this brave, but inconsiderate and light-hearted commander; given, however, by an officer not of his regiment. The honest corporal already mentioned, who was one of Rahl's own men, does him more justice. According to his journal, rumors that the Americans meditated an attack had aroused the vigilance of the colonel, and on the 21st of December he had reconnoitred the banks of the Delaware, with a strong detachment, quite to Frankfort, to see if there were any movements of the Americans indicative of an intention to cross the river. He had returned without seeing any; but had since caused pickets and alarm posts to be stationed every night outside the town.*

Such was the posture of affairs at Trenton at the time the *coup de main* was meditated.

Whatever was to be done, however, must be done quickly, before the river was frozen. An intercepted letter had convinced Washington of what he had before suspected, that Howe was only waiting for that event to resume active operations, cross the river on the ice, and push on triumphantly to Philadelphia.

He communicated his project to Gates, and wished him to go to Bristol, take command there, and co-operate from that quarter. Gates, however, pleaded ill health, and requested leave to proceed to Philadelphia.

The request may have surprised Washington, considering the spirited enterprise that was on foot; but Gates, as has before been observed, had a disinclination to serve immediately under the commander-in-chief; like Lee, he had a disparaging opinion of him, or rather an impatience of his supremacy. He had,

---

* Tagebuch des corporals Johannes Reuber.—MS.

moreover, an ulterior object in view. Having been disappointed and chagrined, in finding himself subordinate to General Schuyler in the Northern campaign, he was now intent on making interest among the members of Congress for an independent command. Washington urged that, on his way to Philadelphia, he would at least stop for a day or two at Bristol, to concert a plan of operations with Reed and Cadwalader, and adjust any little questions of etiquette and command that might arise between the continental colonels who had gone thither with Lee's troops and the volunteer officers stationed there.*

He does not appear to have complied even with this request. According to Wilkinson's account, he took quarters at Newtown, and set out thence for Baltimore on the 24th of December, the very day before that of the intended *coup de main*. He prevailed on Wilkinson to accompany him as far as Philadelphia. On the road he appeared to be much depressed in spirits; but he relieved himself, like Lee, by criticising the plans of the commander-in-chief. "He frequently," writes Wilkinson, "expressed the opinion that, while Washington was watching the enemy above Trenton, they would construct bateaux, pass the Delaware in his rear, and take possession of Philadelphia before he was aware; and that, instead of vainly attempting to stop Sir William Howe at the Delaware, General Washington ought to retire to the south of the Susquehanna, and there form an army. *He said it was his intention to propose this measure to Congress at Baltimore,* and urged me to accompany him to that place; but my duty forbade the thought."

Here we have somewhat of a counterpart to Lee's project of

---

* Washington to Gates.   Gates's papers.

eclipsing the commander-in-chief. Evidently the two military veterans who had once been in conclave with him at Mount Vernon, considered the truncheon of command falling from his grasp.

The projected attack upon the Hessian posts was to be threefold.

1st. Washington was to cross the Delaware with a considerable force, at McKonkey's Ferry (now Talyorsville), about nine miles above Trenton, and march down upon that place, where Rahl's cantonment comprised a brigade of fifteen hundred Hessians, a troop of British light-horse, and a number of chasseurs.

2d. General Ewing, with a body of Pennsylvania militia, was to cross at a ferry about a mile below Trenton; secure the bridge over the Assunpink creek, a stream flowing along the south side of the town, and cut off any retreat of the enemy in that direction.

3d. General Putnam, with the troops occupied in fortifying Philadelphia, and those under General Cadwalader, was to cross below Burlington, and attack the lower posts under Count Donop. The several divisions were to cross the Delaware at night, so as to be ready for simultaneous action, by five o'clock in the morning.

Seldom is a combined plan carried into full operation. Symptoms of an insurrection in Philadelphia, obliged Putnam to remain with some force in that city; but he detached five or six hundred of the Pennsylvania militia under Colonel Griffin, his adjutant-general, who threw himself into the Jerseys, to be at hand to co-operate with Cadwalader.

A letter from Washington to Colonel Reed, who was stationed with Cadwalader, shows the anxiety of his mind, and his consciousness of the peril of the enterprise.

"Christmas day at night, one hour before day, is the time fixed upon for our attempt upon Trenton. For Heaven's sake keep this to yourself, as the discovery of it may prove fatal to us; our numbers, I am sorry to say, being less than I had any conception of; yet nothing but necessity, dire necessity, will, nay must, justify an attack. Prepare, and in concert with Griffin, attack as many of their posts as you possibly can, with a prospect of success; the more we can attack at the same instant, the more confusion we shall spread, and the greater good will result from it. * * I have ordered our men to be provided with three days' provision ready cooked, with which, and their blankets, they are to march; for if we are successful, which Heaven grant, and the circumstances favor, we may push on. I shall direct every ferry and ford to be well guarded, and not a soul suffered to pass without an officer's going down with the permit. Do the same with you."

It has been said that Christmas night was fixed upon for the enterprise, because the Germans are prone to revel and carouse on that festival, and it was supposed a great part of the troops would be intoxicated, and in a state of disorder and confusion; but in truth Washington would have chosen an earlier day, had it been in his power. "We could not ripen matters for the attack before the time mentioned," said he in his letter to Reed, "so much out of sorts, and so much in want of every thing are the troops under Sullivan."

Early on the eventful evening (Dec. 25th), the troops destined for Washington's part of the attack, about two thousand four hundred strong, with a train of twenty small pieces, were paraded near McKonkey's Ferry, ready to pass as soon as it grew dark, in the hope of being all on the other side by twelve o'clock.

Washington repaired to the ground accompanied by Generals Greene, Sullivan, Mercer, Stephen, and Lord Stirling. Greene was full of ardor for the enterprise; eager, no doubt, to wipe out the recollection of Fort Washington. It was, indeed, an anxious moment for all.

We have here some circumstances furnished to us by the Memoirs of Wilkinson. That officer had returned from Philadelphia, and brought a letter from Gates to Washington. There was some snow on the ground, and he had traced the march of the troops for the last few miles by the blood from the feet of those whose shoes were broken. Being directed to Washington's quarters, he found him, he says, alone, with his whip in his hand, prepared to mount his horse. "When I presented the letter of General Gates to him, before receiving it, he exclaimed with solemnity,—'What a time is this to hand me letters!' I answered that I had been charged with it by General Gates. 'By General Gates! Where is he?' 'I left him this morning in Philadelphia.' 'What was he doing there?' 'I understood him that he was on his way to Congress.' He earnestly repeated, 'On his way to Congress!' then broke the seal, and I made my bow, and joined General St. Clair on the bank of the river."

Did Washington surmise the incipient intrigues and cabals, that were already aiming to undermine him? Had Gates's eagerness to push on to Congress, instead of remaining with the army in a moment of daring enterprise, suggested any doubts as to his object? Perhaps not. Washington's nature was too noble to be suspicious; and yet he had received sufficient cause to be distrustful.

Boats being in readiness, the troops began to cross about sunset. The weather was intensely cold; the wind was high, the current strong, and the river full of floating ice. Colonel Glover, with his amphibious regiment of Marblehead fishermen, was in advance; the same who had navigated the army across the Sound, in its retreat from Brooklyn on Long Island, to New York. They were men accustomed to battle with the elements, yet with all their skill and experience, the crossing was difficult and perilous. Washington, who had crossed with the troops, stood anxiously, yet patiently, on the eastern bank, while one precious hour after another elapsed, until the transportation of the artillery should be effected. The night was dark and tempestuous, the drifting ice drove the boats out of their course, and threatened them with destruction. Colonel Knox, who attended to the crossing of the artillery, assisted with his labors, but still more with his " stentorian lungs," giving orders and directions.

It was three o'clock before the artillery was landed, and nearly four before the troops took up their line of march. Trenton was nine miles distant; and not to be reached before daylight. To surprise it, therefore, was out of the question. There was no making a retreat without being discovered, and harassed in repassing the river. Beside, the troops from the other points might have crossed, and co-operation was essential to their safety. Washington resolved to push forward, and trust to Providence.

He formed the troops into two columns. The first he led himself, accompanied by Greene, Stirling, Mercer, and Stephen; it was to make a circuit by the upper or Pennington road, to the north of Trenton. The other led by Sullivan, and including the brigade of St. Clair, was to take the lower river road, leading to the west end of the town. Sullivan's column was to halt a few moments at a cross-road leading to Howland's Ferry, to give

Washington's column time to effect its circuit, so that the attack might be simultaneous. On arriving at Trenton, they were to force the outer guards, and push directly into the town before the enemy had time to form.

The Hessian journals before us enable us to give the reader a glance into the opposite camp on this eventful night. The situation of Washington was more critical than he was aware. Notwithstanding the secrecy with which his plans had been conducted, Colonel Rahl had received a warning from General Grant, at Princeton, of the intended attack, and of the very time it was to be made, but stating that it was to be by a detachment under Lord Stirling. Rahl was accordingly on the alert.

It so happened that about dusk of this very evening, when Washington must have been preparing to cross the Delaware, there were alarm guns and firing at the Trenton outpost. The whole garrison was instantly drawn out under arms, and Colonel Rahl hastened to the outpost. It was found in confusion, and six men wounded. A body of men had emerged from the woods, fired upon the picket, and immediately retired.* Colonel Rahl, with two companies and a field-piece, marched through the woods, and made the rounds of the outposts, but seeing and hearing nothing, and finding all quiet, returned. Supposing this to be the attack against which he had been warned, and that it

---

* Who it was that made this attack upon the outpost is not clearly ascertained. The Hessian lieutenant who commanded at the picket, says it was a patrol sent out by Washington, under command of a captain, to reconnoitre, with strict orders not to engage, but if discovered, to retire instantly as silently as possible. Colonel Reed, in a memorandum, says, it was an advance party returning from the Jerseys to Pennsylvania.—*See Life and Corresp.* vol. i. p. 277.

was "a mere flash in the pan," he relapsed into his feeling of
security; and, as the night was cold and stormy, permitted the
troops to return to their quarters and lay aside their arms. Thus
the garrison and its unwary commander slept in fancied security,
at the very time that Washington and his troops were making
their toilsome way across the Delaware. How perilous would
have been their situation had their enemy been more vigilant!

It began to hail and snow as the troops commenced their
march, and increased in violence as they advanced, the storm
driving the sleet in their faces. So bitter was the cold that
two of the men were frozen to death that night. The day dawned
by the time Sullivan halted at the cross-road. It was discovered
that the storm had rendered many of the muskets wet and useless.
"What is to be done?" inquired Sullivan of St. Clair. "You
have nothing for it but to push on, and use the bayonet," was the
reply. While some of the soldiers were endeavoring to clear
their muskets, and squibbing off priming, Sullivan despatched an
officer to apprise the commander-in-chief of the condition of
their arms. He came back half-dismayed by an indignant burst
of Washington, who ordered him to return instantly and tell
General Sullivan to "advance and charge."

It was about eight o'clock when Washington's column arrived
in the vicinity of the village. The storm, which had rendered
the march intolerable, had kept every one within doors, and the
snow had deadened the tread of the troops and the rumbling of
the artillery. As they approached the village, Washington, who
was in front, came to a man that was chopping wood by the road-
side, and inquired, "Which way is the Hessian picket?" "I don't
know," was the surly relpy. "You may tell," said Captain Forest
of the artillery, "for that is General Washington." The aspect

of the man changed in an instant. Raising his hands to heaven,
" God bless and prosper you ! " cried he. " The picket is in that
house, and the sentry stands near that tree." *

The advance guard was led by a brave young officer, Captain
William A. Washington, seconded by Lieutenant James Monroe
(in after years President of the United States). They received
orders to dislodge the picket. Here happened to be stationed the
very lieutenant whose censures of the negligence of Colonel
Rahl we have just quoted. By his own account, he was very
near being entrapped in the guard-house. His sentries, he says,
were not alert enough; and had he not stepped out of the picket
house himself and discovered the enemy, they would have been
upon him before his men could scramble to their arms. " Der
feind ! der feind ! heraus ! heraus ! " (the enemy ! the enemy !
turn out ! turn out !) was now the cry. He at first, he says,
made a stand, thinking he had a mere marauding party to
deal with; but seeing heavy battalions at hand, gave way, and
fell back upon a company stationed to support the picket; but
which appears to have been no better prepared against surprise.

By this time the American artillery was unlimbered; Washington kept beside it, and the column proceeded. The report
of fire-arms told that Sullivan was at the lower end of the
town. Colonel Stark led his advance guard, and did it in
gallant style. The attacks, as concerted, were simultaneous.
The outposts were driven in; they retreated, firing from behind houses. The Hessian drums beat to arms; the trumpets
of the light-horse sounded the alarm; the whole place was in
an uproar. Some of the enemy made a wild and undirected

* Wilkinson's Memoirs, vol. i. p. 129.

fire from the windows of their quarters; others rushed forth in disorder, and attempted to form in the main street, while dragoons hastily mounted, and galloping about, added to the confusion. Washington advanced with his column to the head of King Street; riding beside Captain Forest of the artillery. When Forest's battery of six guns was opened the general kept on the left and advanced with it, giving directions to the fire. His position was an exposed one, and he was repeatedly entreated to fall back; but all such entreaties were useless, when once he became heated in action.

The enemy were training a couple of cannon in the main street to form a battery, which might have given the Americans a serious check; but Captain Washington and Lieutenant Monroe, with a part of the advance guard rushed forward, drove the artillerists from their guns, and took the two pieces when on the point of being fired. Both of these officers were wounded; the captain in the wrist, the lieutenant in the shoulder.

While Washington advanced on the north of the town, Sullivan approached on the west, and detached Stark to press on the lower or south end of the town. The British light-horse, and about five hundred Hessians and Chasseurs, had been quartered in the lower part of the town. Seeing Washington's column pressing in front, and hearing Stark thundering in their rear, they took headlong flight by the bridge across the Assunpink, and so along the banks of the Delaware toward Count Dunop's encampment at Bordentown. Had Washington's plan been carried into full effect, their retreat would have been cut off by General Ewing; but that officer had been prevented from crossing the river by the ice.

Colonel Rahl, according to the account of the lieutenant who had commanded the picket, completely lost his head in the confusion of the surprise. The latter, when driven in by the American advance, found the colonel on horseback, endeavoring to rally his panic-stricken and disordered men, but himself sorely bewildered. He asked the lieutenant what was the force of the assailants. The latter answered that he had seen four or five battalions in the woods; three of them had fired upon him before he had retreated—"but," added he, "there are other troops to the right and left, and the town will soon be surrounded." The colonel rode in front of his troops :—"Forward! march! advance! advance!" cried he. With some difficulty he succeeded in extricating his troops from the town, and leading them into an adjacent orchard. Now was the time, writes the lieutenant, for him to have pushed for another place, there to make a stand. At this critical moment he might have done so with credit, and without loss. The colonel seems to have had such an intention. A rapid retreat by the Princeton road was apparently in his thoughts; but he lacked decision. The idea of flying before the rebels was intolerable. Some one, too, exclaimed at the ruinous loss of leaving all their baggage to be plundered by the enemy. Changing his mind, he made a rash resolve. "All who are my grenadiers, forward!" cried he, and went back, writes his corporal, like a storm upon the town. "What madness was this!" writes the critical lieutenant. "A town that was of no use to us; that but ten or fifteen minutes before he had gladly left; that was now filled with three or four thousand enemies, stationed in houses or behind walls and hedges, and a battery of six cannon planted on the main street. And he to think of retaking it with his six or seven hundred men and their bayonets!"

Still he led his grenadiers bravely but rashly on, when, in the midst of his career, he received a fatal wound from a musket ball, and fell from his horse. His men, left without their chief, were struck with dismay ; heedless of the orders of the second in command, they retreated by the right up the banks of the Assunpink, intending to escape to Princeton. Washington saw their design, and threw Colonel Hand's corps of Pennsylvania riflemen in their way ; while a body of Virginia troops gained their left. Brought to a stand, and perfectly bewildered, Washington thought they were forming in order of battle, and ordered a discharge of canister shot. " Sir, they have struck," exclaimed Forest. " Struck !" echoed the general. " Yes, sir, their colors are down." " So they are !" replied Washington, and spurred in that direction, followed by Forest and his whole command. The men grounded their arms and surrendered at discretion ; " but had not Colonel Rahl been severely wounded," remarks his loyal corporal, " we would never have been taken alive !"

The skirmishing had now ceased in every direction. Major Wilkinson, who was with the lower column, was sent to the commander-in-chief for orders. He rode up, he says, at the moment that Colonel Rahl, supported by a file of sergeants, was presenting his sword. " On my approach," continues he, " the commander-in-chief took me by the hand, and observed, ' Major Wilkinson, this is a glorious day for our country !' his countenance beaming with complacency ; whilst the unfortunate Rahl, who the day before would not have changed fortunes with him, now pale, bleeding, and covered with blood, in broken accents seemed to implore those attentions which the victor was well disposed to bestow on him."

He was, in fact, conveyed with great care to his quarters, which were in the house of a kind and respectable Quaker family.

The number of prisoners taken in this affair was nearly one thousand, of which thirty-two were officers. The veteran Major Von Dechow, who had urged in vain the throwing up of breastworks, received a mortal wound, of which he died in Trenton. Washington's triumph, however, was impaired by the failure of the two simultaneous attacks. General Ewing, who was to have crossed before day at Trenton Ferry, and taken possession of the bridge leading out of the town, over which the light-horse and Hessians retreated, was prevented by the quantity of ice in the river. Cadwalader was hindered by the same obstacle. He got part of his troops over, but found it impossible to embark his cannon, and was obliged, therefore, to return to the Pennsylvania side of the river. Had he and Ewing crossed, Donop's quarters would have been beaten up, and the fugitives from Trenton intercepted.

By the failure of this part of his plan, Washington had been exposed to the most imminent hazard. The force with which he had crossed, twenty-four hundred men, raw troops, was not enough to cope with the veteran garrison, had it been properly on its guard ; and then there were the troops under Donop at hand to co-operate with it. Nothing saved him but the utter panic of the enemy ; their want of proper alarm places, and their exaggerated idea of his forces : for one of the journals before us (the corporal's) states that he had with him 15,000 men, and another 6,000.* Even now that the place was in his possession he dared not linger in it. There was a superior force under Donop below

* The lieutenant gives the latter number on the authority of Lord Stirling ; but his lordship meant the whole number of men intended for the three several attacks. The force that actually crossed with Washington was what we have stated.

him, and a strong battalion of infantry at Princeton. His own troops were exhausted by the operations of the night and morning in cold, rain, snow and storm. They had to guard about a thousand prisoners, taken in action or found concealed in houses; there was little prospect of succor, owing to the season and the state of the river. Washington gave up, therefore, all idea of immediately pursuing the enemy or keeping possession of Trenton, and determined to recross the Delaware with his prisoners and captured artillery. Understanding that the brave but unfortunate Rahl was in a dying state, he paid him a visit before leaving Trenton, accompanied by General Greene. They found him at his quarters in the house of a Quaker family. Their visit and the respectful consideration and unaffected sympathy manifested by them, evidently soothed the feelings of the unfortunate soldier; now stripped of his late won laurels, and resigned to die rather than outlive his honor.*

We have given a somewhat sarcastic portrait of the colonel drawn by one of his lieutenants ; another, Lieutenant Piel, paints with a soberer and more reliable pencil.

"For our whole ill luck," writes he, "we have to thank Colonel Rahl. It never occurred to him that the rebels might attack us ; and, therefore, he had taken scarce any precautions against such an event. In truth I must confess we have universally thought too little of the rebels, who, until now, have never on any occasion been able to withstand us. Our brigadier (Rahl) was too proud to retire a step before such an enemy; although nothing remained for us but to retreat.

"General Howe had judged this man from a wrong point of

* Journal of Lieut. Piel.

view, or he would hardly have intrusted such an important post as Trenton to him. He was formed for a soldier, but not for a general. At the capture of Fort Washington he had gained much honor while under the command of a great general, but he lost all his renown at Trenton where he himself was general. He had courage to dare the hardiest enterprise; but he alone wanted the cool presence of mind necessary in a surprise like that at Trenton. His vivacity was too great; one thought crowded on another so that he could come to no decision. Considered as a private man, he was deserving of high regard. He was generous, open-handed, hospitable; never cringing to his superiors, nor arrogant to his inferiors; but courteous to all. Even his domestics were treated more like friends than servants."

The loyal corporal, too, contributes his mite of praise to his dying commander. "In his last agony," writes the grateful soldier, "he yet thought of his grenadiers, and entreated General Washington that nothing might be taken from them but their arms. A promise was given," adds the corporal, "and was kept."

Even the satirical lieutenant half mourns over his memory. "He died," says he, "on the following evening, and lies buried in this place which he has rendered so famous, in the graveyard of the Presbyterian church. Sleep well! dear Commander! (theurer Feldherr.) The Americans will hereafter set up a stone above thy grave with this inscription:

> "Hier liegt der Oberst Rahl,
> Mit ihm ist alles all!
>
> (Here lies the Colonel Rahl,
> With him all is over.)"

CHAPTER XLIV.

THE Hessian prisoners were conveyed across the Delaware by
Johnson's Ferry, into Pennsylvania; the private soldiers were
marched off immediately to Newtown; the officers, twenty-three
in number, remained in a small chamber in the Ferry House,
where, according to their own account, they passed a dismal
night; sore at heart that their recent triumphs at White Plains
and Fort Washington should be so suddenly eclipsed.

On the following morning they were conducted to Newtown
under the escort of Colonel Weedon. His exterior, writes Lieutenant Piel, spoke but little in his favor, yet he won all our hearts
by his kind and friendly conduct.

At Newtown the officers were quartered in inns and private
houses, the soldiers in the church and jail. The officers paid a
visit to Lord Stirling, whom some of them had known from his
being captured at Long Island. He received them with great
kindness. "Your general, Van Heister," said he, "treated me
like a brother when I was a prisoner, and so, gentlemen, will you
be treated by me."

"We had scarce seated ourselves," continues Lieutenant Piel, "when a long, meagre, dark-looking man, whom we took for the parson of the place, stepped forth and held a discourse in German, in which he endeavored to set forth the justice of the American side in this war. He told us he was a Hanoverian born; called the king of England nothing but the Elector of Hanover, and spoke of him so contemptuously that his garrulity became intolerable. We answered that we had not come to America to inquire which party was in the right; but to fight for the king.

"Lord Stirling, seeing how little we were edified by the preacher, relieved us from him by proposing to take us with him to visit General Washington. The latter received us very courteously, though we understood very little of what he said, as he spoke nothing but English, a language in which none of us at that time were strong. In his aspect shines forth nothing of the great man that he is universally considered. His eyes have scarce any fire. There is, however, a smiling expression on his countenance when he speaks, that wins affection and respect. He invited four of our officers to dine with him; the rest dined with Lord Stirling." One of those officers who dined with the commander-in-chief, was the satirical lieutenant whom we have so often quoted, and who was stationed at the picket on the morning of the attack. However disparagingly he may have thought of his unfortunate commander, he evidently had a very good opinion of himself.

"General Washington," writes he in his journal, "did me the honor to converse a good deal with me concerning the unfortunate affair. I told him freely my opinion that our dispositions had been bad, otherwise we should not have fallen into his hands. He asked me if I could have made better dispositions, and in what manner? I told him yes; stated all the faults of our arrangements, and showed him how I would have done; and would have managed to come out of the affair with honor."

We have no doubt, from the specimens furnished in the lieutenant's journal, that he went largely into his own merits and achievements, and the demerits and shortcomings of his luckless commander. Washington, he added, not only applauded his exposition of what he would have done, but made him a eulogy thereupon, and upon his watchfulness and the defence he had made with his handful of men when his picket was attacked. Yet according to his own account, in his journal, with all his watchfulness, he came near being caught napping.

"General Washington," continues he, "is a courteous and polite man, but very cautious and reserved; talks little; and has a crafty (listige) physiognomy." We surmise the lieutenant had the most of the talk on that occasion, and that the crafty or sly expression in Washington's physiognomy, may have been a lurking but suppressed smile, provoked by the lieutenant's self-laudation and wordiness.

The Hessian prisoners were subsequently transferred from place to place, until they reached Winchester in the interior of Virginia. Wherever they arrived, people thronged from far and near to see these terrible beings of whom they had received such formidable accounts; and were surprised and disappointed to find them looking like other men. At first they had to endure the hootings and revilings of the multitude, for having hired themselves out to the trade of blood; and they especially speak of the scoldings they received from old women in the villages, who upbraided them for coming to rob them of their liberty. " At length," writes the corporal in his journal, " General Washington had written notices put up in town and country, that we were innocent of this war and had joined in it not of our free will, but through compulsion. We should, therefore, be treated not as enemies, but friends. From this time," adds he, " things went better with us. Every day came many out of the towns, old and young, rich and poor, and brought us provisions, and treated us with kindness and humanity." *

* Tagebuch des corporals Johannes Reuber. MS.

CHAPTER XLV.

EPISODE—COLONEL GRIFFIN IN THE JERSEYS—DONOP DECOYED—INROAD OF
CADWALADER AND REED—RETREAT AND CONFUSION OF THE ENEMY'S OUT-
POSTS—WASHINGTON RECROSSES THE DELAWARE WITH HIS TROOPS—THE
GAME REVERSED—THE HESSIANS HUNTED BACK THROUGH THE COUNTRY—
WASHINGTON MADE MILITARY DICTATOR.

THERE was a kind of episode in the affair at Trenton. Colonel
Griffin, who had thrown himself previously into the Jerseys with
his detachment of Pennsylvania militia, found himself, through
indisposition and the scanty number of his troops, unable to render efficient service in the proposed attack. He sent word to
Cadwalader, therefore, that he should probably render him more
real aid by making a demonstration in front of Donop, and drawing him off so far into the interior as to be out of the way of
rendering support to Colonel Rahl.

He accordingly presented himself in sight of Donop's cantonment on the 25th of December, and succeeded in drawing him
out with nearly his whole force of two thousand men. He then
retired slowly before him, skirmishing, but avoiding any thing
like an action, until he had lured him as far as Mount Holly;
when he left him to find his way back to his post at his leisure.

The cannonade of Washington's attack in Trenton on the

morning of the 26th, was distinctly heard at Cadwalader's camp at Bristol. Imperfect tidings of the result reached there about eleven o'clock, and produced the highest exultation and excitement. Cadwalader made another attempt to cross the river and join Washington, whom he supposed to be still in the Jerseys, following up the blow he had struck. He could not effect the passage of the river with the most of the troops, until mid-day of the 27th, when he received from Washington a detailed account of his success, and of his having recrossed into Pennsylvania.

Cadwalader was now in a dilemma. Donop, he presumed, was still at Mount Holly, whither Griffin had decoyed him; but he might soon march back. His forces were equal, if not superior in number to his own, and veterans instead of raw militia. But then there was the glory of rivalling the exploit at Trenton, and the importance of following out the effort for the relief of the Jerseys, and the salvation of Philadelphia. Beside, Washington, in all probability, after disposing of his prisoners, had again crossed into the Jerseys and might be acting offensively.

Reed relieved Cadwalader from his dilemma, by proposing that they should push on to Burlington, and there determine, according to intelligence, whether to proceed to Bordentown or Mount Holly. The plan was adopted. There was an alarm that the Hessian yagers lurked in a neighboring wood. Reed, accompanied by two officers, rode in advance to reconnoitre. He sent word to Cadwalader that it was a false alarm, and the latter took up his line of march.

Reed and his companions spurred on to reconnoitre the enemy's outposts, about four miles from Burlington, but pulled up at the place where the picket was usually stationed. There was no smoke, nor any sign of a human being. They rode up and found the place deserted. From the country people in the neighborhood they received an explanation. Count Donop had returned to his post from the pursuit of Griffin, only in time to hear of the disaster at Trenton. He immediately began a retreat in the utmost panic and confusion, calling in his guards and parties as he hurried forward. The troops in the neighborhood of Burlington had decamped precipitately the preceding evening.

Colonel Reed sent back intelligence of this to Cadwalader, and still pushed on with his companions. As they rode along, they observed the inhabitants pulling down red rags which had been nailed to their doors; tory signs to insure good-will from the British. Arrived at Bordentown not an enemy was to be seen; the fugitives from Trenton had spread a panic on the 26th, and the Hessians and their refugee adherents had fled in confusion, leaving their sick behind them. The broken and haggard looks of the inhabitants showed what they had suffered during the Hessian occupation. One of Reed's companions returned to Cadwalader, who had halted at Burlington, and advised him to proceed.

Cadwalader wrote in the night to Washington, informing him of his whereabouts, and that he should march for Bordentown in the morning. "If you should think proper to cross over," added he, " it may easily be effected at the place where we passed; a pursuit would keep up the panic. They went off with great precipitation, and pressed all the waggons in their reach; I am told many of them are gone to South Amboy. If we can drive them from West Jersey, the success will raise an army next spring, and establish the credit of the Continental money to support it."

There was another letter from Cadwalader, dated on the following day, from Bordentown. He had eighteen hundred men with him. Five hundred more were on the way to join him. General Mifflin, too, had sent over five hundred from Philadelphia, and three hundred from Burlington, and was to follow with seven or eight hundred more.

Colonel Reed, too, wrote from Trenton on the 28th. He had found that place without a single soldier of either army, and in a still more wretched condition than Bordentown. He urged Washington to recross the river, and pursue the advantages already gained. Donop might be overtaken before he could reach Princeton or Brunswick, where the enemy were yet in force.*

Washington needed no prompting of the kind. Bent upon following up his blow, he had barely allowed his troops a day or two to recover from recent exposure and fatigue, that they might have strength and spirit to pursue the retreating enemy, beat up other of their quarters, and entirely reverse affairs in the Jerseys. In this spirit he had written to Generals McDougall and Maxwell at Morristown, to collect as large a body of militia as possible, and harass the enemy in flank and rear. Heath, also, had been ordered to abandon the Highlands, which there was no need of guarding at this season of the year, and hasten down with the eastern militia, as rapidly as possible, by the way of Hackensack, continuing on until he should send him further orders. "A fair opportunity is offered," said he, " of driving the enemy entirely from the Jerseys, or at least to the extremity of the province."

Men of influence also were despatched by him into different

* Life and Correspondence of Pres. Reed, vol. i. p. 281.

parts of the Jerseys, to spirit up the militia to revenge the oppression, the ravage, and insults they had experienced from the enemy, especially from the Hessians. "If what they have suffered," said he, "does not rouse their resentment, they must not possess the feelings of humanity."

On the 29th, his troops began to cross the river. It would be a slow and difficult operation, owing to the ice; two parties of light troops therefore were detached in advance, whom Colonel Reed was to send in pursuit of the enemy. They marched into Trenton about two o'clock, and were immediately put on the traces of Donop, to hang on his rear and harass him until other troops should come up. Cadwalader also detached a party of riflemen from Bordentown with like orders. Donop, in retreating, had divided his force, sending one part by a cross road to Princeton, and hurrying on with the remainder to Brunswick. Notwithstanding the severity of the weather, and the wretchedness of the road, it was a service of animation and delight to the American troops to hunt back these Hessians through the country they had recently outraged, and over ground which they themselves had trodden so painfully and despondingly, in their retreat. In one instance the riflemen surprised and captured a party of refugees who lingered in the rear-guard, among whom were several newly-made officers. Never was there a more sudden reversal in the game of war than this retreat of the heavy German veterans, harassed by light parties of a raw militia, which they so lately had driven like chaff before them.

While this was going on, Washington was effecting the passage of his main force to Trenton. He himself had crossed on the 29th of December, but it took two days more to get the troops and artillery over the icy river, and that with great labor and difficulty. And now came a perplexity. With the year expired the term of several regiments, which had seen most service, and become inured to danger. Knowing how indispensable were such troops to lead on those which were raw and undisciplined, Washington had them paraded and invited to re-enlist. It was a difficult task to persuade them. They were haggard with fatigue, and hardship and privation of every kind; and their hearts yearned for home. By the persuasions of their officers, however, and a bounty of ten dollars, the greater proportion of those from the eastward were induced to remain six weeks longer.

Hard money was necessary in this emergency. How was it to be furnished? The military chest was incompetent. On the 30th, Washington wrote by express to Robert Morris, the patriot financier at Philadelphia, whom he knew to be eager that the blow should be followed up. "If you could possibly collect a sum, if it were but one hundred, or one hundred and fifty pounds, it would be of service."

Morris received the letter in the evening. He was at his wits' end to raise the sum, for hard money was scarce. Fortunately a wealthy Quaker, in this moment of exigency supplied the " sinews of war," and early the next morning the money was forwarded by the express.

At this critical moment, too, Washington received a letter from a committee of Congress, transmitting him resolves of that body dated the 27th of December, investing him with military powers quite dictatorial. "Happy is it for this country," write the committee, " that the general of their forces can safely be intrusted with the most unlimited power, and neither personal security, liberty or property, be in the least degree endangered thereby." *

* Am. Archives, 5th Series, iii. 1510.

Washington's acknowledgment of this great mark of confidence was noble and characteristic. " I find Congress have done me the honor to intrust me with powers, in my military capacity, of the highest nature and almost unlimited extent. Instead of thinking myself freed from all *civil* obligations by this mark of their confidence, I shall constantly bear in mind that, as the sword was the last resort for the preservation of our liberties, so it ought to be the first thing laid aside when those liberties are firmly established."

CHAPTER XLVI.

GENERAL HOWE was taking his ease in winter quarters at New
York, waiting for the freezing of the Delaware to pursue his triumphant march to Philadelphia, when tidings were brought him
of the surprise and capture of the Hessians at Trenton. "That
three old established regiments of a people who made war their
profession, should lay down their arms to a ragged and undisciplined militia, and that with scarcely any loss on either side," was
a matter of amazement. He instantly stopped Lord Cornwallis,
who was on the point of embarking for England, and sent him
back in all haste to resume the command in the Jerseys.

The ice in the Delaware impeded the crossing of the American troops, and gave the British time to draw in their scattered
cantonments and assemble their whole force at Princeton. While

his troops were yet crossing, Washington sent out Colonel Reed to reconnoitre the postion and movements of the enemy and obtain information.   Six of the Philadelphia light-horse, spirited young fellows, but who had never seen service, volunteered to accompany Reed.   They patrolled the country to the very vicinity of Princeton, but could collect no information from the inhabitants; who were harassed, terrified, and bewildered by the ravaging marches to and fro of friend and enemy.

Emerging from a wood almost within view of Princeton, they caught sight, from a rising ground, of two or three red coats passing from time to time from a barn to a dwelling house. Here must be an outpost.   Keeping the barn in a line with the house so as to cover their approach, they dashed up to the latter without being discovered, and surrounded it.   Twelve British dragoons were within, who, though well armed, were so panic-stricken that they surrendered without making defence. A commissary, also, was taken; the sergeant of the dragoons alone escaped.   Colonel Reed and his six cavaliers returned in triumph to head-quarters.   Important information was obtained from their prisoners.   Lord Cornwallis had joined General Grant the day before at Princeton, with a reinforcement of chosen troops.   They had now seven or eight thousand men, and were pressing waggons for a march upon Trenton.[*]

Cadwalader, stationed at Crosswicks, about seven miles distant, between Bordentown and Trenton, sent intelligence to the same purport, received by him from a young gentleman who had escaped from Princeton.

Word, too, was brought from other quarters, that General

[*] Life of Reed, i. 282.

Howe was on the march with a thousand light troops, with which he had landed at Amboy.

The situation of Washington was growing critical. The enemy were beginning to advance their large pickets towards Trenton. Every thing indicated an approaching attack. The force with him was small; to retreat across the river, would destroy the dawn of hope awakened in the bosoms of the Jersey militia by the late exploit; but to make a stand without reinforcements was impossible. In this emergency, he called to his aid General Cadwalader from Crosswicks, and General Mifflin from Borden-town, with their collective forces, amounting to about three thousand six hundred men. He did it with reluctance, for it seemed like involving them in the common danger, but the exigency of the case admitted of no alternative. They promptly answered to his call, and marching in the night, joined him on the 1st of January.

Washington chose a position for his main body on the east side of the Assunpink. There was a narrow stone bridge across it, where the water was very deep; the same bridge over which part of Rahl's brigade had escaped in the recent affair. He planted his artillery so as to command the bridge and the fords. His advance guard was stationed about three miles off in a wood, having in front a stream called Shabbakong Creek.

Early on the morning of the 2d, came certain word that Corn-wallis was approaching with all his force. Strong parties were sent out under General Greene, who skirmished with the enemy and harassed them in their advance. By twelve o'clock they reached the Shabbakong, and halted for a time on its northern bank. Then crossing it, and moving forward with rapidity, they drove the advance guard out of the woods, and pushed on until they reached a high ground near the town. Here Hand's corps of several battalions was drawn up, and held them for a time in check. All the parties in advance ultimately retreated to the main body, on the east side of the Assunpink, and found some difficulty in crowding across the narrow bridge.

From all these checks and delays, it was nearly sunset before Cornwallis with the head of his army entered Trenton. His rear-guard under General Leslie rested at Maiden Head, about six miles distant, and nearly half way between Trenton and Princeton. Forming his troops into columns, he now made repeated attempts to cross the Assunpink at the bridge and the fords, but was as often repulsed by the artillery. For a part of the time Washington, mounted on a white horse, stationed himself at the south end of the bridge, issuing his orders. Each time the enemy was repulsed there was a shout along the American lines. At length they drew off, came to a halt, and lighted their camp fires. The Americans did the same, using the neighboring fences for the purpose. Sir William Erskine, who was with Cornwallis, urged him, it is said, to attack Washington that evening in his camp; but his lordship declined; he felt sure of the game which had so often escaped him; he had at length, he thought, got Washington into a situation from which he could not escape, but where he might make a desperate stand, and he was willing to give his wearied troops a night's repose to prepare them for the closing struggle. He would be sure, he said, to "bag the fox in the morning."

A cannonade was kept up on both sides until dark; but with little damage to the Americans. When night closed in, the two camps lay in sight of each other's fires, ruminating the bloody action of the following day. It was the most gloomy and anxious night that had yet closed in on the American army, throughout its series of perils and disasters; for there was no concealing the impending danger. But what must have been the feelings of the commander-in-chief, as he anxiously patrolled his camp, and considered his desperate position? A small stream, fordable in several places, was all that separated his raw, inexperienced army, from an enemy vastly superior in numbers and discipline, and stung to action by the mortification of a late defeat. A general action with them must be ruinous; but how was he to retreat? Behind him was the Delaware, impassable from floating ice. Granting even (a thing not to be hoped) that a retreat across it could be effected, the consequences would be equally fatal. The Jerseys would be left in possession of the enemy, endangering the immediate capture of Philadelphia, and sinking the public mind into despondency.

In this darkest of moments a gleam of hope flashed upon his mind: a bold expedient suggested itself. Almost the whole of the enemy's force must by this time be drawn out of Princeton, and advancing by detachments toward Trenton, while their baggage and principal stores must remain weakly guarded at Brunswick. Was it not possible by a rapid night-march along the Quaker road, a different road from that on which General Leslie with the rear-guard was resting, to get past that force undiscovered, come by surprise upon those left at Princeton, capture or destroy what stores were left there, and then push on to Brunswick? This would save the army from being cut off; would avoid the appearance of a defeat; and might draw the enemy away from Trenton, while some fortunate stroke might give additional reputation to the American arms. Even should the enemy march on to Philadelphia, it could not in any case be prevented; while a counter-blow in the Jerseys would be of great consolation.

Such was the plan which Washington revolved in his mind on the gloomy banks of the Assunpink, and which he laid before his officers in a council of war, held after nightfall, at the quarters of General Mercer. It met with instant concurrence, being of that hardy, adventurous kind, which seems congenial with the American character. One formidable difficulty presented itself. The weather was unusually mild; there was a thaw, by which the roads might be rendered deep and miry, and almost impassable. Fortunately, or rather providentially, as Washington was prone to consider it, the wind veered to the north in the course of the evening; the weather became intensely cold, and in two hours the roads were once more hard and frost-bound. In the mean time, the baggage of the army was silently removed to Burlington, and every other preparation was made for a rapid march. To deceive the enemy, men were employed to dig trenches near the bridge within hearing of the British sentries, with orders to continue noisily at work until daybreak; others were to go the rounds; relieve guards at the bridge and fords; keep up the camp fires, and maintain all the appearance of a regular encampment. At daybreak they were to hasten after the army.

In the dead of the night, the army drew quietly out of the encampment and began its march. General Mercer, mounted on a favorite gray horse, was in the advance with the remnant of his flying camp, now but about three hundred and fifty men, principally relics of the brave Delaware and Maryland regiments, with some of the Pennsylvania militia. Among the latter were youths belonging to the best families in Philadelphia. The main body followed, under Washington's immediate command.

The Quaker road was a complete roundabout, joining the main road about two miles from Princeton, where Washington expected to arrive before daybreak. The road, however, was new and rugged; cut through woods, where the stumps of trees broke the wheels of some of the baggage trains, and retarded the march of the troops; so that it was near sunrise of a bright, frosty morning, when Washington reached the bridge over Stony Brook, about three miles from Princeton. After crossing the bridge, he led his troops along the bank of the brook to the edge of a wood, where a by-road led off on the right through low grounds, and was said by the guides to be a short cut to Princeton, and less exposed to view. By this road Washington defiled with the main body, ordering Mercer to continue along the brook with his brigade, until he should arrive at the main road, where he was to secure, and, if possible, destroy a bridge over which it passes; so as to intercept any fugitives from Princeton, and check any retrograde movements of the British troops which might have advanced towards Trenton.

Hitherto the movements of the Americans had been undiscovered by the enemy. Three regiments of the latter, the 17th, 40th, and 55th, with three troops of dragoons, had been quartered all night in Princeton, under marching orders to join Lord Cornwallis in the morning. The 17th regiment, under Colonel Mawhood, was already on the march; the 55th regiment was preparing to follow. Mawhood had crossed the bridge by which the old or main road to Trenton passes over Stony Brook, and was proceeding through a wood beyond, when, as he attained the summit of a hill about sunrise, the glittering of arms betrayed to him the movement of Mercer's troops to the left, who were filing along the Quaker road to secure the bridge, as they had been ordered.

The woods prevented him from seeing their number. He supposed them to be some broken portion of the American army flying before Lord Cornwallis. With this idea, he faced about and made a retrograde movement, to intercept them or hold them in check; while messengers spurred off at all speed, to hasten forward the regiments still lingering at Princeton, so as completely to surround them.

The woods concealed him until he had recrossed the bridge of Stony Brook, when he came in full sight of the van of Mercer's brigade. Both parties pushed to get possession of a rising ground on the right near the house of a Mr. Clark, of the peaceful Society of Friends. The Americans being nearest, reached it first, and formed behind a hedge fence which extended along a slope in front of the house ; whence, being chiefly armed with rifles, they opened a destructive fire. It was returned with great spirit by the enemy. At the first discharge Mercer was dismounted, "his gallant gray" being crippled by a musket ball in the leg. One of his colonels, also, was mortally wounded and carried to the rear. Availing themselves of the confusion thus occasioned, the British charged with the bayonet ; the American riflemen having no weapon of the kind, were thrown into disorder and retreated. Mercer, who was on foot, endeavored to rally them, when a blow from the butt end of a musket felled him to the ground. He rose and defended himself with his sword, but was surrounded, bayoneted repeatedly, and left for dead.

Mawhood pursued the broken and retreating troops to the brow of the rising ground, on which Clark's house was situated, when he beheld a large force emerging from a wood and advancing to the rescue. It was a body of Pennsylvania militia, which Washington, on hearing the firing, had detached to the support of Mercer. Mawhood instantly ceased pursuit, drew up his artillery, and by a heavy discharge brought the militia to a stand.

At this moment Washington himself arrived at the scene of action, having galloped from the by-road in advance of his troops. From a rising ground he beheld Mercer's troops retreating in confusion, and the detachment of militia checked by Mawhood's artillery. Every thing was at peril. Putting spurs to his horse he dashed past the hesitating militia, waving his hat and cheering them on. His commanding figure and white horse, made him a conspicuous object for the enemy's marksmen; but he heeded it not. Galloping forward under the fire of Mawhood's battery, he called upon Mercer's broken brigade. The Pennsylvanians rallied at the sound of his voice, and caught fire from his example. At the same time the 7th Virginia regiment emerged from the wood, and moved forward with loud cheers, while a fire of grapeshot was opened by Captain Moulder of the American artillery, from the brow of a ridge to the south.

Colonel Mawhood, who a moment before had thought his triumph secure, found himself assailed on every side, and separated from the other British regiments. He fought, however, with great bravery, and for a short time the action was desperate. Washington was in the midst of it; equally endangered by the random fire of his own men, and the artillery and musketry of the enemy. His aide-de-camp, Colonel Fitzgerald, a young and ardent Irishman, losing sight of him in the heat of the fight when enveloped in dust and smoke, dropped the bridle on the neck of his horse and drew his hat over his eyes; giving him up for lost. When he saw him, however, emerge from the cloud, waving his hat, and beheld the enemy giving way, he spurred up to his side. "Thank God," cried he, "your excellency is safe!" "Away, my dear colonel, and bring up the troops," was the reply; "the day is our own!" It was one of those occasions in which the latent fire of Washington's character blazed forth.

Mawhood, by this time, had forced his way, at the point of the bayonet, through gathering foes, though with heavy loss, back to the main road, and was in full retreat towards Trenton to join Cornwallis. Washington detached Major Kelly with a party of Pennsylvania troops, to destroy the bridge at Stony Brook, over which Mawhood had retreated, so as to impede the advance of General Leslie from Maiden Head.

In the mean time the 55th regiment, which had been on the left and nearer Princeton, had been encountered by the American advance-guard under General St. Clair, and after some sharp fighting in a ravine had given way, and was retreating across fields and along a by-road to Brunswick. The remaining regiment, the 40th, had not been able to come up in time for the action; a part of it fled toward Brunswick; the residue took refuge in the college at Princeton, recently occupied by them as barracks. Artillery was now brought to bear on the college, and a few shot compelled those within to surrender.

In this brief but brilliant action, about one hundred of the British were left dead on the field, and nearly three hundred taken prisoners, fourteen of whom were officers. Among the slain was Captain Leslie, son of the Earl of Leven. His death was greatly lamented by his captured companions.

The loss of the Americans was about twenty-five or thirty men and several officers. Among the latter was Colonel Haslet, who had distinguished himself throughout the campaign, by being among the foremost in services of danger. He was indeed a gallant officer, and gallantly seconded by his Delaware troops.

A greater loss was that of General Mercer. He was said to be either dead or dying, in the house of Mr. Clark, whither he had been conveyed by his aide-de-camp, Major Armstrong, who found him, after the retreat of Mawhood's troops, lying on the field gashed with several wounds, and insensible from cold and loss of blood. Washington would have ridden back from Princeton to visit him, and have him conveyed to a place of greater security; but was assured, that, if alive, he was too desperately wounded to bear removal; in the mean time he was in good hands, being faithfully attended to by his aide-de-camp, Major Armstrong, and treated with the utmost care and kindness by Mr. Clark's family.*

Under these circumstances Washington felt compelled to leave his old companion in arms to his fate. Indeed, he was called away by the exigencies of his command, having to pursue the routed regiments which were making a headlong retreat to Brunswick. In this pursuit he took the lead at the head of a detachment of cavalry. At Kingston, however, three miles to the northeast of Princeton, he pulled up, restrained his ardor, and held a council of war on horseback. Should he keep on to Brunswick or not? The capture of the British stores and baggage would make his triumph complete; but, on the other hand, his troops were excessively fatigued by their rapid march all night and hard fight in the morning. All of them had been one night without sleep, and some of them two, and many were half-starved. They were without blankets, thinly clad, some of them barefooted, and

* See Washington to Col. Reed, Jan. 15.

this in freezing weather. Cornwallis would be upon them before they could reach Brunswick. His rear-guard, under General Leslie, had been quartered but six miles from Princeton, and the retreating troops must have roused them. Under these considerations, it was determined to discontinue the pursuit and push for Morristown. There they would be in a mountainous country, heavily wooded, in an abundant neighborhood, and on the flank of the enemy, with various defiles by which they might change their position according to his movements.

Filing off to the left, therefore, from Kingston, and breaking down the bridges behind him, Washington took the narrow road by Rocky Hill to Pluckamin. His troops were so exhausted, that many in the course of the march would lie down in the woods on the frozen ground and fall asleep, and were with difficulty roused and cheered forward. At Pluckamin he halted for a time, to allow them a little repose and refreshment. While they are taking breath we will cast our eyes back to the camp of Cornwallis, to see what was the effect upon him of this masterly movement of Washington.

His lordship had retired to rest at Trenton with the sportsman's vaunt that he would "bag the fox in the morning." Nothing could surpass his surprise and chagrin, when at daybreak the expiring watchfires and deserted camp of the Americans told him that the prize had once more evaded his grasp; that the general whose military skill he had decried had outgeneralled him.

For a time he could not learn whither the army, which had stolen away so silently, had directed its stealthy march. By sunrise, however, there was the booming of cannon, like the rumbling of distant thunder, in the direction of Princeton. The idea flashed upon him that Washington had not merely escaped, but was about to make a dash at the British magazines at Brunswick. Alarmed for the safety of his military stores, his lordship forthwith broke up his camp, and made a rapid march towards Princeton. As he arrived in sight of the bridge over Stony Brook, he beheld Major Kelly and his party busy in its destruction. A distant discharge of round shot from his field-pieces drove them away, but the bridge was already broken. It would take time to repair it for the passage of the artillery; so Cornwallis in his impatience urged his troops breast-high through the turbulent and icy stream, and again pushed forward. He was brought to a stand by the discharge of a thirty-two pounder from a distant breastwork. Supposing the Americans to be there in force, and prepared to make resistance, he sent out some horsemen to reconnoitre, and advanced to storm the battery. There was no one there. The thirty-two pounder had been left behind by the Americans, as too unwieldy, and a match had been applied to it by some lingerer of Washington's rear-guard.

Without further delay Cornwallis hurried forward, eager to save his magazines. Crossing the bridge at Kingston, he kept on along the Brunswick road, supposing Washington still before him. The latter had got far in the advance, during the delays caused by the broken bridge at Stony Brook, and the discharge of the thirty-two pounder; and the alteration of his course at Kingston had carried him completely out of the way of Cornwallis. His lordship reached Brunswick towards evening, and endeavored to console himself, by the safety of the military stores, for being so completely foiled and out-manœuvred.

Washington, in the mean time, was all on the alert; the lion part of his nature was aroused; and while his weary troops were in a manner panting upon the ground around him, he was despatching missives and calling out aid to enable him to follow up his successes. In a letter to Putnam, written from Pluckamin during the halt, he says : " The enemy appear to be panic-struck. I am in hopes of driving them out of the Jerseys. March the troops under your command to Crosswicks, and keep a strict watch upon the enemy in this quarter. Keep as many spies out as you think proper. A number of horsemen in the dress of the country must be kept constantly going backwards and forwards for this purpose. If you discover any motion of the enemy of consequence, let me be informed thereof as soon as possible, by express."

To General Heath, also, who was stationed in the Highlands of the Hudson, he wrote at the same hurried moment. "The enemy are in great consternation; and as the panic affords us a favorable opportunity to drive them out of the Jerseys, it has been determined in council that you should move down towards New York with a considerable force, as if you had a design upon the city. That being an object of great importance, the enemy will be reduced to the necessity of withdrawing a considerable part of their force from the Jerseys, if not the whole, to secure the city."

These letters despatched, he continued forward to Morristown, where at length he came to a halt from his incessant and harassing marchings. There he learnt that General Mercer was still alive. He immediately sent his own nephew, Major George Lewis, under the protection of a flag, to attend upon him. Mercer had indeed been kindly nursed by a daughter of Mr. Clark and a negro woman, who had not been frightened from their home by the storm of battle which raged around it. At the time that the troops of Cornwallis approached, Major Armstrong was binding up Mercer's wounds. The latter insisted on his leaving him in the kind hands of Mr. Clark's household, and rejoining the army. Lewis found him languishing in great pain; he had been treated with respect by the enemy, and great tenderness by the benevolent family who had sheltered him. He expired in the arms of Major Lewis on the 12th of January, in the fifty-sixth year of his age. Dr. Benjamin Rush, afterwards celebrated as a physician, was with him when he died.

He was upright, intelligent and brave; esteemed as a soldier and beloved as a man, and by none more so than by Washington. His career as a general had been brief; but long enough to secure him a lasting renown. His name remains one of the consecrated names of the Revolution.

From Morristown, Washington again wrote to General Heath, repeating his former orders. To Major-general Lincoln, also, who was just arrived at Peekskill, and had command of the Massachusetts militia, he writes on the 7th, "General Heath will communicate mine of this date to you, by which you will find that the greater part of your troops are to move down towards New York, to draw the attention of the enemy to that quarter; and if they do not throw a considerable body back again, you may, in all probability, carry the city, or at least blockade them in it. * * * * Be as expeditious as possible in moving forward, for the sooner a panic-struck enemy is followed the better. If we can oblige them to evacuate the Jerseys, we must drive them to the utmost distress; for they have depended upon the supplies from that State for their winter's support."

Colonel Reed was ordered to send out rangers and bodies of militia to scour the country, waylay foraging parties, cut off supplies, and keep the cantonments of the enemy in a state of siege.

" I would not suffer a man to stir beyond their lines," writes Washington, " nor suffer them to have the least communication with the country."

The expedition under General Heath toward New York, from which much had been anticipated by Washington, proved a failure. It moved in three divisions, by different routes, but all arriving nearly at the same time at the enemy's outposts at King's Bridge. There was some skirmishing, but the great feature of the expedition was a pompous and peremptory summons of Fort Independence to surrender. " Twenty minutes only can be allowed," said Heath, " for the garrison to give their answer, and, should it be in the negative, they must abide the consequences." The garrison made no answer but an occasional cannonade. Heath failed to follow up his summons by corresponding deeds. He hovered and skirmished for some days about the outposts and Spyt den Duivel Creek, and then retired before a threatened snow-storm, and the report of an enemy's fleet from Rhode Island, with troops under Lord Percy, who might land in Westchester, and take the besieging force in rear.

Washington, while he spoke of Heath's failure with indulgence in his despatches to government, could not but give him a rebuke in a private letter. " Your summons," writes he, " as you did not attempt to fulfil your threats, was not only idle, but farcical; and will not fail of turning the laugh exceedingly upon us. These things I mention to you as a friend, for you will perceive they have composed no part of my public letter."

But though disappointed in this part of his plan, Washington, having received reinforcements of militia, continued, with his scanty army, to carry on his system of annoyance. The situation of Cornwallis, who, but a short time before, traversed the Jerseys so triumphantly, became daily more and more irksome. Spies were in his camp, to give notice of every movement, and foes without to take advantage of it; so that not a foraging party could sally forth without being waylaid. By degrees he drew in his troops which were posted about the country, and collected them at New Brunswick and Amboy, so as to have a communication by water with New York, whence he was now compelled to draw nearly all his supplies; "presenting," to use the words of Hamilton, "the extraordinary spectacle of a powerful army, straitened within narrow limits by the phantom of a military force, and never permitted to transgress those limits with impunity."

In fact, the recent operations in the Jerseys had suddenly changed the whole aspect of the war, and given a triumphant close to what had been a disastrous campaign.

The troops, which for months had been driven from post to post, apparently an undisciplined rabble, had all at once turned upon their pursuers, and astounded them by brilliant stratagems and daring exploits. The commander, whose cautious policy had been sneered at by enemies, and regarded with impatience by misjudging friends, had all at once shown that he possessed enterprise, as well as circumspection, energy as well as endurance, and that beneath his wary coldness lurked a fire to break forth at the proper moment. This year's campaign, the most critical one of the war, and especially the part of it which occurred in the Jerseys, was the ordeal that made his great qualities fully appreciated by his countrymen, and gained for him from the statesmen and generals of Europe the appellation of the AMERICAN FABIUS.

END OF VOL. II.

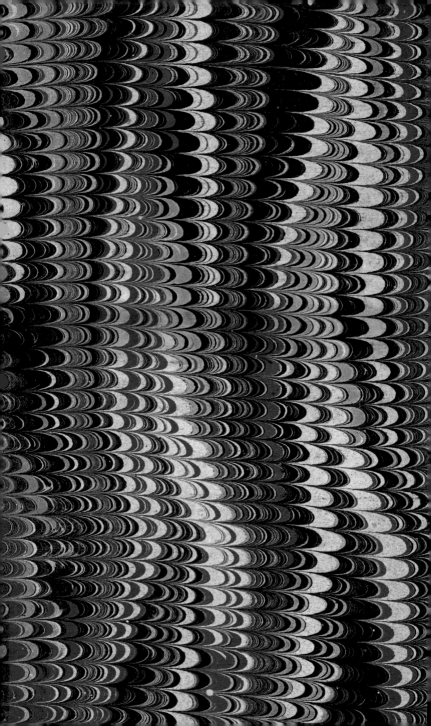